Spirals and Circles

Studies on Themes and Motifs in Literature

Horst S. Daemmrich
General Editor
Vol. 7

PETER LANG
New York • Washington, DC/Baltimore • San Francisco
Bern • Frankfurt am Main • Berlin • Vienna • Paris

Horst S. Daemmrich
Ingrid G. Daemmrich

Spirals and Circles

A Key to Thematic Patterns
in Classicism and Realism

Vol. I

PETER LANG
New York • Washington, DC/Baltimore • San Francisco
Bern • Frankfurt am Main • Berlin • Vienna • Paris

Library of Congress Cataloging-in-Publication Data

Daemmrich, Horst S.
    Spirals and circles: a key to thematic patterns in classicism and realism /
Horst S. and Ingrid G. Daemmrich.
      p.   cm. — (Studies on themes and motifs in literature; vol. 7–8)
    Includes bibliographical references and index.
    1. Classicism. 2. Realism in literature. 3. Literature, Modern—17th
century—Themes, motives. 4. Literature, Modern—18th century—
Themes, motives. I. Daemmrich, Ingrid. II. Title. III. Series: Studies
on themes and motifs in literature; vol. 7–8.
PN56.C6D34   1994   809'.912—dc20   93-27275
ISBN 0-8204-2404-8 (set).   CIP
ISBN 0-8204-2337-8 (v. 1)
ISBN 0-8204-2338-6 (v. 2)
ISSN 1056-3970

Die Deutsche Bibliothek - CIP-Einheitsaufnahme

Daemmrich, Horst S.:
Spirals and circles: a key to thematic patterns in Classicism and Realism /
Horst S. and Ingrid G. Daemmrich. - New York; San Francisco; Bern;
Baltimore; Frankfurt am Main; Berlin; Wien; Paris : Lang.
NE: Daemmrich, Ingrid:

Vol. 1 (1994)
    (Studies on themes and motifs in literature; Vol. 7)
    ISBN 0-8204-2337-8
NE: GT

Vol. 2 (1994)
    (Studies on themes and motifs in literature; vol. 8)
    ISBN 0-8204-2338-6
NE: GT

Contents

VOLUME ONE

VOLUME 2

Spirals Within Circles. The Coexistence of Classical
  Figure Conceptions and Realistic Restrictions
Developmental Personality Restricted by
  Social Forces
Adaptation to and Manipulation of Changing or
  Dominant Circumstances

Doubt
Ambivalence
Optimism

The Journey into the Realistic Landscape
Journey into Historical Space and Time
Broad Panorama and Narrowing Focus.
  The Growth of Detail
The Signature of Fluid and Empty Space

Humor and Ambiguity: The Accommodation of
  Developmental Figures to Realistic Structures

Preface

This study extends our previous investigations of themes and motifs to two periods that are firmly established in the development of many national literatures: classicism and realism. By providing detailed analyses of typical thematic constellations, we hope to answer several substantive questions raised by prominent critics in reviews of *Wiederholte Spiegelungen, Themes and Motifs in Western Literature: A Handbook,* and *Themen und Motive in der Literatur: Ein Handbuch.* The juxtaposition and comparisons of works from different national literatures and distinct historical periods establish new dimensions for classicism and realism that can serve as a basis for the future comparative studies called for by Manfred Beller, Sander Gilman, and Wolfgang Paulsen. In the sections in which we discuss the coming-of-age theme and the motifs linked to the development of human potential, we examine the relative importance of external factors and internal evidence for the appraisal of literary texts and thereby answer Horst Hartmann's query concerning the relative importance of historical and social factors for the formation of motifs and themes. The impetus emerging from changed historical and social conditions clearly contributes to the clustering of motifs and the preference for certain themes. Yet, it can explain neither the unique configuration of specific patterns nor the confluence and concurrence of classical and realistic features during the same historical period. Thematic analysis reveals an interdependence and linking process of figure conception, motif, and theme that modifies the specific referential signification of textual details to social and historical processes. Themes and motifs establish functional relational patterns and structures. They are dynamic, open to variation, and within the literary tradition, indicators of approximation rather than sources. Themes are mediated. They are informed by stylistic tendencies of a period and by traditional patterns that leave a residue in both derivations and creative transformations. They not only reshape but also create literary traditions and therefore play an important role in determining stylistic features of periods.

The present study therefore examines the interrelationship of themes and motifs with other stylistic features in English, French, and German classicism and realism. In addition to analyzing themes and motifs in individual works, we examine their role in the conception of figures, the portrayal of events, and their general structural significance both intra- and intertextually. Our study shows the scope of these themes and patterns in the works of individual authors and in literary currents. Specific thematic analyses of canonized texts in conjunction with comparisons of lesser known works by once popular novelists and dramatists disclose recurrent motifs and unique patterns in thematic exposition and resolution that give coherence to distinctive literary currents. However, such dominant stylistic features can persist in the literary tradition even though the system of conventions, ideals, norms, and formal characteristics that were perceived to be primary indicators of a period have been replaced by new sets of values. Conversely, the theme and motifs of an individual work may be predictors of periods to come. Hence, we identify parallels as well as differences among authors and periods. Finally, we focus on characteristic differences in the thematic representation of human development by tracing the pronounced differences in representations of the coming-of-age theme when it is fused with either that of exemplary behavior or that of accommodation to forces which are apparently beyond individual control.

When figure conceptions are viewed in their relation to characteristic themes of the periods, it becomes apparent that the representation of human relations and personal conduct displayed in attitudes toward the other, the stance toward the physical world and society, and perceptions of history are linked to configurations of approach and withdrawal, proximity and distance. The primary themes show recurring spatial alignments in the conception of social interaction that give rise to two distinct structures:

(1) the centrifugal pattern of classicism moving from enlightened individual development and crossroads decisions outward to an ever-expanding circle of other like-minded individuals, upward to successively higher planes of individual encounters with universal principles that provide increased historical understanding, and forward to an acceptance of contradictions in life;

(2) the centripetal pattern of realism moving from an increasingly restrictive outer circumference of socioeconomic or other impersonal forces inward to individual consciousness and action, downward from the human to comparisons with animal- or machine-like behavior, and backward from the present to a fragmentary, often illusive memory of the past.

We trace each pattern by analyzing representative works in each period. The classical themes of personality development and individuation, narrative voice and figure conception, crossroads, coming-of-age, wilderness - garden - civilized landscape, exemplary conduct, renunciation, and reform circle prove to be equally central to French classical drama, English neoclassicism, and works in Germany during the age of Goethe. The themes of personality development restricted by ambivalence and doubt, the narrowing of broad panorama, the loss of historical perspective, the loss of individual freedom, confinement, and disintegration structure works of realistic literature from the seventeenth century to the present. The continuity of themes and motifs leads at times to schematization and overdetermination in texts, at others, to ambivalences and contradictions. However, the study indicates a continuous dialectic between two basic dispositions toward life. The classical thought structure postulates the freedom of the will and the possibility of unrestricted self-determination. The realistic view transfers the principle of mechanical causation that is assumed to govern phenomena in the physical world to the realm of human endeavor and social interaction. But thought structures persist in the Western cultural tradition as a dialogue that contributes to a process of clarification of thematic patterns. The comparative evaluation establishes that the thematic focus, rather than the contemporary historical or philosophical orientation, shapes the literature of classicism and realism. The thematic approach reveals spatial configurations and structural patterns that permit a new view of periods in literature. It is our hope that the present study provides a model for the thematic reexamination of other national literatures, periods, authors, and works.

The first chapter offers a systematic review and evaluation of previous research focusing on past and current definitions of themes, motifs, motif sequences and clusters, and figure conceptions, as well as of the periods known as "classicism" and "realism," in English, French, and German literature, and for realism, American literature as well. It is obvious that we are indebted to many scholars, and that the study contains a sustained inquiry into the arguments advanced by Erich Auerbach, Manfred Beller, André Billaz, Ernst Robert Curtius, Tzvetan Todorov, Alexander Zholkovsky, and Theodore Ziolkowski. We have refrained from all polemics, not only because we have learned much from other critics but also because we know that it is easier to make errors than to correct them.

We wish to thank all reviewers of our previous work for pointing out the need for a study of the role of themes and motifs in periodization and acknowledge in particular the generous assistance given by the University of Pennsylvania Research Foundation for the publication of our research.

CHAPTER 1

Previous Perspectives

Themes, Motifs, and Periods in Literature

Themes and motifs are basic components of literary works. Their arrangement, distribution, repetition, and variation form an intricate system of relationships that is an integral part of the textual structure. The system also provides the signals which guide the reader's perception of organization and signification. Since themes and motifs recur not only in texts of an author but also in other works, contemporaneous and distant, they establish a literary tradition that transcends time and location. Authors from different ages and nations grasp the threads of this available network to form new patterns. These characterize the individual works but also continue long-established models. Thus the study of themes and motifs reveals unsuspected relationships between literary works not usually linked together by literary historians or critics.

Critics have tended to view themes and motifs either as identifiable units to be isolated and catalogued as they recur and develop through centuries of Western literature or as integral elements of individual texts to be included in detailed textual analyses. The first approach led to the German concept of *Stoffgeschichte* and the publication of reference books which trace the continuation and variation of specific themes and motifs.[1] The second approach has resulted in numerous studies analyzing the role played by a specific theme or motif in a given work, author, or literary period.[2] Each of these perspectives has its advantages and disadvantages. Studies tracing the development of themes or motifs over a wide range of time and space should be the central domain of literary history according to Petriconi, one of the most ardent supporters of thematology. By concentrating on the literary heritage gradually built up by the repetition and development of a certain theme or motif instead of biographical data, social conditions, or historical events, these studies focus on the impulses that authors receive from the vast literary tradition and point to the authors' choices of themes.[3] Such studies are often limited by the tendency to merge their broad concerns into a history of ideas and eventually relegate internal textual relationships to secondary importance. On the other hand, it is rather obvious that narrowly focused thematic examinations of an author or a period are confined by their concentration to results which frequently reinforce traditional interpretations. Moreover, some studies disregard the important creative transfigurations of well-established or little-known themes by authors who reshape them according to their individual perspectives. Inasmuch as such works in turn become part of the literary heritage from which other writers can draw according to their individual needs, the creative transformation of themes and the variation of motif sequences give an added dimension to the history of themes.

Although the terms "theme" and "motif" are commonly used, especially by recent critics, their definitions still vary widely. A work's main theme is generally conceived to be its central idea, the element which organizes the author's material, or content, into the form of a literary work and represents the complete action with a beginning, development, and conclusion. Beller views the theme as operating between the material and the form, thereby establishing a connecting link between formal analysis and the exegesis of content.[4] For Poulet, the theme links literary form and a dominant idea in a given work. He has done extensive studies on universal themes such as time, space, and the circle but also sees the theme as an expression of the writer's inner being or time.[5] This position has been strengthened by the thematic studies of Richard, who utilizes a dominant theme that runs like a thread through the entire work of an author in order to reconstruct his "sensibility" or psyche.[6] The most radical use of themes in exploring the writer's hidden soul has been made by Weber. His method enabled him to infer important stylistic patterns in authors' works from specific childhood incidents.[7]

Far more productive in advancing the understanding of literature are the definitions of "theme" by Levin and Trousson. Levin perceives the theme as an avenue for the introduction of ideas into literature, not only philosophical thoughts but also characterizations as well as clusters of images, such as the expression of England's decadence through images of the overgrown, neglected garden in several of Shakespeare's plays. In conceiving a theme, writers draw from a common stock of associations and memories as well as from their own observations or experiences.[8] Trousson views the theme as the individualization of the motif, or chief concept or situation, described in a given work. This individualization is embodied in either mythical, legendary, or literary figures with long traditions such as Prometheus, Faust, and Dido, or Antigone, Oedipus, or Pandora. Situational themes are particularly attractive to the playwright who dramatizes a theme rather than its philosophical implications.[9] The relationship of theme to genre is examined by other critics, such as Klotz, who argues that the theme of the city dictates that its literary treatment should assume the form of the novel.[10]

Relating thematic analysis to other modes of criticism, Trousson presents an important consideration. From a thematic point of view a text belongs to a cluster of works with the identical theme. The comparative study of themes can overcome therefore the limitations of textual interpretations that focus on isolated works or consider them only in their relation to other texts of a period. Themes can be widely scattered throughout Western literature. They can form clusters during a given period or may occur as primary constellation in creations of an individual author. Viewed from this broad perspective, themes undergo many variations which add to their attractiveness. Trousson argues that without the potential to be varied, a theme fades away. Yet, themes can be resurrected after long periods of disuse when an author's experience or changing institutions promote their revaluation.[11] Trousson fails to observe that thematic analysis is not only compatible with structuralism but, as Zholkovsky has demonstrated, furnishes essential information for any structural model. Insofar as themes from which variant forms may take their ideational content can persist over periods of changing literary conventions, it is possible that some, as for instance the coming-of-age theme, ultimately serve as basic configurations which over time assume the function of a prototype.

In fact, Todorov approaches thematic analysis by looking at clusters that transcend individual themes. Stating that studies which address themselves exclusively to either visual images (Bachelard, Frye, Jung) or abstractions (Lévi-Strauss, Freud, Marx) are of limited value, Todorov proposes instead to group themes together within the dynamic relationship between the self and the world. He establishes two contrasting clusters: a passive group of themes describing the perception of the world by the individual consciousness (perception themes or *thèmes du je*) and a dynamic group describing the active interaction of the self with the world, or more specifically, with other individuals (sexual themes or *thèmes du tu*).[12] In the first group, interaction is limited to the ego's conscious observation of the surrounding world, while in the second group, encounters, conversations, and contact of the ego with others assume an important role. Todorov furthermore restricts the critic's task to identifying the elements of a literary text. In contrast to other critics' varying interpretations of a given text, he assures that his method will achieve objectivity. For our present study, Todorov's view has proven valuable. His division of themes into two clusters based on active and passive interactions of the self with the world and other individuals closely corresponds to our grouping of themes into "classical" ones supported by the motifs of genuine dialogue, the helping hand and the giving heart, and "realistic" ones, based on images of confinement and such motifs as the closed window and lack of dialogue.

Moreover, Todorov's insistence that themes are dynamic components in a literary text expressing the relationship of the individual consciousness to the world, linking elements of the work with each other and with the whole structure, emphasizes the expansive nature of themes. They can range from specific problems to be solved, such as how a youth reconciles his dreams with the demands of an adult world, to general human concerns of love, success, failure, and perseverance. They bridge the space between the specific and the general, the author and the reader, the past, present, and future. Goethe's poem "Der neue Amadis" opens with the recollection that the speaker was left to himself as a young boy. The following four stanzas capture his imaginary heroic adventures fighting dragons and freeing the beautiful Princess Fish. The final stanza raises the question of why the world of fantasy has disappeared so quickly: "Tell me, where is the country/ Where the path leading there?" In correlating the figure with the theme and motif, a thematic analysis observes first a speaker who reconstructs in highly concentrated form critical moments of a person's coming of age. The sequential alignment covers: loneliness ("locked up, alone as in a womb"), release ("golden fantasy helped me pass the time"), a series of imaginary adventures that help the youth to resolve conflicts successfully, acquire highly prized skills, and realize his full potential (built and destroyed castles, threw a javelin, sought affection, married), and the expression of regret that the speaker, though he can recollect it, cannot relive the past ("what magic bond could keep her from sudden flight?"). Yet, any nostalgic sentiment is tempered by the technique of combining the remembrance with literary allusions and a touch of irony. The poem's caption aligns the six stanzas with the interminable late medieval romance of Amadis and the whole tradition of knightly adventures from Rodriguez de Montalvo to Wieland. The names, Prince Pipi and Princess Fish, allude to a French fairy tale, and the description of the princess as "enameled" by sunshine evokes associations of the lustrous surface of a porcelain statuette, a gimcrack depicting a mermaid. Thus, the speaker reminds the reader that dreams, be they inspired by a mundane trifle or a long and rich literary heritage, constitute an important aspect of individual growth. Critically, yet fondly recalled fantasy forges a link between a specific moment in time and a general human experience.

The observations in the poem unfold almost imperceptibly a unique dimension of the coming-of-age theme that enables readers to perceive a pattern which may be encountered in other works. To cite just one example: in "Fern Hill," Dylan Thomas explores the confluence of observation and potential action, of present, past, and future in a young boy's dream world by accenting sentiments similar to those expressed by Goethe. Metaphors and allusions in "Fern Hill" establish relations to a rural setting ("apple boughs, grass green, trees, barn, stable") and to the human dream of paradise ("the farm, like a wanderer white / With dew . . . it was all / Shining, it was Adam and maiden"). The speaker recalls the "green and carefree" youth, the role-playing ("I was prince of the apple towns"; "I was huntsman and herdsman"), and the miracle of fantasy ("Time let me play and be / Golden; And nothing I cared, at my sky blue trades"). In the final lines, the poem gives a hint of nostalgia ("Oh as I was young") and succinctly captures the tension between captivity and freedom: "Time held me green and dying / Though I sang in my chains like the sea." Yet, "Fern Hill," like Goethe's poem, not only reaffirms precious moments of adolescent fantasy but also focuses on the continuous interaction of the youth and the world, thereby linking fantasy to the coming-of-age pattern.

In addition to determining the situation, possible stance toward life, tone, and metaphoric field, the juxtaposition of fantasy and reality as the primary aspect of the coming-of-age theme shapes the figure conception and can integrate the action-resolution sequence on a narrative plane. Wilhelm Raabe's *Prinzessin Fisch*, for instance, explores the challenge of a materialistic world to a sensitive individual who seeks to retain the quality of his dreams as he is confronted by the disparity between professed goals and selfish practice, visions of widely forgotten ideals and deterministic factors shaping society. The story traces the growth of Theodor Rodburg from an initial preoccupation with himself through adolescence to the point in life where he understands his place in the community. It emphasizes the significance of dreams in the process of individuation. Orphaned as a young boy, Theodor creates for himself a world of fantasy that offers release but also enables him to anticipate future roles he will have to play in life. He dreams about adventures, projects himself into the role of Robinson Crusoe, and explores far-off lands. As the years pass, the demands of reality intrude more firmly into fantasy. Yet, the imaginative world also expands to capture visions of love and beauty. As he looks through the window of his study, he perceives a fleeting smile of a neighbor's wife and quickly sees a beautiful princess in a charmed garden. Dreams continue to soften the transition from one stage of his development to the next until he is fully awakened by experiences of success and failure. Finally, as Theodor prepares to bid farewell to the world in which he grew up, he recognizes that his dreams were not futile but an experience of beauty which permanently enriched his life and prepared him for the activity in the world that awaits him. Avoiding stale approximations and artificial "naturalness," the three authors find the appropriate expression to depict a period of life everyone has known. The spirit, sentiments, and dreams of youth are present. The reader recognizes that fantasy is as important to growth as the rational perception of the world.

Associations, comparisons, and revaluations during subsequent phases of aesthetic perception not only reinforce such a pattern retention but also contribute to a heightened awareness of thematic constellations. Overcoming restrictions set by time or national boundaries, the reader, like the critic, begins to assimilate a structural pattern. This imprinting enhances and shapes perception in subsequent reading experiences. It also is reinforced, modified, challenged, or undermined in encounters with texts as diverse as Joseph Conrad's *Lord Jim,* Richard Wright's *The Long Dream,* and Gustave Flaubert's novels. All present fantasies as vital to a person's development and self-identity. But Jim who envisions detailed scenes in which he battles hurricanes, saves shipwrecked sailors, or masters extraordinary obstacles fails when he is confronted by a real emergency. Overpowered by his imagination, he sees chaos and destruction, is paralyzed, becomes incapable of rational action, and deserts ship and passengers. By showing the precarious balance of dreams and action, of volition and deeds in human nature, the narrative raises an important question concerning individual growth: Is self-knowledge even feasible without a test of one's perception in the world? Wright's novel, spanning the life of Rex Tucker from childhood to adulthood, exposes the black boy nicknamed Fishbelly to a succession of experiences that severely test his ability to retain the glimpse of a pure vision in an environment that seems designed to prevent the development of human potential. Fishbelly learns to adjust to prejudice and to failure. He finds accommodation with corruption, deceit, and fraud. He mistakes sex for love and quick success for true achievement. Often he is almost too scared to breathe. Yet, throughout his extended nightmarish ordeal, he clings to the hope to wake up and find a world that might be worthy of dreams. Flaubert's protagonists discover that the simultaneously rigid and shifting circumstances of their environment undermine all attempts to realize their dreams. Emma Bovary (*Madame Bovary*) cannot find in life the fulfillment of her dream of romantic love, fed by the romances she read as a young girl. Frédéric Moreau (*L'Education sentimentale*) is unable to realize his dreams of professional and romantic success during the chaotic time of the 1830 Revolution

in Paris. Bouvard and Pécuchet's vision of being independent gentle-
men farmers is continuously shattered because of their inability to
master the complexities in pursuing their dream.

The relationship between characters, plot, and theme is complex.
Not only does the theme mold other elements to achieve unity of
structure, but it is also shaped by these other literary components
when the figures move toward self-insight, when they are confronted
by situations that could either support or inhibit their growth, or when
they encounter strong characters linked to other themes. The central
theme can shift, intensify, diminish, or even be supplanted by a new
theme, as the plot progresses and characters develop, meet new challenges, or change radically.

By shaping setting, characters, and action and by creating dramatic tension, themes provide forceful stimuli for a reader's initial perception of texts. They give readers the opportunity to reexamine their
existence, their attitudes toward others, and their understanding of social or historical questions. Nevertheless, themes do not promise simple solutions. Since they reflect both the recurring human concerns
and the intellectual shifts occasioned by changing historical conditions, they project alternative relationships between the individual and
the world which may be ambiguous. Indeed, the uncertainty factor
plays an important role when readers attempt to relate solutions suggested by themes to their own personal, economic, social, and historical circumstances.

Definitions of "motif" vary even more widely than those of
theme. The concept, first used in the *Encyclopédie* of 1765 to describe a musical piece, later gained popularity in literary criticism.
Motifs have been variously identified with single units of action, psychological traits, attitudes, poetic principles, situations, and images.
Nearly all definitions begin with its etymological and semantic origin,
deriving from the Latin *movere* in the sense of moving or convincing
by persuasive means. Its function has always been more important
than its essence: it must *do* rather than be. What the motif does is to
recur. It links elements with one another and thus contributes to the
structural unity of a work of art. In music, the motif is defined as the
smallest identifiable melodic unit and its variations. In art, it is a recurring figurative unit that can be identified as contributing to the formal composition of the piece, be it the S-configuration of sculpture,

the repetitive sheaves of wheat on bas-relief, the bases of columns or the bundling of pilasters in architecture. In his comparison of the use of motifs in the various arts, Czerny finds that literary motifs can be defined least precisely, because they combine the traits of musical and artistic motifs with intellectual characteristics foreign to other forms of art which depend more upon the senses than does literature. In literature, the motif, which he defines as a "unit-limit of structure and expression . . .the indissoluble unit of thought and action," not only recurs, is varied, is enlarged or diminished, but adds on new details and relationships with each recurrence.[13] A succession of motifs linked to each other becomes an integral part of the overall design of the work.

Literary motifs are often defined as schematic patterns of typical, mythical, or archetypal traits indicating a recurring human situation. Goethe observes in his *Maximen und Reflexionen*: "What we call motifs are therefore actually phenomena of the human spirit which have been restated and will be reproduced again . . ."[14] As archetypal phenomena of the human mind, motifs can assume symbolic meaning, as for instance, the motif of the dragon killer that symbolizes attempts to tame chaos. Unlike symbols, motifs are not ambiguous in meaning. Therefore they do not lend themselves to conflicting interpretations. Psychological motif studies open interesting perspectives on the universality and consistency of the human experience but tend to lead away from literary criticism, since they isolate the motif from its context. Frequently folklorists have also used the concept in reference to universal experiences.[15] Accepting Lüthi's definition of the motif as "the smallest unit of a narrative that has the potential to survive intact in tradition," Frenzel traces the occurrence of 54 motifs through Western literature with occasional references to non-Western literature. She is not concerned with their function within a given text but rather with their appearance and reappearance in literature as they build up a long tradition, as for instance, the motif of the man loved by two women has done.[16] The inventory of motifs that express basic human experience prompts Frenzel to classify them as moving, retarding, anticipating, or pointing back, empty, blind, ornamental, or filler motifs. Frenzel's approach fosters the tendency to ignore the specific function of motifs in a given text or period and also leaves the impression that motifs are superimposed on literary texts.

Of greater interest to the literary critic is the author's adaptation of

motifs to fulfill certain structural needs. These are often prefigured in
the poet's imagination. Goethe observes: "Certain important motifs,
legends, ancient traditions have so impressed themselves upon my
mind that I have retained them in my inner being alive and working
for 40 or 50 years; my most treasured possessions seemed the renewal
of such valuable images in my imagination."[17] Analyzing Goethe's
writings, particularly those between 1771 and 1776, Krogmann confirms the persistent presence of the motif of the "Friederike experience." Rooted in the poet's abandonment of the young Friederike
Brion in Strassburg in 1771, the motif combines unfaithfulness with
the pain of desertion and the pangs of guilt. In his effort to measure
the impact of this emotional experience on Goethe's writings,
Krogmann sets up an elaborate system classifying the motif's "intensity" or centricity to a work's structure, its "extrensity" or proliferation within the work, its constancy, its linking to allied literary motifs
of unfaithfulness, abandonment, and guilt, and finally its transfer from
actual experience to becoming a literary source for further creations.[18] With this system, Krogmann can show the origin, moment of
intensity, decline, and transformation of the motif from life to art during an important period of Goethe's career.

Essentially Krogmann is using a system of classification of motifs
in order to arrive at an understanding of the motif's various functions
in literary texts. Petsch and Frenzel share both Krogmann's objective
and procedure and the limitations of the method. Defining the motif
as the single element of a literary work's content which has the function of strengthening or expanding its structure, Petsch proceeds to
differentiate between "central motifs," which give the text a strong
unity, "frame motifs," which expand its structure, and "filler motifs," which "are not closely connected to the content" but offer possibilities for variation.[19] For Petsch, motifs expand the questions
raised by a literary work, determine the direction of its action,
strengthen textual unity, and stimulate the reader's imagination. His
statement that motifs are the fundamental building blocks of literature
is misleading, however, since this function belongs to the theme, not
the motifs of a given work. Although the motif of "birds of prey"
has organizational functions in Charles Dickens's *Our Mutual Friend*,
for example, the theme of the novel is not bestiality but environmental
determinism.[20] Both Falk's definition of motifs as visual carriers of

ideas that support themes by translating them into images that can
have symbolic meaning and Curtius's conception of the motif as the
objective representation of the theme that moves and organizes the
theme in the realization of a work relate the motif more closely to its
function within the text.[21]

At the same time, such a view clearly shows not only the wide span
covered by definitions of motifs but also the need to allow in a definition for occurrences that cannot be fully anticipated. If we try to remain flexible, we must grant that a motif is a verbalized expression
which has a sensory basis but also a cognitive value. It can characterize behavioral traits and point to or even interpret a whole network of
actions. The motif, because of its position, repetition, and relationship
to other textual components, performs essential functions in literary
works that cannot be assumed by other elements. Its effectiveness in
texts depends far more on the relationships it creates than on the sensory detail from which it originates. Thus in Goethe's *Novelle,* the fire
has the qualities of an image in the distinct pictorial basis, but its recurrent use at specific moments of the narration and subsequent identification with human emotions not only move the action along but
also raise questions of the renunciation of passion in civilized behavior. The motif of bestiality in realistic narratives illustrates the difference between the functional and representational characteristics of the
motif. In contrast to the visual quality of the motifs of fire, fog, sun,
labyrinth, or trap, the recurring animal metaphors or similes that constitute the motif are frequently abstract and general. Few details speci-
fy the visual aspect of the "birds of prey" in Dickens's *Our Mutual
Friend.* The numerous animal metaphors used by Honoré de Balzac
in *Le Cousin Pons* to describe Fraisier's complex plot to gain possession of Pons's art collection emphasize the lawyer's actions. The comparison of Chaval to a horse in Emile Zola's *Germinal* is based on the
phonic similarity of his name with *cheval,* not on any similarity of appearance with a horse. In "Der kleine Herr Friedemann," Thomas
Mann reduces Gerta von Rinnlingen's snake-like characteristics to the
movement of her tongue and her glittering eyes. Friedemann is characterized as squirrel-like, as he sits with hunched back hastily munch-
ing under a walnut tree. The allusion to Bucephalus, the steed of
Alexander the Great, in Kafka's "Der neue Advokat" points to the
loss of historical perspective. Perhaps most abstract is Zola's align-

ment of Jacques's insatiable thirst for killing in *La Bête humaine* with his primitive ancestors who strangled beasts for survival. The deliberately nonvisual quality of the motif suggests that its symbolic and literary functions are more important to the writer than the external appearance of a specific animal. The functions of the motif of bestiality vary from pointing to a specific theme, as in Kafka's "Der neue Advokat" or characterizing figures, as in Zola's *Germinal* or Mann's "Der kleine Herr Friedemann," to organizing a part of the plot, as in Balzac's *Le Cousin Pons* or Dickens's *Our Mutual Friend.*

Conversely, one has to guard against the temptation to look upon a rhetorical figure as a motif when an author skillfully employs it at a time when its meaning is no longer easily recognized by the reader. When Thomas Mann uses the figure "an ocean to drink" in "Schwere Stunde" (1905), he has recourse to a common eighteenth-century expression for a difficult task. The expression perfectly fits the situation of Schiller in Mann's story who contemplates the difficulties confronting him in his work on the *Wallenstein* trilogy. Since motifs, particularly when they recur in works of differing historical periods or national origin, stir the curiosity and creative imagination of readers, they tend to link repeated images, similes, or metaphors. In the process, they often discover variations or established motif forms. For example, a reader may note that in Alfred de Musset's *La Confession d'un enfant du siècle* as well as in Tennessee Williams's *The Glass Menagerie*, dead leaves falling from a tree are compared to disillusionment. Czerny has speculated that readers form a motif from this simile in their minds by following five steps. They must compare the works, focus on the recurring detail, eliminate conflicting elements, exclude concrete particulars, and search for the pattern while overlooking difference in content, characterization, style, period, and theme.[22] Consequently, readers overlook such concrete details as the fact that Musset places the simile of the falling leaves in the panoramic second chapter of his novel, and Williams uses it to close his play, while recognizing that the motif supports the theme of disillusionment, common to both works.

But the necessary precision for the interpretation of motifs can only be gained by detailed comparisons, not by uncertain parallels. To appreciate the function of the path in Goethe's poems "Wandrers Sturmlied," "Der Wanderer," and "An Schwager Kronos," we must not only grasp the function of the detailed descriptions of the path as muddy, strewn with rocks, overgrown by roots, leading upward or downhill for the individual poem but also understand the path's relationship to the figure of the wanderer. The specific interplay of path, wanderer, and shelter opens the perspective to the fulfillment of human potential, life's goals, and possible failure. It also forms the connection between departure and arrival, life's beginning and end, restlessness and rest, seeking a new mode of existence and retaining or protecting the present one. In spanning both concrete detail and general abstraction, the path becomes a motif which functions to organize the spheres of physical, emotional, and intellectual experience into a meaningful statement about life that is precise and yet demands our continuous reflection.

The motif's application can be quite specific. When in "Zum Shäkespears Tag" and "Von deutscher Baukunst" Goethe speaks of Shakespeare and Erwin von Steinbach, the builder of the Strassburg Cathedral, as "wanderers," he does not merely use the conceptualization of existence as undertaking a voyage, searching on the way, and setting a goal. Rather, he addresses their special need as artists to create out of a multiplicity of natural and historical phenomena an object of value and permanence. Their "wanderings" are their struggles with various modes of artistic expression and form-endowing forces. Here the motif expresses a concrete situation and mediates between the specific character traits and the conflicts and triumphs of the artist which together form the theme of the two essays.

The motif of the path can also be split into two contrasting images and form a polar sequence. The biblical "narrow" and "wide" paths are familiar. In Friedrich Schiller's *Wallenstein* the characters face a choice between two modes of conduct, succinctly conveyed by the contrasting "straight" and "crooked" paths. They can choose the "straight path" of ethical conduct and remain true to a high standard unmoved by circumstances or events. Or they can accommodate their actions to the changing demands of the times and follow like the "course of rivers" the "twists and bends" of life. Max and Thekla model their actions on the "straight path," while Octavio and Butler choose the "crooked path" of accommodation. Here the split motif, which recurs consistently in the pictorial imagery of the play's rich language, sets a polar framework of powerful tension around which the dramatic action is structured and the characters are defined throughout the trilogy.

Since such pairing of contrasting or complementary images for structural rather than visual purposes occurs frequently in literature, we have assigned the term "motif sequence" to them. Like the motif, the motif sequence should be viewed in terms of its function. It conceptualizes and retains the threads of an action and links it with the characterization of figures, the theme, or other images. The tension resulting from the polarity contributes in a great measure to the dynamics of literary works. The coupling adds an open-ended quality to motifs because the reader is asked to reflect upon sharp contrasts as well as ambiguous relations, different meanings, and alternative solutions. The reader is forced to make comparisons and grope for explanations even if one of the poles is clear, perhaps single-minded in its characteristics. In *Wallenstein*, the crooked path identifies the disintegration of human trust, destruction, death, and ultimately the decay of civilized society. Yet, Octavio's plea for accommodation to changes in life cannot be dismissed simply because he is a political opportunist. Given a different constellation, his diplomatic advice could prove beneficial. His son's insistence to follow the straight path of honor that is dictated by the voice of his heart opens a vision of a form of existence as yet unfulfilled. The death of Max, however, raises serious questions, perhaps not of the validity of his views but of the practicability of a life dedicated to immutable ethical norms. Whenever a motif sequence incorporates powerful antitheses, it heightens the dramatic suspense and tends to further climactic resolutions of the action.

It is not uncommon that reversals in the personal fortunes of writers or economic and social change cause shifts in motif sequences. In Horace's *Odes* I. 4, for example, the coupling hut – palace appears as complementary: death visits equally the inhabitants of both. In his odes written in exile, however, Horace emphasizes the antithetical nature of the sequence. He contrasts the peaceful, virtuous, moderate life possible in a simple hut with the luxuriant, immoral, and worrisome existence of the palace dwellers. Herman Meyer has shown how the ideational fixation of the sequence transformed it into a *topos* which persistently reappears in Western literature.[23] Toward the close of the eighteenth century, a sharp revaluation of the individual poles and their interrelationship took place. As a consequence, topos and expanded motif begin to coexist. In novels advocating social reform, in the literature calling for a return to nature, in several poems by Goethe and Schiller, as well as in Goethe's *Faust,* the motif sustains the call for crossroads decisions and motivates ideational conflicts experienced by wanderer figures. In France, the anti-regime philosophical and political writers used the topos in order to express succinctly and powerfully the recognition that the existing unjust distribution of wealth and the resulting poverty demanded social change. "War on palaces, peace for huts!" became a political slogan used by French patriots, by Napoleonic troops marching into foreign lands, and later by European revolutionaries who employed it as a rallying cry to advocate civil war.

Motif sequences, like motifs, can also be structured around abstract concepts, such as fertility / sterility. The poles of this sequence provide a large, expansive framework for Thomas Mann's *Joseph und seine Brüder.* The concrete basis, Pharaoh's dream of seven fat and seven lean cows, seven full and seven empty ears of corn, is expanded to include carefully linked sequences of images from plant and sex life, as well as characterizations of such figures as the dwarfs, Potiphar and Mut-em-enet. The motif sequence serves to connect the problems of human concerns and provision with self- and world-insight. It illuminates not only Joseph's personal development but also the growth of human consciousness. Thus it appears in multiple variations, ranging from incestuous desires to far-reaching economic resolutions.[24]

Furthermore, motif sequences assist in organizing a text around a specific conflict. Molière, for instance, consistently uses the sequence"sentient heart" / "possessive hand" in his comedies in order to establish the pattern of a recurring dramatic situation: the conflict between persons who espouse generosity, trust, sincerity, self-sacrifice, and respect coupled with concern for another person's well-being and those figures who seek to abrogate the freedom of others by means of intrigues, lies, games, beatings, confinement, and contracts, who, in short, treat others as objects. This contrast is repeatedly reflected by the recurrent use of "heart" and "hand" in dialogues and monologues.

> HENRIETTE: A heart, you know, can't belong to two,
> And I feel that Clitandre has made himself master of
>   mine
> . . . .

TRISSOTIN: The gift of your hand which I have
  been promised
Will yield to me this heart which Clitandre possesses . . .
              (*Les Femmes savantes* V. i. 1481-82; 1489-90)

Les Femmes savantes illustrates the dialectic of opposing forces. The characters, as in all of Molière's major comedies, are divided into two groups, representing the sentiments of the "sentient heart" and the behavior of the "possessive hand." The motif sequence encompasses two antithetical courses of action. Figures who listen to the voice of the heart struggle to realize their faith in ethical behavior in a world clearly dominated by actions of the "possessive hand." In the comedies, the proponents of the "sentient heart" win, but only after adopting temporarily the tactics of the "possessive hand" or with the help of external forces, such as an authoritarian figure. The motif sequence forms a consistent framework that links and unifies characters and action. It also shapes the language of Molière's most mature comedies.

Since the function of themes and motifs is to establish a network of relationships both within and without the structure of a text, it is logical that themes and motifs can also play a key role in determining stylistic characteristics of literary currents. Literary historians have generally recognized that few periods lend themselves to absolute precision in definition. Periods provide a convenient system of classification that locates and describes sets of predominant stylistic characteristics. The spirit of a time, the intellectual disposition of a generation, a group's philosophic, aesthetic, and political declarations, linguistic norms, or strict adherence to formal categories have been admitted as primary indicators of literary periods.[25] A century or even a few decades can incorporate several distinct periods. In France, the seventeenth century saw the rise of baroque, mannerism, and classicism; in Germany, Goethe's lifetime spanned enlightenment, Storm and Stress, classicism, and romanticism. This situation has contributed not only to the tendency to apply such morphological analogies as growth, maturity, and decay to the rise and decline of periods but also to the predisposition to view literary movements as competing with or confronting each other. For the purpose of periodization, scholars have consistently grouped some of Goethe's plays, notably *Götz von*

Berlichingen, and Schiller's early tragedies *Die Räuber* and *Kabale und Liebe* with the works of such playwrights as Heinrich Wilhelm Gerstenberg, Jakob Michael Reinhold Lenz, and Friedrich Maximilian Klinger. The classification appears to be convincing: the authors share common interests in Shakespeare, a reform of the theater, and the revaluation of the art of the Renaissance and Reformation. In addition, the literature of Storm and Stress shows such common characteristics as a revolt against reason, the rejection of the ideals of the enlightenment, a preference for spontaneity of expression, absolute self-assertion of the individual, and a combination of exaggerated pathos with sentimental reflection, or of stark realistic detail with improbable situations. Yet, the dominant stylistic features of a succession of conflict motifs (brother conflict, the struggle between father and son, infanticide, revenge), the recurring theme of powerful self-assertion, and the attempt to arouse the audience by conveying high-pitched emotions seem to indicate that the series of amorphous tragedies, tragicomedies, and farces published between 1768 and 1784 share their essential characteristics with a literary current that reaches back to Seneca, gains great popularity among Shakespeare's contemporaries, manifests itself in the British and Spanish tradition of revenge tragedies, bursts forth again in the nineteenth-century literature of sensationalism, leaves its imprint on European naturalism, and reemerges in the post-modern fiction of the past decade.

Similarly, classicism and realism have distinct dimensions as periods in the national literatures of Europe. The criteria chosen for their periodization must take into account, among many other elements, the literary debates of the seventeenth and eighteenth centuries concerning formal characteristics of plays, the shift from historical verisimilitude to psychological probability, the struggle between tradition and innovation, and the specific social, political, and economic factors that left their mark on the period. Such considerations tend to influence the subsequent choice of pertinent evidence. Consequently, periodization creates an order of synchronically described clusters arranged in a succession of discontinuous temporal units. Thematic analysis, however, not only shows the coexistence and interaction of styles but also translates the persistence of important features into a persuasive literary account. Much of the focus in Europe's so-called regional literature of the nineteenth century or the unresolved tension between social determinism and individual freedom in the works of Berthold Auerbach, Elizabeth Gaskell and Jeremias Gotthelf, for instance, has its roots in a classical figure conception that cannot be sustained by the primary motifs and themes. Conversely, several salient works of the classical periods in France and Germany show a significant number of features usually associated with late realism.

The conviction that realistic works depict as accurately and truthfully as possible the world in which we live, see, hear, feel, and think may offer limited, but perhaps misleading results, if we note how details commonly associated with reality frequently change meaning in metaphoric fields. The motif of caged existence, for instance, is not only highlighted by stark imagery of industrialized urban environment but also sustained by closed windows, dim rooms, or the inability to move from mansion or palace to the open landscape. The contrasting analysis of landscapes which include vistas of unspoiled nature, the cultivated landscape, nature as stage setting, and the industrialized environment has shown distinct patterns in classicism and realism. Yet, the comparisons also reveal parallels that cannot be explained fully by the impetus emerging from changed historical or social conditions. To gloss over these indicators by focusing on elements conforming to dominant characteristics of the period[26] is essentially as misleading as the recent attempt by some scholars to stress those qualities in texts that seem to anticipate future events.[27] However, by concentrating on the basic constellation of themes and motifs, we can distinguish literary constants that are generated by the reciprocal relations of figure conception, theme, and motif from unique stylistic features that govern a literary period. Therefore our analysis of primary themes and motif clusters should not only provide new insights into salient characteristics of classicism and realism but also advance our understanding of the nature of literary currents.

Structure and Function of Motif and Theme

In our previous research of the occurrence, dissemination, and renewal of motifs and themes, we have observed a series of distinctive, formal qualities that also characterize their function in classicism and realism. The often incompatible definitions of motif and theme advanced by literary historians derive from the fundamental nature of these concepts and the hesitation to render explicit apparent contradictions. The concepts are based on a synthetic judgment that admits: (1) dual relationships by referring to the semblance of phenomena and fluctuating position in texts, (2) a series of relational patterns and a selective principle that classifies concordant phenomena on the basis of frequency of occurrence. Thus motifs have been classified according to similarities of attributes (eye, mirror, heart, horse, ship, shipwreck), imputed effects of an identifiable agent on an author and a text (Friederike / Charlotte – Goethe – text), and as dominant, subordinate, ornamental, or even blind motif. The concept, then, can only characterize functions, that is, the inherent structure of relationships.

Motifs leave their imprint on a wide range of features in a text.[28] They can be examined on the basis of seven primary relations:

(1) Semblance. Motifs either convey the appearance of a concrete, actual substance (place / topos, object / image, comparison / metaphor, figure / characteristic) or function in relational patterns (action / structural dimension) that permit the identification with observable qualities. The primary set of attributes is enlarged as a result of a linking process with other textual elements which adds new signification.

(2) Positional alignment. Motifs serve as coupling devices on the narrative plane that provide for and facilitate integrational relations with successively different planes of signification. If one assumes a hierarchical perspective, the motif functions like a switch that guides the reader to a new plane. Each subsequent recurrence in its original or altered appearance elicits secondary associations that initiate a continuous process of reflection. In Goethe's works, for instance, we can trace a succession of references to atmospheric conditions that either obstruct vision or permit a clear view of the landscape, human activity, and by extension, life. The reappearance generates a chain of signifiers (fog: haze, mist, dense to refractive atmosphere; descending clouds / lifting fog, light, clarity; brilliant sun: inability to face directly, waterfall, rainbow / translucent reflection, capacity to see) that enhance the reader's perception.

> Brilliantly rising from this rage,
> The tinted bow vaults in transfigured continuity
> Now clear, now dimmed, in cool sweet vapor blended.

> So strive figures on our mortal stage.
> This ponder well, the mystery closer seeing;
> In mirrored hues we have our life and being.
> (*Faust* II. i. 4721-27)

The motifs, then, occur on a plane but are also distributed like nodes on an axis.

(3) The principle of polar dimension. Motifs are positioned as textual units in an indefinitely large number of linguistic sequences generated in literature. They appear transparent because they illuminate in a condensed textual unit complex situations, individual choices, and basic existential issues. They crystallize, for instance, affective states into common experiences that cover a wide range of emotions (father - son conflict: authority - individual assertion, self to other person, attraction / repulsion). Yet, this apparently one-dimensional signification is frequently balanced by (a) the linking process with figures and themes that call forth conflicting associations such as horse - rider: joyous affirmation of life / lack of foresight / early death; (b) connections established to objects (mirror, window: space) or phenomena perceived as natural (heart, hand, sea), and products of culture (palace, garden, park) that have acquired multiple meanings. These relations enhance a process of recognition, thinking, increased awareness, new observation, and continuing reflection.

(4) Tension. The tendency of motifs to occur in clusters or to be joined in sequences such as heart / hand, straight / crooked path, ship - shipwreck / harbor, or aggressor / victim creates powerful contrasts and provides alternate solutions to questions of human development. Motif sequences contribute to the formation of a textual field of tension and reinforce thereby the process of reflection.

(5) Schematization. The continued use over long periods of time, in addition to the pronounced reductive characteristics of some motifs, can foster schematized action sequences. Such basic game plans characterize, for instance, plays and narratives employing deception, disguise, homecoming, labyrinth, or revenge. It is possible that schematization encourages reader response to the pattern with a simultaneous devaluation of individual textual details. It is certainly significant that our analysis of realism discloses increased schematization in works that focus on human isolation.

(6) The principle of supporting themes. Motifs sustain and clarify themes by supplying concrete details and by establishing in concert a basic grid of references in the form of primary and secondary associations.

(7) Textual organization. In addition to the aforementioned functions, motifs contribute to the textual arrangement by initial foregrounding and subsequent restatement. The early introduction raises anticipation. Ensuing recurrences can heighten suspense and point toward a resolution. Motifs serve the textual cohesion by motivating behavior and coordinating action. As the ruins and garden motifs demonstrate, they can establish significant temporal and spatial relations. These functions combine to create a dynamic quality in texts.

Changing historical, cultural, and socioeconomic conditions have not only added new dimensions to motifs but also subtracted specific components and influenced their use. Motifs have furthermore been transformed or inverted to create humorous, ironic, or tragic effects. These transformations do not, however, alter their intrinsic function.

The designation "theme" has been so firmly established in general use that critics have resorted to a broad application of the concept. They have also arrived at definitions that reflect specific aspects of language patterns or have functional application to a mode of inquiry. Curtius, for instance, analyzes *sapientia et fortitudo* (*armas y letras, Waffen und Wissenschaft,* weapons and letters) as a "topos"[29] but in numerous other instances also identifies the ideational component of the topos as a theme. Yet, the questions of rank, prominence, and basic stance toward the world raised by linking sword and pen have served as motivating forces in the clash of personalities (Tasso and Antonio in Goethe's *Tasso*) and as a motif sequence that elucidates the self-perception of writer-figures who look upon the word as a finely honed weapon for criticism (Balzac, *Les Illusions perdues*; Thomas Mann, "Tonio Kröger"). The theme, supported by the motif, captures the struggle of gifted writers with society and their evolving capacity for self-knowledge. However, the theme's orchestration and resolution differ in these texts. Goethe's play closes with a desperate outcry that links personal shipwreck and the endurance of a great work. Balzac's Lucien de Rubempré's social position is destroyed when his weapon-pen fails him. Mann's narrative ends on a note of faint resignation coupled with hope.

Literary tradition shows numerous reciprocal relationships between figure conception and unique traits, specific situations, or actions. Thus a figure may be identified consistently with a situation, or conversely, a situation may call for a suitable figure. But it is a figure's reference to events, decisions, actions, and reactions, not the static location, that shapes thematic configurations. A figure in a room is not a theme unless it enters into an interrelationship with an event, decision, or reaction. Persons fighting for justice or survival (Schiller, *Maria Stuart*), coming to terms with their confinement (Raabe, *Wunnigel*), trying to escape a deadly environment (Crane, *Maggie: A Girl of the Street*), pleading for acceptance (Kafka, *Die Verwandlung*), struggling at midnight with the difficult conception of a play (Thomas Mann, "Schwere Stunde"), awakening in the bedroom and continuously reflecting upon the creative interrelationship between the artist and the world (the figure of Goethe in Mann, *Lotte in Weimar*) provide the necessary ideational substance for thematic development. Themes are supported by a wide range of details that characterize situations, events, experiences, or action-reaction sequences. They can be linked to motifs or abstract concepts. They can reflect changing historical perspectives but also capture fundamental questions of human interrelationships. They embody the ideational substance of texts and extend, as for example the theme of confinement, from the sociopolitical sphere to the metaphysical realm.

The literature of classicism and realism provides strong evidence for the following six characteristic features of themes:

(1) Concept. The study of a theme must consider its substance and properties. Aggression, renunciation, and self-development are abstract concepts, the properties of which are derived from numerous observations. A theme's concept classifies individual occurrences in terms of common characteristics. The substance of a theme resides in qualitative (meaning) and quantitative (occurrence) properties. The properties are organizations of qualities actualized in various group combinations that are relational (action, metaphors, motifs) and therefore dependent, that is, of adjectival nature. A theme, then, must be substantive, capable of supporting itself and its dependents. Since we cannot perceive a theme's substance apart from its properties, the activities linked to it, and the effects it generates, we tend to locate the theme in subject-object relations: identified aggressor – aggression –

identifiable effect – victim; person – desirable goal – sacrifice for a higher end; individual – exposure to formative influences – learning – development – developed personality. At this juncture, the theme itself is considered a quality supporting the embodiment of potentially numerous characteristics. Yet in classifying the properties of aggressors, persons capable of renunciation, and developmental figures, we can only establish a meaningful coherence either by verifying figure relations or by referring to a primary correspondence between the theme and its embodiment. Since aggressive acts can range from facial and verbal expressions to rape and murder but are substantially alike, their variety springs from their specific organization.

(2) Probability. Themes appear both logically and psychologically probable. A theme cannot contradict its meaning (support system). Since they posit meaning in terms of being, themes are represented through concrete, observable illustrations, comparisons, and associations that reflect modes of perception and thinking which are comprehensible to the reader.

(3) Delineation. Texts can either be organized around one central theme or interweave several themes. Secondary supporting themes have been linked to a central theme to support the main theme (individual development in reciprocal relationship with social reform and creation of a new community, confinement supporting disintegration or disintegration supporting confinement), to create ambiguity or point in the direction of the unknown (Goethe, *Egmont*: affirmation of life / lack of foresight – joy / failure; Raabe, *Alte Nester*: cheerful expectations for life / disappointment, retreat – adventure / indeterminate end). However, a theme remains a distinct conceptual unit no matter how much it may overlap with others. When supported by contrasting motif sequences, it can project possible alternate resolutions.

(4) Function. Themes are central organizational units of texts. Themes, figures, motifs, motif sequences, and metaphoric correlates are mutually dependent.

(5) Recurrence. Themes that recur over long periods of time retain their underlying support system. It is apparent, however, that their continued vitality springs from the historic sense of authors who weave the typical pattern into a new and unique fabric.

(6) Recurring primary themes in classicism and realism have consistently focused on human individuation. They have raised serious

questions concerning personality structure, the possible coexistence of opposites, limits of self-knowledge, the individual and society, and the relationship of the individual to the principles governing the universe. As a result, such themes have contributed to a powerful literary tradition reflecting a continuing struggle for self-realization in a fictional realm that accommodates patterns of conservation and radical change, a dialogue with the past and a vision of the future.

The Nature of Figure Conceptions

Most studies of literary figures (conventionally identified as characters, protagonists, or heroes) have been guided by the intent to elucidate the forces that prompted specific actions, motivational patterns, or unique character traits. Consequently, a wealth of research underscores the singular achievement and conveys the impression that noticeable similarities of figures result from timeless traits of human nature or recurring typical social, economic, or political conditions. Scholars who delineated typological features either focused on a series of dramatic situations that determine characterization [30] or stressed action-response sequences that establish a specific radius of possible movement.[31] Typological investigations have the advantage of systematizing textual invariance by showing the structural configuration underlying the apparently unlimited figure interactions. The text begins to resemble a chess game: the figures' movements are defined by the narrative function. Such analyses tend to arrive at a level of abstraction that interferes with the recognition of stylistic indicators of literary currents. In contrast, the study of dominant character traits presupposes that individual behavior is organized and rooted in a distinct personality structure. Depending on the focus of the research, such inquiries have advanced implied definitions that stress biological, juridical, theological, psychological, sociological, and biosocial factors. Even if a description of socio-psychological factors were purely mechanistic, it would presume a definition of the text as a cultural product that is blurred by references to a natural sphere. It is rarely clear whether the laws of nature should render the text meaningful, or whether the text should contain information that would aid in deciphering manifestations of nature.

Thematic analysis cannot resolve issues of mimesis, determinants of genre, or chance circumstances. It can show that figure conceptions are congruent with the principles governing the function of themes and motifs. It also enables us to anticipate the occurrence of distinctive figure constellations that are compatible with these principles.[32]

Literary figures attain their unique features through descriptive detail and particular behavior patterns assigned to them. The threads of a narrative sequence or actions represented in plays usually converge in principal figures. Once they have been linked to basic themes or motifs, their actions and reactions appear to be in consonance with these textual elements. This connection is especially valid for works that seek to create a semblance of reality by means of psychological probability. Specific works have provided singular and unforgettable portraits of figures who even influenced popular imagination to the extent that a person may be identified as having a Werther disposition or a Scrooge mentality. The features associated with primary figure conceptions show, however, a high correlation of recurring thematic patterns. Figures have a wide sphere of potential action, but they cannot move contrary to the support system established by themes or motifs. It is therefore more essential to ascertain the figure – theme – motif relationship than to pursue parallels between figure and subject matter. The marked differences in the Iphigenia tradition, for instance, are obviously rooted in dissimilar thematic conceptions of her personality: victim of circumstances, acquiescent servant of the divine will, loving daughter, a woman cherishing a new vision of ennobled life. Figures like Faustus who are identified with a powerful determination to overcome all limitations imposed by society or even human nature always attempt to move beyond established boundaries. Consequently, they may appear less restricted than chessmen. Yet, even in the Faust tradition, the various strands of themes, motifs, and symbols associated with the quest for self-realization and for the understanding of the world converge in the figure's dynamic expansion, thereby fusing person, situation, and action.

Figures can be conceived of being capable of intellectual and spiritual growth. They may also perceive in a moment of recognition their errors in judgment, the frailty of institutions, or a web of circumstances that impeded the full development of their capacities. In such instances, the action is usually designed to convey a vision of human potential to the reader or audience and to raise serious questions about the conviction that existence is foreordained. Alternately, figures may be presented in a series of encounters that convey the impression that they are carried along by events without comprehending the forces shaping their behavior. They can be portrayed as victims of circumstances who either helplessly struggle, acquiesce, or search for a form of accommodation that seems to promise their survival. Consequently, such primary themes as confinement, accommodation, aggression, coming of age, search for self-perfection, or self-realization tend to be linked to distinct personality structures.

Preferred figure conceptions during classicism and realism comprise five basic types: the person who is capable of development, gains self-knowledge, and acquires an understanding of the world; the exemplary individual; the character who evokes criticism; the ordinary person who meets with experiences that merit telling because they elucidate life; and the individual who encounters seemingly incomprehensible forces that eventually destroy self-determination or life itself. A frequently recurring feature linked to these figure conceptions is the representation of conflict situations in which an individual's self-evaluation and outlook on the world clash with group values or those expressed by contrast figures. Such encounters establish a pattern that duplicates the problem-solving process. In Schiller's *Maria Stuart*, for instance, a series of moves and countermoves is predicated on a delayed execution. The time span covers strategies of political intervention, aid by friends and lovers, force, the possibility of securing a pardon, and the clash of personal desires with the interest of the state. Each step designed to free her opens new avenues but is subsequently followed by a countermove that checks the maneuver until she finds a solution that frees her spiritually while claiming her life. She accepts injustice as deserved punishment for previous sins, renounces the world, and forgives her enemies. Thus the tragedy first raises the expectations of the central figures and the audience by promising fulfillment of a task set from the beginning, then eliminates all possibilities, and thereby strains expectations to the fullest. The conflict is resolved through a solution that permits Maria to mature to a point where she can renounce all temptations and preserve her integrity.

In *Tristram Shandy*, Lawrence Sterne juxtaposes two approaches to problem-solving that illuminate the difficulties in establishing probability factors for what can happen in a person's life. Toby Shandy, immersed in his hobby of model building, assembles and dismantles fortresses and cities. Consulting his extensive library on the subject, he designs ever-new arrangements which, however, not only incorporate but also lead to predictable patterns. Tristram journeys through the world, stumbles into adventures, and accepts unpredictability as an integral element of existence. Both learn and apply the acquired knowledge to new problems.

Noah, the central figure in Raabe's *Das Odfeld*, attempts to comprehend the complete disruption and disorder occasioned by war by relating his observations of the tumultuous events to his vast knowledge of myth, literature, philosophy, and history. At the end of his teaching career, he is forced from shelter, traverses a battlefield, and returns at the end of the day to his room. The continuous confrontations of contradictory perceptions of the present with the knowledge derived from studying the past reveal how an individual can slowly master apparently irreconcilable expressions of human thought and can begin to understand the regularity of recurring patterns through an unremitting process of inquiry. The diverse points of view in the narrative combine external movement with internal reflection and embrace the contrast between an ordered world and one governed by chance. They juxtapose moral imperatives and amoral processes, perfectly executed maneuvers and involuntary actions, the rational and the irrational. The points of view underscore the figure conception of an individual who moves through stages of intellectual growth while experiencing setbacks and moments of increased awareness. The interaction of figure and theme conveys the view that human development requires a dialectic process in which the present meets the past and historical certainty is balanced by unpredictable occurrences in the future.

The quest for self-knowledge and insight into the world has been associated consistently with a thematic development that represents human individuation as an interplay between personal motivation and social integration. The course of narrated action usually exposes the central figure to formative influences in five comprehensive areas: personal interaction, social conduct, nature, the cultural tradition, and scientific, philosophical, and political thinking. Consequently, those narratives shaped by the coming-of-age theme show a distinct stratification in the formative influences that mold the person's character.

Central figures are exposed to them during a course of action covering vast areas of human experience. During childhood and early
youth, they absorb impressions at home, in school, and in the immediate circle of neighbors in their village or town. Parents, friends, and
helpful guardians provide the first standards of social interaction. The
initial response to the world is conditioned by impressions of birth,
love, friendship, conflicts, and death. Conscious learning experiences
during the years of personality formation span conflicting, even contradictory sentiments and values in society. The young person leaves
home, moves to a large city, travels to a foreign country, feels love and
despair, encounters the forces of materialism and idealistic visions, and
gains insights into historical thinking, science, and the arts.
Frequently, a series of encounters with representative characters and
groups initiates a cognitive maturing process that eventually enables
the individual to gain self-knowledge and insight into the world.

Works generally follow the pattern of a triadic process in character
development. The initial response to the world is shaped by primary
events that the individual absorbs in a series of unreflected observations. Depending on the narrative point of view, scenes depicting early
impressions can be introduced at the beginning or at critical junctures
of the narration, when flashbacks, a stream-of-consciousness technique, or the device of dreams may serve to reinforce contrasting evaluations. The first experiences are recalled, enhanced, transformed,
and supplemented by conscious learning during the years of personality formation. A cognitive maturing process initiates the final phase
of individual growth, which requires the conscious perception of phenomena, the ability to objectify sentiments, and the intellectual curiosity to raise questions concerning human interrelationship with nature,
society, and the forces of the universe. Representative figures either
arrive at true self-insight or reach a level of maturity that enables them
to apply their knowledge to a wide spectrum of human thought and
action. By continuously examining contrasting views and reassessing
previous insights during successive experiences, the narratives project
a vision of increasing human consciousness. Once initiated, the process of reflection persists and accelerates. Cognition is projected onto
the existential plane with the ultimate goal of the complete liberation
of human imagination or is transposed into the social realm and becomes a philosophy of conscious activity, either freed from the dehu-

manizing effects of economical, political, or social determinism or directed toward a rational concern for the future of society.

The cornerstone of this thinking is the postulate that the present becomes intelligible by understanding the past and the future becomes predictable because a finite number of archetypes or invariant human tendencies can be identified behind the seemingly bewildering variety of events. Indeed, figure conception of developmental personalities presupposes a teleological view of history or at least the conviction that cause and intent can be established for all historical events. In his lecture, "Was heißt und zu welchem Ende studiert man Universalgeschichte?," Schiller counseled historians to select from the mass of data only those events that had "an essential, irrefutable, and easily demonstrable influence on the *present* constitution of the world." Ten years later, Novalis surmised in *Heinrich von Ofterdingen* that the historian and artist alike combine coincidences into an instructive whole. Both express thoughts deeply rooted in the classical tradition, current at their time, and of far-reaching consequence for the nineteenth century. By relating incidental occurrences to a plan, they have effectively excluded chance from historical thinking.

The absence of a causal correlation appears to be the most important element in figure conceptions that portray persons whose actions are prompted by unpredictable incidents or who fail to comprehend the forces that shape the environment. Like Frédéric Moreau and his companions in Flaubert's *L'Education sentimentale*, they react to events and circumstances rather than shaping them or searching for their meaning, because they cannot control or comprehend them. Linked to confinement, supported by a metaphoric field of life as a prison, the motifs of empty dialogue or silence, the destructive hand, and the circular path, such figures reflect a general human condition of "each person carrying his own room within him" (Kafka, "Brief an den Vater"). Isolated among others, even condemned to solitary confinement, they may seek liberation in acts of sudden violence designed to create the illusion of self-determination but are always trapped in the labyrinth of chance and the unknown. Yet, the paradox remains that confinement calls forth visions of freedom. The resulting dialectical relationship between the two themes creates powerful tensions in texts and readers alike. Fears of solitude, uncontrollable actions, and unpredictable events invariably arouse the desire for an explanation that will restore the semblance of order. If we consider such figure – theme – motif correlations as central building blocks in simulated narratives of human development, then the implied explanation that either assigns to or withholds from individuals a necessary place in nature and society should help us identify basic configurations in literary currents.

The narrative voice can also play a role in determining both theme and outlook of protagonist. In Charlotte Brontë's *Villette*, for example, though the coming-of-age theme shapes the chronological order of the protagonist's experiences and maturing process, it is undermined and supplanted by the theme of confinement. This theme reflects the narrator's outlook that in the nineteenth-century society of England and Belgium described by the text, the development and self-determination of women are restricted to a narrowly prescribed parameter defined by social convention. By having the same figure, Lucy Snowe, play the double role of protagonist and narrator and by placing considerable time between the two roles, Brontë can play both themes and figures ironically against each other. The effect is that in assuming the major role, confinement as theme bolsters the narrator's point of view over the protagonist's experiences expressed in the coming-of-age theme.

Classicism

In Joseph Addison's *Cato: A Tragedy*, the young Numidian prince Juba explains to his skeptical countryman Syphax his attraction to the noble old Roman senator Cato. The martial arts of directing troops, controlling fiery steeds, and guiding ponderous elephants through battle, skills cultivated by the Numidians in order to survive and conquer the vast deserts of their homeland, are "virtues of a meaner rank," when compared with the Roman values exemplified by Cato:

> A Roman soul is bent on higher views:
> To civilize the rude unpolish'd world,
> And lay it under the restraint of laws;
> To make man mild, and sociable to man;
> To cultivate the wild, licentious savage,
> With wisdom, discipline, and lib'ral arts;
> The embellishments of life: . . .[33]

The "soul bent on higher views," the civilizing influence on the "rude unpolish'd world," the "restraint of laws," human sociability, the cultivation of the "wild, licentious savage, / With wisdom, discipline, and lib'ral arts"—these are considerations associated with "classical" thinking. Critics agree that the term was derived from a phrase used by the late Latin writer Aulus Gellius quoting Cornelius Fronto in his miscellany *Noctes Atticus* (173 A.D.): *classicus scriptor non proletarius* to mean "first-class or excellent."[34] Fleischmann traces the two designations to Roman tax law. *Classicus* was the highest income level; *proletarius* was income below the taxable level. The *scriptor classicus* addressed the elite, while the *scriptor proletarius* wrote for the populous classes.[35] The oft-noted elitism of classical writings is then intimately connected with the origin of the term.

As Wellek points out, the adjectives "classical," "classique" and "klassisch" are considerably older than their corresponding nouns "classicism," "le classicisme," and especially "die Klassik." The nouns were applied by nineteenth-century critics to a specific period and style in literary history,[36] while the adjectives have acquired a multiplicity of meaning over the centuries. During the Renaissance, "classical" was synonymous with "good" (Thomas Sébillet, *L'Art poétique*, 1548) or "canonical" (Erwin Sandys, *Europa Speculum*, 1599).[37] "Classical" literary works were canonical texts approved for study in schools. Their language and style were to be imitated by the young. The use of the adjective, defined by Magnus Felix Ennodius in his sixth-century dictionary as a derivation from *classicus* —a student attending school—, became widespread among French and Italian critics of the Renaissance, the seventeenth and the eighteenth centuries.[38]

Canonical texts were selected from the writings of the ancients. Luck points out that scholars in Alexandria practiced the "authorization" of works already during the Hellenistic era. Faced with the necessity of choosing the most noteworthy well-established Greek texts for preservation in their library, they drew up lists of such works, called *kanones*. "Classical" literature was literature deemed worthy to be "classified" or catalogued in the collection. The authors on the list were the "sanctioned ones," "great ones," in short, Gellius' *classici*.[39] Post-Renaissance thought molded the Latin and Greek cultures into a single "classical" tradition that was firmly rooted in two ancient treatises on poetics: Aristotle's *Poetics* and Horace's *Art of Poetry*.[40] These works occasioned numerous translations that gave rise to critical debates and revaluations. They also inspired a continuous flow of imitations, interpretations, and expansions. Admiration for and preoccupation with these treatises directly influenced the formation of "classical doctrine" with its well-defined rules and procedures in France and England. The assimilation of classical tenets was strongly affected in Germany by the concurrent reception of French thought. Indeed, the system of classical principles that emerged in Germany had been filtered through successive reappraisals.[41]

The gradual fitting of ancient literature into a narrowly defined "classical mold" gave rise to continuous efforts either to modify or to apply norms derived from works of antiquity and classical poetics to contemporary literary currents. The tradition assimilated three orientations: the Aristotelian, the Horatian, and the changing perceptions of modernism. At times developing independently, at others converging, the trends were sustained by:

(1) commentaries, exegeses, and revaluations of Aristotle by Giangiorgio Trissino (*Poetica*, 1529/1563), Lodovico Castelvetro (*Poetica d'Aristotele vulgarizzata e sposta*, 1576), Jakob Masen (*Ars nova argutiarum*, 1649 and *Palaestra eloquentia ligatae*, 1654), Albrecht C. Rotth (*Vollständige Deutsche Poesie*, 1688), Gotthold E. Lessing (*Hamburgische Dramaturgie,* 1769), Johann G. Herder (*Über Bild, Dichtung und Fabel,* 1787), and Goethe ("Nachlese zu Aristoteles' Poetik," 1827);

(2) poetics that were deeply indebted to Horace's *Art of Poetry,* as for instance, Hieronymus Vida, *Poeticorum ad Franciscum . . .* (1520/1527) or Martin Opitz, *Buch von der Deutschen Poeterey* (1624) and adaptations of stylistic features or recommendations of Horatian principles by such diverse authors as Ben Jonson, John Milton, Edward Phillips, Alexander Pope, Joachim Du Bellay, Pierre Ronsard, and Nicolas Boileau;

(3) successive debates between authors defending classical principles and those who raised their voices in support of modern compositions. The most influential literary debates were provoked first in Italy during the sixteenth century by works initially regarded as unconventional (Ariosto's *Orlando furioso*, Dante's *La Divina Commedia*, Tasso's *Gerusalemme Liberata*). The dispute erupted in France

between 1688 and 1697 into a clash between the "Ancients" (Nicolas Boileau, Jean Racine, Pierre Daniel Huet, Jean de La Fontaine, Jean de La Bruyère) and the "Moderns" (the brothers Perrault, Jean Desmaretz, sieur de Saint-Sorlin). It was rekindled in 1714 by the contrasting evaluation of Homer by Antoine La Motte and Anne Dacier. The arguments continued in England with Pope's assertion in his *Discourse on Pastoral Poetry* (1709) that Virgil's refinement of Theocritus is superior, because each imitation is an improvement over its predecessor, and in Germany with Lessing's attack on the unreflected application of classical norms. In addition to a thorough revaluation of classical poetics, these debates contributed to a growing awareness that literary forms are not immutable.[42] Theoretical considerations in Germany from Johann Joachim Opitz to Johann Gottsched and Christoph Winckelmann to Lessing further contributed to a canon of critical thought that ultimately shaped the changing attitudes toward the role of mimesis, historical truth, psychological probability, illusion, and aesthetic distance in literature.

The persistent attention to the classical tradition not only colored self-evaluations or arguments defending artistic innovation but also influenced the reasoning of those critics who drafted poetics in the vernacular for contemporary audiences.[43] Moreover, the recurring tendency to think in terms of a hierarchic order of literature that extended from present-day creations to a timeless classical form persuaded a succession of authors to imitate past perfection. As a result, ancient literature, or specifically the theoretical canon linked to it, eventually became associated with an anti-modern and anti-progressive literary convention in the thinking of those writers who struggled to liberate themselves from the yoke of the past. Classical principles became the target of bitter polemics in debates between defenders of antiquity and proponents of modern tendencies. Rejecting the tyranny of classicism over the European mind, the "moderns" felt that artistic creativity could not be sustained by emulating past achievements. Literature should capture the unique spirit of contemporary life. However, the most persistent charge leveled against Neo-Aristotelians and Neo-Horatians appears to be based on the conviction that the entire classical canon rested on a mimetic theory that was misleading and poorly understood. The moderns looked for fantasy, not reality in literature. Madame de Staël, one of the great popularizers of "Northern" romanticism, summarized this sentiment accurately in the influential *De l'Allemagne* (1810): "Ancient literature is for modern people a transplanted literature; romantic or chivalric literature is indigenous to us."[44] In her brief discussion of *classique*, she also rejects the most widely accepted connotation of classic as it occurs in the caption "world classics": a model, an authoritative literary work, the perfection of which is so generally admired that it becomes a permanent, outstanding example of a given national literature.

Still, the meaning of national or world classics has persisted to the present.[45] Sainte-Beuve's "Qu'est-ce qu'un classique" (1850) and T.S. Eliot's "What Is a Classic?" (1944) come to the same conclusion: a true classic is a "mature work," fully exploiting the possibilities of language and the spirit of the nation it represents. "It is the importance of that civilization and of that language, as well as the comprehensiveness of the mind of the individual poet, which gives universality."[46] It is written by an author "who has enriched the human spirit, . . . who has discovered an unequivocal moral truth or grasped an eternal passion . . . who has rendered his thought, observation, or invention in some great and grandiose, delicate and sensitive, healthy and beautiful form . . . easily the contemporary of all ages."[47] In our time, Levin reversed Walter Pater's generalization that "all good art was romantic in its day" by stating: "all good art that survives its day is classical."[48] Yet, by extending the term to such dissimilar authors as Homer, Virgil, Dante, Shakespeare, Milton, Racine, Molière, Goethe and Schiller, to cite but a few true "classics," the standard practice simply puts a stamp of approval on so-called masterworks without regard for any unifying traits.

The application of the terms *classicism, le classicisme,* and *Klassik* to a unique style and historical period can be traced to the onset of European romanticism. Though writers and critics alike had discussed the art of antiquity, studied classical literature, and debated the merits of modern works by contrasting them with those of the past, the romantics took advantage of the term to create an ideologically charged concept that embodied the antithesis to their program.[49] Defining their movement as progressive, revolutionary, independently creative and original, they identified the traditional literature as dominated by reason, regularity, rules, and traditions. Each nation discovered the presence of these traits in its own literature at a specific time.

The French romantics found them in the age of Louis XIV which combined Cartesian reason with Aristotelian poetic regulation and a Horatian sense of proportion and balance.[50] The German romantics, particularly the Schlegel brothers, singled out their immediate predecessors, especially Schiller, as perpetrating these values.[51] The English had the most difficult time of all. Reason, regularity, and rules characterized the writings of Pope, Swift, Addison, and Dryden. Measured against Shakespeare and Milton, whose works could certainly not be called strongly traditional, or compared with the European renown of Racine and Molière, these writers seemed insignificant and colorless. The designations "classical" and "classicism" used approvingly for the French writers of the seventeenth century did not fit the English authors of the eighteenth century, despite the fact that they admired and consciously imitated the French.[52] Since French classical writers already imitated ancient models, it was felt that the English acquired their art from previous imitators. For this reason, nineteenth-century critics called them "pseudo-classical" or "neoclassical." The latter term has persisted, together with "Augustan" and simply "classical." Even today, "classicism" is not a firmly established term in English literary history.[53] The spirit of the romantics was not felt to be a powerful reaction or to be completely antithetical to the views espoused during the age of Pope, Dryden, and Swift.[54]

German critics, in contrast, assigned the term *Klassizismus* to those authors who consciously imitated ancient or French classical modes. First used by Hermann Hettner in *Literaturgeschichte des achtzehnten Jahrhunderts* (1856-1857) to designate French classicism, it became a convenient name for Otto Harnack in his study *Goethe in der Epoche seiner Vollendung* (1887) to distinguish such writers as Gottsched, J.E. Schlegel, and Wieland from the true *Klassiker* Goethe and Schiller. Although Walzel still applied *Klassizismus* to the writings of Goethe and Schiller in 1922, *Klassik* has become the accepted designation for Goethe's and Schiller's mature work.[55]

Nineteenth-century literary historians found that for several reasons the first efflorescence of post-Antiquity classicism occurred in France from 1660 to 1700. These years marked the coincidence of Louis XIV's most active interest in literature and the arts with the height of creativity of the era's greatest writers.[56] After years of religious, political, social, and cultural turbulence, the court of Louis XIV affirmed the king's absolute authority, upheld the hierarchical order of the aristocracy, and set specific standards of elegance in manners and language. The medieval, chivalric code of conduct became outmoded.[57] A new concept, that of *honnêteté*, or civilized behavior, dominated relationships at the court.[58] A period of stability and peace, though broken at times by such events as the criminal activity of the *Fronde* and the poisonings, gave the nobility gathered at Versailles leisure to occupy themselves precisely with those "lib'ral arts" lauded by Juba in Addison's *Cato*.[59] They formed a discerning appreciative audience for works which in turn reflected essential values in their courtly functions: politeness, refinement, elegance, and precision of expression, restraint, rules, and an appeal to reason as the guide to human relationships. Later generations admired and envied this harmony between literature and its audience. They often identified the classical outlook as reflecting the true French spirit. Indeed, simultaneous with French political hegemony, the norms set by French classicism dominated much of European literature throughout the following century.[60]

Like the French court of Louis XIV, classical writers had their supreme authority against which they measured their work: that of antiquity. Yet like their Renaissance predecessors, they based their understanding of ancient society and literature on an internalized image which did not necessarily correspond to historical facts. As aggressively modern in their time as writers are today, they did not hesitate to transform history or add to it in order to fit their needs and the patterns of their society.[61] In focusing on the intense personal confrontations and decisions made by long-admired but distant heroes of old, they created works of singular vivacity. The gradual shift of emphasis from emotion to reason, already noticeable during the years of French classicism, but fully apparent in the following century had three consequences. Classicism was acknowledged as the acceptable literary style by the proponents of Enlightenment, particularly by Voltaire. Certain aspects, above all, clarity of thought and design and elegance of expression became international hallmarks against which the value of an author's work was measured. Finally, the loss of the emotional intensity of a tragedy by Racine or a comedy by Molière in the interest of rational arguments established a new period in literary history: neoclassicism.[62]

In contrast to the short and precisely defined age of classicism in French literature, English literature had a number of classical "moments" or "aspects" over a period of nearly a century and a half.[63] Most literary historians have agreed that the ascent of Charles II to the English throne paved the way for classicism in England which continued to flourish until the second half of the eighteenth century. In reestablishing the monarchy after the radical politics of the Commonwealth, the need for order, authority, restraint, and refinement was perhaps even greater in England than in the France of Louis XIV. Prominent persons in the government established by Charles II encouraged those writers who stressed clarity, elegance, design, and morality in their writings.[64] Grateful for the prospect of a new age of peace and prosperity after the discord and upheaval of the Commonwealth, Restoration writers responded by repeatedly drawing parallels between the reinstituted monarchy and the golden age for the arts in Rome under Augustus. As critics have pointed out, Dryden's *Astraea Redux* (1660), his translation of the *Aeneid*, and even Pope's translation of the *Iliad* were among the many attempts by writers to give expression to their hope that under the monarchy, an "Augustan" age for the English language, literature, and monarchy would arise.[65] English authors turned especially to Virgil and Horace as reliable long-proven models for shaping public life and morality through their works. Imitations of Horace and Virgil were popular. While building on the traditional models, however, English classicists, like their French predecessors whom they read and admired, carefully adapted their work to the English situation. Finding satires, epistles, and pastorals to be well-suited to the English scene, they polished, expanded, and transformed these genres to express their moral stand on the political, social, and aesthetic issues of the day. The epic, in contrast, with its particular view of the individual's relationship with the universe, was unsuitable as a means of reacting to the urbanity and rising mercantilism of eighteenth-century England. Finally, the tendency of English classicists to preach morality in every literary creation stifled their attempts at tragedy, which had been the glory of French classicism.[66] They did, however, create novels that are still widely read, such as Jonathan Swift's *Gulliver's Travels* (1726) or Daniel Defoe's *Robinson Crusoe* (1719).

German classicism is one phase of a general intellectual development in Germany which saw an unprecedented ascent in creative forces and is characterized by a distinct acceleration of stylistic and cultural change. During the brief span of 1770 to 1830, three literary movements, Storm and Stress, classicism, and romanticism reached their apexes. In addition, the period covers not only the publication of Lessing's critical appraisal of theological thinking, his play *Nathan der Weise* (1779), and *Die Erziehung des Menschengeschlechts* (1780) but also the productive years of Friedrich Hölderlin, Heinrich Kleist, and Jean Paul. The music of Gluck, Haydn, Mozart, and Beethoven captured Europe. The American Declaration of Independence and the French Revolution generated a ferment of ideas. Napoleon's expansionism and the War of Intervention brought the threat of violent changes and aroused nationalistic sentiments. Johann Gottfried Herder laid the foundation for a new appraisal of myths, folklore, and national literatures. Achim von Arnim and Clemens Brentano compiled *Des Knaben Wunderhorn* (1806-1808), a collection of folk songs and poems that in their opinion expressed the German spirit. Jacob and Wilhelm Grimm published their collection of fairy tales (*Kinder- und Haus-Märchen*, 1812-1815) and sagas (*Deutsche Sagen*, 1816-1818). Kant laid the foundation for philosophic idealism and formulated a philosophical system that was to dominate completely the thought of the nineteenth century. As an unintentional result of his and Johann Gottlieb Fichte's investigations, the theocratic view of history, already questioned during the Age of Reason, fell into further disrepute. Moreover, anthropological studies, the growth of the scientific spirit, and the beginning of comparative interpretations of religion nurtured an increasingly skeptical attitude toward religious dogma, with its proofs of God's existence, as well as toward theism itself. Suddenly, individuals had to adjust to the idea of a transcendental God in a transcendental world.

In literature and the arts, the entire period is characterized by conflicting tendencies. To be sure, many works show striking similarities in such thematic concerns as coming of age, the individual's precarious existential situation, and broad issues of human development. But solutions of central questions range from the affirmation of the faith in reason and the evolution of a rational society or the confidence that individual potential could develop freely under the right circumstances to explorations of unconscious anxieties and visions of disintegrating personality structures. Stylistically, the period shows experiments with forms and modes of expression extending from the restoration of classical forms to the abandonment of traditional genre-oriented requirements. Goethe's and Schiller's works also show clear signs of stylistic innovation. They do not always adhere strictly to the Aristotelian unities or the regularity of form typical of French classicism. Instead, Goethe and Schiller strove for an organic form, one in which subject matter, action, themes, motifs, and stylistic characteristics were fused. Furthermore, they expressed a view of the individual's relationship to society and to an ordering principle in the universe that differed fundamentally from the thinking of the romantics.

Weimar classicism, also known as *Hochklassik*, has traditionally been dated to coincide with Goethe's first Italian journey (1786-1788), the years of collaboration with Schiller, the efforts of both authors to reappraise the role of art in society, and Goethe's increasing interest in symbolic forms.[67] A distinctive characteristic of Goethe's and Schiller's artistic concern is the search for a mode of representation that would adequately express confidence in the individual's ability to shape the future and guarantee human dignity while acknowledging inner drives, fears, and potentially restrictive sociopolitical forces. It is also clear that the ideas of individual and social perfection expressed by Goethe, Schiller, Herder, and Wilhelm von Humboldt contributed a unique dimension to German classicism. While the views expressed by these men were in a sense too imaginative and personal to constitute a "theory of culture," they acted as a unifying factor first in the cultural and later in the political life of Germany.

In a collection of essays entitled *Von deutscher Art und Kunst* (1773), Herder, Goethe, and Justus Möser stressed three ideas of major consequence for the development of the German concept of culture: first that nature, culture, and art follow the same evolutionary path (an idea of organic growth); second, that great art is based on common cultural values (appreciation of the Middle Ages); finally, that a variety of forms, called nations, develop in the evolutionary process of society, though the measure of cultural progress differs from nation to nation. In his *Ideen zur Philosophie der Geschichte der Menschheit* (1784-1791), Herder restated his belief that the pure national spirit is to be found in a people's myths, sagas, songs, and rituals. While asserting the view that artists are prompted by their historical period, culture,

and personal needs, Herder stressed that the finest national art transmits the heritage and destiny of the whole human race, as well as furthering human perfection.

The cultural heritage presented itself to Goethe not as fact but as a
challenge. Its validity and ultimate significance depended entirely on
society's ability to awaken the past and infuse it with new life. Despite
the fact that he viewed history essentially as intellectual history, he accepted technical and industrial developments as important steps in the
progressive quest for self-liberation.[68] Goethe's approach to the understanding of the past and the present was one of active participation;
he felt that true insight into cultural, historical, and natural phenomena
could best be gained by establishing an almost personal relationship
to objects. Thus he transformed them into subjects with whom he
could enter into a dialogue. A cathedral became an intimate friend, a
great artist of the past, his brother, and nature, the primeval mother
who nourished him. Such continuous communication, for instance,
generated the great immediacy with which he experienced antiquity
during his Italian journey. Indeed, Goethe felt that such a dialogue
that demands constant reflection and reappraisal of one's own position, could expand the individual's cultural consciousness and thereby
lead to self-knowledge. He was also interested in cultural achievements that express the dignity of humanity by providing standards
and values that enable individuals to reach their potential fully and
harmoniously.[69]

Schiller saw culture primarily as a regulative process that was at
once liberating and restraining, and as a system of institutions promot-
ing human existence and welfare.[70] All political and social institutions
must be evaluated "insofar as they further the growth of all of man's
faculties, insofar as they advance the development of culture or at least
do not impair it."[71] In accordance with the spirit of his age, Schiller
believed that the unsurpassed cultural achievements of Greece can be
attributed to the equilibrium established between individual desires
and the demands of society, between sensuous needs and intellectual
capacities. Although he questioned some of the conclusions reached
by Winckelmann in his influential studies on Greek art, Schiller
agreed with Winckelmann's genetic account of the evolution of styles
and ideas, especially with the view that an interrelationship exists between sociopolitical forces and the arts. Based on the "noble simplic-

ity and calm grandeur" of Greek sculpture, Winckelmann's picture of
the harmonious Hellenic personality seems overidealized. Yet, compared to the fragmentation and specialization of modern life with its
internal tensions and external conflicts, Greek culture can teach individuals how to reach a harmonious balance of all faculties and desires.
The society envisioned by Schiller has essentially the same characteristics as the Rome described by Juba in Addison's *Cato*: continuous reform, a balance of looking forward to the future while being enriched
by the past, the humanization provided by the arts, and harmony between all its segments:

> Lasting reforms must begin with man's character. . . .
> The state, political freedom, and civil rights depend on
> the character of the citizen. . . . Political freedom and
> civil liberties will always remain our most sacred pos-
> session, the highest goal to be achieved, and the mag-
> nificent center of all culture. But this marvelous struc-
> ture can only be built upon the solid foundation of
> man's ennobled character. It will be necessary to edu-
> cate citizens for a constitution before you can give a
> constitution to citizens.[72]

In order to delineate classicism, literary historians have established
a series of characteristics for a "classical" work. Many of these were
already stressed by French classical writers and their contemporary
critics. Over the years, they have occasioned heated debate, have been
rejected and resurrected. The true classical work teaches by entertaining (*docere cum delectatione*). "The cardinal rule of rules is to
please," says Dorante in Molière's *Critique de L'Ecole des femmes*
(1663), while in his preface to *Tartuffe* Molière defines the goal of
comedy "to correct men by entertaining them."[73] While convinced
that ancient literature, history, and mythology furnish the most inspiring and entertaining material available, the creative classical writers
search for precisely those moments that will touch their own audiences. Although carefully avoiding gross distortions of their models,
they readily change elements that repel their contemporaries and add
characters or scenes which they feel their audiences will need.
Racine's prefaces demonstrate the classical writer's delicate balance between fidelity to his ancient sources and the demands of contemporary
viewers. On the one hand, he defends Pyrrhus' barbaric ferocity in

Andromaque with the remark that his character "had not read our [courtly] novels; he was violent by nature." On the other hand, he has changed the tradition: Andromaque's concern for her son fathered by Pyrrhus is transferred to Astyanax, Hector's son. The new figure conception conforms better "to the idea we now have of this princess," and therefore the spectators' tears will flow more abundantly. While in his first preface to *Britannicus* Racine states that he strove to please a "small number of wise men" like Homer, Virgil, and Sophocles, he is equally pleased to discover that the spectators of his *Iphigénie* are moved to tears by the same passions that once moved the ancient Greeks in Euripides' tragedy.[74]

That "the taste of Paris" should be the same as Athens' points to another classical precept: emphasis on the universality of the human emotional and rational nature. All human beings, according to this conception, share in being a "Chaos of Thought and Passion, all confused."[75] Classical writers attempt to make order out of this chaos. It would be in their interest to attract spectators' or readers' attention by showing the domination of passion over human action and reason. Racine justifies his choice of topic in his preface to *Bérénice*, "because of the violence of the emotions which it could excite." At the same time, allegiance to the classical doctrine of teaching by entertaining requires him to emphasize the "disorder" that passion creates.[76]

In order to discern this disorder, the audience should not completely identify with the passions portrayed. This requirement necessitated a number of distancing techniques. First, the supremacy of reason, recognized by classical audiences as the final and universal arbiter of human conduct, served to restrain and refine any direct expression of emotion.[77] Good judgment and taste, as defined by the elite audiences that classical writers strove to please, limited their depiction to the socially and, by extension, morally acceptable. Moreover, a number of rules established in France prior to the flourishing of classicism spelled out clearly what was considered to be presentable. In the hierarchy of literary genres, the tragedy was the most narrowly prescribed. In addition to the Aristotelian unities of time, place, action, and conception of character, the writer of tragedies must observe both contemporary propriety (*bienséance*) and historical plausibility (*vraisemblance*). The preoccupation with producing works "according to the rules" led to an emphasis on correct form and precise structure. Thus, the French insisted on Alexandrine verse, while the English classical writers preferred the heroic couplet. Reason was interpreted as dictating that classical works exhibit the characteristics of clarity and simplicity of design, elegance, and correctness of expression. To achieve these goals, the writer had to practice self-discipline, self-effacement, and orderliness, to be "modestly bold" and "humanely severe." Finally, a certain serenity and noble grandeur became the recognized traits of a truly classical work and of its ideal hero or heroine.[78] The adjectives noble, formal, precise, correct, balanced, even cold, have dominated traditional discussions of the classical style. Certainly, the reader encountered intense emotional struggles in classical literature. But reason, order, judgment, and above all, a propensity for analysis and self-analysis more than counterbalanced emotion, with the result that the spectator's response was guided by detached reflection and admiration, rather than by emotional involvement.[79]

Recent literary historians have questioned this rather restrictive characterization. If all manifestations of classical literature were only serene, universal, impersonal, and concerned with general truths and public morality, the entire period or style would have shared the fate of English classical tragedy.[80] Critics have argued, however, that even the oft-noted humanistic interests of classical writers were actually directed at the civilized courtly or urban audience for whom they primarily wrote.[81] Nevertheless, were one to consider the oft-experimental approaches of classical writers to contemporary problems, their skillful application of rules to increase spectator suspense, the scarcely suppressed realm of the passions lurking beneath the smooth polished language and highly ordered structure of their works, the strong tensions not to be soothed by insistence on serenity or equilibrium, and the portrayal of many characters as victims of other characters, circumstance, or "fate,"[82] then classicism becomes far more complex and ambiguous a term than had been traditionally assumed. As a result of these investigations, there have been inquiries about the continued utility of the designation "classicism" and even calls for its abolishment. Rousset has proposed integrating French classical authors into the general European movement of the Baroque.[83] Many non-German critics have persistently classified Goethe and Schiller as romantics.[84] English classicism could be considered as a manifestation of the Enlightenment. What common features does classical literature exhibit other than respect for and adherence to ancient literature?

A second look at Addison's *Cato* can assist in answering this question. Juba, we recall, is attracted to the noble spirit of the Roman senator because of certain features long regarded as "classical": nobility of outlook, civilized conduct, wisdom, discipline, concern for others, and culture: " . . . virtues like these / Make human nature shine, reform the soul, / And break our fierce barbarians into men." Unconvinced, Syphax questions whether these "wond'rous civilizing arts" would not "change us into other creatures / Than what our nature and the gods design'd us?" Juba not only acknowledges this consequence but strongly affirms its potential: "There [in Cato] may'st thou see to what a god-like height / The Roman virtues lift up mortal man . . ."[85] In proclaiming a radically different form of existence from the realist's recognition of human weakness, anxieties, and inherent aggressiveness, Juba expresses the classical belief that an individual has the capability to transform himself, that is, raise himself from the barbarian to the civilized, cultured, socialized creature and from that refined state to a height of virtue achieved by the gods. We propose that it is this dynamic movement away from the restraints dictated by one's surroundings toward the freedom of determining one's actions and attitudes despite circumstances that characterizes all truly classical works of art.

The classical work of art denies neither chance occurrences in life nor the reality of the hostile environment. On the contrary, viewers of Addison's *Cato* witness the growing power of evil spreading from Caesar's menace to ancient Roman liberties to reach into Cato's shrinking camp. Caesar's tactics of aggression influence Cato's former allies Sempronius and Syphax to mutiny against Cato. Overcome by the futility of his increasingly lonely moral stand against Caesar's military might and popularity, Cato takes his own life. But in dying, Cato exemplifies self-sacrificing generosity and concern as he arranges for the safe escape of his comrades and a secure future for his children. Even his corpse is to be "A fence betwixt us and the victor's wrath; / Cato, tho' dead, shall still protect his friends." (V) In continuing his protective role after death, he has achieved the god-like status of eternal life.[86] At the same time, his steadfastness and generosity are to be exemplary for his family, comrades, and for the spectators of the tragedy.[87] The centrifugal spiral that corresponds to the expansive pattern of Cato's behavior as it first ascends from barbarism to civilization and next to divinity, then moves outward from individual to community and finally to universal reform. This pattern of moving upward, outward, and forward is one of the features of the classical attitude toward ancient Graeco-Roman history and literature. While regarding the ancients as models of human conduct and literary excellence, true classical writers in all three countries sought to establish in their works new models to be emulated by their successors and public. The authors clearly searched for a new basis of existence and an order that would reconcile individual aspirations with a broad concern for the interests of society.[88]

Realism

In 1833 Honoré de Balzac declared in a letter to his sister Laure that he sought to portray the human condition with scientific accuracy. Later in his "Preface" to the *Comédie humaine* (1842), he observed that "French society was going to be the historian; I would only be the secretary. "[89] As secretary of a large, diffuse, and complex society, the novelist "would choose the principal events of Society and compose types by linking together the traits of several homogeneous characteristics," that is, by weaving the multiple threads into a cohesive pattern. The emerging picture in his novels reveals the individual's dependence on society, the far-reaching impact of the milieu, and a preponderance of character traits antithetical to those promulgated by classical texts. After Emile Zola applied this "realistic" point of view in *Les Rougon-Macquart,* several contemporary reviewers praised both the astonishing accuracy of detailed scenes and the sweeping panorama of typical social conditions. The dominant literary convention of nineteenth-century realism is certainly shaped to a considerable extent by attempts to account for the conditions influencing individual development and social interaction. The most outspoken adherents of the view that human existence was entirely determined by socioeconomic forces were convinced that individuals had no free choice and no power over their destiny. In "Die naturwissenschaftlichen Grundlagen der Poesie" (1887), Wilhelm Bölsche called for a realistic assessment of the individual's potential in the light of these well-established "facts." Ultimately, such thinking paved the way for judgments like Theodore Dreiser's, who summarized the essence of life bereft of any spiritual dimension in his essay "The Essential Tragedy of Life":

> How could there possibly be success for a watery, bulbous, highly limited and specially functioned creature . . . made apparently not in the image and likeness of anything superior to himself but in that of an accidentally compelled pattern, due to an accidental arrangement of chemicals, his every move and aspiration anticipated and accounted for by a formula and an accidentally evolved system long before he arrives, and he himself puling, compact of vain illusions in regard to himself, his "mission," his dominant relation to the enormous schemes of Nature, and ending, if "life" endures so long, in toothless senility and watery decay, dissolution.[90]

The term *realism* (related to the Latin *res* and real estate) first occurred in scholastic philosophy to denote the recognition of the objective reality of the external world and of ideas.[91] In philosophy, realism stands in opposition to the doctrine of essences which maintains that the external world or ideas represent abstractions. From its beginnings, then, the focus of realism was on the authority of experience rather than preconceived patterns of thought or structure. Thomas Reid, Kant, Schiller, and Schelling used the term in contrast to idealism. Realism identifies a view of the world that assigns a primary value to the observable or what "the normal human consciousness" can absorb through the senses.[92] Wellek traces its first application to a literary technique to Schiller's letter to Goethe on April 27, 1798, which states: "realism cannot make a poet." The first truly literary adoption of the term appears to have been by an article in the *Mercure Français* of 1826 that defines realism as the "doctrine which leads to faithful imitation not of the masterworks of art but of the originals offered by nature."[93] This goal, which contrasts sharply with the classical emulation of historical, mythological, or literary examples, was seconded by the preface written supposedly by Champfleury for the catalogue to Courbet's personally staged exhibition entitled "Le Réalisme" at the World's Fair of 1855. Its proclamation, "to depict the manners, ideas, and appearance of my time as I see it, in short to produce living art," has been declared "the true manifesto and charter of the school [of realism]."[94] In emphasizing the superiority of the artist's individual experience to all previously heralded literary traditions, realists accepted the new limitations that these experiences inevitably brought with them. By restricting their works to "true-to-life," everyday lives, they gained accuracy and precision in their descriptions of environment and portrayal of characters.

Other critics and novelists, notably a group of authors in Germany who formulated a program for realistic writing, called for a literature that not only recreated the social conditions faithfully but also upheld a sense of human dignity and gave direction to the search for a new basis of existence. The specific requirements for this type of realistic narration were outlined by Julian Schmidt, Gustav Freytag, Emil Homberger, Rudolf Gottschall, Hermann Hettner, and Karl Gutzkow after 1848 in such leading literary journals of the period as *Die Grenzboten, Deutsches Museum, Europa,* and *Blätter für literarische Unterhaltung.* The critics agreed on a series of principles that would insure "realistic" portraits in contrast to the "idealistic" characterizations of classicism. The realist should not only observe social phenomena objectively but also capture the persistent vitality of life. The narrator should be truthful. But in addition to complete accuracy in depicting the inner substance of reality (*Gesetz der Wirklichkeit*), poetic veracity required the ability to rise above the profusion of nature's unique manifestations. The narrator was to be highly selective and capture in the text a central, unifying idea that would give not only significance to the story but also meaning to life. Such artistic transfiguration would lend poetic form to the aspirations of the reading public.[95] Theodor Fontane expressed the essential thrust of such criticism when he asserted that art should enhance freedom, not negate it. He admitted that the characters, milieu, and individual concerns portrayed in Zola's novels seem to be true to life. Yet, the cross-section of society lacks an essential element: "The whole appears as a negation of the individual's *free will.* A person has no soul, *that through its own power,* despite all weakness and temptation can achieve something great, beautiful, noble, or heroic. People always act under an influence."[96]

The primacy of meticulous observation and analysis of mundane occurrences and circumstances became, according to most critics, a hallmark of realism. But Duranty's call for dispassionate, impersonal objectivity in his short-lived journal *Réalisme* (1856-1857) also led to the sacrifice of writers' traditional role of mediation between their work and their audience. Writers were to absent themselves and instead of moral judgment, sympathy, or even antipathy, were to present a strictly amoral viewpoint. Needless to say, few of the early realist writers heeded this demand.[97] It did result, however, in a shift away from the traditional emphasis of literature on feelings, thoughts, and personal development to a concentration on the world of objects: rooms, streets, cities, clothing, money and property, and by extension, the particular historical moment with its social and economic conditions. These were often of a sordid nature; for portraying realistically the common, everyday lives of industrial workers, homemakers, or farmers meant the depiction of their drab surroundings and hopeless circumstances.[98] The seriousness with which some realists treated this milieu and their refusal to romanticize it underscored their adherence to a philosophy of determinism. The actual worker, soldier, homemaker, or farmer, they reasoned, is dominated not by mysterious forces or a personal destiny but by impersonal physical, economic, social, and hereditary circumstances. Endowed with such limited intellectual and emotional capabilities that they cannot even comprehend their situation, these men and women turn to their instincts, particularly sex, anger, and flight in order to relieve at least temporarily their fear and anxiety. However, because figures cannot escape the circumstances that determine their existence, realistic texts show that such retreats are as illusory as the retreat from the city to the simple life in the idyllic village.

Many nineteenth-century critics derived the model for realistic literature from prose narrations in which setting, major characters, and theme reflected concerns of the middle class. Consequently, the earliest critical concern with realistic writing focused on the substance of texts. When George Meredith distinguishes in a letter to A. Jessop on September 20, 1864 between a "high and generous" and a "low and groveling reality," he resorts to a frequently advanced argument of the period. Realistic art should not reproduce the aimless, noisy, and turbulent here and now but show a "meaningful" pattern which would capture a vision of human individuation that contrasted favorably with the existing social strife. In a review of Flaubert's *L'Education sentimentale,* Homberger uses the distinction to criticize the novelist's cold and detached point of view. Flaubert, he argues, describes the world faithfully. However, since he reports everything with the same "indifferent" objectivity, he fails to convey an understanding of the period's historical dimension.[99]

Literary historians have echoed nineteenth-century characterizations of realism as the literary expression of the rising middle class and of the dominating bourgeois society of the nineteenth century. Reflecting the growth in importance of merchants, manufacturers, and traders during the Restoration in England, a literature that viewed trade, commerce, and industry with favor and adopted middle-class attitudes toward life arose and took its place next to that of neoclassicism. Specifically, it was the realistic novel that began in England with Defoe, Richardson, and Fielding; in France with Stendhal and Balzac, in Germany with Gustav Freytag, Otto Ludwig, Friedrich Spielhagen, and Wilhelm Raabe; and in America with the popular literature after the Civil War that most faithfully represented the middle-class work ethic and the goal of acquiring wealth, power, and prestige through industriousness, and if necessary, through speculation or manipulation of the system.[100] Some novelists felt that the aspirations and the spirit of the middle class could best be shown by describing people at work, at home, and among their circle of friends. Other authors sharply criticized the negative effects of the Industrial Revolution, attacked the inhumane working conditions, probed the increasingly impersonal relationships, and called for social, political, and economic reform.[101]

The connection between realists and middle-class values is illustrated in their passionate embrace of history and historical studies. Their fascination with the past expressed itself in two forms: a proliferation of historical novels and fictionalized historical accounts and a consistent turning back toward the past in narratives of contemporary life that contrasts sharply with the forward-looking spirit of classicism. Balzac's first signed novel, *Les Chouans,* was a historical novel. Throughout Europe and especially in Germany, historical novels and fictionalized history enjoyed immense popularity. They often glorified the actions of heroic individuals, national spirit and mission, the rise of the middle class, and its virtues of work, patriotism, and order. Historical novels like Victor von Scheffel's *Ekkehard,* mentioned only in passing in literary histories today, were immensely popular: 330,000 copies of *Ekkehard* were sold by 1900. The success of such historical novels as Gustav Freytag's *Die Ahnen* can be traced to their presentation of a dynamic past that explained to readers the positive characteristics of the contemporary German people. Critics have differed in their assessment of the significance of these novels for realism. While Lukács asserts that historical novels are of critical importance, Müller-Seidel considers only a few to possess aesthetic quality, and others, like Broch, condemn the genre as an escape into the idyllic.[102] A study of their themes and motifs could aid in evaluating the importance of historical novels for the development of realism. In examining the question of the individual's comprehension of sociopolitical forces, authors like Raabe (*Das Odfeld*) certainly do contribute to the thematic development of realism.

In addition, realist narratives and dramas set in contemporary times from Balzac and George Eliot to Raabe, Henry James, and Nathalie Sarraute, are filled with detailed descriptions of old houses, streets, towns, collections of antiques, art objects, and other collectibles. These assume widely ranging primary functions in the texts. They inspire nostalgia for the "lost paradise" of a past time when life was comprehensible and events were controllable that contrasts starkly with the incomprehensible, uncontrollable forces of the present. The objects from the past symbolize stability and endurance at a time of inexplicable, threatening change. The impulse to collect, trade, and retain old and beautiful objects is one expression of the accumulating and possessive instinct of many of realism's most memorable figures (Balzac's Pons, Raabe's Wunnigel, Henry James's Osmond, Sarraute's Tante Berthe). Perhaps most importantly, the focus on the glorification of the past indicates a turning backward to the old that is the antithesis of the classical stance of affirming the opportunities to shape the present and future, as exemplified by Goethe's *Egmont, Faust,* and *Wilhelm Meister.*

Two considerations, the representation of an individual's free will and the historical roots of social forces, were inherent in the comparisons between the emerging literary convention and the classical literature of the past that served to highlight the new realistic style. These comparisons, as well as the tendency to focus on the narrative's substance, left their imprint on subsequent literary histories of the period.

Thus, Heselhaus and Brinkmann note that literary historians consistently stressed the material substance of realism and yet did not succeed in arriving at a definition that accounted for substantive and formal elements.[103] More recently, several scholars have applied Bakhtin's concepts of multiple voices and the centrifugal and centripetal forces to account for certain narrative techniques in realism.[104] Structuralists have demonstrated that the apparently accurate portrait of reality, especially the description of objects, reveals not only significant changes in human interaction but also important shifts in literary figure conceptions.[105] Various critics in Germany have attempted a complete revaluation of realistic writing by analyzing the dialectics of perception, selection, and signification in the process of artistic creation.[106] Scholars of the period agree that realism parallels the sweeping changes in the philosophical thinking of the nineteenth century and the social reorganization set into motion by the Industrial Revolution. No one doubts that realists not only portray a changed society and the effects of social institutions on individuals but also explore new thematic concerns and develop new motif clusters.

Nevertheless, a thematic analysis of the stylistic cross-currents between 1850 and 1910 indicates significant shifts in artistic concerns as well as the persistence of traditional narrative techniques, classical figure conceptions, established themes, and a high prevalence of stylistic inconsistencies that occur when, for instance, the idea of a free personal development is contradicted by other dominant textual patterns. Such recurring inconsistencies point to a central problem in the evaluation of realistic features in texts. The authors select both details and significant patterns from a vast number of individual phenomena. Their arrangement is determined by compositional considerations. Since the realistic principle requires not only a semblance of reality but also the representation of every scene in such a natural manner that it would appear accurate, the author has to superimpose upon the narrative a series of details which create the illusion that the text no longer obeys the laws of composition but directly reflects social reality. However, authors, like other observers, organize the diverse, changing impressions of reality, select specific details according to their needs, and establish a hierarchical order of the observed data in a continuous process of clarification that combines personal insights with culturally determined views. Consequently, even the reproduction of a specific realistic detail might tell the critic more about the subjective interests of the author than an objective observation.[107]

For some authors, then, the most adequate narrative technique was to create the impression of an objective stance that was true to life because it avoided all direct explanations. Some preferred an analytic point of view that enabled the narrator to characterize the motives of the figures and reveal the hidden meaning of the events. Some used the technique of multiple voices; others preferred the omniscient authorial mode. Some tried to record social change; others attempted to uphold ideals of individual freedom and human dignity. Many incorporated or created myths or an entire mythology to frame or structure their works. Several distinguished authors envisioned social and political utopias. A considerable number of popular writers maintained established literary conventions. For many realists, existence was characterized by the struggle for survival in a world determined by purely physical needs, a continuous struggle of competing wills to power, and incomprehensible economic forces. It is hardly surprising, then, that one of the central issues in the critical exchange of ideas among artists of the period was the appropriate mode of representing the human condition. Should the writer become the statistician of his age and simply record with utmost precision faithfully the all-pervasive misery? Did social criticism require authors to enter the political arena and fight ever-changing battles? Should they become prophets of doom or point to reform by upholding a sense of human dignity?

Responses to such questions varied considerably. They ranged from stark portraits of total hopelessness and pessimistic projections of social catastrophes to descriptions of spiritual regeneration and political reform. Nevertheless, over the last two hundred years, the "realistic" assessment of the individual's situation in life gave rise to a dominant theme: that of the loss of freedom and control over human destiny. Artists, whether painters or writers, have sought to observe, analyze, and portray with all the power of their art, often with innovative techniques, the subservience of humans, both outwardly and inwardly, to the outside forces of an essentially materialistic world. In doing so, they have assigned to material things, be they surroundings, possessions, sociopolitical, economic, or physiological-psychological conditions, a supremacy that sharply separates their works from those of classical writers, with their emphasis on the individual's capacity for self-determined development.

Many realists were not only intensely fascinated by the interests of the middle class and drawn to philosophical determinism but also approved of the scientific temper of their time. They reasoned that the scientific method of observing, collecting, analyzing, experimenting with data, and reaching conclusions based on these procedures resembled their own approach to their material. Their stance as observers and collectors of facts, the careful documentation, the reliance on often minute detail, and the tendency among writers to keep exhaustive notebooks filled with massive, precise information, were in some instances a conscious imitation of the scientific method. The specific branches of science to be imitated changed: whereas Balzac sought to apply the principles of the naturalists Lamarck, Cuvier, and Saint-Hilaire to his writings, Zola modeled his theory of the "experimental novel" after those of Darwin and the doctor Claude Bernard. Freud's exploration of the subconscious led to the more recent realists' interest in psychology, in the mediation between the individual's consciousness and subconsciousness and text-external phenomena, or as Hector Agosti stated, "the translation of reality through a temperament."[108] The rise of indeterminacy and chaos theories in twentieth-century physics has been echoed by experiments with non-chronological, polyvoiced, even anti-pyschological fiction. Thus, a case could be made for tracing the varying aspects of realism to its accommodation of changing scientific interests: from an early emphasis on observation and cataloguing to later experimentation and case histories to a more recent concern with evolutionary biology, psychology, and theoretical physics. Much of this development is directly related to the question: what is reality? Whereas the first realists were satisfied with presenting data gathered by an individual's sense perceptions, later realists became increasingly skeptical of the usefulness of this "endless bookkeeping of existence," as they probed the problems of relating this limited perception to the complexity of external phenomena and internal processes of thought and feeling.[109]

A large number of approaches in the representation of reality arose as response to the "matter of fact" narrations of Charles Reade and the focus on the problems in large cities by Eugène Sue and Zola. Most widely known and imitated was Zola's naturalism with its attempt to relate the cause and effect of observed social and economic phe-

nomena, its concentration on lower-class conditions, human degrada-
tion, its strident criticism of the social structure, and its pessimism.[110]
In marked contrast, socialist realists, while upholding the other tenets
of naturalism, returned to the optimism of earlier realists as they strove
to "depict actuality in its revolutionary development," by combining
historical accuracy with a socialistically ideological transformation of
society.[111] Despite Becker's assignment of the year 1893 as the termi-
nal date of realism as a literary movement, post-realist writers have
continued its and naturalism's traditions. Indeed, many authors who
have been identified as Expressionists, creators of the "new novel" or
representatives of the "absurd theater," have explored and refined the
tradition. They assure the continued viability of realism, for, as
Becker points out, even the most recent literature is "still intoxicated
with exploring the vast territories to which the realists lay claim."[112]

In order to transmit their perception of reality to readers, realists
developed a number of specific literary techniques. Most common
among these is the "slice-of-life" device. Based on the awareness
that unless a work is a verbatim report of an actual incident, such as
Martin du Gard's inclusion of actual court documents from the
Dreyfus trial in *Jean Barois* (1913), the "slice-of-life" technique
comprises procedures such as beginning and ending a work in mid-
stream, including well-known or precisely detailed features of actual
persons, milieus, and occurrences, reproducing actual speech patterns,
and characterizing individuals through their speech, including distinct
phonetic patterns that form a "phonetic mask," and behavior rather
than through author description.[113]   In order to duplicate the
monotony of ordinary living, as well as to show the influence of outside factors on the lives of average persons, realists deemphasized narrative plot in favor of dialogue and detailed description of milieu.
Thus in their hands, the novel, which traditionally had been a narrative
epic in prose, began to exhibit features of verbal paintings, dramas,
and films.[114] In the *nouveau roman,* narration has become so mini-
mal that it is the reader who must construct the story. It is no easy
task, as the reader attempts—often in vain—to arrange several superimposed "slices-of-life" in a meaningful pattern.

The reader's difficulty in constructing meaningful patterns from
the fragmented, often contradictory, data presented in more recent
post-realist works testifies to the realists' successful creation of a num-

post-realist works testifies to the realists' successful creation of a number of literary techniques specifically designed to convey the meaninglessness of life in a materially oriented universe. These include the use of massive panoramic scenes on the one hand and the highly subjective "stream of consciousness" on the other, the substitution of multiple or shifting points of view for that of a single narrator or series of narrators, the ostensible absence of moralizing, and the preference for metaphors and similes based on commonplace articles.[115] Finally, the disintegration not only of structure but also of syntax and character in contemporary literature reflects fully adherence to the philosophy enunciated by Dreiser, that all life in the material world ends "in toothless senility and watery decay, dissolution."[116]

Recent criticism has focused on these "realistic techniques" as the true hallmarks of realism. According to Kolb, the traditional definitions of realism are based on the fundamental error of confusing the realists' creation of the *illusion* of reality for reality itself. Realistic details, real experiences, and the absence of moral preaching are simply conventions developed and used by writers of the post-romantic era in order to create a specific style and mode of writing. Its main characteristics are: an anti-omniscient point of view, complexity, ambiguity, and the use of the image rather than the symbol.[117] We would take Kolb's evaluation one step further: the stylistic features present in realistic writing are themselves but reflections of a basic assumption made by all realists concerning individuals and their relationships with their surroundings. In exact antithesis to the classicists, realists view individuals as unable to determine themselves, because they are not autonomous beings, but infinitesimal parts of an immensely complex, inexplicable, absurd system governed by physical, social, political, and economic forces that can no longer be comprehended, controlled, or conquered and from which the individual can no longer withdraw.

Literary works having as their premise the view that the individual is but a reflection of these external forces express this outlook through their themes, structure, narrative technique, motifs, images, and characterizations. The overriding theme of realism, as exemplified in Dreiser's sentence at the beginning of this chapter, is the consequential restriction and loss of freedom of self-determination and individual action. This theme is conveyed by a number of secondary themes.

Primary among them is the establishment of a rigid outer circumference to which figures either willingly mold their inner beings through accommodation or are reshaped or destroyed by its pervasive force. Another closely related theme is the crowding out of the human dimension by a money- and material-oriented environment. A number of motifs support these themes. Dominating them is the radical transformation of the milieu, be it the city, village, town or country, a mansion, cabin, or a single room, into a space resembling a prison or cage in which individuals perceive themselves locked. Attempts to escape are doomed. The closed window, whether it cuts figures off from the outside world or from interior shelter and comfort, portrays their isolation from nature, from others, and ultimately from self-identity. The labyrinth, together with the fixed sphere, the circular path and other round, self-contained objects, conveys the futility of trying any escape from this condition. The aggressive, manipulative hand that expresses the values of the materialistically oriented outer circumference dominates, reshapes, or crushes sentiments of the heart. Shipwreck in storms is more prevalent than safe harbor or confident piloting. Finally, the motif of empty or uncommunicative dialogue, that identifies the use of language either to conceal true emotions or as a weapon to subdue others and in its extreme form, becomes chatter in the void, forms the bridge between the individual's sense of alienation and an autonomous, impersonal society. Deprived of the classical means for communication, the spoken word and the shared gesture, society in the literature of realism no longer allows for a group of like-minded individuals to extend their exemplary behavior outward but rather forces them inward toward withdrawal and contraction.

These themes and motifs coordinate to create a definite pattern exhibited in the progressive development of realism as well as in its individual manifestations: that of the centripetal spiral that begins with the external socioeconomic, political and psychological forces, draws individuals into a rigid, constricting pattern that conforms to an outer circumference of values, and increasingly restricts thereby their freedom of choice and action. The spiral catches all figures within its outward circumference and forces them into a downward, contracting centripetal movement. As realism progresses, the outer circumference of the spiral itself narrows and intensifies. Balzac, at the beginning of nineteenth-century realism, drew a wide and complex circumference, layered with many spheres dictated by social, political, or economic exigencies. His individual figures, as reflections of the many spheres within a complex society, are finely differentiated, even while exhibiting common values and behavior patterns. Later realists such as Dickens, Thackeray, Flaubert, George Eliot, Raabe, and Fontane, as well as naturalists like Zola or Dreiser, continued the wide panoramic view of a multi-faceted society in their portrayal of complex personalities and plots. Nevertheless, the tendency of later forms of realism, especially village or provincial literature, to subject individual figures to ever more precisely and restrictively defined social, political, economic, or psychological conditions increasingly shrinks the outer circumference. Consequently, the choice of conduct and values of individuals within this circumference progressively narrows. The constrictive motion of the centripetal spiral reaches its culmination in the literature of the absurd. In Samuel Beckett's *Play*, for example, the three characters, locked up to their necks in individual jars and responding only when specifically challenged by an external spotlight, exhibit in their extremely reduced radius of reaction an ultimate imprisonment by incomprehensible, and therefore uncontrollable, forces. The narrowness of their outer circumference allows for no movement whatsoever. Dissolving the human body into its component parts or the individual consciousness into a fragmentary moment in the present with no memory of the past or hope in the future contracts the outer rim to a minuscule, and ultimately meaningless, point in space and time.

Many individual realistic works also follow the pattern of the centripetal spiral. They begin with a detailed description of the protagonists' physical, historical, social, or economic environment, then describe the physical attributes of the characters, and at last move in to concentrate on the characters' responses to the specific situation that defines their limited development. For example, in *Madame Bovary*, Flaubert draws at first a fairly wide circumference that begins with Charles's family and education, habits and character, marriage, meeting with Emma, death of his wife, and courtship of Emma. This larger circumference includes smaller circular forms such as his "composite hat" and also sets up the circular framework with such details as Emma's tongue touching the outer rim of her glass, which will be closed at the end of the novel with the reappearance of Emma's tongue, now hanging out of her mouth in her final agony. The description of Emma's school years with her romantic dreams forms the next circumference within the outer one. Thereafter, the circles forming the spiral progressively narrow as the novel concentrates increasingly, though not exclusively, on Emma's thoughts, feelings, behavior, memories, hopes, and dreams. As Emma's yearning for "felicity, passion, and intoxication" is systematically shattered by her experience of the monotony of existence, the novel moves to the far more constrictive concerns with money. The circles become ever smaller, as the dynamic motion of the novel spins downward to the mundane and inward toward exclusive self-preoccupation, which ends in her suicide. Although the novel in its closing statement about Homais's election to the Legion of Honor maintains a nineteenth-century rapport with the large circumference, the closing emphasis on the decay of Emma's corpse and the corresponding deterioration of Charles's and Berthe's financial and psychological condition presage the twentieth-century theme of disintegration.

CHAPTER 2

Figure Constellations in Classicism

Personality and Individuation: The Core of the Spiral

Works displaying the centrifugal or centripetal spiral patterns share pronounced similarities in thematic structure, preference for supporting motifs, and an expressed or implied conception of the physical universe. This view of reality, at times clearly articulated by the poetic voice or figures in the text, frequently conspicuous in the narrative stance, and occasionally veiled in the dramatic constellation, affects a wide range of attitudes captured in the texts toward individual freedom, human interrelations, and the ordering principle in the universe. The underlying philosophical assumptions may occur simultaneously with the speculative thought of a period, anticipate, reflect, or question significant change in the philosophical tradition, but may also persist after new theories have gained wide support. They are instrumental in shaping prominent figure conceptions, thereby advancing the vision of a unique personality structure.

The considerable accord among writers of diverse literary periods who sought to depict the full development of human potential as a desirable goal of personality formation should not blur the essential difference in regard to individuation between the literature of classicism and realism. Whereas realists accentuate dominant traits that are shaped by the social environment, the classical tradition affirms behavior patterns that reflect a confluence of individual volition and a so-cially determined self-perception. Whereas texts organized around the theme of confinement portray static figures who are unable to de-velop freely because their actions are determined by the environment, classical literature portrays individuals who are in the process of be-coming. The shifting perspective of reality always has a center of sta-bility in developmental figures. Their self-realization ranges from the passionate affirmation of existence to the search for individual perfec-tion, from direct identification with a spiritual entity to the critical evaluation of failure, and from renunciation of personal desires to the active dedication to life and communal interests.

In classical plays and narratives, figures can display one of three distinct modes of individuation: (1) enlightened persons endowed with a level of insight that enables them to act in a manner consistent with high ethical norms and values (Henriette in Molière's *Les Femmes savantes;* Thekla in Schiller's *Wallenstein;* the Baroness of C. in Goethe's *Unterhaltungen deutscher Ausgewanderten;* the prince and the animal keeper in Goethe's *Novelle*); (2) developmental per-sons who are exposed to a sequence of learning experiences that at each stage augment previous knowledge until they reach an advanced level of self-knowledge and understanding of the world (Clitandre in *Les Femmes savantes;* Max in *Wallenstein;* Wilhelm Meister in Goethe's *Wilhelm Meister* novels); (3) persons portrayed as unwilling to develop beyond their assigned personality traits of aggressiveness and possessiveness who nevertheless are exemplary in their struggle (Alceste in Molière's *Le Misanthrope;* Wallenstein; the figures in Goethe's *Die Wahlverwandtschaften*). The dramatic action of classical plays develops and exposes the conflict between the various personali-ties, as they struggle to make their vision the dominant one, either through ruthless aggression and possessiveness, or conversely, through persuasive dialogue and actions. The narratives establish a pattern of a triadic process in the character development. Initial responses to life are molded by primary emotive impressions that are later recalled, en-hanced, supplemented, and transformed by a wide range of conscious experiences. The literary figure and, by extension, the reader objecti-fy the learning during a cognitive maturing process and gain a com-prehensive view of interpersonal relations, society, history, culture, and nature. The constantly expanding intellectual and spiritual horizon of the figures conveys the impression that individuals can master their destiny through a continuous process of reflection. This conviction is perhaps most succinctly expressed in the poetry of Pope, Schiller, and Goethe. Either directly addressing the reader or entering into a dialogue with the implied audience, such poems as Pope's *An Essay on Man,* Schiller's "Die Götter Griechenlands," and Goethe's "Selige Sehnsucht" seek order in the infinite variety of human encounters during a life span by establishing a fundamental unifying principle: all living organisms in nature evolve toward optimum form and therefore display a degree of stability that can be described by a set of principles. The evolution toward optimum form in the human personality can be understood in terms of increasing intelligence, that is, the capacity to think, but not as a biological phenomenon of physical perfection. Human individuation is rarely perceived as a biological phenomenon, but rather as a spiritual-intellectual and social-historical development. As a consequence, the slowly emerging coherent set of concepts for the description of personality formation focuses on clusters of associations that take cognizance of historical and social change and altered modes of perception, adaptation, and affection.

The developmental personality is conceived as a figure who is capable of intellectual and spiritual growth, learns to acknowledge the preeminence of reason and the rational solution of conflicts, and recognizes that shared interests and human vulnerabilities necessitate that the personal desire for maximum freedom must be tempered or balanced by the needs of society. By linking the full development of the individual's potential with a freely accepted social restraint, classical authors advance an ingenious mode of adaptation that differs from the social accommodation portrayed in realistic texts, because the meeting of individual and society is rendered feasible by a combination of personal responsibility and the restraint of a civilized society. The recurring criticism of a society in which rigid conventions have replaced the spirit of cooperation (Molière, Goethe) and of individuals whose passionate assertion of their will threatens the basis of communal life (Racine, Addison, Schiller) confirms the prevailing conviction that the rational behavior of individuals can foster public reason. Hence, the prototype of the developmental personality would be the ideal citizen in a society in which private efforts precede communal action and lasting reforms depend on the individual's desire to learn and to mature.

Immanuel Kant in "Was ist Aufklärung?" and *Idee zu einer allge-meinen Geschichte in weltbürgerlicher Absicht*, as well as Schiller in *Über die ästhetische Erziehung des Menschen, in einer Reihe von Briefen* advance principles of individual and collective action that cor-respond to a considerable extent to the thinking represented in the lit-erary works. Individuals are challenged to cultivate, enhance and ex-pand their intelligence. They should accept full responsibility for their actions and develop the "courage" to use reason in secular and spiritual matters.

The insistence on reason favors a philosophical inquiry that starts with logical analysis and seeks to arrive at truth by this method. The approach has far-reaching consequences for the figure conceptions of Schiller and Goethe. Schiller, like Kant, distinguishes between empiri-cal knowledge that is inferred inductively from experience and a pri-ori knowledge that is demonstrable because judgments are stated with an absolute generality that permits no exception. Applying the law of causality to phenomena of nature,[1] Schiller considers reality as well as its artistically created semblance as entities that, together with their fea-tures, exist objectively and independently of observation. It can be ar-gued, therefore, that within such an ontology of realism (*natura mat-eraliter* and *formaliter*) the coming of age of a person and all human development are a condition for, not the result of, experience. In ad-dition, it becomes axiomatic that the development toward optimum form necessitates a struggle with absolutes. Under these circum-stances, the developmental process is frequently either projected as unrealized promise upon a dramatic confrontation or portrayed as in-ternalized conflict between either-or alternatives. The philosophical implications and likely social consequences are outlined by Kant in the fourth principle of his *Idee zu einer allgemeinen Geschichte in weltbürglicher Absicht* and Schiller in *Über die ästhetische Erziehung des Menschen*: the struggle for power among persons and the antago-nism of individuals and society foster the growth of societies and phy-logenetic evolution while simultaneously retarding or impeding the full development of the individual's faculties (ontogenetic ideal).

However, a significant number of Schiller's poems and plays, among them, "An die Freude," "Der Spaziergang," "Die Götter Griechenlands," "Das Ideal und das Leben," *Don Carlos,* and *Wil-helm Tell*, indicate different considerations. The struggle to win a desired objective, be it self-recognition, power, assertion of the will, or mastery of any absolute, is desirable for the art of drama. Still, Schiller's poems and play demonstrate that the classical concept of individual perfection is preferable for building the consensus necessary for the human community. Most systematically expressed in Goethe's narratives and scientific writings, the view of optimum development of individuals is based on the conviction that direct confrontations of win or lose contests are undesirable for both individuals and communities. They should be avoided and replaced by strategies of adaptation and cooperation. In addition, Goethe does not accept uncritically Cartesian causation, the notion of mental substance, and Newtonian mechanics. He formulates the concepts of polarity and enhancement-augmentation and applies them to formed matter in nature (*Urpflanze*) as well as to ethical and social concerns of society (the Pedagogic Province in *Wilhelm Meisters Wanderjahre*).

Coming of Age

The coming-of-age theme represents a prominent configuration of self-realization. It occurs frequently in narratives of individual development. Occasionally, it provides a continuous thread in the action sequence of plays. In a highly crystallized form, it can determine the decision for or against a course of action captured in poems. Social psychologists agree that behavior is organized. Depending on the focus of their research and their historical position, they have advanced definitions that stress biological, juridical, theological, psychological, sociological, and biosocial factors. [2] Similarly, literary works have either emphasized unique dominant traits that give stability to the personality or accentuated behavior patterns that are shaped by socially determined self-perceptions and adjustments to the environment. In a broad sense, the theme of self-realization encompasses all distinct behavior patterns that preserve the integrity of the unique individual personality in social interrelations and underlie such specific thematic constellations as coming of age, affirmation of life, exemplary conduct, renunciation, the search for self-perfection as well as accommodation and the fatalistic acquiescence in forces that are perceived to be beyond individual control.

Prevailing conceptions differ over time. Thematic resolutions vary with changing social conditions and dominant philosophical currents. However, both correspondences and striking contrasts in thematic emphasis not only sum up the artistic aspirations but also elucidate the structural patterns of the classical and realistic traditions. Coming of age in classicism invariably includes a moment in which the figure's subjective volition and the narrator's objectified perception merge in the conscious recognition that a unique stage of individuation has been reached or clearly beckons to be attained. Such moments capture an essential characteristic of classical figure conceptions: individuals are not controlled by the environment but act freely and are capable of shaping their destiny. Moreover, they identify specific thematic resolutions. Scholars who traced the tradition of the *Bildungsroman* have argued that the progressive formation of individuals is represented as an organic process and imposes therefore thematic limitations on texts.[3] While it is true that narratives of self-development show a high correlations of recurring patterns, the thematic constellations range from the exploration of the intuitive unconditional affirmation of life to the gradual, continuous exposure to the cultural heritage and from considerations of a transformation inspired by a sudden, disruptive experience to a continuous search for self-perfection. All works selected for analysis, even those that seem to focus almost exclusively on character development, have a significant social or an important historical dimension.

Narrative Voice and Figure Conception

Narrative voice and literary representations of human development extend from unequivocal affirmation to remarkable ambivalence and from apodictic projections of the unifying order of a chain of life to discontinuous change occasioned by chance. Alexander Pope, for instance, announces in the "Design" of *An Essay on Man* the reason for the universal perspective of the poem: "more good will accrue to mankind by attending to the large, open, and perceptible parts, than by studying too much such finer nerves and vessels, the conformations and uses of which will for ever escape our observation."[4] In demanding that the reader focus not on isolating factors of human existence but on the "great chain that draws all to agree" (I. 33), Pope proclaims a unity of existence that encompasses all forms of life, God, and human society: "All are but parts of one stupendous whole, / Whose body nature is, and God the soul . . ." (I. 267-268). Within this cosmic community, each individual, no matter where placed on the chain of being, is to work for the preservation and extension of the divinely ordered universe: "Heaven's greatest view is One, and that the Whole" (II. 238).

The metaphor of an organic chain that binds nature and spirit into a continuous, all-inclusive community constitutes one of the basic principles in *An Essay on Man.* Perfection is possible within the totality of being, and the question of free will is answered by insisting that God, world, and individual are in equilibrium. Highlighting the "chain of love" within the chain of being, Pope explains in Epistle III how individuals can advance the envisioned unity by "embracing" their neighbors. Reaching others, the individual is strengthened while enriching others: "Heaven forming each on other to depend . . . / Bids each on other for assistance call, / Till one man's weakness grows the strength of all" (II. 249, 251-252). Giving and receiving aid forms a continuous pattern binding society together from the heads of state who discover that practicing justice and benevolence benefits their rule far more than brutality to the most insignificant subject in the realm. Indeed, the poet reminds those in power that the basis for the state is the human need for interaction and communication. As persons are inspired to rise from private concerns to the altruistic consideration of the common weal, they merge with a community whose actions are based on model behavior: "All served, all serving: nothing stands alone" (III. 24). Using the verbal picture of the concentric circles made by a pebble thrown into a still lake, Pope ends the poem by tracing a dynamic movement that links successively a single act of kindness to the universal whole:

> Friend, parent, neighbour, first it will embrace:
> His country next; and next the human race;
> Wide and more wide, th' o'erflowings of the mind
> Take every creature in, of every kind;
> Earth smiles around, with boundless bounty blest,
> And Heaven beholds its image in his breast. (IV. 367-372)

Pope challenges the reader to weigh each potential act, to "[a]sk your own heart" (II. 215) and choose those that benefit society. Structured in a series of expansively concentric circles that relate all parts to the whole, Pope's *Essay on Man* presents readers with a broad, all-encompassing framework within which to judge and reach each decision.[5]

Though Goethe and Schiller establish ordering principles which detail the relation between the self and the world and God, they no longer adhered to Pope's simple faith that "One all-extending, all-preserving Soul / Connects each being, greatest with the least" (III. 22-23). They acknowledge the growing distance between individual and God occasioned by Cartesian thinking and the mechanistic philosophies of the eighteenth century. Schiller characterizes the situation in a world in which thinking is determined by scientific laws of mechanics as one of spiritual loneliness: "Arduously I scan in the realm of ideas, fruitlessly in the world of senses.[6] Beatrice in *Die Braut von Messina* experiences the dislocation and isolation of an individual who has broken with tradition and entered upon a new path: "Hurled like a leaf from the tree, I am losing myself in infinite space" (II. 1. 15-16). Both Schiller and Goethe are also fully aware of the ever-increasing estrangement among individuals and the successively impersonal relations that are prompted to a considerable extent by a combination of spiritual disorientation, rigid conventions, and the failure to comprehend the nature of historical and social change.

Furthermore, Goethe's scientific investigations (*Farbenlehre, Botanik, Geschichte meines botanischen Studiums*) confirm that he realized the necessity of formulating empirical observations without reference to God or creation. Not persuaded by the arguments of Descartes and Newton and conscious of the fact that observers could alter any phenomenon during the process of perception, Goethe proposed a dialectical inquiry that mediated between subject and object through a continuous process of refining questions. The method requires an observer who is capable of adopting a stance characterized by Goethe as a composite of inquiry, dialogue, and exegesis. During the inquiry, the observer begins to comprehend that all questions formulated in a predetermined linguistic system may not only focus the research but align it in the direction of specific desired results. The dialogue combines the ability of transforming the material substance of the object of investigation into a meaningful essence, a subject that responds to questions with the readiness to modify the line of inquiry. The exegesis incorporates own observations, the existing critical tradition, the historical dimension of evolutionary change which provides for a great variety of forms to evolve, and the recognition that accidental occurrences can augment any given class of structures. The recognition that chance may indeed influence human development is expressed frequently in Goethe's and Schiller's works either through the contrast pattern destiny / chance or the artistic technique of describing a whole range of possible interpretations of an occurrence by relating the reactions of different figures instead of presenting a single observation. The disparity between individual destiny perceived as the ultimate goal of freely determining one's future and chance as an unpredictable element in existence is captured with exceptional skill in Schiller's *Wallenstein* and *Die Braut von Messina.*

Jonathan Swift's *Gulliver's Travels* provides an excellent example for the inclusion of the irrational in the developmental conception, as well as the interrelation between a satirical narrative voice and an ambiguous developmental figure. Within the framework of a highly imaginary satire of a travelogue, *Gulliver's Travels* traces the development of an ordinary sea surgeon into a unique individual whose simultaneous rejection and exhortation of his fellow human beings can be viewed as both ingenious and insane. The four voyages to imaginary lands provide the narrator-protagonist with multiple occasions to prove himself, to compare and contrast hitherto unquestioned values and practices, and to gain insight about human nature and himself. The results are a curious ambiguity: human nature covers an enormous territory spanning from the bestiality of the Yahoos to the capability of imitating the example of the enlightened Houyhnhnms. The potential for both self-development and regression is always present, but also constantly negated by Gulliver's clownlike features, his foolishness, adaptability, and resilience to physical abuse, and also the emphasis on physical and especially scatological activities.[7] Because an individual's choice depends upon a combination of self-determination and desire or need to conform to the social environment, the outcome is seldom decisive or final. As a satire, the narrative voice challenges readers to rethink their values and conduct.

Gulliver's report of his own development is an example of this ambiguity. His motives for repeatedly deserting his family and setting out to sea reflect the values of his society: esteem for accumulation of wealth ("getting some addition to my Fortune") and adventure ("having been condemned by Nature and Fortune to an active and restless Life"). Critics have pointed out Gulliver's propensity for lying and manipulating others, as for example in talking his way out of trampling on the crucifix in Japan. But he also hesitates to inflict unnecessary pain upon others.[8] Thus, Gulliver functions as a representative for the satirist's vision of English and European culture of the eighteenth century. Moreover, in contrast to Robinson Crusoe's self-reliance, he immediately hunts out and discovers other creatures as soon as he lands on alien shores in order to satisfy his basic needs. In accepting food, shelter, protection, and clothes from these creatures, Gulliver surrenders his independence and is even encaged on occasion. In these new situations and circumstances, old values become radically reordered. Long-accepted assumptions such as a preference for immortality or the ascendancy of the human race over other species are challenged when Gulliver learns the true nature of the immortal Struldbrugs, the humanlike Yahoos, and the horselike Houyhnhnms. In structuring the successive voyages to move from the pettiness of the Lilliputians to the nobility of the Houyhnhnms, the narrative traces Gulliver's corresponding development from a self-determined rejection of Lilliputian values to acceptance of the Houyhnhnms' "first Principles of Honour, Justice, Truth, Temperance, public Spirit, Fortitude, Chastity, Friendship, Benevolence, and Fidelity" (240).[9]

In each new encounter, the text emphasizes the need for a conscious decision. Thus, Gulliver refuses to become "an Instrument of bringing a free and brave People into Slavery" (32). He willingly separates himself from Lilliput. Likewise, he refuses to become an encaged object of display and thus resolves to leave the Brobdingnags. In contrast, he makes a "firm Resolution never to return to human Kind, but to pass the rest of my Life among these admirable *Houyhnhnms* in the Contemplation and Practice of every Virtue . . ." (210). It is the first decision that is thwarted. Cast out from Houyhnhnm society, forced by succeeding circumstances to return home, Gulliver nevertheless makes two decisions based upon his acceptance of the Houyhnhnm principles. He will shun both mendacity and humans. "The many Virtues of those excellent *Quadrupeds* placed in opposite View to human Corruptions, had so far opened mine Eyes, and enlarged my Understanding, that I began to view the Actions and Passions of Man in a very different Light . . ." (210). By rejecting both the vice and its perpetrator, Gulliver isolates himself from human society, "smitten with Pride," which could be, but is not, corrigible. His final resolution to "enjoy my own Speculations in my little Garden . . . to apply those excellent Lessons of Virtue which I learned among the *Houyhnhnms*; to instruct the Yahoos of my own Family as far as I shall find them docile Animals" (242) indicates that his ambiguity toward himself and others is based on an unambiguous decision to follow the distant example of an imaginary non-human race that is ultimately "a mere fiction out of my brain" (xii).

The theme of exemplary conduct functions as another point of ambiguity in *Gulliver's Travels*. While Gulliver protests that without the constant "example" and "incitement" of the Houyhnhnms (210, 229) he would be unable to continue his commitment to their principles, he becomes in fact so exemplary in his devotion to Veracity, "that it became a Sort of Proverb among his Neighbours . . . when any one affirmed a Thing, to say, it was as true as if Mr. *Gulliver* had spoke it" (xxv). Nevertheless, neither his example nor that of the Houyhnhnms contained in his published account "hath produced one single Effect according to mine Intentions" (xxii). Thus, despite his own enlightenment, Gulliver concludes "that the *Yahoos* were a Species of Animals utterly incapable of Amendment by Precepts or Examples . . ." Without their conscious decision to change their nature, humans both individually and collectively will remain unaffected by models, both real and imaginary.

Two closely linked motifs support the themes of self-realization and exemplary conduct in *Gulliver's Travels*: language and conversation (constructive dialogue). In turning to alien creatures for his needs rather than depending upon his own resources, Gulliver immediately attempts to communicate with them through language and gesture. Though his audience invariably does not comprehend "a single word" and responds with equally incomprehensible sounds, a foundation for dialogue is established. Each side speaks and listens, and each grasps that the other is using the organized patterns of language: "He [the Brobdingnag servant] appeared pleased with my Voice and Gestures, and began to look upon me as a Curiosity: much wondering to hear me pronounce articulate Words, although he could not understand them" (63). The acts of speaking, listening, and responding appropriately establish the first conscious links between Gulliver as stranger and the alien societies that he encounters. The spoken word is the means for communicating, integrating, and organizing in each of the societies described in the four voyages. Thus, Gulliver's first self-imposed and also readily accomplished task in each of the voyages is to be tutored in the alien tongue. The finest scholars in each kingdom undertake to tutor him. Moreover, Gulliver's boast of his language-acquisition abilities reflects his willingness to adapt to others, which in turn provides for self-development by engaging in enlightening dialogues. These function in two ways. By communicating through his discourses the customs, values, and attitudes of his fellow Europeans to creatures unfamiliar with them Gulliver becomes aware of their absurdity and later, depravity. By learning the vocabulary and structure of the strange tongues, he gains insight into entirely different perspectives. These range from the Laputians' focus on geometrical figures and astronomical phenomena to the Houyhnhnms' lack of vocabulary for evil, pride, lies, and crimes.

Furthermore, as an outsider, Gulliver becomes aware of the diverse functions of the spoken word, whether to initiate the Lilliputians' release of hundreds of tiny arrows into his left hand or to "make us understand one another, and to receive Information of Facts" (195) as in the general discourses among the Houynhnhnms. Indeed, it is in the society of the Houynhnhnms that Gulliver discovers the supreme delight of a truly enlightened conversation, during which reason, benevolence, and friendship become fully realized and thus provide the ideal setting for self-insight. After its fullest expansion at the end of the fourth voyage, however, the motif's role shrinks and becomes subjected to the ambiguity which characterizes both Gulliver's insight into human potential and his limited potential for exemplary conduct. For in contrast with his approach to the alien societies, when confronted with his own, Gulliver retreats into sullen silence or pleads to be left alone. While the novel closes with the projection of permitting conversation with his wife and even a neighbor, leading to a potential reestablishment of contact through language, the letter to Cousin Sympson (placed at the beginning of the novel, but actually the last in the chronology) reveals that "Conversing with a few of your Species" will lead to new corruption.

An examination of representative texts from Pope, Goethe, and Swift demonstrates that the interrelationship between narrative voice and figure conception depends on differing views on the human capacity and desire to develop and conform to certain models of conduct. Texts like Pope's *An Essay on Man,* dominated by an optimistic monovoiced speaker, affirm the potential of all individuals to develop themselves mentally and morally into beings that support a universal design of goodness. Goethe's scientific texts question the monovoiced perspective and propose a dialectic method of inquiry rather than a single viewpoint. Finally, polyvoiced texts like Swift's *Gulliver's Travels* interlace skepticism with optimism and satire with idealism, as the narrator-protagonist both aims to reform his fellow citizens and yet realizes that they may be unreformable.

CHAPTER 3

Crossroads Decision: Diverging Paths. Loss of Direction. Affirmation of Life

The Choice of Path in Three Early Tragedies of Corneille and Racine

By contrasting Gulliver as narrative voice with Gulliver as limited developmental figure, Swift projects a picture of personality development that captures the potential of self-realization as well as the factors curtailing individual growth. The individual is summoned to make a decision that will ultimately guarantee the mastery of existence. Frequently, the initial choice appears to be between clearly defined alternatives such as adventure, the lure of the unknown, and uncertainty or predictability, stability, and control over events. Supported by the motif of the crossroads, the central figures in the major texts of classical literature must choose from different paths beckoning the wayfarer. Unlike the sharp delineation offered in Matthew 7: 13-14 and Luke 13: 24 between the broad, easy road leading to destruction and the narrow, hard way offering salvation, the right path of hard labor and the wrong path of pleasure before Hercules, and even the diverging roads envisioned by Robert Frost in "The Road Not Taken," the contrastive, frequently non-visual patterns of paths depicted by Corneille, Racine, Goethe, and Schiller afford much greater variety.

In their early tragedies, both Corneille and Racine place characters at a figurative crossroads.[1] Faced with alternate courses of conduct, these figures are forced to make a decision. Should they continue old patterns of behavior and follow a course of action that satisfies their self-interest or their passions? Or should they venture into the unknown and strike out on a different, untried path, one that calls for the renunciation of the old order and ultimately leads to a commitment to a new mode of existence? If the decision remains isolated from the chief dramatic interest, it is assigned a less crucial moment, and its influence is restricted or negated by the dominant action. If, however, their choice of path affects not only their self-development but also the fate and development of the other figures, the crossroads is placed at a strategic point in the design of the work, at the beginning, the climax, or the dénouement. The choice of path becomes exemplary for others.

Three motif sequences assist in defining the choices faced by the figures at the crossroads: (1) the two contrasting paths, one leading to a rupture with the past, the other, to a return or reinforcement of past patterns; (2) the antithesis of genuine, constructive dialogue and violent confrontation or silence; and (3) the opposition of the sentient heart and the manipulative hand or oppressive arm. The motif clusters are as follows: open dialogue / violent confrontation or silence; sentient heart / manipulative hand or oppressive arm). The dialogues that constitute most of the action in the French classical theater interweave the individual motifs of the sequences into two opposing textual fields that organize the abstract clash between a new and an old view of life into a verbally expressed conflict. Thus, an enunciated decision for the new path is accompanied by an expressed desire for constructive dialogue and the values associated with the sentient heart. The decision to continue old patterns of behavior is enunciated by clusters of images reflecting violence, self-interest, inhumanity, oppressiveness, and manipulation depicted by the motifs of silence, aggressive dialogue, and the violent, menacing hand. By their textual recurrence at significant moments in the dramas, the three motif sequences function together to focus attention on each individual's right, need, and responsibility to choose his or her own course of conduct and then to model or promulgate it to others.

Both Corneille and Racine gradually developed the concept of freedom of choice. Their early dramas show figures whose capability or desire to choose a radically different course of action is limited either by a rigid social code of honor (Corneille, *Le Cid*; *Horace*), their passions or an inexplicable fate (Racine, *Andromaque*; recurring in his later play *Phèdre*).[2] The motif sequence of the two opposing paths is absent. The constitution and function of the other two motif sequences reflect the acceptance of aggressiveness and possessiveness as the social norm. The emphasis on "knowing" in the exchange between the two lovers after Rodrigue has killed Chimène's father demonstrates the validity of this code in Corneille's *Le Cid*:

> RODRIGUE: You know how a fist blow to the face
> touches a man of heart.
> CHIMENE: Yes, I know what honor after such an out-
> rage
> Demanded of the ardor of an abundant courage
> . . . .
> But also, in fulfilling [your duty], you have taught me
> mine
> . . . .
> I will follow your example . . .
> (III. iv. 875, 909-12, 953)

Located at the center of the play, this brief dialogue represents one of the few attempts to achieve an enlightened conversation: that is, one in which the participants share their thoughts rather than confronting each other.[3] The code demanding that injured honor must be restored through an aggressive counteract engenders a series of actions designated textually as those of the hand or arm and those of the heart. Rodrigue, as a model defender of honor and duty, is repeatedly characterized as both *homme de coeur,* that is, endowed with the aristocratic virtue of courage, and as the hand or arm, supporting first his father against Don Gomez's insults, then Spain against the Moors' invasion.[4] When Elmire calls Rodrigue "a man of the heart" (I. ii. 30), when Don Diègue asks him, "Rodrigue, do you have a heart?" (I. v. 261), or when Rodrigue evaluates his forcefulness by "having enough heart" (II. ii. 416), they are linking the heart to decisive action in defense of honor. The strong arm or hand becomes an extension of courage, perceived as the heart. Don Diègue defends his son's courage before the King: "He has lent me his hand / . . . I am the head, he is

only the arm" (II. viii. 717,724), then argues: "preserve for yourself
the arm that can serve you" (728). Listening to her confidante's re-
counting of Rodrigue's subsequent triumph over the Moors and his
taking of two kings as prisoners, Chimène asks: "And the hand of
Rodrigue has done such miracles" to which Elvire replies: "His hand
has conquered them; his hand has taken them" (IV. i. 1110, 1112).
Reinforcing his example, Chimène decides to "attack without any fear
this triumphant hand" (1127, 1141) by calling upon another "hand"
to avenge her family's injured honor and promising her hand in marriage as prize. Finally, the strong hand is rewarded with the promise of
possessing the one it strove for: "To possess Chimène, and for your
service. / What can I be commanded that my arm cannot accom-
plish?" (V. vii. 1833-34). To the end, then, the code's integrity is upheld by the persistent recurrence of the heart as seat of courage and
the hand or arm as its embodiment.

By joining the traditional topos of the strong heart as the seat of
courage with a decision resulting from a congruence of mind, heart,
and hand, the motif conveys a hierarchical system that aligns the individual to the king's and ultimately God's authority. When individuals
are called upon to shape their own destiny, the center of true authority
becomes increasingly internalized in the inner voice of the heart,
whereas the external rule of power falls prey to corruption and manifests itself in destructive actions of the hand. Nevertheless, Corneille's
play captures already a few isolated moments when the insistence on
honor, duty, courage, and the strong arm is challenged by the radically
different perspective of a sentient, grieving heart. Generally conceived
as a mute, pliant object to be conquered or possessed by the actions of
a strong arm (DON DIEGUE: "Come back as conqueror / It's the
only means to regain her heart" III. vi. 1095-96; the KING: "And
possessing already your mistress's heart" V. vii. 1838), this alternate
conception of the heart quietly asserts itself as a counterpoint to the
prevailing perception of heart as courage. In contrast to the buoyancy
of heart as courage, the sentient heart is associated with pain, as indicated by the words "Pierced to the depth of my heart" that begin the
oft-cited stances of Rodrigue (I. vi. 291). Duty becomes painful
("such a cruel duty," III. iv. 983) whenever the heart's tender sentiments begin to dominate perception. Other values, such as mutual
love and self-sacrifice, come to the fore and form the basis for a dia-

logue between the lovers:

> DON RODRIGUE: O miracle of love!
> CHIMENE: O height of misery!
> RODRIGUE: What unhappiness and tears our fathers
>   will cost us.
> CHIMENE: Rodrigue, who would have believed it?
> RODRIGUE: Chimène, who would have said it?
> CHIMENE: That our happiness was so near and so
>   soon lost! (985-88)

This brief duet of two grieving hearts opens the way for a radically different relationship based on individual feelings, not family allegiances. Chimène's refusal to listen and her demand that Rodrigue withdraw ("Leave, I tell you again, I will not listen to you any more" 992) signify her decision to return to the dominant code of behavior. But the sentient heart is not silenced. It asserts itself and successfully contradicts the values of the court, when Chimène openly avows her true feelings for Rodrigue in court but refuses to become the prize for his strong, winning arm. Challenging the propriety in dictating the decisions of the heart ("For what he does for you should I become the prize?" V. vii. 1810), she succeeds in obtaining the postponement of her marriage. With that victory, she finally achieves independence from society's norms and paves the way for individual freedom of choice.5

As in *Le Cid,* only one figure in Racine's *Andromaque* breaks out of the established pattern of conduct to achieve independence: Andromaque herself at the conclusion of the play.6 Although all of the figures are repeatedly placed at figurative crossroads where they have the opportunity to abandon their prevailing passionate possessiveness in favor of self-transcendence, they consistently fail. Thus, the freedom of individual choice remains an unrealized ideal in this early play of Racine. The reality of being enslaved to an overwhelming passion dominates.7 Oreste's early statement that it was not his choice but a destined love that "makes me seek here an inhuman [lover]" (I. i. 25) is reiterated by Pyrrhus: "One look [from Andromaque] would make me forget all" (II. v. 640), in Oreste's question: "Was I master of myself? / Fury overcame me" (III. i. 725-26), and in Hermione's anguish: "My heart, my cowardly heart still is attached to him?" (V. i. 1404).

The resulting inability to make a decisive commitment afflicts all alike. All demure, agonize, and if possible, flee or attempt to rescind previously made decisions. Thus, Pyrrhus proclaims he will follow a new course of action and protect Andromaque's son. But a cold glance of Andromaque in response to his advances causes him to revert to the previous stance of adversity, and he reasserts the old enmity.[8] Andromaque's plea that Pyrrhus base his new course of action on generosity, not passionate possessiveness "to respect the misery of an enemy, / To save the misfortunate, to return a son to his mother, / To combat the rigor of a hundred peoples for him / Without making me pay for his safety with my heart . . ." (I. iv. 305-8) falls upon deaf ears. His willingness to turn her over to Oreste and the Greeks reinforces old patterns. Similarly, given the chance to act magnanimously toward Andromaque, Hermione flees. Despite Céphise's words, "of your fate you would still be mistress" (III. viii. 978), Andromaque seeks advice at her husband's grave and devises an "innocent strategy" instead of facing independently the choice between saving her son and being faithful to Hector. Having commissioned Oreste to kill Pyrrhus, Hermione draws back, unwilling to shoulder the consequences of her passionate decision. Likewise, Oreste demures, torn between the desire to prove his love and his revulsion against the assassination.

Nevertheless, it is Oreste's decision for aggression that instantaneously frees the other figures from the inactivity of non-choice by forcing them into decisions that will not be rescinded: Andromaque into the new course of adopting Pyrrhus' interests and avenging his death, Hermione into the old pattern of rejecting Oreste, and Oreste in facing his solitary destiny. Oreste's murder exemplifies the close alignment of aggression with passion that characterizes much of Racinian action. This association is particularly evident in the use of the term "heart" as the seat of passion, possessiveness, and violence, and its consistent association with actions of the hand or arm. Oreste's expository speech in the play's first scene is characteristic of this motif pattern: "My rival bears elsewhere his heart and his crown . . . / I come to see if one can tear out of his arms / This child . . . / Happy if I could . . . / Instead of Astyanax take by force from him my princess!" (I. i. 78, 91-94). Pyrrhus' words in announcing his marriage with

Hermione continue the association: "Tell her that tomorrow / I expect, with the agreement, her heart from your hand" (II. iv. 624). In commanding Oreste to murder Pyrrhus, Hermione endows the heart / hand connection with double meaning: "I will pierce the heart I could not touch; / And my bloody hands, turned on myself, / Will join our destinies at once despite him" (IV. iii. 1244-45). Pyrrhus' confession, combining the two opposing motifs of sentient heart and the acts of the possessive hand, signals irrational action: "Andromaque tears from me a heart that she detests. / Dragged by each other, we run to the altar . . . / despite ourselves . . ." (IV. v. 1298-1300). Indeed, Oreste's final words that he will offer Hermione his "heart to devour" (V. v. 1644) intimate that the ultimate effort of their pairing will lead to murder.

As a result of the continual confrontations that structure the play, as well as the pairing of the heart and hand motifs, the sentient heart and constructive dialogue remain elusive dreams.[9] The sentient heart is almost always questioned, negated, or relegated to fantasy. Thus Andromaque asks: "Must such a great heart show so much weakness?" (I. iv. 298). In announcing his breaking of their engagement, Pyrrhus declares to Hermione: "Our hearts were not made to depend upon each other" (IV. v. 1353). Hermione imagines Pyrrhus speaking to Andromaque "about the heart" (IV. v. 1379). Finally, she accuses Oreste of not reading her heart: "And didn't you perceive in my outbursts / That my heart contradicted my mouth at every moment?" (V. III. 1548). It is clear that the negation of the existence of the sentient heart not only bolsters the pairing of the possessive, passionate heart with the aggressive hand but also restricts the potential for making any rational decision at the numerous figurative crossroads built into the play's structure.

In Corneille's *Horace*, the crossroads is formed by the contrast pattern of two distinctive significations of the heart: on the one hand, courage, pride, and nationalistic heroism; on the other, personal and humane feelings that transcend patriotism. A decision for the former leads to conflict and aggressive brutality, whereas the latter demands harmony with others and self-sacrifice.[10] As in *Le Cid* and *Andromaque*, the textual language reflects these tensions by coupling the first conception of heart with the aggressive arm or hand and the second with the selfless emotions of grief and love. Thus, Horace rejects the pain of combating his brother-in-law as unworthy of a "generous heart" (II. i. 399): "Rome has chosen my arm, I examine nothing: / With a lightheartedness as full and sincere / As I married the sister, I will fight the brother" (II. iii. 498-500). His decision is seconded by others, notably his father, who names Camille "a heart so little Roman" (V. i. 1413) when she refuses to admire the thrice repeated "strong, generous" arm of Horace that has killed her husband (IV. v. 1251-53).[11] Enlightened by Valère that Horace has single-handedly killed his three opponents, the old man denies Camille the domain of human emotion in echoing his son's commitment to violence and glory: "In the death of your lover you only lose a man / Whose loss is easily repaired in Rome; / After this victory, there is no Roman / Who would not glory to give you his hand" (IV. iii. 1179-82).

The decision against this barbarity glorified as patriotic heroism leads to the embrace of more human values. These also are signaled by the word "heart" which now recurs not in justification of the deeds of the strong arm or hand but in opposition to them. Those figures who choose this attitude confront the prevailing value of nationalistic glory with a universal love. Curiace recognizes that in battle "my heart will be terrified" (II. iii. 474), not because of the fear of the battle itself but because of the inhumanity of fighting his future brother-in-law. Camille decides to let her "heart degenerate" in antithesis to her brother's heroism: "It's glory to pass for a broken heart. / When brutality becomes the highest virtue" (IV. iv. 1241-42). Sabine identifies the combatants as "inhuman hearts" (II. vi. 657). Though they do not triumph over the prevailing patriotisms, their decisions do effect a modification in the general brutality. The play closes with reconciliation and the prospect of a future harmony which promises to include Horace's decision for patriotic heroism without its attendant brutality.[12]

Corneille and Racine recognized early in their play-writing the central significance of crossroads decisions for representing the motivation of the figures and turned to the three motif sequences of the two paths, genuine dialogue / confrontation or silence, and aggressive hand / sentient heart in order to portray the problematics of the theme. Using the dramatic components of dialogue and confrontation, these early plays examine the individual's options and decision-making process within a culture of glory, violence, and pride and thus prepare for the later dramas which, in probing the motif sequences in far greater complexity, show a far deeper and richer growth of personality configuration.

Bloody Crossroads: Loss of Direction

An analysis of the crossroads in the three early plays of Corneille and Racine indicates that the range of thematic constellations associated with the quest for self-development generates clusters in which themes intersect and motifs overlap. At times, the threads of several themes are interwoven in a single text; at others, a contrasting theme underscores the specific thematic resolution. Hence, restriction exists alongside expansion; factors impeding individual development materialize next to those highlighting the desirable course toward the fulfillment of human potential. Themes like freedom, justice, or the renunciation of personal desires for the common good call forth contrasting views of confinement, injustice, and the assertion of self-interest. The decision at the crossroads does not spare figures from error, guilt, or even despair. Moreover, the representation of successive stages in human growth incorporate not only renewed choices but also increasingly complex motivations in the behavior of contrast figures. Any analysis of major thematic alignment should neither blanket the important function of counter-currents nor obscure the fact that centrifugal and centripetal forces can coexist in the same text. While events threatening the loss of freedom activate the impulse toward liberation, patterns of confinement can dominate a textual structure and only reflect opaquely the ideal of a humane existence. Schiller captures throughout his dramatic works the persistence of social and political institutions that obstruct the reorientation sought by forward-looking individuals. Similarly, Goethe explores frequently the clash between personalities driven toward innovative action and forces that deter change. The struggle in itself may simply reinforce the spiral pattern. However, in such works as Schiller's *Die Braut von Messina* and Goethe's *Torquato Tasso*, the unyielding conventions of traditional thought overwhelm the impulse toward development. The spatial restrictions and hierarchical distribution of the contrast pairs self-sacrificing love / passion, heart / hand, dialogue / silence, and immortals – order / society – discord announce the persistence of individually colored and socially oriented modes of perception that thwart personality change.

The events in Schiller's *Braut von Messina* commence with the plan of Queen Isabella to reunite her family that is at war with itself and thereby to bring peace to the land torn apart by warring factions. The dramatic action opens with her having summoned her two sons, dispatched a faithful servant to bring her daughter who has been raised in secrecy, and anxiously awaiting the reconciliation. The homecoming exposes a world in which self-deception and deceit permeate human relations. Passion, strife, and hate overpower the desire for love, accord, and cooperation. The violent action centers on overt brother conflict and incestuous passion. Both brothers love Beatrice without knowing that she is their sister. Don Cesar, stunned when he sees her in the arms of Don Manuel, murders his brother in a jealous rage, persists in his passion even after he knows the truth, and kills himself. The allusions to strained relations between father and son and mother and son, to Oedipal identification and incestuous tendencies create a web of motivational factors. They seem to indicate that the conflict is rooted in subconscious processes controlling the family relationships.[13] The complex, formal alignment of dominant and subordinate motifs suggests an identity crisis that mirrors a general social problem in the personal experience. The behavior of the figures is determined by subconscious motives, conscious planning, and recurring attempts to understand their role in society, that is, to reach a cognitive level that provides knowledge of the world.

All motifs point in the direction of a confining circle of existential anxiety captured already by Dante in the image of the absence of a path in the "dark forest" in the opening lines of the *Divine Comedy:* "Midway the journey of this life I was 'ware / That I had strayed into a dark forest, / And the right path appeared not anywhere."[14] With no path to lead them, the figures in *Die Braut von Messina* do not venture forth to meet the other. They adhere to a stance determined by inverted values. Deception, aggression, and the reduction of others to objects become modes of self-realization. As a result, the play affirms positive values only in the mirror of a negative dimension. The incest motif signals unresolved problems in self-development. It accentuates the persistence in adult years of factors that influence child development and contributes to the appearance that a personality shaped in childhood is unlikely to change significantly later in life. The figures in the play shrink from change. Deception, arrested or misleading dialogues, and delusive monologues point to the refusal to search for truth. The recurrent efforts to seize the moment of good fortune and master the "demon envy" that threatens ephemeral advantages underscore the latent fear of existence. Don Cesar's wish to possess Beatrice as if she were a precious object adorning his palace is a striking example of transfiguring individuals into objects by draining them of their human essence. The motif of fated existence establishes that the figures disavow full responsibility for their actions.[15] They are spiritually ensconced at the gateway to a possible humane existence.

All the figures in the play voice sentiments most clearly expressed in Isabella's lament: "These events / I suffer innocently, yet the oracles are still esteemed / And the Gods are saved" (ll. 2507-09). Attempts to fathom the meaning of dreams (ll. 1307 ff., 1333 ff.) result in confusion. Efforts to understand oracles beget error. Since the gods are immovable (1.1558), the "art of prophesy is vain nothingness. / Prophets are deceivers or deceived" (ll. 2371-72), and "winged fortune hard to grasp, hard to secure" (ll. 650-51), the mortals seem to be incapable of escaping fate or shaping their destiny. What is gained by faith?

> It is as impossible
> To find the Gods residing on lofty heights
> As it is to shoot an arrow into the moon.
> The future is walled in for mortals
> And no prayer pierces the iron sky. (ll. 2386-90)

Yet, the perception that a mysterious, unknowable fate rules life attests only to the maze of self-deception fashioned by the figures. Their decisions, always powerful assertions of a will that recognizes no limitations, are prompted by the wish to shape events to personal advantage. Fearful and suspicious that others covet what they prize at the moment (demon envy – fate: ll. 658, 1144 f., 1278, 1698, 2182), they seek to wrest from life everything that will enhance the illusion of power and thereby strengthen their sense of autonomy. As a result they are incapable of freeing themselves from their limitations, reflecting upon their motives, considering their mutual dependence, and attaining a level of self-insight and understanding of human relations that guarantees the respect for others. Consequently, the fateful rivalry for the affection of Beatrice becomes the most visible sign of a power struggle in a world of spiritual isolation.

The feud among the brothers, spawned in their childhood, provides the surface pattern for the basic conflict of the autonomous individual with the own self. Isabella avows that the discord can be traced to a fateful incomprehensible origin (ll. 24-25), a chain of events initiated by her husband who had forcefully taken her as his wife though she had been his father's intended bride (ll. 960-68, 2504-06). Yet, Isabella broods over the possibility that she herself might have caused the strife. Twice she emphasizes that she has shared her love equally with her two sons, indicating that she has never shown a preference for one alone (ll. 29-30, 305). Later in her agitation she confesses that she had loved Don Manuel more than Don Cesar (ll. 2127, 2501). The envy that poisons Don Cesar's life (ll. 2700, 2728, 2739) springs from the fear that his mother preferred Don Manuel. This anxiety, coupled with a jealousy of Manuel's position as first-born son (ll. 1410-11), constitutes a major factor in the conflict that affects all the figures of the play. Schiller identifies the elemental personal passion through the motif of fire – flame and captures the poisoning of the social fabric in the frequent clashes between Don Cesar's and Don Manuel's men. The former pride themselves in their youthful strength and are hardly able to control either their seething blood (ll. 149) or passionate hate (ll. 1706 ff.), while the latter prize their wisdom, reason (ll. 155-57), and rights as first-born (ll. 1706 ff.). When the Chorus is not divided in partisan factions, it reflects on polar forces that characterize human endeavor. It praises love, the healing power of language (ll. 168), peaceful coexistence, and nature's serenity (ll. 871-79). But it also lauds war, the struggle for power, and teeming life (ll. 879-91). Hence, the capacity to affirm or negate love and hatred is ever-present.

But when the power to choose is exercised, it is countermanded by hesitation born of inner uncertainty or strategies to conceal and disguise the truth. Isabella, for example, once elected the path of love. She saved Beatrice when her husband ordered the child's execution in order to forestall the bloody ruin of his house. But since she could not master the courage to defy her husband openly, she became entangled in deception and secrecy. Likewise, when Beatrice falls in love with Don Manuel, their relationship is cloaked in secrecy. It is also overshadowed by Don Manuel's ominous, instinctive disposition to avoid truthfulness and his desire to possess her. His omission of informing Beatrice of his family, his apprehension that ever-changing fortune could deprive him of her love (ll. 650, 666), and his fear of a revelation concerning Beatrice's origin point toward his possessive self-assertion in the face of ominous signs portending disaster for their relationship. This trait is reinforced by his unwillingness to probe into her family history (ll. 757-58) and his decision to abduct her at the moment when her identity is to be revealed (ll. 769-99). Even the transcending quality of his love, expressed best when he contemplates her beauty as the embodiment of grace, is counterbalanced by his need to possess her. This impulse manifests itself most clearly when he envisions her arrival at the palace.[16] He will reveal his identity as ruler, festively attired and surrounded by his knights. She is to enter not as a "homeless refugee" but as a noble princess (ll. 1800-10), to be decked out with sandals, gown, sash, coat, and precious jewels furnished by him. As he paints a verbal picture of the pageant and adds lavish details to enhance Beatrice's beauty, her identity slowly recedes into the background and she is finally transformed into an object. While he veils his bride, Don Manuel unveils his self-deception. His bride is to magnify his own wealth and power.

Don Manuel's deception, secrecy, and possessiveness toward his sister are echoed by his brother Don Cesar. Relating his first encounter of Beatrice, he conveys the impression that an elemental force, a subconscious affinity of hearts aroused him (ll. 1534-38). Haughty and proud, he is certain that she will be his. When he confronts her a second time, he asks no questions but proclaims her his wife (ll. 1145-47). Even though Beatrice trembles and shudders silently during this confrontation, he acts with confidence that she will return his feelings. Single-minded in his drive to power, he ruthlessly asserts his will and affirms his belief in the elemental forces that compel them to couple (ll. 1120-24).

The figure conception of Beatrice points most clearly to the disorientation associated with the inability to decide freely on a constructive course of action (the motif of the straight path). She is perhaps best characterized by an acute sense of existential anxiety. She grew up without knowledge of her roots. She had to grope with the idea that her family exiled her in obedience to a mysterious, fateful command.

She has therefore no family or community for orientation and submits to the unknown: "I am not permitted to lift the dark veil" (l. 1024). When she leaves her protective confinement, she becomes immediately entangled in deception and secrecy. Her encounter with Don Cesar at the father's funeral deeply disturbs her (ll. 1092-1101; 1891-98). Her silence delays Don Manuel's discovery that she is his sister at the most critical moment (ll. 1643-60) when this knowledge could have averted the murder. When she allows herself to be taken from the convent and decides to follow Don Manuel, she again feels that the events have been fated (l. 1039). Confronted by the world's turmoil, she is lost: "Hurled like a leaf from a tree / I lose myself in infinite space" (ll. 995-96). Deprived of the inner voice of truth that gives direction to Goethe's Iphigenie, she lacks the certainty that could initiate the reorientation in human relations.

The inner and outer confinement of the two brothers in repetitive roles of deception, aggression, and possessiveness are further clarified by their reaction to the discovery of Beatrice's true identity. While Don Manuel stoically submits to fate (1858-59), Don Cesar kills the hated rival and believes that he has finally outwitted "fortune's tide and ebb and demon envy" (ll. 1143-44). But at the moment of triumph, he is denied his prize. Searching for the external forces that have caused his misery, he rages against his mother, whose "secrecy" has caused his anguish, cursing the womb that bore him (ll. 2472-76). Vacillating between hate (ll. 2555-58) and love, he recalls her affection and also his deep-seated envy: "Envy poisoned my life, / Although we shared your love equally" (ll. 2728-29). Don Cesar reveals his ambivalent mood in the discourse with his sister. To the end, he continues to covet her in the face of opposing religious and societal pressure. The thought that she loved Don Manuel enrages him (ll. 2533-35). When Beatrice pleads with him to spare his life, his passion flares up, as he hopes for a final assurance that his love has been answered (l. 2816). For Don Cesar, then, the transgression of the incestuous barrier is a sign of supreme love for the feminine element in the world, a love that knows of no taboos but leads to superhuman agony (ll. 2655-57). By acknowledging the sentiments that infected his life, he finally accepts responsibility for his actions, purges his passions, and atones for his deeds by his death. Consequently, the typical classical insistence on full accountability for personal behavior dominates the play's resolution.

The tragedy shows individuals in search for identity, exposed to dangers from within and without, and living in a state of apostasy from all principles essential for the free development of human potential. Schiller's representation of their condition focuses on the assertion of the will to power, the disregard for the concerns of others, self-deception, intrigue, and lies. The view of history expressed by the Chorus is cyclical. Individuals caught in the "rising and falling ebb of the ocean" share in a rhythm of eternal recurrence that lacks direction. The possible reconciliation of the family holds the promise for reform. However, when Isabelle implores her sons to look into each other's eyes (l. 383), thereby challenging them to be truthful, they settle the feud by denouncing others for having continued the conflict.

> DON MANUEL: The mighty are cursed because the
>   rabble controls their ears.
> DON CESAR (*quickly*): That is how it is, the servants
>   are guilty! (ll. 487-89).

They refuse to account for their action and resist the call to ponder society's disorder. While, as the Chorus declares, the world is equally ready to follow established patterns of aggression or pursue a road leading to peaceful coexistence and increased understanding of life, the brothers have never exercised this choice of path. Since they persisted in continuing traditional patterns of aggression, deception, and possessiveness, the Chorus can only close the circle with the traditional but appropriate observation: "Life is *not* the highest treasure, / However, the greatest evil is *guilt*" (ll. 2838-39).

Error, misconception of socially transmitted traditions of thought, and the rejection of convention, "the trifles of etiquette," can determine decisions at the most critical junctures in life that inspire a crisis in faith or love and ultimately lead to the tragic destruction of a noble mind. The clash between individual and convention, between heart-love, subjective / objective truth and mind, between constructive dialogue and the discourse of society, and between truthful sentiments and the oppressive hand in Goethe's *Die Leiden des jungen Werthers* and *Tasso* identifies circumstances in which personal and collective error are inextricably interwoven. In *Werther*, the motif sequence sentient heart / possessive hand, in conjunction with the landscape motif,

conveys the immediate impressions, innermost emotions, and changing sentiments of the narrator-protagonist. Initially, the sentient heart
seems to dominate as Werther experiences spring, the season of bursting life, as an elemental force that warms his trembling heart and enables him to experience God's presence. A miraculous clarity unfolds
in his heart, as he absorbs the myriad details of life. The heart becomes "the mirror of eternal God," is self-sufficient, and a mirror of
self-indulgence (JA 16: 4-6). Werther bemoans the fact that historical
and social development has established a barrier preventing direct
identification with either others or the universal spirit. His increasingly severe criticism of conventional behavior, purposeful, practical actions, pragmatic thinking, and social orientation, reveals a deeply felt
antagonism of heart - nature - God - truth and society - convention -
artificial relations. He completely identifies with those "simple souls"
who have retained a feeling heart and sinks into despair when they are
misunderstood by society (16: 17,112). Upon meeting Lotte, he responds to her as she appears in a natural setting, subsequently attributes to her those character traits missing in others, and sees her behavior as a perfect harmony of heart and mind (16: 65). Werther
transfers his yearning for oneness with nature and God to her, reads in
her eyes "true interest," and believes that she loves him. When Lotte's
engagement to Albert prevents the desired union of hearts, Werther
again encounters the unbridgeable gulf between convention and pure
emotion. He feels uprooted. Despair, nausea, and the awareness of
entrapment displace the previously experienced bliss of unity with life.
After his various attempts to preserve the essence of his personality by
repudiating society, escaping from the situation, and redefining nature
have failed, he elects suicide in the hope of achieving a union with ultimate love in a realm beyond earthly existence.

The motif sequence sentient heart / possessive hand establishes a
pattern of contrasts that are transposed through the coupling of heart
and nature, silent glance and dialogue onto a higher plane on which
they are critically redefined. The novel's landscape representations establish that Werther's reasoning is shaped by a common linguistic
structure. Moreover, they show that his thought and mode of perception have been influenced by literary conventions. Similarly, Werther's
conceptualization of "heart" is indebted to a prevailing distinction
between heart as intuitive emotion and mind as rational reflection in

the philosophical discourse of the eighteenth century. The narrative technique is designed to expose Werther's self-deception. He is not only engulfed by his emotions but also encircled by the very conventions that he abhors. He mirrors himself in a Homeric landscape and heightens his bliss by imitating a cultural tradition. Later he identifies with Ossian and intensifies his grief. Werther seeks the experience of grace promised in Scripture in his heart but feels ever-mounting uncertainty because the sentiments of the heart intersect with the emotions of others and with social convention. The disorientation is evident in Werther's exclamation: "My God! my God! why have you abandoned me?" (16: 99)

Under these circumstances, the constructive dialogue, the silent communication of eyes meeting understanding in the other, and even introspection ("my heart") ultimately lose meaning as communication is saturated with ambivalence. Werther's letters show that he rebuffs dialogues that would entail a critical reappraisal of his perception of events. He is either puzzled by the inability of others to share immediately his views or irritated by their "cold" reasoning (16: 51, 52, 70, 76). Similarly, when Lotte admonishes Werther, he relies on his intuitive perception of truth in her eyes. Can her eyes be fathomed? Werther sees in them affection, kindness, interest, love, and pity (16: 100). Each glance corresponds to his emotions. But at the last meeting, the narrator's observation establishes beyond doubt that Lotte is capable not only of love but also of the renunciation and self-insight that Werther cannot muster. Werther finally reconciles the polarization of values by reintegrating his love, the sentiments of the heart, and the desire for orientation in absolute truth in the vision of an enduring realm of love (16: 136-37). Simultaneously, he resolves his identity crisis by escaping from the "soulless" world through suicide.

The motif of the sentient heart clarifies the central conflict organized around crossroads decisions in *Tasso*.[17] The specific sequence heart – intuitive impression of order – voice of the immortals / convention – silence and the contrasts of heart / mind and heart / hand identify the conflict between individual and social convention at critical junctures of the action sequence. The motif's distribution reinforces the circular pattern. Blending easily into dialogues and monologues, the poetic articulation of "heart" appears appropriate to setting, figures, and action. For example, Leonore Sanvitale resorts to a conventional expression when she characterizes the Princess as having a lofty mind and noble heart (1. 11). She underscores her view by subsequently praising the wide intellectual horizon of the Duke's sister (1. 139). The relationship between "heart" and "mind" appears complementary and is congruent with efforts of writers during the age of sensibility who sought to establish a balance between emotion and reason, "coeur" and "esprit." In other instances, when Leonore observes that the "full heart" (1. 86) forces her to speak, or that every heart rejoices over Tasso's poetry (1. 196), when she exclaims, "I sympathize with the noble, beautiful heart!" (1. 1914), or when she uses "heart" to identify a noble friend (1. 2101), she avails herself of standard expressions that had become stereotyped during the vogue of sentimental novels.

These linguistic patterns identify Leonore as a voice of convention commenting in a subdued mode on the view of human self-realization expressed by Alfons who primarily states and restates one idea: the individual can only develop fully in contact with society (ll. 293-301). A person must reach out to the world and understand the judgment of others (mind) in order to comprehend the inner self (heart). Thus Alfons, despite his good intentions, cannot fully understand Tasso's tendency to retreat into solitude. Similarly, when Leonore offers to help Tasso, she must fail. Her assistance fuses self-interest and consideration. Furthermore, her conventional view prevents her from recognizing in Tasso the absolute purity of a love that culminates in complete self-abandonment.

In contrast, Tasso's use of the word "heart" is sheltered from this conventional use. In fact, in terms of his heart, he perceives himself as a distinct individual. As we listen to him, it becomes apparent that the self's true inner core is characterized by gratitude (1. 450), truthfulness (1. 785), the desire to interact with the world (1. 789), deep devotion (1. 902), and the capacity for love. However, Tasso completely trusts this subjective perception, refuses to consider arguments that threaten the primacy of his intuition, and rages when misunderstood (ll. 936-37, 1388-93). After his clash with Antonio, Tasso turns to Alfons with the exclamation: "My own heart, my Lord, / acquits me; yours will surely do the same" (ll. 1466-67).

The conflict between Tasso and Antonio has its roots in an antagonism between noble sentiments and rational views, between introspection and criticism that requires reorientation.[18] It is precipitated, however, by Antonio's rejection of the offer of friendship ("my heart") that far surpasses the conventional gesture. What appears on the surface as headlong, youthful behavior has in Tasso's eyes the dignity of a solemn, almost sacred act. Just prior to the scene, Tasso had told the Princess how he quietly "dedicated his heart to her" (1. 911). The linguistic sign "sacred vow" establishes a direct relation with Tasso's vision of the "divine" in his exclamation: "When my heart unfolds itself to praise you, / To thank you, then only do I feel / The purest joy that humans feel; / What is truly divine I experienced through you" (ll. 1066-70). The self experiences the divine in the archetype of virtue and beauty (1. 1098). These overtones are present as Tasso approaches Antonio and offers him his heart and hand in friendship (1. 1200). When he encounters an apparently insurmountable obstacle in his plea for direct communication (heart to heart) and suffers not only mounting resistance but disapproval, he resorts in a flash of emotion to a challenge of violent action (hand against hand, sword against mind).

The play's further development presents an increasingly unresolvable conflict between heart and mind and heart and convention. The juxtaposition of opposites becomes a symptom of the inability to resolve categorical propositions. Tasso's unrestrained outburst is a transgression of the socially accepted code of behavior. His challenge to a duel is a violation of a law decreed to safeguard society's interest. Tasso misunderstands his own action and also all attempts by others to help him. Alfons seeks to mediate between the poet and the world. He only requests that Tasso retire to his room. But Tasso's reply indicates the breakdown in communication: "Your sacred word obeying / I bid my innermost heart to remain absolutely silent / . . . Whatever my heart may say, I am a captive" (ll. 1538-39, 1545). It seems no longer adequate to read these lines as the statement: I obey you and shall remain silent. Whatever I feel, I am a prisoner. Instead, we hear a desperate command and final plea: I honor your word. The word is sacred because it has the power to heal. But does your heart speak or do I hear the voice of convention? I now order my heart (sincerity) to be mute. Whatever my heart (truth) speaks—can't you hear me?—I must obey the rules of civilized behavior and convention. That the motif refers at this point to a conflict between heart and convention, voice of the heart and failure to understand is confirmed by Tasso's reflection and behavior after he retires to his room.

While the Princess, Leonore, and Antonio plan a course of action designed to help Tasso, he is desperately groping alone for an answer to his sudden fall from grace. He laments, "I know myself no longer!" (l. 2262), tells Leonore that it is foolish to be open-minded toward the attitudes of others and to recognize the interest of society, because such honesty destroys self-integrity (ll. 2342-49), and concludes that although Alfons is duped, he cannot show him the real deceivers (ll. 2483-84). Tasso finally resolves the conflict by resorting to deception. He attempts to be diplomatic, to speak the language of the court, and seeks to suppress his true feeling. But he senses that he is no longer truthful and is violating the commands of his "heart" (ll. 2796, 2807, 3098). He calls Leonore "a crafty heart" (l. 2496) and is even convinced that the Princess is heartless (ll. 2541-43). Clearly Tasso plays the role of deception in an effort to achieve a degree of personality integration in the face of a direct assault on his person by what appears to him a monstrous perversion of the truth intuitively felt by the heart.

Tasso becomes his true self again precisely when the Princess conveys her real sentiments: "I have to leave you and yet my heart / Can not give you up" (ll. 3220-21). But instead of benefiting him, the conversation creates a complete identity crisis. He misunderstands the Princess while she cannot comprehend his emotional response which is conditioned by his perception that body and mind are united in true love. The moment of truth-finding and its catastrophic consequences highlight the collision of individual and society in a civilized world in which personal aspirations and common concerns have been equally poised in a code of behavior that ultimately requires the renunciation of self-interest.

In the third act, in the very center of the play, the Princess laments that we forget to obey the "pure, subdued signal / of our heart" (ll. 1670-71). To forget is to "unlearn" (*verlernen*) the signals of the heart by acquiring social interaction and the linguistic ability that enables humans through the manipulation of signs to exist in their environment. The prevailing language of the Court of Ferrara reflects a precarious balancing act of social interaction (*Sitte*) that must not be disturbed by demands for absolute truth or forthright expression of pure emotions. Therefore, the heart can only give hushed hints. Yet, the Princess attributes sacred importance to these signals. If we listen, we hear a "God speak ever so softly / and yet quite audibly in our bosom" (ll. 1672-73). The heart speaks with the voice of an order that is superior to the language of convention. Hence, self-inquiry focuses on the intuitive perception of truth as a critical moment in the centrifugal movement toward self-insight. The signification of "heart" echoes that of Tasso. The Princess comprehends the absolute sincerity of Tasso's emotion. However, she attributes to his vision a dimension which he himself had alluded to in his description of their first meeting. The pure confluence of hearts, silently established through glances, can heal the distancing effects of civilization by establishing a bond between individuals without resorting to ambiguous verbal signs (ll. 875-880). The Princess considers this convergence of kindred spirits attainable within the existing social structure of society. She had therefore already admonished Tasso to renounce his longing for the unrestrained freedom of the golden age, a time where "whatever pleases is allowed" (l. 994). Her orientation in life is determined by the maxim: "What is befitting is allowed" (l. 1006).

The mnemonic spatial dimension inherent in the irreconcilable clash between the judgment of the Princess and Tasso's view points to diverging paths, both of which lead to isolation. The Princess hears the call to seek vertical orientation but remains restricted in the horizontal perspective of convention. Tasso insists that the path to truth leads inward and thereby denies the vertical orientation. He expects total commitment to a vision that must be lived, not distilled in a poetic structure, neither contemplated nor reasoned. His confession of love not only violates her conception of truth in living but also terrifies her because his passionate language defies the civilized code of the court (ll. 3252-83). Her cry, "Away!" as she flees sets the stage for reactions in the face of an incomprehensible situation. Alfons's exclamation, "He has lost his senses" and Antonio's statement, "we have nothing to compare this to" represent the courtly response to the outburst of passion. Grasping Antonio for support, Tasso expresses his grief: "When humanity is silenced by torment / A God gave me the power to voice my suffering" (ll. 3432-33). Thus the poet preserves his artistic integrity even in the "shipwreck" of his life. Yet, the spectator is left to contemplate the fact that the articulation of pure sentiments has not closed but widened the gulf separating individuals. The individual is retrained by language when expressing emotions ranging from ecstatic bliss to the desire for a supra-personal order. Society is confined by the ritual of convention. All are troubled by their uncertain judgment. The figures are suspended in an unresolvable conflict between human passion and the vision of pure love, between the need for the affirmation of life and the renunciation of personal hopes. The tension between ideals and the all-too-human can propel individuals to a new plane of self-knowledge. It can also lead to error, guilt, and the tragic circle of confinement. Convention, a form of social consensus, may become a source of hidden oppression. While Schiller and Goethe recognize this possibility, they do not advocate reforms espoused by writers at the turn of the nineteenth century that called for the abolition of cultural and social institutions. Instead, they stress the classical stance of the individual's decision to turn from old, inherited, confining patterns of aggression, deception, and possessiveness to new models dictated by mutual understanding, open, unequivocal communication, and concern for the well-being of others. In failing to make the crossroads decision, the protagonists Don Cesar, Don Manuel, Werther, and Tasso remain confined to the old patterns. But in the words of the secondary figures of Beatrice and the Princess, the audience can hear the potential for a crossroads decision that points to a mode of existence shattering the walls of confinement in traditional patterns.

The Wanderer at the Crossroads: Diverging Paths in the Works of Wieland, Klinger, Goethe, and Schiller

I

The young German poets and playwrights who became identified with the generation of Storm and Stress (G.A. Bürger, Friedrich H. Jacobi, J.M. Miller, Friedrich Stolberg, J.A. Voss, J.M. Lenz, F.M. Klinger) frequently used the motif of the journey to express a deeply felt desire for change. They conceived the figures of wanderers as nonconformists who seek to escape the confinement of convention, demand social and political reforms, and often yearn for unrestrained expression of individual desires. Since the motif also lends itself to express a character's restlessness, the impulse to seek the unknown, and the promise of full development, it can underscore the dynamic process of personality change. More importantly, the motif reveals the far-reaching effects of social change. Indeed, it is a reliable indicator of an author's recognition or critical comprehension of historical development. The differences in such contrast patterns as civilization / nature, inspired by Rousseau's thinking, or castle / hut, derived from a topos of antiquity, provide evidence for the marked difference in the historical consciousness of the writers of the period. Furthermore, the decision at the crossroads that initiates the journey may serve to introduce choices that, even though they are not seriously contemplated, will appear conceivable and thereby intensify narrative suspense. The crossroads decision is also frequently designed in such a manner that it dictates subsequent choices of the figures and thereby determines the narrative action. It affects the structural patterns and shapes the interplay between the figures in the text. Such foregrounding becomes pronounced in the eighteenth century. It can be observed in the works of such diverse writers as Christoph Martin Wieland, whose works breathe the spirit of Enlightenment, Rococo, and classicism, and Friedrich Maximilian Klinger, whose play *Sturm und Drang* gave the literary movement its name.

As a supporting motif of the coming-of-age theme, the excursion, journey, or voyage often elucidates increasing individual understanding or even growing collective consciousness. The complex thematic structures of such works as Wieland's *Geschichte des Agathon*, a novel that initiated the trend toward extensive novels of human development in Germany, or Goethe's *Die Wahlverwandtschaften* illustrate this technique. Conversely, the motif can retain the unequivocal quality of the Hercules in bivio tradition. The continued fascination with the artistic possibilities of representing diverging value systems at the crossroads is apparent not only in Goethe's early poems but also in Wieland's *Die Abenteuer des Don Sylvio von Rosalva*. The imaginative, entertaining journey of the youth Don Sylvio, the central figure in the first really modern German novel,[19] spans the brief period when he awakens from dreams of adventure to the demands of reality. Orphaned at the age of ten, Sylvio is raised by his aunt Donna Mencia who believes that the rules and customs of chivalry expressed in the tales of knight-errantry and heroic novels of the seventeenth century will prepare Sylvio for his future life as nobleman on a small estate in Spain. However,

Sylvio's perception of the world is completely shaped by his reading of wondrous fairy tales. He accepts fiction as truth and is convinced that the world is populated by beautiful and ugly fairies, by dwarfs, nymphs, sylphs, elves, goblins, sprites, and sirens who can change their shape, understand the mysteries of nature, and are either benevolent or mischievous and evil. Sylvio builds a tree house in a secluded grove, dreams of the adventures awaiting him in the world, and finally, beckoned by the melancholy glance of a butterfly, sets out to liberate the lovely princess who in his opinion had been transformed into the insect by an evil fairy. Further spurred on by discovering in the grass a medallion enclosing a miniature portrait of a beautiful girl and also his aunt's plan to marry him to a rich but ugly heiress, he single-mindedly pursues his goal, undeterred by accidents and events that contradict his belief in the "perfectly normal occurrences" of an enchanted world. In the tradition of Cervantes' *Don Quixote,* he is accompanied on his journey by his trusted servant Pedrillo. After numerous breathtaking adventures, during which he not only meets the brother of his future bride who seeks to teach Don Sylvio the difference between reality and a magic world but also finds his sister who had been abducted by gypsies as a child, he wins the lady of his dreams, Donna Felicia, who resides in a resplendent, palatial estate close to his own home. The narration closes with the preparation for his as well as Pedrillo's wedding, a vision of harmonious nature, and the hopeful outlook for fulfillment in life.

The novel examines conflicting value systems that offer clear alternatives for a decision at the crossroads. It incorporates philosophical inquiries into literary composition, the differences between idealism and materialism, and the subjective perception of nature and the verifiable, objective view of reality. Nevertheless, the prevailing view among Wieland scholars that the novel addresses the dangers of an excessively subjective perception of life[20] fails to consider several salient thematic features. To be sure, Don Sylvio is willing to admit at the end of his journey that his perception of reality was strongly colored by literature. However, Sylvio's individual characteristics, his attitudes and personal development, and also the descriptive detail of the social environment support the literary conception of an archetypal young dreamer who awakens to the demands of adult life. Don Sylvio is characterized consistently as a naive idealist whose imagination is influenced by literary tales that delight in unequivocal contrasts of good and evil and present the reward of successful self-realization to those who resist all temptation to deviate from the right path, retain a pure heart, and trust the innate goodness of nature. In behavior, outlook, and desire, he resembles the simpleton of the fairy tale who journeys into the world to win a fair princess. Moreover, Don Sylvio does not reach a high level of enlightenment or learning because he, as those around him, completely relies on intuitive perception and is not disappointed because in essence, the world corresponds to his dreams. However, he admits that his identification of life and literature has to be modified when he beholds Donna Felicia's beauty which triumphs over his "aesthetic" expectation.[21] He also questions the verisimilitude of fairy tales after Don Eugenio invents and relates the fantastic tale of Prince Biribinker in whose realm nature's laws have been suspended (VI: 268-69). After contemplating Felicia's and her brother's estate, the groves, arbors, garden houses, paths, fountains, cascades, temples, and pedestals set into a cultivated landscape, he recognizes that the "enchanted region was an artistic creation that had been created by combining the loveliness of nature with the beauty of art." He speculates that human fantasy may indeed "be the true mother of the miraculous which as a result of his inexperience he had until now considered part of nature" (VI: 270). Similarly, he modifies his view that the very essence of historical writing becomes suspect if the stories told in fairy tales are not truthful (VI: 118, 254). However, his experience of history appears in a timeless frame. Hence, he tentatively agrees that alternative perceptions of life are possible and begins to distinguish between imagination and reality. Yet, by affirming Don Sylvio's childlike stance, the novel suggests that fantasy is as important for human individuation as the rational perception of the world.

Just as Wieland projects in his novel an ever-recurring, ever-possible moment of human individuation, so Don Sylvio experiences a world in which historical processes are suspended. The dreams of victory over evil, the liberation of captive princesses, the acquisition of immense wealth, and the vision of unfathomable beauty, depicted by comparisons to gold, precious stones, and jewelry, find a direct parallel in Sylvio's encounter with the world. He meets Donna Felicia, whose beauty surpasses any description in the tales Sylvio has read and whose wealth appears to equal that of a fairy princess. She loves him at first sight, sees the future in the light of an Arcadian idyll, and offers him the fulfillment of his dreams at her side on the estate Lirias which her grandfather Gil Blas of Santillan had received as a gift. The direct reference to Lesage's literary creation underscores the novel's intended resolution: Don Sylvio awakens from the dreams of youth to face reality. The world, however, not only offers good fortune and personal success but also appears to be suspended in an ahistorical continuum in which all conflicts can be resolved and everyone finds fulfillment. Pedrillo, who consistently compares the market value of the jewels worn by fairies to the price of farms, is appointed supervisor of the estate; Jacinte, searching for nobility of spirit, marries the gentle and truthful Eugenio; and even the crass materialistic desires of Donna Mencia are rewarded with a pension of 6000 Taler. Before concluding the charming adventures, Wieland makes a brief reference to Don Sylvio's travels through "the most elegant regions of Europe" (VI: 300), a tour designed to enhance and develop his potential to the fullest. Yet, what he perceives, thinks, or learns during that time remains hidden from the reader. Indeed, any elaboration of the complex factors that determine the full development of an individual's potential would have detracted from the novel's primary interest of voicing a plea for sensibility and imagination. Don Sylvio awakens at a critical moment in life and succeeds in retaining his fantasy in the face of the world's opposition. This ability not only softens the transition from youth to adulthood but also gives rise to a good-humored acceptance of reality.

During the last quarter of the eighteenth century, the spirit of tolerance for philosophic differences that characterizes Wieland's narrative stance and especially his resolution to the awakening of youth to the demands of society is less frequently linked with the coming-of-age theme and the motifs of the journey and the crossroads than with either almost dogmatic philosophical assertions of the valid resolution of social change or antithetical arrangements which highlight the protagonist's agony in choosing the right direction in life. The confrontation with two irreconcilable attitudes toward the social realm, portrayed as the straight path of truth and the devious road of accommodation, tends to inject into narratives a recurring clash between utopian visions and the acquiescence to social demands. If the initial dialogues in Goethe's "Urfaust" or Klinger's *Fausts Leben,*

Thaten und Höllenfahrt illustrate the technique of fusing the motif of the crossroads decision with a defiant rejection of the established, oppressive order, then Wieland's *Agathon* and Klinger's *Geschichte eines Teutschen der neuesten Zeit* offer striking examples of a process of abstraction in which representational characterizations give way to an ideational conception. Furthermore, the existential situation that either precedes or follows the decision at the crossroads of life of the central figures in these novels clarifies the motif's signification in Goethe's and Schiller's works. Klinger's *Faust* is the first in a series of nine novels in which the author tries to account for the moral primacy of existence as well as the natural and artificial relations in social life. Klinger states in his preface that he will spread before the reader the complete panorama of the human condition: "Society, government, religion, the sciences, the high idealistic perception, the sweet dreams of another world, the glowing hope for a purer existence beyond the world—their value and futility will be cast into bold relief through their proper use and abuse."[22] Yet, both Faust's quest and Ernst von Falkenburg's education (*Geschichte eines Teutschen*) appear to be restricted by irreconcilable differences in the conflicting philosophical systems that promise answers to the question of human individuation. Furthermore, historical processes and social interaction follow a timeless pattern of recurring conflicts, the assertion of individual wills at the cost of social concern, and a general disregard for others. *Fausts Leben* links Faust's adventures with a succession of pointed attacks against the feudal system, the orthodox church hierarchy, and the immorality of the ruling classes. The hopes of those who seek reforms are continuously stifled and the aspiration of the rising middle class, represented in the figure of Faust, is suppressed. As a result, the novel projects a misleading historical transparency.

Historical processes follow a mythic pattern of rise and decline; human nature appears unchangeable; individuals are forever condemned to face the same decision on the crossroads of life. When the momentous discovery of printing fails to endow Faust with wealth, increased knowledge, and unlimited personal freedom, he enters upon a path of self-discovery that leads to destruction. He becomes immoral in order to understand immorality, commits crimes in order to penetrate evil, and philosophizes in order to comprehend the essence of thinking. Still, he fails because the universe envisioned in the novel is

entirely enclosed within the either/or structure of good and evil. The
narrator's observation at the end of Faust's journey confirms the pre-
destined existential situation: "Boldly, the scholar's courageous soul
soars to the heights of conceptions that approach the inconceivable
and inexplicable until the feeling of human limitation paralyzes the
wings of the spirit and it plunges back in a dizzying whirlwind into the
darkness, to awaken in desperation."[23]

The temper of moderation that characterizes both action and
philosophical debates in Wieland's *Agathon* also determines the wan-
derer-at-the-crossroads motif's primary use. Agathon is conceived as
a wanderer who surveys his age and in the process of development
achieves an exemplary balance of reason and sensibility. The motif of
traveling unifies the stages of Agathon's growth and provides decisive
junctures throughout the composition. The journey includes numerous encounters that are designed to evoke the appearance of successive decisions by Agathon. However, the novel's pedagogic purpose
defines his choice and hence the road to be traveled. To be sure, the
events capture the excitement of travel, captivity, slavery, and the exploration of foreign lands. But the action never projects a serious
threat to Agathon that would seriously weaken his faith in himself or
give rise to profound inner turmoil, indecision, and ambivalence.
Instead Agathon meets persons whose attitudes and lives elucidate
conflicting but representative views of the world. Their formative influence on Agathon lays the foundation for a desirable education of
an enlightened citizen. The encounters, especially those with the intellectual mentors Hippias and Archytas, initiate a process of reflection
that guides the young person in his decisions. Agathon is educated as
an enlightened citizen and statesman for a community whose government guarantees the open exchange of ideas and encourages the participation of all citizens.

The pronounced ideational component of conflicting philosophies that vie for Agathon's commitment gives direction to the pedagogic intent, enhances the conversations, and places the novel in the
tradition of the philosophical journey. The discourses, covering a
wide range of topics from self-fulfillment to subordination of the individual will under the state's interest, convey the conviction that social
reform is possible. The novel contains several sharp attacks on auto-
cratic rulers, as for instance Dionysus, who waste the resources of the

country, lack wisdom, and have no ethical commitment. Wieland also consistently draws parallels between the text's fictitious historical setting and the contemporary scene in order to show that arbitrary rule destroys the moral fiber of society.[24] In contrast, the republican form of government appears to be threatened by anarchy, because individuals are unwilling to subordinate personal desires under the common interest.

The action's historical setting is Greece in the fourth century B.C. However, the spirit of the debates and the conversations at the country estates in Smyrna, at the court of Dionysus in Syracuse, and in Tarent is much more reminiscent of late Greek culture, of Rome under Claudius I, of the court of Louis XIV, and even the gallant Rococo temperament of Wieland's own time because the quest for absolute ideals has been tempered by an ironic acceptance of the contradictions of life. From the outset, Agathon believes in the possible spiritual and political reform of the state. In Athens and Syracuse he observes how civilization has corrupted the moral fiber of society and is persuaded that only the cultivation of sincere affections will provide a solid foundation for cultural, social, and political progress. He is exposed to the thinking of the Sophist Hippias who has mastered the art of successful living through a joyous acclamation of the world's material wealth. Agathon is tempted by this apparently felicitous solution to the interplay of individual self-realization and the social weal. His love for Danae, a friend of Hippias, seems to pave the way for his acceptance of the Sophist's philosophy. Disillusioned by the revelation that she is a former courtesan, he leaves Smyrna. After further disappointing attempts to instruct the ruler of Syracuse, he finally comes to the Republic of Tarent, where he meets Archytas whose life and thinking correspond to Agathon's vision of human development. Archytas becomes his mentor. His own exemplary conduct as ruler convinces Agathon that reason coupled with a deep respect for all manifestations of life will provide the foundation for a wise reform of society.

In Agathon's education, Wieland apparently envisioned not only the coming of age of a world citizen but also a dialectic process of formation. The stress that necessarily results when conflicting philosophies compete for the individual will ultimately give rise to "harmony, wisdom, and virtue" (493). Agathon realizes that only a civilized person following a path between the extremes of self-gratification and an uncompromising idealism (175 ff.) can hope to join with others to sustain a civilized society. Consequently, social reform is initiated with the individual who has learned to balance heart and mind, conquers all fanatical attachment to either emotions or ideals, and affirms the contradictions of life.[25] Agathon advances in his thinking through a continuous interaction with the world portrayed in the novel. His journey along a path of critical junctures is a quest for individual moderation and social stability. His ethical and intellectual development provides orientation for those who value enlightened discourse and seek knowledge by cultivating tolerance and cooperation.

Klinger's *Die Geschichte eines Teutschen* is typical for a tendency in German novels at the turn of the eighteenth century to link the journey motif to a clearly defined orientation in personal development and specific proposals for social reform. As a result, the motif's function of initiating a process of increased understanding of historical developments is restricted. Klinger's narration of Ernst von Falkenburg's life, for instance, assigns to the crossroads decision the role of persuading Ernst of the validity of Rousseau's philosophy. The decision, then, limits rather than expands human growth. Similarly, the other figures in the novel are distinctly identified either by philosophical positions or social attitudes. They are arranged in a persistent pattern of parallels and contrasts. Ernst is aligned with the educator Hadem, his father, and an enlightened prince. His antagonists, grouped around a powerful uncle, who is president of the privy council, include the educator Renot, the nobility, and the state bureaucracy. The motif cluster of crossroads decision and journey into life is directly linked to the coming-of-age theme and assumes primary importance in the narrative structure, since a major portion of the novel is devoted to the formative years in Ernst's life. Ernst is persuaded by Hadem to adopt Rousseau's ideas. The lengthy, often critical intellectual debates between mentor and pupil and subsequently his friend Ferdinand and his uncle heighten Ernst's awareness of the necessity for social change. His convictions are severely tested when Hadem is dismissed and replaced by Renot, a tutor who espouses the philosophical materialism, sensualism, and enlightened self-interest set forth by Claude-Adrien Helvétius in *Le Vrai Sens du Système de la Nature*. Whereas Ferdinand accepts the materialistic outlook and develops into a political opportunist whose professed ambition is worldly success, Ernst remains un-

compromising in his belief in human equality. He supports the agricultural reforms that are rejected by the nobility, favors the declaration
of human rights, attacks the corruption and despotism of the German
princes who sell their citizens as soldiers to England, travels to Paris
where he meets Franklin, and visits Rousseau's grave in Ermenonville,
where he voices sentiments that echo Schiller's laudation "Rousseau."
After a visit to England, he returns home only to find a country in
which his ideas are completely rejected. All his hopes appear to be
shattered when in quick succession his father is killed in battle against
the French revolutionary army, his little son dies, and both his wife and
his best friend Ferdinand betray him. This descending, apparently
ever more restrictive spiral of his existence is suddenly arrested with
the return of Hadem, who instills new hopes in Ernst by reminding
him of Rousseau.

The novel's conclusion confirms that the expansive motif loses
much dynamic potential when the figure of the wanderer is cast as a
person who, after an initial choice and under firm guidance, adheres
unflinchingly to an idea, a concept, or a philosophical system that
leaves no room for further development. While the novel seems to
offer a new choice for individual growth and the reform of society, the
basic thrust that "only the rejection of nature introduced evil into the
social process" (II: 311) provides no real basis for a critical evaluation
of historical processes. Consequently, the novel cannot resolve the
contradictions of the period's revolutionary change. In Goethe's and
Schiller's works, in contrast, the basic conception of the wanderer presupposes movement in space with a real or visionary departure, the
confrontation with a choice (crossroads), the quest in the world, and
the arrival at the destination or failure to master the circumstances.

II

The metaphoric field of the wanderer in Goethe's writings encompasses exclamations of personal identification, comparisons to the creative urge, and subtle associations with such motifs as rider – horse or
helmsman – ship – shipwreck / harbor. The representations range
from brief allusions, as in "Drei Oden an meinen Freund Behrisch,"
to pivotal structural patterns, as for instance in *Die Leiden des jungen
Werthers* and *Wilhelm Meisters Wanderjahre*. It is clear, however, that

in poetry, the signification of the wanderer at the crossroads often surpasses the critical juncture of doubt or inner certainty, rebellion or acquiescence, success or failure, because a poem's conclusion can align
the call to action with a shifting perspective that suggests a definite
course of action.   With the exception of lyrics such as "Unbeständigkeit" or "Mit einem gemalten Band," which adhere to a conventional Anacreontic mood, the poems from the early 1770s are
characterized by strong internal tensions and resolutions that point to
different possibilities of individual growth.

"Willkommen und Abschied" gives a clear indication of the view
that the capacity to love is indispensable for human individuation.
Tracing the anticipation, meeting, and farewell of the lovers, the poem
succeeds in establishing a dynamic balance of conflicting emotions
through the association of fear and fulfillment, sorrow and bliss with
the natural rhythm of day and night.   Yet, the most forceful sentiment
sustaining the rider's awakening to future action is the full affirmation
of life.   The readiness to view life as an adventure becomes a prominent feature of the motif in all the poems that hold forth the promise
of a successful journey through the world.   The traveler in "An
Schwager Kronos" acclaims the vitality of existence.   His vision
blends with the motion of the galloping horses of time that speed him
on the journey through life toward his ultimate destination of death.
Opening on a note of urgency, the poem spans the swift departure
(youth), the uphill struggle to the zenith that offers a sweeping view of
creation (maturity), and the rapid descent to Orcus.   The stanzas are
accentuated by exclamations urging the traveler to look forward, be
active, self-reliant, and ready to experience the vitality of existence.
As the traveler, "an ocean of fiery light in the foaming eye," is hurled
toward the realm of death, it appears as if the sun has permanently
conquered darkness.

The sequence of the traveler's ride in the stagecoach in "An
Schwager Kronos" provides a series of significant junctions that illuminate the formation of thematic patterns.   The traveler's challenge to
the coachman to hasten the journey articulates self-reliance and the
exuberance of youth.   At the zenith of life, he experiences the potential of love ("Gesundheitsblick") and divines the eternal spirit of creation.   Finally, sweeping aside the fear of old age, he confronts death
and acclaims his mode of existence.   Missing in the constellation of

the youthful acceptance of life are the motifs and themes of dialogue / silence, heart / hand, and renunciation that assume major importance in the representation of a model of excellence, social reform, and the stages of individual growth that necessitate the careful consideration of historical change and its effect on society. The unflinching commitment to the immediacy of experience, untroubled by existential anguish, intellectual reflection or worry, appears, then, as a valid, if one-sided possibility of self-realization.

"Wandrers Sturmlied," in contrast, conveys a vision of the precariousness of existence. Confronted with the crosscurrents of changing artistic styles and philosophical views, the wanderer-poet winds his way through mud, rain, hail, and snow squalls. As he defiantly challenges the Muses under the most adverse circumstances and probes the extent of his freedom, it becomes apparent that the faith in a universal order that had nourished society's spiritual existence in previous centuries can no longer sustain him. The recurring call to inspiration which fuses plea and defiance in a rhythmical incantation reveals the ambivalence of the individual who seeks to assert autonomy and yet experiences the deep anxiety of a person who is not certain of his destination. He hesitates, prompted by the fear of having lost faith in his inner self. A farmer eagerly returning to his warm shelter impresses upon the wanderer the difference between a life following the straight path of certainty and the struggle with the agony of doubt. At the same time, the wanderer recognizes in the search for protection a general tendency of the age to look for security that threatens creativity. The poet rejects the materialistic tendencies of society as well as the conventional art of the day that has gained a false security by imitating the past. He realizes that he can reach his destination only by building a genuine confidence that springs from an inner certainty gained in the continuous, active participation in life. This recognition elates the wanderer and gives him courage to look for a new order in the world. The poem's exuberant lines, accentuated by frequent exclamations, summon the reader to face the world joyously even under the most desperate circumstances. It also reveals strong subjective tendencies in the personalized conflict between the poet and his age. The reiteration of "genius" and the asseveration of the "heart's" primacy not only underscore the difference in the perception of self-realization expressed in the poetry of Enlightenment but also indicate shifting patterns in Goethe's representation of human nature. The final appeal to gain sufficient strength to reach a destination that permits an overview of the landscape suggests that the broad vision which guarantees the right decision for future action has yet to be attained.

Similarly, in "Prometheus" the individual also appears freed from conventional beliefs and the burden of tradition. Characterized by a powerful assertion of the will, creating his own world, forming humanity "in his own image," and relying only on his own "divinely glowing heart," the individual seems to triumph over divine order which holds forth its promise only for "children and beggars." The wanderer gains strength by pitting his free will against the oppressive tradition. He has been awakened, derives joy from inner strength, but still remains at the crossroads of life. In "Ganymed," Goethe once again fuses mythological elements with concrete images to express the search for a secure basis of existence. The poem, marked by a strong centrifugal movement, points to a new direction in the quest for self-realization. The hymn links spring, the season of renewed life, to the individual's desire to partake of nature's rejuvenation. Responding to the enchanting summons of a nightingale, the poet hesitates momentarily—"where to?"—then finds the direction: "upwards." As the spirit rises and the clouds respond by descending, the individual achieves momentarily a complete fusion with nature and God.

The cosmic dimension in "Ganymed" appears more pronounced than the historical perspective in "Der Wandrer." However, the poem, written as a dialogue between the wayfarer and a young woman nursing her child, extends the consideration of self-development to a concern for the intellectual heritage and the interrelationship of art and nature. The conviction that human growth is impossible without historical awareness is stated emphatically in several stanzas. Goethe juxtaposes two distinct voices in the poem: the wanderer's, as he contemplates the setting, reflects, and gains a critical insight of his situation, and the woman's, as she comments on her plain life in a hut built in the remnants of an ancient temple. Unaware of the past, untouched by the fallen pillars, and even unaffected by the cycles of nature intertwining growth and decay, she lives in complete harmony with her small world. Her actions of tending the baby, waiting for the husband to return from the field, and offering a slice of bread and water from the well to the wayfarer reflect a life untroubled by the challenge of a crossroads decision. Yet, while her naive existence confirms nature's seemingly boundless energy to renew itself, the wanderer's reflection establishes that the creative spirit seeks to comprehend the meaning of life. Contemplating the ruins, the wanderer initially laments the apparently transitory character of society's great aspirations, then considers the possibility that historical cycles reflect nature's rhythm of birth, growth, and decay, but finally resolves to look into the future for an as yet unfulfilled optimum form of human development.

Each of these poems captures vividly the concrete detail of specific observations related to journeys. At the same time, they raise serious questions of human destiny. By focusing on the wanderer's relationship to nature, the capacity for love, the attitude toward death, and his view of the ordering principles in the universe, they embody the moment of awakening that is of critical significance for a person called to make decisions at the crossroads. The resolutions point to a strong affirmation of life, to potential self-perfection, and historical insight but also hint at possible failure. The existential signification inherent in the alignment of the wanderer with decisions at the crossroads of life is also discernible in the motif sequence helmsman - ship - harbor / shipwreck. Goethe captures the doubt and insecurity, the visions of hope and potential of failure encountered in the journey into life in the three poems "Seefahrt," "Meeresstille," and "Glückliche Fahrt." The first stanzas of "Seefahrt" focus on the activity and excitement of departure, give expression to the sentiments of onlookers who urge an immediate start, and introduce the captain patiently awaiting favorable winds. After lifting anchor and steering a straight course under sunny skies, the ship is overtaken by gusts that threaten to force it off its direction. The captain adjusts to the ever-changing squalls. Although he appears to seek accommodation with the world, the poem asserts that he remains "true" to his course even "on the crooked path" by outwitting the elements and finally reefing the sails when a storm overtakes the ship. Doubt, worry, and dismay overwhelm both crew and friends on shore whose observations function like the commentary of a chorus. But while wind and waves play with "the fear-filled ball," the captain remains steadfast at the helm. "Breaking apart or landing safely," he believes in himself and trusts his gods. The concluding lines intensify the feeling that individuals can master destiny by relying on the inner certainty that is born of the conviction of having singled out the right path. To deviate temporarily in the face of overpowering forces is an indication of sound judgment. The willingness to face death unflinchingly seems to spring from a deep emotional source. The accord of reason and sentiment, inner strength and faith in a natural order ("Godsent wind") shows a desire for a dynamic balance of conflicting tendencies in human individuation. It clearly opens up a new perspective on the single-minded choice between right or wrong at the crossroads of life.

In presenting both the experience of facing death and the joyous acclamation of existence, the poems "Meeresstille" and "Glückliche Fahrt" illuminate the crossroads decision between contemplating the certainty of death and looking forward to the activity of life. "Meeresstille" evokes the chilling stillness of an elemental power in a compact single strophe that projects the appearance of a landscape frozen in time. Moving almost imperceptibly from the opening observation of the profoundly calm water to the deep apprehension of the sailor looking at the "polished" surface, the poem focuses in continuous restatement on one fear-inspiring situation. The comparison of the ocean with a product of human craftsmanship locates the sailor at a moment in history when society has been led to believe that nature has been conquered. A polished surface, resembling table tops or lacquered chests, creates familiarity and lessens fear. Nevertheless, the attempt fails. After a brief glance that takes in the calm atmosphere which resembles a void, the sailor faces the absolute silence of death. The ocean's immense space is frozen into the single aspect of a world without motion. Self-deception is no longer possible. The depth of the ocean resembles a fathomless destiny: the polished surface appears as opaque as the future. The joyous acclamation of the voyage and the quickening impulse to affirm existence under hoisted sails in the poem's twin break the deadly spell. In a single stanza, "Glückliche Fahrt" presents the rapid movement of time during the journey through life: the fog lifts, the sky brightens, Aeolus comes to assist. The "anxious pennant" flying in the breeze alludes briefly to the fear that held the helmsman captive. But the waves part as the wind activates the sailors; the horizon approaches, and the shore is within reach: "Already I see the land!" Suddenly destiny can be mastered: The destination appears within reach as the individual looks forward and upward toward sky and wind rather than down toward the water.

In their representation of the crossroads decision, several poems written in 1815 during a journey to the Rhineland almost appear to be sequels to the lyrics of the early seventies. They illustrate the immediacy of perception and the continuity and change in tracing the individual's stance and level of awareness at the decisive moment of reaching a decision. "Vollmondnacht" depicts the solitude and anticipation of an expectant lover. At the same time, it strengthens the individual's precarious hold on life by pointing to the fulfillment of love's desire. Each of the poem's three stanzas, spoken by a lady's faithful attendant, is followed by a single-line response introducing and reiterating the woman's desire to be united in a kiss with her absent lover. Her resolve is firm and unclouded by any possible doubt. The attendant's observations introduce significant alternate considerations. They advance from a description of the immediate atmosphere and the praise of nature's timeless beauty to reflections of a universal order and the absent lover's struggle to reconcile his love with the ever-changing demands of an active life. Unaffected by these reflections, the woman persists in her single-minded perception which beholds the world as an extension of her sentiment and does not admit any possible conflict between senses and intellect. Disdaining any mind – body antithesis and rejecting the thought of a possible separation between individual and cosmic spirit that propels the voice in "Ganymed" to seek a renewed unity of being, she expresses her vision in the elemental exclamation: "I want to kiss! Kiss! I say. "

If this experience crystallizes powerful emotions enunciated in "Ganymed," then "Wiederfinden" parallels and simultaneously enhances the stance toward life expressed in "Willkommen und Abschied." Once more, the sorrow of separation and the joy of togetherness are linked to the crossroads motif. "Wiederfinden" opens with an almost joyous disbelief that after the torment of separation, two lovers will see each other again. Reflecting on past sorrows that still appear to shroud the present, the speaker accounts for his personal situation by projecting it onto a universal plane. He calls forth a myth of creation incorporating three successive stages to render the individual existence meaningful. The act of creation, accompanied by the delight of the creator to bring forth variant forms from the homogeneous matter, is followed by the dispersion of all elements. The universe expands. Light parts from darkness. Each living organism follows its own path and begins to search for autonomous self-determination. Suddenly, God himself feels isolated from the continuously expanding universe. He conquers his solitude and simultaneously the fragmentation of the world by bringing forth a new element of fusion: the colorful "resounding" light of dawn that issues in the era of love and new creation. The new order of the world, outlined in the poem's fifth stanza, assigns to human existence the duty to emulate life's creative urge. Instead of the Promethean defiance of God and the insistence upon autonomous self-determination, the individual is asked to channel the will directed toward powerful personal self-assertion into the resolve to work for a collective interest. "We" work to create "his" world.

The poem concludes with the conscious recognition that polar forces are essential principles of life and that individuals partake equally of light and darkness. In assigning to love a central function in the creative process and by affirming that love alone enables the individual to break out of subjective, restrictive self-concern, the poem offers the vision of human growth through a shared existence. The line "We both are on earth exemplary in joy and sorrow" reinforces the title's significance. To rediscover what was once united, yet find it on a higher plane of conscious recognition signals a new awareness of the individual's existential situation. The poetic voice no longer strives for immediate access to the absolute order portrayed in "Ganymed" but searches instead for the principles governing creation. Systole and diastole, expansion and contraction, growth and metamorphosis appear as necessary stations on the road to self-insight.

These poems, some marked by the pathos of youth, others already containing the chiseled outlines of classical works, strike us as immediate expressions of sincere feeling despite the fact that all of them show great technical perfection. "Willkommen und Abschied," "An Schwager Kronos," "Wandrers Sturmlied," and "Prometheus" evoke the impression of immediacy because they portray crossroads decisions that are determined by an inner certainty that disavows the doubt and ambivalence occasioned by the contemplation of alternate modes of individuation. As a result of the forceful, urgent thrust toward the unreflected, direct acceptance of life, the poems attain extraordinary clarity in revealing one basic trait in the personality structure of the developmental individual. That Goethe considers the willingness to affirm all manifestations of life as a primary characteristic of any view of existence as a continuing learning process becomes evident in those poems, plays, and narratives in which the motif cluster of awakening, crossroads, and wanderer is either subordinated to or absorbed by other themes or motifs. Usually, the shift from portraying the temporary yet timeless moment of awakening to the exploration of recurring choices at different junctures in successive stages of individual growth is attended by a modulation of the narrative voice. The urgency, even impatience, of exclamations is then either balanced by thoughtful reflection, as, for instance, in "Der Wandrer," "Daimon," "Nachts, wann gute Geister schweifen," and "Selige Sehnsucht," or replaced by the tone of contemplation that characterizes such vistas of life as for instance, "Zueignung" and "Warum gabst du uns die tiefen Blicke." Nevertheless, even in the poems of the *West-östlicher Divan,* the real or implied wanderer often expresses youthful yearning, a demand for immediate reform, and a desire for unique resolutions in the meaningful search for individual development.

III

It is also possible to locate in Schiller's works moments of awakening and decisions on the crossroads of life that are linked to a youthful stance toward the world. However, Schiller not only shifts the accent to pronounced existentially homeless individuals but frequently also represents personal awakening and choice in a tragic constellation at a moment when death is immanent. Consequently, figures like Karl Moor, Ferdinand Walter, Posa, Max Piccolomini, Maria Stuart, and Don Manuel experience doubt and error, reject convention, and face failure. In addition, Schiller prefers the finely honed contrast between an absolute ideal and worldly imperfection that leaves no room for the acceptance of insoluble contradictions of existence. Indeed, the stark antitheses frequently thwart the slowly maturing perception that a person ought to be able to advance in and also withdraw from a course of action without forsaking the final goal.

The dominant motifs and motif sequences of brother conflict, conflict between son and father, subject and ruler, and individual and Fate that support the critical junctures of the crossroads and the stages

in representations of the coming-of-age theme in Schiller's writings
trace deep-seated antagonisms, discord, and deadly encounters. In
Die Räuber, both brothers are characterized with dramatic precision.
They typify unmistakable and irreconcilable attitudes toward life.
Karl is impressed with the shallowness, pretensions, and conventions of
society, rebels against the loss of ideals and condemns his whole century in sweeping generalizations (I. ii.). He seeks fulfillment in righting
the injustices of society and attempts to restore a natural order to the
world. He dimly perceives the path to virtue but becomes guilty in his
struggle. As a dedicated revolutionary, he embraces violence, is corrupted by followers, and falls from grace. After laying waste to the
land, he reflects upon his transgressions. Initially, Karl seeks to mini-
mize his responsibility. Claiming that his victims were nothing but
"links in a chain of fate" (IV. v.), he sees himself as a prey of existence ordained by powers beyond human comprehension. He next
considers suicide as escape but finally accepts responsibility for his
life and decides to atone for his crimes by facing a trial.

His brother Franz, essentially weak and malicious, is a theatrical
villain, schemer, thief, and despicable worm, who embodies all imagin-
able ills of society. He hungers for power and believes that everyone
has the potential for success or failure, for extraordinary achievement
or an existence of submission to others. His choice of action is dictated by his will to triumph in life. The conqueror decides right or
wrong and accepts only the limits of his power as law (I. i.). He betrays father and brother, lusts after Karl's fiancée, and tries to kill his
father by starving him to death in a dungeon. When his end approaches, he is tormented by fears of the last judgment, collapses in
terror, and commits suicide.

The violent action, the alternation of wild rapture and grief, of
half-delirious exaltation and gloom, vengeance and retribution capture
and sustain the audience's attention. Yet, the real center of interest is a
dimly perceived ideal of human perfection. Near the end, Karl speaks
of the longing for a bliss that is a foretaste of heaven (IV. v.), a bliss he
sought to snatch from turbulent strife. He failed. Life ensnared him.
But after the conceit of Franz is annihilated and his own pride has
been destroyed, Karl no longer justifies his actions by pointing to the
wrongs he suffered. Instead, he looks forward to the expiation of the
crimes committed by him. The events and his own spiritual arrogance

break Karl. He embraces a penitent state of mind and looks toward salvation through suffering.

In "Das Ideal und das Leben," Schiller summons his readers to a crossroads where they are presented with the challenge to leave the stupefying pursuit of narrow goals for the freedom offered by the contemplation of ideals. The uncompromising choice advanced in the poem, succinctly restated in the epigram "Die Idealische Freiheit," makes no allowance for the continuous struggle in life that does not expend itself in judgments of good and evil but in answering the challenge to exist. Two roads are open in life: "One leads to the ideal, the other to death. / Try to escape without delay freely on the first, / Lest the Parcae carry you off by force on the second." As an accomplished dramatist, however, Schiller finds the choice of the wrong path and human error even more interesting than the right path of virtuous aspirations. Consequently, many poems accentuate unequivocal alternatives and extol the road less traveled while the tragedies tend to probe the reasons for individual failure to search for the golden thread leading to ideas of lasting reform. Certainly, the focus is on a comprehensive personal, social, and political reform.

In several poems, the poet's authoritative voice decrees the need for a complete transformation of existing transitions. "Die Herrlichkeit der Schöpfung," reminiscent of Friedrich Gottlieb Klopstock's odes, portrays nature's beauty. The poet-seer contemplates the sunbathed landscape after a storm, conveys the ecstatic joy of soaring into the light and, joining the "lyre of nature," extols the rhythm of creation. The vision of nature's organic evolution as alternative to civilization's disjunctive development recurs briefly in later poems, notably in "An die Freude," "Die Künstler," "Die Macht des Gesanges," and "Das Glück." However, Schiller did not share the faith of many Romantic poets that unspoiled nature could serve as model for cultural regeneration. As a result, the orientation of the poems shifts toward human interaction, perception, emotion, reason, and choice. *Nature:* "Fable brought it to life; learning robbed its soul; reason will return to it renewed creative life" ("Die drei Alter der Natur"). The road to a naive return to nature is closed. The poet probes the universe, sets sails for the cornerstone of creation, but confronted by infinity, casts his anchor in the world ("Die Größe der Welt"), where he confronts all those who individually or collectively have charted a course to worldly success. He voices the cries of humanity tormented by wars of conquest, curses the vain search for glory, and condemns the conqueror to eternal punishment ("Der Eroberer"). He lauds the noble spirit of true friendship that prevails over natural disasters, life-threatening physical attacks, and personal needs ("Die Bürgschaft"). Undaunted by skepticism, he relates how such exemplary conduct and loyalty can move a tyrant to renounce his previous conduct ("Die Bürgschaft" ll. 134-140).

The individual's ability to reject the lure of glory and relinquish power for a supra-personal ideal becomes the ultimate measure of genuine achievement in the final scenes of *Fiesco*. Fiesco has planned to overthrow Genua's tyrant and carefully considered his options when joining a group of idealistic conspirators. Success appears certain. Allured by the prospect of becoming the next Duke of Genua, Fiesco hesitates and determines that "it is *great* to gain a crown in battle. It is *divine* to cast it aside" (*Fiesco* II. xix.). Nevertheless, although his decision is based on careful reflection, the temptation recurs until he succumbs at the moment of victory. He trusts that he can be a just ruler, rejects the plea by his friend Verrina to disavow power, proclaims himself Duke, and is killed by Verrina (V. xiii., xvi.). The play's Mannheimer stage version that culminates in a scene in which Fiesco breaks the crown and embraces the citizens shows the importance attributed by Schiller to the complex interrelation between choice, self-assertion, and renunciation. The decision at the crossroads must be reaffirmed at successive stages in life. Political and personal freedom beckon but are unattainable if the individual remains enslaved by personal aspirations. Fiesco is free. He can espouse the suprapersonal interest of all citizens. He can also seek his own advantage, assert his powerful will, and lose freedom.

The pre-eminence of free choice and the implications of self-absorbed, deterministic action are exceptionally concentrated in the representation of a spontaneous, visible act of the will in "Der Taucher."[26] The ballad relates the events touched off by a challenge perceived as a test of courage. The king casts a priceless golden goblet into the Charybdian water and challenges the attending knights and squires to retrieve it. Offering the precious goblet as reward, the king dares the silent retainers three times. A handsome young page springs forward and flings himself into the sea's hissing cauldron. Contrary to expectations, he returns, relates the horrors of the ocean's depths, and is challenged again by the king to brave the water in order to explore the abyss. When the king's daughter interrupts, beseeching her father to forgo his demand, the king hurls the goblet and offers her as bride and prize. The page dives into the water, never to come back up.

This action sequence is crucial for the development of the crossroads decision. The ballad introduces a frivolous monarch, curious, devoid of compassion, and incapable of love, since he counts his daughter among his possessions. He functions as amoral tempter. His daughter, moved by profound pity to intercede, unwillingly makes the renewed challenge irresistible. The courtiers play a twofold role. They refuse to risk their lives but bow to tyrannical rule. They also function as a chorus by commenting on the action. The page initially responds spontaneously. His will, courage, graceful motion of doffing his cloak, and descent are one. The extraordinary feat is characterized through a detailed description of the monstrously rising, seething, roaring, and hissing sea that extends over three stanzas and the reflection of those left behind who would not dare the plunge even if they were to gain a kingdom. The page returns. A grace beyond comprehension has saved him. The group jubilates and listens to his report. He brings news from an abyss never seen by human eyes: purple darkness, terrifying creatures, and utter loneliness without "human emotions," without "human speech." He experiences the existential terror of being truly autonomous and simultaneously alone. When he responds to the appeal to repeat the descent, he is no longer innocent but looking at the maiden. Thus, he consciously risks "life and death" for a prize (ll. 155-56). His decision to follow the path to fortune and life was indeed one for an illusory realm of shadows, for the abyss, for death.

A test of courage, the choice of action when confronted by temptation, and the struggle to maintain human dignity are also linked in "Der Handschuh" but resolved decisively in a firm rejection of the traditional expectations of social convention. The speaker captures the tone of popular ballads. The ballad's narrative point of view, however, is ironic and accentuates the uncompromising stance toward flawed ideals. The setting evokes the spirit of chivalry and heroic deeds. King Franz and his retinue prepare to watch a fight among wild animals. When the lion, tiger, and leopards are in the arena, Lady

Kunigunde drops a glove into the ring. Mockingly, she appeals to Knight Delorges to prove his love and fetch the glove. To everyone's "surprise and alarm," he retrieves it, and while her eyes promise imminent good fortune (ll. 62-64), brusquely throws the glove in her face.

The stunning breach of courtesy is transformed into an instant universal judgment through the juxtaposition of artificial convention and a natural, unaffected stance toward life. Schiller depicts society at a stage of development when the allegiance to cultural and, by implication, political ideology has guaranteed social integration and the efflorescence of civilization. The crucial consequence of the successful cohesion is a powerful hold on the imagination and affection of the individuals who accept the code of convention and can no longer express sincere emotions or voice critical reservations. While society appears to be highly refined, it is instead ossified. A series of tableaux, underlined by the ironic manipulation of popular linguistic clichés, captures the atmosphere of a spectacle performed for an insouciant group. The king, surrounded by the important figures of his realm and on a balcony with a circle of ladies, watches the arena, a "lions' garden." The entering animals raise the expectation of a fierce struggle designed to stir excitement. However, the description of their behavior is designed to convey the artificiality of the performance, society, and life. The knight quickly enters the arena, calmly plucks the glove from the center formed by the yawning, lying, crouching, circling beasts, and "serenely" returns it to its owner. Courageous and self-reliant, he defies general expectations, renounces the courtly code by rejecting his reward, and through his action, unveils society's pretentiousness.[27]

While great courage is admirable, it is only exemplary when grounded in thoughtful reflection. Similarly, good fortune becomes praiseworthy for Schiller only when tempered by renunciation. In "Der Ring des Polykrates," Schiller captures the moment in Polykrates' life when he is at the height of power, favored by fortune, and content. Polykrates is visited by the Egyptian King who observes with mounting fear the limitless success and ever-increasing abundance of worldly goods bestowed upon his host by the munificent gods. He implores Polykrates to consider the events as a summons to a crossroads decision, to reorient his life, balance the account and, if all else fails, summon misfortune. Polykrates obeys. But his mind is still preoccupied with material wealth, not with life-sustaining values. He casts into the ocean his most precious possession, a priceless ring, which is returned to him the next morning.

In the ideational concentration of the decision at the crossroads of life, the ballad anticipates modern parables. The narrative integration is achieved through the articulation of a sequence of fortunate events that are considered by the guest in the light of possible calamity. Since Polykrates was later in life lured to Persia and crucified by Oroetes, the ballad can be read as an account of capricious fate that blesses mortals at one moment and destroys them at another. However, the exclusive focus on wealth, victory in battles, and surrender of a priceless ring point to a different significance. The ballad opens with Polykrates surveying Samos from the battlement of his palace and exclaiming: "All this serves me . . . admit that I am happy." Successive tableaux add to the picture of his wealth. The ballad never refers to his capacity for love, interest in others, acquisition of knowledge, or desire for wisdom. He is bound to the material world and is willing to tithe an object to appease fate. But he fails because he loses his friend who leaves him (ll. 93-94). By choosing power and wealth over friendship, Polykrates has committed himself to an existence governed by illusion. He sees the shifting panorama of life without penetrating the essence of being.

A decision at the crossroads is taken between the world of shadows and the realm of ideals. Notwithstanding the unequivocal choice delineated in "Das Ideal und das Leben," the ideals advanced by Schiller encompass those that give new direction to human development. They require a firm decision for an active participation in social and political reform. They demand a reorientation of personal objectives. They hold the promise for human relationships not based on material advantage but spiritual values. This stance forms the basis for the correspondence in the thematic and motif patterns found in Goethe's and Schiller's works. In opting for thoughtful reflection and a natural stance toward life instead of an unreflected continuation of artificial conventions, Goethe's and Schiller's figures choose the difficult "road less traveled."

Spontaneous Affirmation of Existence in Goethe's *Egmont*

The summons at the crossroads is consistently accompanied by an awakening to the obligation to reflect on the present, reconsider the past, and look for new directions in life. In several of Goethe's poems, the poetic voice articulates the joyous acclamation of the adventure promised by the journey into a new world. The departure conveys the exuberance of youth and the sensation of open, expansive space. Emotional intensity and youthfulness also characterize Egmont's stance toward the world. However, the unique thematic alignment in *Egmont* of the crossroads decision with the obligation to serve the community calls attention to the almost unresolvable conflict in an individual who must subordinate his desire for freedom to the demands of society. The thematic constellation links a central struggle between heedless youth and agonizing age, the rejection of existential anxiety and troubled anticipation of the future, action and reflection, self-fulfillment and self-mastery, the recognition of historical change and an appropriate response.[28] To delineate the principles that govern Egmont's vital presence and spiritual potential, Goethe introduces a group of major and minor figures whose attitudes reveal fundamentally different modes of self-realization. The technique of externalizing perceptions that are simultaneously personal and supra-personal, since they are inextricably interwoven with historical change, affects the dramatic action, the design of tableaux, and the resolution culminating in a lyrical vision of freedom that is accompanied by music. As a result, the tragedy diverges from the classical canon of playwriting while nevertheless objectifying an intrinsic concern of classicism.

The representation chosen by Goethe is characteristic for the manner in which he probes the theme. Furthermore, it presents clear evidence for the internal dynamics, interrelations, and creative resolutions of spiral and circular patterns. In his investigation of light and colors, Goethe perceived the phenomenon of "entoptic colors": colors that become visible in crystals when light passes through several reflective planes and generates unusual shapes. Subsequently, he gave poetic expression to a correspondence between scientific observation and a possible artistic expression. "Entoptische Farben" is a contemplation of the effect of repeated reflections and the symbolic interrelationship of individual and universe. "Here a mirror, there a mirror, / Double position, unique selection; / Twixt them persons darkly drearier / Sleep in crystalline perfection" (JA 2: 257). The poem continues by alluding to the increased variety and precision of the "color magic" that results from the inclusion of additional segments of crystals. Thus, fragments fuse into symbolic unity through repeated reflection. A process of continuous mirroring forms the foundation of the dramatic technique in *Egmont*. It gives unity to apparent digressions, connects figures, reinforces motifs, distills from a historical event an element of universal significance, and raises Egmont's coming of age to a level that is exemplary in both failure and success.

The historical situation and Egmont are linked immediately in the opening scenes. Soldiers, archers, artisans, and citizens express uncertainty. Some anticipate war; others distrust revolutionary change and hope for a peaceful resolution of conflicts. Some are confident that their Flemish leaders will guide them to victory; many dread the wrath of the Spanish Crown and the arrival of Alba, the king's general. Everyone desires freedom. The hopes and anxiety of the population are expressed poignantly in exclamations that initially build up to a musical canon and later into a chant. The calls for "Security and peace! Order and freedom!" (I.i.) "Freedom and privileges! Privileges and freedom!" (II.i.) raise the questions of how to reconcile the demand for guaranteed rights and the longing for freedom, how to resolve the conflicting tendencies toward accommodation and change. Goethe withholds the answer until the final scenes. The play's action, however, shows that the population is paralyzed by fear after Alba's arrival and easily subdued. Moreover, the worried anticipation of Margarete of Parma, the regent of the Netherlands, proves correct: Egmont and the other nobles face destruction and the people will be oppressed.

The diverse opinions and contradictory views of soldiers, people, ruling class, and the revolutionary Vansen are interspersed by remarks about Egmont. In the reflected light of these comments Egmont appears as a person who is admired, trusted, and loved by everyone. Egmont not only accepts with naive self-assurance the admiration, friendship, and love of those around him but is also oblivious to the warning of impending disaster and seems truly surprised when Alba

has him arrested. One could add to these engaging characteristics
Schiller's judgment that Egmont is a wonderful and truly humane figure but ineffectual because he fails to act and therefore lacks dramatic
potential.[29] In order to charge the situation and figure with dramatic
energy, Goethe relies on the strategic placement of the motifs of the
horse, the sleepwalker, and anxiety, as well as the prison scenes. These
components illuminate dramatically Egmont's paradoxical character
traits: his extraordinary strength and his vulnerability because of his
unreflective, almost boisterous commitment to immediate experience.
The motifs fuse Egmont's physical and spiritual essence. They also
externalize his demon.

The motif of the horse captures the ambiguities of Egmont's character traits and relationships with others. The prancing horse is consistently used to identify Egmont. The horse was shot under him in the
battle of Gravelingen; Klärchen is overwhelmed by a woodcut portraying the scene; Egmont visits her cloaked in a rider's coat; he meets
Ferdinand on horseback; Alba's spies report that Egmont, untroubled
by the presence of the Spanish soldiers, devotes his time to riding
through the streets and the countryside; Egmont comes to the meeting
with Alba on horseback; Alba watches as Egmont pats the horse and
resolves at that moment to destroy him; Egmont yearns for his horse
in prison and reflecting upon the freedom of riding into the open
land, compares himself to Antaeus. In the play, rider and horse are simultaneously united and distinct. The galloping horse carried
Egmont on his heedless advance into life: "As though whipped by
invisible spirits, the sun's horses race away with the light chariot of our
destiny" (II. ii.). The rider responds to the neighing horse, mounts, is
released from the oppressive concerns of the daily routine, and experiences the joys of liberation. In prison, separated from his horse and
uprooted from the open space, Egmont begins to reconsider his former freedom and concludes that it was a "terrible freedom raging like
a hailstorm through meadow, field, and forest, wreaking destruction"
(V. ii.). After the admission he can finally contemplate the meaning
of his life.

The scenes in Egmont's home and in Klärchen's room provide direct insight into his innermost being. Egmont steps out from the twilight of the observations by others. He is in his milieu. He discusses
the details of daily routine with his secretary, talks about the manage-

ment of the province, considers requests by soldiers, and is forced to answer an earnest, truthful letter of admonition. It becomes immediately apparent that for Egmont, the days devoted to life at court or ruling the province are not filled with significant events. They lack a memorable or extraordinary incident. Yet, they are the days of decisive historical change. Egmont cannot acknowledge this fact, because his whole nature rebels against anticipation of and planning for the future. He prefers to leave essential preparations for the daily administration to his secretary, is compassionate and therefore sympathetic to requests that should be denied, and refuses to think about tomorrow since such thoughts destroy the freedom to enjoy the present: "Does the sun shine for me today that I may ponder what happened yesterday, that I may fathom and link that which is not to be fathomed or linked—the destiny of a future day?" (II. ii) To consider the future is to experience anxiety and contemplate death. Comparing himself to a sleepwalker, Egmont wonders whether it would be helpful to awaken him and answers the question by insisting on his existence firmly bound to the immediacy of life.

The meeting with Wilhelm von Oranien reinforces and augments the characterization of Egmont. In the mirror of the other statesman who considers the appropriate course of action carefully, weighs alternatives, charts the future, and proposes a plan to insure the freedom of the country, Egmont appears considerate, dignified, and blind. He refuses to accept Oranien's proposal to leave the court. In his opinion, such action could precipitate the bloody war he hopes to avoid. He is deeply troubled by the thought to take up arms for the cause of freedom when the decision could create the impression that it was motivated by self-interest: "When you have to tell yourself: it was for my safety that I took them" (II. iii.). He is mindful of the havoc wreaked by war but rejects Oranien's foresight as false anxiety and blindly trusts in the protection of the Order of the Golden Fleece.

The denial of worried concern for the future and the unshakable confidence in the chain of the Golden Fleece, emphasized especially in the meeting with Klärchen and the encounter with Alba, highlight the singular quality of Egmont's youthful stance. They also have profoundly symbolic meaning since Egmont must not only experience and master anxiety but also face death bereft of all hope and false security at the moment of his coming of age. Brackenburg, who serves as a contrast figure to Egmont, exemplifies the existential failure of a person held in suspense by a permanent, all-pervasive anxiety. He cannot reach decisions, lacks the courage to act, is dejected, contemplates suicide, and fails to muster the strength to either live or die. He bemoans his "wretched, despicable state" and "simply languishes away in the midst of turmoil" (I. iii.). The Duke of Alba, on the other hand, fears neither present nor future. His ideal of serving unquestioningly an absolute monarch steels him for his duties as first servant of the state but also corrupts his humanity. His decision to promote the state's interest is a manifestation of his aggressive will to power. He plans his strategy with utmost care, even provides for unexpected events, but dimly and only fleetingly perceives his limitations as his freedom of action slips away when Egmont enters the palace. Time presses. Alba reconsiders: "Thus fate compels me, the invincible! How long I pondered it! How great and alluring the plan! How close my hope to its aim! And now, at the moment of decision, I am placed between two evils" (VI. ii.). The ensuing debate between Alba and Egmont underscores their irreconcilable world views and the two diverging paths of outlook and conduct. Alba is prepared to sacrifice the aspirations of the community and the values of a free existence represented by his antagonist for his fanatical mission of restoring a political order that is doomed because it cannot accept Egmont's vision of respect for life, the individual, and the community.

During their confrontation, Alba asks Egmont: "What is permanent in this world?" The audience, seeing the immediate success but ultimate failure of Alba's design, realizing that those who appear invincible are compelled to act by an unfathomable fate, and witnessing the destruction of Klärchen and the preparation for Egmont's execution, may wonder what hope there is for individuals whose destiny is weighed by inaccessible "silent judges on black scales." The prison scenes in the final act provide an unequivocal answer. They introduce the most important elements for Egmont's coming of age: conscious reflection, recognition of the inner daimon, and transmission of self-insight to a young heir. Alba's son Ferdinand comes to prison, confides to Egmont his deep admiration for him, and remonstrates with the fate that destroys his hopes for the future by taking the person whose name "shone like a star of heaven," who had captured his imagination since childhood, and whose life served as a model for his own aspirations. The boy who has dreamed in the reflection of Egmont's spirit gropes hopelessly in the dark. "What should I do? You conquer yourself and us; you endure; I survive you and also myself" (V. iv.).

Egmont has already reflected upon his existence. He knows that any hope for rescue is futile. He has mastered anxiety and suddenly intuits the true significance of the encounter. His reply justifies and reaffirms the form into which he has shaped his existence and holds forth the promise of a self-realization in which the intuitive affirmation of life is augmented by conscious reflection. Destiny's caprices make life uncertain at every step. At moments Egmont pursued his goal like a "sleepwalker, balanced on the knife-edge of a rooftop"; at others he faced worry and death. But holding fast to the "careening chariot of time," his energies at their highest pitch, he always responded with cheer to the challenge of the day. Now, as he calmly accepts the end, he is suddenly aware that not only his life but also his death can give direction to Ferdinand's quest for understanding the world. His death illustrates the peril besetting a person who scorns the paralyzing, unremitting anxiety that is rooted in the fear of the future but in the process spurns the necessary core and foresight that provides orientation. His life exemplifies the joyous acclamation of an elemental energy that is unleashed when a person loves the world. "If my life to you was a mirror in which you liked to contemplate yourself, let my death be the same . . . Every day of my life I was glad to be alive, every day I did my duty with quick efficiency, as my conscience demanded . . . I cease to live; but at least I have lived. Now live as I did, my friend, gladly and with joy, and do not shun death!" (V. iv.).

The final scene contours the initially intuitive and subsequently conscious allegiance to the living form into a myth of eternal youth. Egmont rests in darkness. Suddenly a brilliant vision merging freedom with Klärchen, music with language, illuminates the stage. The vision holds more than a promise of liberation from political oppression. It offers hope for spiritual regeneration. Egmont accepted a gift from nature. He praised and cultivated its essence through his love. As the beloved transforms herself into manifold forms in the lover's heart, Egmont experiences the devout emotion expressed by Goethe in the "Marienbad Elegie" (1823): in the purity of our innermost being, we desire to "devote ourselves thankfully and freely to ele-

ments higher, purer, and unknown" (JA 2: 209. ll. 129-34). Egmont
loved the world but also mastered himself. This achievement is truly
his own ("Die Geheimnisse") and enables him to spiritualize
Klärchen and everything he loved.   On the ideational plane the
tragedy is structured to move through stages of intuitive affirmation,
conscious reflection, and reaffirmation to a vision of potential freedom inherent in self-insight. The play's resolution shifts the crossroads decision to the audience, transmutes chance into necessity, the
historical moment into timeless recurrence, and death into rebirth.
When Egmont avers his daimon, it becomes apparent that the road to
self-knowledge leads through an active life. When the technique of
repeated mirroring that links the figures and the political-philosophi-
cal considerations to the existential concern blends into the motif of
life's mirror. The semblance of Egmont's presence, his real existence,
passes into the realm of myth. The specific instance is lifted into the
sphere of the general: Egmont's compulsion is transfigured into creative regeneration.   Renewal – rebirth and continuity in a chain of
spiritual life are the prominent poles in the myth of eternal youth.
These visions are truly classical and frequently superimposed on thematic developments. They represent the antithesis of the acceptance
of aging and the finite destruction of figures when they are either expelled from society or severed from the intellectual tradition which
signal realistic resolutions.

CHAPTER 4

Classical Space: Civilized Landscape

Theoretical Considerations

Authors writing during the seventeenth and eighteenth centuries still benefited from compositional features rooted in classical antiquity. Landscape metaphors that strike readers as too elaborate or emotionally expressive can frequently be traced either to ancient literary traditions or to carefully designed innovations. Specific descriptive details have been conventionally associated with specific literary genres, such as love scenes, the bucolic or idyllic setting (*locus amoenus*), the journey into the unknown (mountain, desert, forest, or sea), security (sacred temple), or power (palace, temple). Toward the end of the fifteenth century, the terms *lantschaft* and *paysage* were used to identify a segment of nature that evoked pleasurable sentiments in the observer. After Dutch *landscap* paintings had become widely known in the sixteenth century, the term landscape (*landscip*) was adopted by English painters in the following century and spread throughout Europe. Eventually, it characterized appealing scenes in literature. The interest in landscape painting and pictorial representations of seasons, meadows, or woodlands coincided with an interest in spatial patterns that contrasted surface and depth and also with a growing enthusiasm for formal garden arrangements.

Well into the seventeenth century, landscape descriptions relied on

literary conventions of setting, topos, and allegory. They were broad-
ened in scope as a result of changing perceptions of nature, philosophical opinions, scientific attitudes, discoveries, explorations, and
journeys into "new" lands.[1] Blending individual observations with
greatly embellished scenes from travelogues, the landscape seemed
designed for an observer looking at a homogenous spatial aggregate.
The space affords pleasure, reminds the observer of paradise, creates
the illusion of a vision that allows an overview of life, or even appeals
to colonizing instincts. An increasing connection between landscapes
and self-awareness in the actual or implied observer marks representations during the eighteenth century.[2] The open space gives way to
groves, areas in which flowers, running brooks, and shrubs complement each other, and parks that provide sanctuary. The landscape begins to echo the individual's intense emotions, responds to the yearning for protection, becomes a true friend, and finally a brother with
whom one can share intimate sentiments.

The literary tradition was further enriched during the later eighteenth century by poetic innovations that, together with the repertory
of established compositional and rhetorical devices, gave rise to new
conventions in landscape representations. Hence, we can observe the
appearance of a variety of features that identify Homeric, Anacreontic,
Ossianic, pantheistic, and desolate poetry or the lyrics inspired by the
contemplation of ruins and the graveyard. Poets consistently expressed specific attitudes of the speaker-observer through features of
the landscape. However, in the works of Jean La Fontaine, Pope,
Wieland, Schiller, and especially Goethe, the details of the landscapes
serve as important guides for the reader's evaluation of narrative intent. By the time   Goethe completed the *Novelle* in 1827, the range
of narrative functions is impressive. Representations in Goethe's
works extend from precise, descriptive details (the oak in
"Willkommen und Abschied"; the stony path in "Wandrers
Sturmlied") to designations of natural phenomena that can be observed and experienced but express essential characteristics in abstract
form. The "night and wind" in "Erlkönig," for instance, are further
defined and charged with signification through the child's voice, his
anxiety and mounting fear of the elf, and ultimate death.

The conditions that determine the inclusion or omission of specific detail frequently comprise: (1) the subgenre (pastoral, drinking

song, religious hymn); (2) the motif (excessive praise of friendship, love, seasons); (3) the convention of established topoi and figures of speech, as for example: "mild vines," "hedges abundantly covered with roses" (Friedrich Hagedorn, "Anakreon"); "radiant attire," "Luxuriance . . . smilingly radiating the fragrance of colorful ornament" (Johann Peter Uz, "Gott, im Frühlinge"); (4) commencing social criticism that may either be innovative or traditional in linguistic practice (Johann Heinrich Voß, "Die Leibeigenen": "They devour bloody human flesh and drink seething tears"; Matthias Claudius, "Der Schwarze in der Zuckerplantage"); or (5) the author's specific intent. Jacques-Henri Bernardin de Saint-Pierre, for instance, reports in 1773 with great accuracy his observations on the journey to Réunion, noting onerous insects, desolate areas, and the absence of flowers (*Voyage à l'Ile-de-France*). In his narrative *Paul et Virginie*, the same island appears as a lovely, exotic setting for the two women who seek refuge from a civilization that has mistreated them. Similarly, Goethe notes minute detail with great precision during his Italian journey ("Rom 1787, 1788, Das römische Karneval"). Yet, in the *Römische Elegien*, the landscape incorporates myth, history, art, love, and Eros to form the design of a vibrating substance that envelops the observer. The writings of both authors indicate furthermore a qualitative shift in language use that characterizes literary landscapes in general: linguistic units are rarely descriptive; instead, they are arranged to create value-charged or emotionally laden pictures that support such contrasting patterns as cultivated land / wilderness (civilized / original state), open land / closed room (idealized setting / harsh reality), and space – window – room (open window – access; closed window – isolation). Finally, landscape representations are conditioned by the cultural heritage and social conditions affecting an author. The idylls of Johann H. Voß show his sound knowledge of the Greek tradition and also his intimate familiarity with the oppression of serfs. The landscapes in Ulrich Bräker's *Lebensgeschichte und natürliche Abenteuer des Armen Mannes im Tockenburg* betray the struggle with the adverse circumstances of an impoverished life and serve as the setting for the misery of recruits, peasants, and tradesmen who could never envision the bucolic scenes captured in the works of Bräker's contemporaries.

Landscapes, then, may (1) provide a dramatic, poetic, or narrative setting; (2) frame the action; (3) reflect a wide range of emotions voiced by omniscient speakers or characters whose sentiments are in harmony (Goethe, "Mailied") or discord (Goethe, "Prometheus") with nature; (4) project the vision of a divine presence in the world; (5) indicate the speaker's or onlooker's separation from or inability to comprehend nature (motif sequence light / fog - haze in Goethe's works); (6) create moods; (7) serve as ornamental element; (8) characterize events; (9) motivate behavior; and (10) function as an important spatial motif.[3] The motif's dominant features evolve over a long period. They are of singular importance for identifying not only the classical and the realistic stance toward reality but also the level of historical awareness represented in literary texts. In essence and by specific application, single features can be so clearly delineated that they constitute a unique motif, as for instance, the garden, the domain of agricultural reform, the literary, beautified, or civilized landscape, within the general landscape motif.

Our research has established that the spatial motif of the landscape has seven primary functions:

(1) By aligning spatial coordinates with an open expanse, the motif conveys the appearance of unrestricted movement and thereby either generates or underscores the view that the real or implied observer has an almost unlimited potential for development.

(2) The vision of the landscape gives rise to emotional identification in a joyous acclamation of life or the fear of harm or death. Frequently, the observer seems to tap the boundless energies of nature.

(3) Contemplation of the landscape initiates the desire to understand the principles that define nature and life in general. The onlooker's attitude and changing sentiments convey the conviction that the forces of nature should not be experienced emotionally but grasped intellectually. The analysis of this stance yields insight into changing perceptions, both correct and incorrect, of historical and social transformation.

(4) The motif identifies the observer's viewpoint of the landscape and simultaneously exposes fundamental misconceptions of nature or the lack of self-knowledge that encouraged the particular view. A manipulative attitude is expressed in attempts to beautify nature or transform it into an object for aesthetic contemplation. As a result of the bipolar focus, the motif initiates in readers critical revaluations of the

mode of perception, the capacity for self-knowledge, and the behavior of figures in a text. The expert control of the motif often blends contrast patterns, subtle irony, and a skillful manipulation of established literary conventions. Goethe, for instance, shows that Werther's attitude toward nature is shaped by expectations that arose from his reading of Homer, *Ossian,* and contemporary poets. In *Satyros,* Goethe employs the motif to satirize the effects of Rousseau's call for a return to nature, and Schiller exposes Karl Moor's panegyric to a sincere pre-civilized form of existence in *Die Räuber* not only as a simplistic belief but also as evidence for a misunderstanding of historical development.

(5) During the last decades of the eighteenth century, the garden motif assimilated several functions of the landscape motif. In addition, it developed distinct configurations that illuminate the stance of the narrator or individual figures in a text toward life, social change, and historical awareness. Despite exceptions, the most common occurrences show a high frequency of referential scope. First, as extension of the house, palace, mansion, or hut, the garden attests to a partnership between society and nature. Second, descriptions of gardens or parks that either appear to have grown naturally or, once established, duplicate nature disclose historical dislocation. Only specific analyses and comparisons can identify whether an author expresses the spirit of the age, naively confuses original nature with a nature controlled by human design, or consciously seeks to expose the garden's annexation of nature as illusory. Third, elaborate designs of gardens or parks that create pleasure or kindle aesthetic contemplation are frequently indicators of social imbalance or a deep-seated misunderstanding of both nature and art. Fourth, the grove, a place of harmony between the individual and nature, opens a path to the intuitive perception of timeless truth. The listener hears the "voice of the Gods" in the rustling leaves, murmuring brooks, and warbling thrushes. Fifth, the secluded grove forms a stark contrast to the world's turmoil. While offering a sphere for introspection, it symbolizes the existential anguish and fear of figures who, like Beatrice in Schiller's *Braut von Messina*, leave the sanctum. Sixth, the garden blends into a cultivated landscape of fields, meadows, farms, and villages. The observer recognizes that human activities have changed the environment. Seventh, wild growth has choked the garden. Remnants of garden houses, tumbled pillars, pilaster, hermae, and paths that ap-

pear labyrinthine hint at the ephemeral character of human efforts and the transitory nature of life.

(6) The representation foregrounds cultivated regions in which farms, estates, villages, and cities dot the landscape. Planned forests, agriculture, and commerce blend to form a picture of purposeful activity. Upon reflection, observers accept inevitable social and historical change. Rejecting the dream of a possible return to a pre-civilized, naive unity of individual and virgin nature, they begin to search for a new stance toward the source of life. The motif of the civilized landscape initiates in the reader a continuous process of reflection extending from historical considerations to environmental concerns and vividly distinguishes the classical from the realistic perspective.

(7) The constraining cityscape of closed rooms, cages, oppressive buildings, circular paths, and impenetrable or labyrinthine streets reinforces representations of figures who are unable to develop their potential and appear to be entrapped by a milieu that is beyond individual control or even comprehension. The motif sustains the circular pattern of confinement.

Our examination of spatial coordinates of successive landscape representations in works by Racine, Corneille, La Fontaine, Pope, Wieland, Goethe, and Schiller will show their prominence in delineating the classical space and important characteristics of the developmental personality. In their multiple functions of framing action, providing settings, reflecting emotions, and motivating behavior, landscapes and settings in classical literature assist in focusing and developing a number of classical themes and motifs: the building of a community that permits free development, enlightened dialogue, sterility / fertility, and especially the rejection of past patterns of aggressiveness and restrictiveness in favor of a vision that enables the individual to affirm a continuous and expansive process of growth. Thus, landscape descriptions often reinforce the dynamic outward, forward, and upward motion of the classical centrifugal spiral.

Palace / Wilderness / Garden in Representative Classical Dramas and Poems

Central to the representation of the civilized space in many classi-

cal works is the palace, the setting with which a seventeenth- or eighteenth-century aristocratic audience could readily identify.⁴ The
palace can provide either restrictive shelter or expansive stimulation,
depending on whether it is portrayed as a closed structure of impenetrable walls confining its occupants at the edge of the sea, as in several
of Racine's plays,⁵ or as an open facade interacting with the gardens
and surrounding fields and woods, as in Jean de La Fontaine's *Le
Songe de Vaux* or *Les Amours de Psyché et de Cupidon*. The palaces
in Racine's plays force the characters they enclose to use their inner
resources in order to come to terms with themselves and each other.
The settings in La Fontaine's works promote interaction between figures and the unique aspects of a harmony between palace and surrounding landscape. As the characters freely wander through and
gaze upon the palace's sculptural ornamentation, galleries of paintings,
gardens, groves, grottos, woods, and panoramic settings, they are liberated from self-absorption and ready to participate in imaginary re-cre-
ations of myth, history, and fantasy. These in turn link them with the
human community and the divine order.

   The motif sequences wild (savage) external setting / civilized (ordered) internal setting and sterility / fertility support these antithetical
concepts of the palace. The *Prologue* of Racine's *Esther* defines the
palace as sanctuary: " . . . this place [Saint-Cyr] inhabited by Grace, .
. . far from the tumult," lies under the protection of the king. The
play opens with Esther's contrast between her present asylum under
the protection of Asuérus and the past misery and homelessness from
which he has rescued her. The motif sequence of outside, savage
wilderness / inside, civilized sanctuary is sustained by: (1) Elise's description of her wanderings in the desert with no prospect of security,
contrasted with the safe haven she has now found in the palace(I. i. 10
ff.), (2) Esther's awareness of the opposition between her present security and glory on the throne on the one hand and the deserted, ruined
temple of God in Jerusalem on the other (83-88), and (3) her explanation of the savage "threats of death" that keep even the king immobi-
lized in his palace (I. iii. 193). Aman's treatment by the mob outside
the palace at the end of the play reinforces the contrast between the
palace as ordered sanctuary and its surroundings as threatening
wilderness.

   Racine's previous plays invariably portray the palace as offering restrictive but protective shelter against a hostile landscape, most frequently comprising the sea, but variously also mountains, empty land, ruined cities, a harsh climate, or enemy armies or mobs.   Thus, Andromaque expresses her belief that Pyrrhus' palace would be a safe asylum for her son (III. v. 937), since, as Oreste reports in the play's exposition, Troy is "a deserted country" (I. i. 202).   Because in *Bérénice,* the palace is filled with her beloved Titus' presence (I. i.), leaving it means entering a sterile, deserted world for Bérénice. The seas separating the lovers (IV. v. 114) are symbolic of the emptiness of all settings outside Titus' palace.   The landscape outside Amurat's encaging seraglio-palace in *Bajazet* consists of the empty sea, the hostile mountains abutting the distant shore, and the savagery of the remote battlefield.   Pharnace's urging of Monime to "Come flee the prospect of this savage climate" for a "happier sky" (*Mithridate* I. iii. 227) indicates that the palace functions as a protective sanctuary against the wilderness of the surrounding land and sea.   Finally, despite the fact that the palace in *Phèdre* is polluted by Phèdre's illicit passion which threatens its sanctuary, leaving it means facing the death-dealing savagery of the sea, as Hippolyte, and to a lesser extent, Oenone discover. The only other route of escape is that of Phèdre's "slow descent" to the underworld.[6]

At first glance, the closed interior space of French classical drama, set in antithesis to a hostile landscape of sea and desert, battlefield or city, would seem to prohibit the development of a centrifugal spiral within the dramatic structure.[7] But the elegant, polished setting of the palace room that gives its inhabitants security from the crude forces of the savage environment outside furthers the values of civilization: the focus on the human perspective, enlightened discourse rather than confrontation, and spiritual power over others that can expand to universal proportions. The palace room signifies a spatial unit shaped by and for human use. The very emptiness of its setting allows for a concentration on character, dialogue, and action, undisturbed by external, non-human elements. The identification of the palace room as civilized space with the specifically human dimension is apparent in the recurring allusions to an intimate connection between the palace or a room in the palace and its owner or occupant.[8] When Rodrigue enters Chimène's house after the fatal duel in Corneille's *Le Cid* (III. i.), he is penetrating the very shadow of the Count he has killed. Oreste in

Racine's *Andromaque* confesses: "These guards, this court, the atmosphere around me / All depends on Pyrrhus" (III.i.718). Narcisse in Racine's *Britannicus* asks: "Can anyone hide from Néron in this palace?" (II .ii. 410). As Junie discovers and communicates to her lover, Néron's presence is everywhere in the palace.[9] Bérénice senses that the "luxury of this place [Titus' office] . . . superb and solitary" is filled with the glory of the Emperor's presence. Hence, the civilized space of the closed palace room can facilitate human interaction, specifically, thinking of, talking, and listening to others. In contrast, the savage landscape of the open sea or country, the battlefield or the city calls for action and confrontation. Figures confined to palace rooms develop their mental, emotional, social, and spiritual capabilities, while those engaged in struggling against the open sea, in the battlefield, or on the open street need physical prowess instead. Only as they enter the palace and interact with those figures within it are they confronted with the need of becoming fully "civilized."

This matching of the palace's civilized space, in contrast to that of the savage landscape outside the palace, with the figures' actions and responses is already apparent in Corneille's *Le Cid.* Confrontations take place outside on the street (the challenge and duel) and on the battlefield. Enemies (the Moors) approach by sea. Dialogue in the form of talking and listening to one another is placed within the walls of Chimène's house, where the two lovers can expose their emotional conflicts, and the royal palace, where Chimène voices her feelings and Rodrigue's longing is promised future fulfillment. While in *Horace* confrontation suddenly penetrates the palace, as brother and sister face each other in deadly conflict, and dialogue between the Romans and Albans temporarily supersedes fighting on the battlefield,[10] the sharp division between the civilized space of the palace and the wilderness outside predominates in *Cinna* and *Polyeucte.* It is in the magnificent throne room that Auguste confers with Cinna and Maxime about abdicating his throne, then listens to Livie and accepts her suggestion to substitute clemency for revenge. In contrast, both the conspirators' plotting of Auguste's assassination and Maxime's threat of suicide occur outside the civilized space of Auguste's palace in the savage space of the city. In *Polyeucte,* a large vestibule opening to all the apartments in Félix's palace provides a common meeting ground for the dialogue between the characters that eventually leads to a common goal that all share and thereby to a new sense of community. The destruction of the old community gods and the martyrdom of Néarque and Polyeucte take place outside this sanctuary, in the temple and the prison.[11]

Racine's plays continue the division between the setting of dialogue and understanding in the civilized space motif of the closed palace room and action and conflict in "savage" areas outside. But the contrast is complicated by the frequent occurrence of aggression within the sanctuary. In addition, by becoming a place of confinement, the palace is identified with characteristics of the savage setting motif. Thus, in *Andromaque, Mithridate, Bérénice,* and *Esther,* dialogue continues to take place in the closed space of a palace room, while violence occurs outside in the temple, on the battlefield, or on the city street. But the palace isolates the title characters of *Britannicus, Bajazet,* and *Phèdre* from communication with those they love and eventually becomes the site of their deaths. In *Iphigénie,* the entire setting is moved to Agamemnon's tent in the middle of the Greek camp, far from the security of the palace, as Agamemnon points out to Clytemnestre: "You are not in the Atrean palace here. / You are in a camp . . ." (III. i. 802-803).[12]

Faced with the intrusion of the brutality appropriate to the savage space into the security of the civilized space or even the placing of the entire setting within the savage space of a military camp, Racine's figures are challenged to create their own "civilized space." The setting in Pyrrhus' palace in *Andromaque* is only a passage to the residences of various figures. While this space could represent a common meeting ground, as in Corneille's *Polyeucte,* characters are often shown passing by rapidly (Andromaque on the way to her son), unwilling to listen (Pyrrhus), or even intent on avoiding one another (Hermione's snubbing of Andromaque). Mithridate, arriving in his palace from distant battlefields, finds that both his sons and his bride flee his presence. Inside his palace, suspicions breed, and he responds with threats against the lives of those closest to him. True dialogue is possible only at the end of an annihilating battle after Xipharès' generous, self-sacrificing action on the battlefield. Faced with imminent assault by the invading Romans, Xipharès and Monime, the two loyal beneficiaries of Mithridate's parting blessing, can only flee from the now unsafe sanctuary. Likewise, Bérénice discovers that Titus avoids the office situated between their apartments whenever she occupies it. Esther faints when she must enter the terrifying presence of her husband. As both Britannicus and Bajazet discover, the palace room can become a trap; its walls can have inimical eyes and ears, and in other palace spaces, death awaits them. Phèdre's disclosure of her passion to Hippolyte and her tale of Hippolyte's supposed passion for her to Thésée within the civilized setting of Thésée's palace directly results in Hippolyte's flight into the "savage landscape" outside the civilized setting and a monstrous death. In the "savage landscape" of the Greek military camp anxiously awaiting wind in order to embark on their campaign against the Trojans, Iphigénie discovers that her father refuses to speak with her; that at this time and place, he can no longer be a loving father (*Iphigénie* II. ii .556); that she must keep silent before Achille's questions; and that he refuses to listen to her pleading for her father. The eruption of her jealousy of Eriphile is nurtured by the circumstances and setting.

In order to achieve an enlightened dialogue despite the abolition of the clear separation between civilized and savage settings, Racine's figures must create an internalized space no longer dependent on their surroundings but on the human qualities of comprehension, admiration, and imitation.[13] This internalization of space already occurs in Corneille's *Cinna* and *Polyeucte*. The human quality of Auguste's magnanimity and Polyeucte's fervor touches first those immediately around them, that is, within their fictitious physical environment. But their values are abstracted from this immediate setting to serve as models for future generations throughout the space vaguely defined as "all the provinces" or "everywhere" (*Cinna* V .iii. 1773; *Polyeucte* V. vi. 1814), but actually referring to the civilized world and specifically to the audience. So also Junie's escape from Néron's palace, Bérénice's renunciation of Titus, Iphigénie's self-sacrifice for her father and the Greeks, Bajazet's final adherence to his true feelings, and Esther's willingness to risk her life to save her people create a purely human landscape, no longer dependent on physical elements. Once liberated from the restrictiveness of any physical environment, their exemplary behavior can expand, like a centrifugal spiral, outward to encompass all people and upward to reach—or in the case of Iphigénie, to challenge (III. vi. 1045)—the sphere of the gods.

Not bound, as his French counterparts, to the convention of a single locus,[14] John Dryden shifts the settings of his plays among a variety of locations: palaces, temples, prisons, open countryside, groves, caves, and battlefields. The distinction between the inner "civilized" setting of the palace and the outer "savage" landscape of its surroundings is obliterated by the ubiquitous appearance of violence. Thus, though *Aureng-Zebe* takes place in a palace next to a neighboring plain covered by an "Iron Harvest" of armed men, the outside forces do not present as severe a threat as the passions of both the emperor and his queen unloosed within the palace or brought by Morat into the palace. The potential for violence is equally present everywhere, as figures overcome with passion burst into temples or palaces to rescue those they love or destroy those they hate. Acts of passion even penetrate the secured walls of a prison. Almech, for example, penetrates Cortez's prison cell to avenge her brother's death in *The Indian Emperour*. Indeed, the landmarks of the civilized space motif, the temples and palaces of *The Indian Queen* and *The Indian Emperour*, become synonymous with savage landscapes. Aztec temples are the locations of human sacrifice. The Aztecs have been warned that their nation will fall "when bearded men in floating Castles Land" (I. ii. 124). Furthermore, the "pleasant Indian countryside" that the arriving Spaniards admire for its "natural fruitfulness" (I .i.) is turned by war into a "field grown thin" (II. ii.). Cut off from its once fertile fields, Mexico City under the Spanish siege experiences famine (III. iii.). Resting in a "pleasant grotto," the Spaniards are taken prisoner by the intruding Indians (IV. iii.).[15]

Faced with the sudden intrusion of the landmarks of the savage landscape and its links with aggression within the inner sanctuary of the civilized landscape, Dryden's characters must, like Racine's, create their own inner, purely human space if they wish to develop the human values of dialogue and community. Few figures show a willingness or capability to rise above their environment to create new patterns of behavior: Montezuma and Orazio in *The Indian Queen*, Guyomar and Cortez in *The Indian Emperour*, and Aureng-Zebe and Indamora in *Aureng-Zebe*. The settings in which they will build their communities based on dialogue are both the familiar palace in *The Indian Queen* and *Aureng-Zebe* and the savage land of snow-covered mountains with "Thin Herbage in the Plains and Fruitless Fields" harboring neither the gold nor the silver coveted by the Spaniards in

The Indian Emperour (V. ii.). Both settings are marked more by the promised, future absence of violence than by any identifiable features of a "civilized" landscape.

In contrast to the palace surrounded by a savage landscape, the palace set in a civilized landscape inspires stimulation, self-development, and fruitful dialogue in its observers-participants. Their interaction with both the palace and its setting is to match the harmony established between the palace and its surroundings. This contrast with the restrictive, protective palace is especially apparent in the position assigned to persons. Whereas Racine consistently places his figures as trapped inside the palace, threatened with danger or loss if they leave it, La Fontaine portrays his figures in *Le Songe de Vaux* and *Les Amours de Psyché et de Cupidon* as freely wandering through the gardens, woods, and halls of the palace, marveling at the ever-fresh vistas. The perspective forms the basis a continuous dialogue between human and natural order and between individual and collective consciousness as expressed in art, history, myth, and especially literature.

The function of literature to organize the diffuse elements of a complex spatial conception consisting of panoramic views and close details, works of art and of nature into a harmonious whole is evident in the fragments comprising La Fontaine's *Le Songe de Vaux*. When Sleep first presents the narrator with a succession of generalized images: "a magnificent palace / mansion," "grottos, canals, a superb portical," "plants, marbles, liquid crystals, animals, and men," he confesses himself "confused" by the multiplicity of components. But Sleep comforts him with the promise of ordering principles which "Need neither marble nor tools to build, / Make flowers and shadows grow in a moment, / And, without the assistance of time, compose their works."[16] Even the ensuing allegorical contest among Architecture, Painting, Horticulture, and Poetry that together form the essence of the vision is characterized by dialogue and mutual respect and admiration. Nevertheless, it is clear that by ending the contest with the assembly's admiration for Calliope, as well as by continuing the vision with an assortment of legends, imitations of myths, songs, and verses, literature is given the role of organizing the diversity of the palace's internal and external details into an order that conveys an expanded role for the palace of Vaux. Just as the surrounding woods, gardens, sculptures, as well as the halls richly ornamented with paintings of mythical subjects work together to free the narrator from his self-pity because of his beloved's coldness, so the loose, fragmentary organization of the *Songe* around the exterior and interior of Vaux is to liberate readers from their preoccupations and transport them into the world of art.

The four friends whose conversation forms the framework of La Fontaine's *Les Amours de Psyché et de Cupidon* choose a grotto in the gardens of Versailles for their reading and commenting of the new work for the same reason. In order to fulfill their desire to ban academic discourse and to discuss and absorb the new work uninterrupted by city noises, the friends have walked to Versailles, the ultimate achievement of the palace as civilized space. Though this setting includes plants and animals in its arboretum and zoo, these have been so selected and designed that while they call forth the friends' admiration for "the art and diverse imaginings of nature" (406), they actually represent human ingenuity and aesthetics. Similarly, the grotto in which the friends discuss the new work has been skillfully constructed, is cooled by a carefully designed fountain, and is decorated with arcades with bas-reliefs. Representing scenes from ancient mythology, these bas-reliefs complement, as does the entire civilized landscape of palace and garden, the re-creation of the myth of Psyche and Cupid. Conversely, the tale itself mirrors the civilized setting of Versailles by portraying Psyché's marble palace "enlivened" with sculptures narrating other myths, set in a woods cleared of all sinister beasts, idyllically fresh and cool, surrounded by waterfalls and grottos that provide the fitting background for Psyché's moods and emotions, as she comes to terms with her peculiar fate. Returning to the framework of the cultivated gardens at Versailles, La Fontaine focuses on their capacity to expand the participant-observer's own frame of mind toward a contemplation of art, myth, royal and divine order. Its walkways organized in star formation allow the eye to wander in orderly fashion from works of nature to works of art and engineering design, to admire each separately as well as the design of the whole, and the mind to reflect upon the glory of the royal gardens that uplift the human spirit to the divine.

The capacity of the motif of civilized space to link art with nature, the individual elements with a broad panoramic view, individual emotions with community goals, the present with both the past and the future, and royal order and stability with divine intention forms the structuring principle of Alexander Pope's *Windsor Forest.* The capability of the setting to harmonize the oppo-site features of "hills and vales, the woodland and the plain, . . . earth and water"[17] is indicative of an order that promises dialogue, shelter (the grove), and a fertility (green, fruitful fields, "springing corn") that surpasses that of the ancients. This present order of shelter and fertility contrasts with past chaos, hostility, misery, and sterility captured in the images of "A dreary desert and a gloomy waste," "savage beasts and savage laws," "empty wilds and woods," "Cities laid to waste . . .," "ravished fields" and "gaping tombs" (45-65). The Stuarts' reestablishment of peace and fertility allows "Fair Liberty, Britannia's Goddess" to reign (91). In assuring present and future freedom from past violence and its consequences of sterility and chaos, the now civilized landscape gives the poet the impetus to allow his imagination the same free reign that his eye has enjoyed. Moving from comparisons of individual elements with other famous landmarks to myths delineating the activities of gods and nymphs, and finally to a vision of a worldwide "Pax Britannica" brought about by the expansionist activities of the British navy, the poet skillfully builds a series of concentric circles. Centered on the fertile landscape of Windsor Forest, these expanding circles function as a centrifugal spiral enlarging the observer's perspective to include not only the increase of British power but also its wholesome effects on the community of nations in the abolition of slavery that was introduced by the Spaniards, the promotion of harmony among all people, and the binding of discord, along with pride, envy, care, terror, ambition, vengeance, and rebellion (400-421). Having reached this outermost circumference, the poet's final task is to evoke in his reader through his verse ("First in these fields I sung the sylvan strains" 434) admiration for Stuart and British hegemony, as well as for his and other poets' contributions to it through their writings. The harmonious, fertile landscape of *Windsor Forest* has thus become the springboard for the most civilized of human endeavors: the writing of poetry.

A comparison of the role assigned to the arts in advancing the vision of a harmonious community in Pope's *Windsor Forest* with Goethe's *Torquato Tasso* establishes a remarkable extension of the motif's function. Goethe's play is set in Belriguardo, the country chateau of the Duke of Ferrara. The continuous action converges in a clash between Tasso's imaginative, subjectively colored view of existence and the court's inflexible canon of propriety. Tasso longs for paradisiacal happiness and innocent bliss. He expects the world to conform to his fantasy and, by failing to comprehend the social code originally designed to ensure civilized interaction, is provoked into rash action, emotional outbursts, and erroneous self-analysis. Tasso's misconception together with the inability of those around him to perceive that civilized conduct has been absorbed in a constrictive formality that adheres to its own rules finally propel Tasso to the verge of self-destruction.

   In addition to identifying the precarious balance between individual desires and society's expectation, the landscape motif draws attention to the inevitable but perilous progression from untamed nature to cultivated land and from the civilized landscape that serves as a measure of human achievement to the ornamental garden that mirrors the ossification of life. The play opens in a formal, geometrically aligned garden of the Italian Renaissance. The setting is flanked by the hermae of Ariosto and Virgil. The garden's symmetry complements the castle's interior and underscores the cadence of courteous, urbane discourse among the figures. The garden and the opinions expressed by Alfons, Antonio, and Leonore Sanvitale indicate that in the refined, courtly society the arts serve and enhance civilization. The artistically or even artificially created semblance of the confluence of nature and culture has become natural. Indeed, it has replaced nature. Tasso presents a copy of his work to Duke Alfons, is lauded for his poetic achievement, and crowned with a laurel wreath. The subsequent action exposes the imperiled state of Tasso's existence and the instability of the civilized world. The incompatibility of Tasso's yearning for freedom and social restrictions is underscored by the garden motif that identifies polar views of society. By alluding to Tasso's *Aminta*, Goethe calls attention to a work that created a paradisiacal vision of both a pastoral and an enchanting garden. Those who identify with the unfettered mode of existence in the enchanted realm do not experience conflicts between personal desires and social demands. Love and sensuous passion find immediate fulfillment. Since Tasso sees the courtly world through the eyes of his own creation, he fails to comprehend the sentiments of Princess Leonore whose vision of society and human interaction is inspired by a virtue rooted in self-denial. As a result, subdued emotions change into open passion. Hidden desires and fears burst forth. Misunderstanding turns into strife. Discord displaces reserve, restraint, and cool detachment. Harmony is broken by jarring dissonance. When the play ends in the garden, Tasso, clinging despairingly to his antagonist Antonio, voices his ultimate faith that despite searing pain, the poet retains the ability to articulate the human condition in a world at the brink of chaos. By locating the play in time at the critical moment in cultural change when civilization has succeeded in subduing raw passion but is endangering human growth by stifling the expression of deeply felt emotions, Goethe points to a fundamental danger inherent in social development. The formality of etiquette can encircle society and suffocate the very essence of the civilized relations it was to protect. Under such circumstances the poet can express sorrow and hope, but the artistic creation may fail to bridge the chasm between individual and society.

The Theatrical Landscape: Wieland

The person-space relations, then, range from figures actually present in a delineated place to reports describing distant areas, and from observations of immediate surroundings to contemplations of visionary localities. In some works, the spatial relationships form a basis for a topological order that enables the reader to identify space as spiral and expansive or as circular and restrictive. When a primary figure is linked with the motif of the journey and experiences the exploration of different countries as a form of self-development, both change and persistence in basic landscape patterns can be of great importance for determining the level of self-knowledge that is attained. The spatial relations in Christoph Martin Wieland's *Die Abenteuer des Don Sylvio* underscore the plea for retaining a childlike spark of fantasy throughout life. The travel to different lands and the adventurous encounters in *Geschichte des Agathon,* in contrast, capture a search for balance in human development. Agathon learns to temper sentiment, enthusiasms, and passion. He retains the ability for a spontaneous, even emotional response in a highly conventional society, because he has retained the ability to listen to the inner voice of his heart, is capable of entering into an enlightening dialogue with others, and experiences true love. Consequently, Agathon does not have to recover like Ferdinand Walter the traits stunted by civilization, nor does he submerge himself, like Werther, in a cult of nature. Essentially, he is a person of rational, enlightened moderation.

In *Agathon,* Wieland delineates strong contrasts between pure feeling and syllogistic reasoning, between attachment to unspoiled nature and frivolous conventions, between sincere, generous character traits and the self-interest of persons who find accommodation with existing conditions. The idea of the supreme worth and dignity of the individual is emphasized throughout the novel. The criticism of historical forces that contributed to cultural accomplishments while impeding the full development of individual potential shows significant differences from the classical pattern that evolves in Goethe's and Schiller's works. Agathon's development is expansive. Yet, if one positions the stages of his growth as nodes on an ascending, open spiral, it becomes apparent that he matures into a sensible, rational world citizen. Whenever Agathon appears to lean toward or even contemplate seriously any extreme position, the narrator guides him back to a steady course. Any exposure to thinking or behavior that could impede his ultimate perfection contains already the seed for corrective measures. True love counteracts the danger of unbridled enthusiasm current at Wieland's time. Visions of an ideal community allay the temptations of succumbing to a materialistic society. The intuitive moral guide of the "heart" that inspires sincere emotions mitigates the search for truth controlled by pure reason.

The impression that Agathon's life follows a planned, orderly course is reinforced by the person-space relations. The descriptive detail framing the action conveys a uniform picture of a stage setting including proscenium, up- and downstage, flies, and wings with a scenery of painted flowers and shrubs. While changing in detail, the landscape retains the immediacy of a stage. The polar forces of expansion and contraction appear to achieve equilibrium. When the novel opens, Agathon has been driven from his homeland, is lost in a forest, and falls asleep next to a murmuring spring. He is awakened by a group of dancing Thracian women who celebrate a Dionysian festival. This scene, a presentation of a playlet, is followed by the invasion of Privates who capture the group, bring them to ship, and subsequently sell Agathon in Smyrna. The series of tableaux is followed

by descriptions of Smyrna, the staging of receptions, parties, and plays
in the house of Hippias, and similar depictions of Danae's country estate. The detail of cultivated land, dwarf lemon trees, myrtle bushes,
flowers, fountains, paths, and secluded groves enriched by processions
of dancers accompanies the further stations of Agathon's development. Indeed, the narrator identifies the change of environment as the
"transfer to a new and great theater."[18]

The representation of a nature which does not admit the intrusion
of elemental or destructive forces is an outstanding example of a refined, civilized landscape. Whereas in *Don Sylvio* the description of
nature is essentially an extension of the fairy-tale world encountered
by Sylvio in his reading, the landscape in *Agathon* reflects a philosophical and social consciousness of the human intellect as the rational
and moderate force that shapes a world in which conflict is resolved
by reasonable action. Any potentially realistic appearance is subordinated to the principle of order in the universe and faith in the harmonious development of the human potential. Wieland writes in the prologue that the narrative "truth" that can be demanded from a work
like *Agathon* is to be found in "the congruence of everything with the
course of events in the world and in the fact that characters are neither
arbitrary nor shaped solely by the author's fantasy and desires but are
taken from the inexhaustible storehouse of nature."[19] The novel's literary landscape, however, authenticates the obstacles in creating the
appearance of probability and reality in works that restrict the coming-of-age theme to the developmental person who is guided by pure
reason and moderation in an agreeable environment.   Neither
Agathon nor his mentors Hippias and Archytas ever encounter unsur-
mountable obstacles. Psyche always follows the voice of her heart;
Danae's attitudes are changed fundamentally through Agathon's influence; and slaves perform essentially pleasant services as dancing
nymphs, satyrs, and attendants.

The society in this fictive world that stresses moderation and decorum exhibits not only many symptoms of conventional rigidity but
also the characteristics of a theatrical lifestyle.[20] In addition, it is apparent that the timeless panorama and ahistorical thinking obliterates
all historical differences, thereby creating the illusion of a permanent
recurrence of the forces that influence cultures. Both *Don Sylvio* and
Agathon present visions of the eternally human and portray important

stages in the process of individual development. The novels consciously raise questions in regard to the fairy tale and theatrical landscape. Nevertheless, their appearance in literature at a time when Goethe was almost scientifically delineating the problems encountered by a society that has transformed nature into a civilized landscape must be considered as an indicator of profound, if hidden, change in the artistic conception of the thematic pattern of self-realization.

Journey and Classical Landscape: Multiple Motif Function in Goethe's Works

Goethe's landscape representations form a spatial constellation of spirals and circles. These exhibit four primary motif patterns: as a landscape perceived by observers as literary, as land to be beautified, as land for agrarian use, and as a cultural landscape. Linked and developed thematically, the motifs shed light on different attitudes toward nature and distinct perceptions of self-realization. The motifs have multiple function. They integrate texts and clarify a rational program for a social reform that is based on a fundamentally changed view of nature.

The dominant features of the classical landscape in Goethe's writing evolve over a long period. Landscape metaphors in early poems establish associations with light, colors, haze, spring, the morning or evening setting, or capture vividly a characteristic detail. Landscape metaphors reveal or accentuate characters' emotions and contain veiled commentaries on a person's intellectual capacity to understand nature or history. In addition, they serve as a technique to evaluate the literary tradition to gain distance from contemporary philosophical currents.[21] The changing landscape representations reveal shifts in the view of nature and historical processes.[22] The glimpses at nature in Goethe's early poems variously accent the playful spirit of Anacreontic poetry ("Das Schreien," "Unbeständigkeit"), the joyous acclamation of life ("Mailied," "An Schwager Kronos"), pantheistic views ("Ganymed"), and cultural change ("Der Wandrer"). Yet, the strong yearning for and complete identification with nature that characterize Werther's attitude and Faust's initial outlook are balanced by a technique of infusing literary allusions into the landscape, a technique that introduces critical reservations into the desire for complete identification with nature.

Though traditionally and justifiably considered the most representative text for the sentimentalism that swept Europe in the 1770s, the immediate action in *Werther* is filtered through a critical representation of an exaggerated sentimental attitude toward nature, the self, and oppressive convention. Werther records his sensibility and exuberance in identifying with and ardently devoting himself to a cult of nature. But he also notes his rising irritation as he observes the "unfeeling" attitudes of others. While he experiences changes in mood ranging from highest bliss to the most profound doubt and despair (JA 16: 29-30),[23] the descriptive scenes of landscapes show that these different emotions are evoked not by contact with a wild, untamed nature, but with a thoroughly cultivated region interspersed by settlements, gardens, and parks. Furthermore, by assigning to Werther's observations the linguistic expressions current among the ardent devotees of excessive sensibility (*Schwärmerei*), especially the literary circles in Göttingen and Darmstadt, Goethe shows that literary and philosophical impressions shape Werther's attitude.[24]

Werther's descriptions of his harmony with nature allude to the fact that his vision is colored by literary impressions. He identifies with spring as "the season of youth" bursting with life, as an elemental force that warms his trembling heart.[25] A "miraculous clarity" has unfolded in his soul as he absorbs life's myriad manifestations. He seeks to immerse himself in fields and would like "to become a June bug to float in an ocean of fragrance and find all the nourishment in it" (5). In the letter of May 10, he remarks that in his excitement he cannot draw a single line. Yet, never before has he been "a greater painter than in those moments," when he lies in the grass near a brook and shares the vitality of life. His sensations finally approach a state of cosmic consciousness in which he senses the presence of God. Heaven has entered Werther's soul. Since Werther concludes his letter by observing that it is altogether impossible to express his experience in a work of art, it becomes apparent that his stance toward the world is purely receptive: "O! If you could express again, could breathe into paper that lives warmly and fully in you, then it would become a mirror of your soul as your soul is a mirror of the eternal God." He ends by stating that he completely "succumbs to the force of the beauty of this pageant" (5). Sitting spellbound at the village fountain, he extols the Homeric procession of the girls who fetch the water, feels close to the ancients, reads Homer, and "spoils his dear heart" like a sick child: "Everything it desires will be permitted" (7).

Through an astute choice of diminutives, contrived metaphors, and the pastoral setting, Goethe points to the profusion of Anacreontic and sentimental elements in Werther's perception. The reader is told that the small town is unpleasant. The surrounding landscape, however, breathes "inexpressible beauty." Werther is immediately drawn to a small park designed by "the feeling heart" of a nobleman where he can shed a tear for the inspired creator. Looking to the distant forest, he notes the "impenetrable darkness"; glancing at the immediate area, he sees "small grasses," the "stirring of the little world," the innumerable, "inscrutable figures of all the little worms, and the tiny gnats" in the blades of grass (6). This small world which thrills his heart and dims his eyesight is, however, a tract of countryside that has been transformed already by human activity. Nevertheless, for Werther, it has the qualities of a bucolic landscape. Consequently, when he meets the girl who arouses his deepest passions, he sees her in the center of a pastoral scene which affects him as a completely natural setting. Nothing is "artificial" in his eyes. That his search for the spontaneous and unaffected is shaped by literary undercurrents becomes readily apparent in the scene following the excursion to a dance. A thunderstorm has passed; Werther and Lotte step to a window; he recollects the events in the lyrical style of a sentimental novel: "The marvelous rain whispered on the land and the most invigorating fragrance rose to us in the richness of a warm air. Lotte's eyes filled with tears; she clutched his hand, and remarked: 'Klopstock!'" (28)

The association with Homer, Klopstock, Goldsmith, sentimental journeys, and Ossian not only determines Werther's perception but also contributes to a unique feature of the landscape in *Werther*: the emotions evoked by nature appear too intense when compared to the descriptive detail that characterizes phenomena; the language employed to create the semblance of reality is also colored by an ironic contrast between the phenomenon and its representation. As Werther's life unfolds, as his journey describes a circle combining recollections of childhood with glances at forests and valleys that are covered by a "welcome haze," as he loses his thoughts in a rushing brook or feels

the foreboding of autumn, and as the natural rhythm of seasons finally creates ennui, it becomes apparent that his seeing does not evolve
into understanding. He identifies with artistic and literary conventions
which he projects onto a landscape. He experiences changes in weath-
er and notes that language fails to describe the "inexpressible beauty" of raging storms or boiling fogs. He cannot comprehend that he
looks at a landscape that is not a great unified cosmos animated by the
breath of life but one that reflects the technological advance, social
patterns, and historical dimension of his age.

To be sure, the recurring pictures of mist, twilight, and haze indicate Werther's inability to give definite form to his experience in a
work of art (44). In addition, they point also to the failure to grasp
the transformation of the land by society and helplessness in the face
of historical change. Despairing, Werther finally perceives nature as a
soulless "eternally devouring and regurgitating monster" (59). His
ultimate isolation from nature becomes obvious in the letter of
November 3, in which Goethe skillfully interweaves the motif of the
closed window with Werther's existential anguish. Standing at the window, Werther experiences the landscape as a varnished miniature painting (97). This characterization succinctly captures his inability to find
the key to the conflict between the sentient heart and unfeeling community, idealized nature, and oppressive convention.[26] Appropriately,
Werther is completely overwhelmed by deep sorrow and despair (133)
when he seeks to resolve these irreconcilable differences by evoking
the misty Celtic past and the spirit of Gaelic poetry. His sensibility is
so deeply touched when he reads the "songs of Selma" to Lotte that
he is shattered by the thought of being left in a soulless world.

The discrepancy between the cultivated appearance of the landscape and its perception by a figure given to emotional, unreflective
identification with "nature" defines the basic existential crisis portrayed in the novel. Werther's powerful yearning far outweighs his intellectual cognitive faculty. Unable to comprehend nature's formative
principles and incapable of seeing that society's transformation of nature makes any return to a prehistorical noble simplicity illusory,
Werther cultivates his introspection and seeks within himself the key
that unlocks the secret of life. While simultaneously critically apprais-
ing others and rejecting their judgment, he cannot develop the critical
ability to see himself. The exaggeratedly sentimental attitude toward

nature and the inability to understand what he is actually seeing contribute to Werther's inability to develop his potential. The novel's centripetal movement of Werther's spiritual quest and his circular journey
clearly identify that he cannot establish a productive dialogue with nature and society that would initiate the growth of self-knowledge.[27]

The landscape in *Die Wahlverwandtschaften* conveys perhaps even
more forcefully than the novel's action the struggle between a freely
chosen existence and a restricted form of life apparently shaped by
powers beyond individual control. Closer inspection of the recurring
attempts to manipulate nature for personal pleasure or profit reveals,
however, that these forces are created by society. Consequently, the
novel already advances the realistic perspective of individual preoccupation with harnessing nature's energy for personal gain. Thereby it
identifies the self-imposed limitations of individual development. The
novel traces the failure of two couples to fulfill their inner potential.
It shows the weakness of a social class and by pointing to one character's renunciation of personal wishes, contrasts the inability of others
to renounce their desires in favor of a common goal. As a consequence, the landscape descriptions underscore the circular pattern created by the novel's motifs and thematic structure. The circle in turn
accentuates the inability of the figures to transcend their limited views
and strive for a full development of their potential. The fine irony
embedded in a narrative voice of a detached observer who almost scientifically records the events and repeatedly delights in playing with
expressions denoting action exposes social stagnation and the
grievous, oppressive results of adultery. The narration delineates central problems of individuation by contrasting possible freedom with
behavior that is governed by ideas sanctioned by society and self-determination in purposeful action with a life of leisure that lacks not
only direction but also meaning. The apparently brisk activity that is
generated by plans to change the management of the estate and by the
desire to survey the land disguises but cannot conceal the essentially
monotonous existence on the estate.

The description of the immediate setting, the estate of Baron
Eduard, focuses attention on the cultivated landscape. As the novel
opens, Eduard is informed by the gardener that the construction of a
small pavillon, designed by his wife Charlotte, has been completed.
The ensuing discussion, as well as the conversations during the follow-

ing days and weeks, shows that Eduard and the baroness also plan to expand the park, build a new road, and construct a larger chalet more suitable for parties than the intimate pavillon. The narrator-observer, overlooking the estate and villages from a hill, concludes that the landscape has "a peaceful character" and that the individual parts were well-suited "if not for painting, then for living" (JA 21: 135). The perception of the landscape by Eduard, Charlotte, and the Major clearly indicates that they view nature as an object for beautification. Eduard approaches the pavillon by following a path constructed for a leisurely walk, at times resting on a bench placed at a "suitable spot." In the garden house, his wife offers him a seat that enables him to see "through door and windows the different pictures as it were in a frame" (4). Returning from the inspection, he takes with his wife a direct path leading across the churchyard "which he normally tended to avoid" (7). With pleasurable surprise, he notes that even here, Charlotte has changed the scenery to suit "sentiment." Under her direction, the tombstones have been rearranged and newly ordered, transforming the cemetery into "a pleasant space" that attracts "eye and imagination." The grouping of the stones as ornaments along the wall and around the foundation of the church and the subsequent planing and reseeding of the gravesites are consistent with the overall design for the estate that transforms it into a great park. The landscape has been redesigned for Charlotte's and Eduard's pleasure. But the narrator's ironic stance is noticeable in the juxtaposition of the observation that "no one could deny that this arrangement presented the pious visitors on Sundays and holidays with a joyous and virtuous sight" (146) with the reaction of the distressed villagers.

Indeed, all figures in the novel are engaged in activities that enhance the civilized but also artificial appearance of the landscape. On several occasions, the narrator, using the impersonal pronoun "one" to identify his detached stance as observer, presents glimpses of village, castle, hills, valleys, river, and lakes. The scenery indicates that the land has been farmed for generations. However, Eduard is not interested in cultivating the land. He is excited by the survey of the area and welcomes the topographic map that will facilitate the systematic planning in converting the land from agrarian use into a park. The thrust of the project is not to restore but to improve upon nature. A path should not follow the contour of the landscape but should be-

come agreeable "to saunter along and provide a pleasant view." A
properly positioned bridge would not only shorten the distance but
also "grace the landscape." An area must be timbered to provide a
picturesque effect. It is hardly surprising to read that persons strolling
along see a "cheerful little forest," a "pleasant little wood," a "beautiful resting place," or delight in the idea of combining three ponds
into a lake. Circling the estate, the couples unanimously express the
wish that the slightly strenuous walk be made more comfortable. The
path should be rearranged, so that one could promenade together
"with pleasure" (64). To finance the "improvements," Eduard plans
to sell a section of land not included in the design. "Thus we enjoy
cheerfully on a priceless walk the interest of well-invested capital"
(65). Such a "reasonable, moderate" view of the land finds general
approval.[28]

Significantly, all the planned roads lead in a circle from the castle
and back to the point of origin. The only recommendation for a
change in the project comes from Ottilie who feels that the chalet
should not face the castle but be placed on the summit of a hill opening a view to a different world. The advice is adopted: "We look for
change and foreign impressions" (66), because after all, one travels
long distances for a meal that "would not have tasted like this at
home" (66). While the two men find "new reasons for activity" (67)
in this rearrangement of the landscape, it does not foster the anticipated pleasurable experience and fails to unite the group in a common
effort.

The picturebook park mirrors the inhibiting conventions that govern life on the estate. Just as wild growth is controlled in the landscape, so free development is impeded by conformity and deterministic factors in society. Goethe attributes characteristics of the classical
personality structure to the figures in *Die Wahlverwandtschaften* but
simultaneously shows the process of ossification that curtails the
essence of free development. The figures are portrayed as gifted,
pleasant, and considerate. They avoid behavior that tends to disturb
the equilibrium of life; they know what is proper and faithfully observe the conventions of their class in language and appearance. Both
Charlotte's and Eduard's previous marriages to wealthy partners had
been based on social considerations but had remained untroubled and
without emotional attachment. She acquired a good sense for busi-

ness transactions. He was spoiled by an older lady and never learned "to forego anything he desired" (12). While they accommodate themselves to changing circumstances, they also anticipate a quiet, loving life, untroubled by any thought of the constraints imposed by their environment. Similarly, the Major, a tactful man of learning, endowed with understanding and many excellent qualities, nevertheless conforms to the outlook of his class and is unable to assert himself openly. Before his arrival, he notes in a letter to Eduard that he has decided to accept a position that promised a life of "boredom among wealthy and genteel people who hoped that he would relieve" them from ennui (20). Even the lively discussions among the friends about the chemical properties of acids, bases, solvents, and compounds emphasize scientifically predictable interdependencies. They foreshadow the attraction of the adulterous affinities that these figures experience and simultaneously reveal a "fateful," realistically deterministic aspect in their relationships.

From the beginning, the atmosphere is tinged by the veiled anxiety that the civilized, protected world surrounded by the artificially created landscape might be endangered. Social problems are glossed over or ignored. Beggars are to pass quickly through the village to prevent the disturbance of the calm appearance. The children from the farms are dressed in identical "charming" clothing in order to create the impression of a pleasant arrangement (131). The daily concerns of the villagers remain a mystery to Eduard and his friends who simply delight in their attire when they come to celebrate the completion of the chalet (114 f.). Above all, the figures appear apprehensive when contemplating their future. Only the continuous planning of activities seems to prevent the recognition of a vacuum in life. The preoccupation with impressing upon nature the stamp of society and the attempts to transform the landscape into a setting which provides enjoyment and peace conceals a fear of elemental forces. The conversations occasioned by the visit of a widely traveled English lord point to the destructive tendencies in society. The lord, "at home everywhere," finds it more appropriate that others "build and plant." A well-informed admirer of formal gardens, he is greatly interested in everything "that ornaments and enhances life" (228). He notices every aspect of the estate and the future potential of different sections. In his presence, the women really begin to "enjoy" the landscape.

He points to a spring which, when cleaned up, will adorn a group of bushes. He observes a cave that should be cleared and expanded to provide a grotto for rest. This world of illusory activity and appearance, punctuated by moments of weariness and boredom, by scientific discussions and slightly frivolous conversations about adultery and the ethics of marriage, trembles when strong emotions seize Eduard, then Ottilie, and finally Charlotte and the Major. While Ottilie matures and becomes capable of renouncing her love, Eduard persists and draws inward to focus on his feelings. Moments before his death, he perceives that his whole "endeavor was only imitation, a false effort" (301), thereby raising the question whether his love was as conventional as his beautification of the landscape.

The dichotomy between artificial landscape and organic growth mirrors the contradictions in human relationships in the novel. The dialogue in *Die Wahlverwandtschaften* is civilized, stylized, and like the landscape, artificial. At times, it is marked by truthfulness; at others, the conversation is used to conceal real feelings or becomes a strategy to trap persons in order to discover secrets (91). Some instances, such as the dinner conversation during the visit of the count and his mistress, show a lack of sensitivity. Others, as for example the scene in which Charlotte's daughter Luciane dominates the conversation, reveal how language widens the chasm between individuals. Yet, the real tragedy is that the figures cannot understand each other because they tend to listen only to themselves. To be sure, Ottilie who is transformed by her love from a shy girl into a person capable of profound reflection, listens faithfully to Eduard. But by dedicating herself so completely to the idolized man that she even imitates his errors when accompanying his fluting on the piano (69), she also fails to enter into a meaningful dialogue. Persons may reveal their emotions in a letter, but when it is read, it is suddenly robbed of conviction. By laying bare the centripetal force inward that characterizes the narrowness of the characters' vision, *Die Wahlverwandtschaften* presents a panorama of the human condition in which tragic dilemmas do not arise because of evil design or reckless assertions of individual will, but because the figures fail to understand the essence of nature, love, meaningful activity, and a constructive dialogue. The right conditions for free self-determination have been stifled by convention. By deliberately reversing the centrifugal pattern, Goethe shows the tragedy of human confinement. Society is not presented as in realistic or naturalistic works as a force which inexorably destroys human freedom or impedes individual self-development. But the novel shows a situation in which individuals are trapped by forces that they fail to understand. By unconsciously attributing conventional, artificial, or even theatrical qualities to nature, by seeking accommodation with society, and by relying on tradition without understanding it, the figures in the novel adhere to a lifestyle that prevents them from gaining true self-insight or real understanding of the world. Their existence, then, is essentially "decorative," the term used by the narrator to characterize the architect's archeological collection (153).

In contrast to the contracting perspective that highlights in *Die Wahlverwandtschaften* the inability of the figures to comprehend social change, the *Römische Elegien* offer vistas of a broad historical and social panorama. The elegies blend city and nature, social setting and past, intellectual history and artistic achievement into a unique literary tapestry. The first elegy introduces dialogue as the technique for the articulation of a continuous dialectic process of raising questions in viewing life, searching for possible answers in the landscape, reflecting, and renewing inquiries. Even in instances of introspection when the poet speaks to himself, he appears to ask questions and receive answers by reconsidering previous impressions. He thereby raises them to a new plane of understanding. By appealing to the streets, churches, and palaces of Rome to awaken and speak to the stranger, by walking through vineyards and fields, and by sharing noble aspirations, love, and daily worries, the observer is transformed into a participant. He learns and gains distance from the encounter without losing the immediacy of experience. Consequently, the "past and present speak louder and more charmingly" than before (JA 1: 157). The dialogue brings the past to life; myths are reborn and become animated; old texts suddenly reach into the present; and just as the harvest season is transformed into a great celebration of fertility, so the landscape is transfigured into a living form. "Live joyously, and antiquity may live in you! . . . Here you saw a world arise, saw a world here in ruins / And from the wreckage arising an almost mightier world!" (167). Since such a continuous dialogue may contribute to a vision of a vibrating organism that subsumes historical and social upheaval because it appears timeless, Goethe repeatedly refers to contemporary political events. As a result, the past and present coexist in a landscape that calls for renewed evaluation. The landscape, then, arouses historical awareness and becomes a beacon that guides the individual to a new understanding of human achievement.

The cityscape as human artifact, comprising life that ranges from the trivial to the highest aspirations and includes the vile as well as the sacred, mirrors the collective expectations of society and appears in its totality as a dynamic force that constantly regenerates itself. Even the knowledge of death enhances life because it is not colored by futile despair, but by the recognition that just as the seed will be put in the ground and sprout again, so human actions can inspire future generations in a living chain. By broadening the image of the lovers' union to an embrace of society and the cultured landscape, the poet shows that the road to self-realization leads through the world. Individuals cognizant of human fallacy and aware that reform is necessary must learn that they cannot return to a blissful state of nature. They cannot negate the past or society's transformation of the world. They must look forward, if they hope to contribute to a lasting reform of life. By portraying the wanderer who participates in the harvest festival, by showing the poet guided by immediate sensuous perceptions in his understanding of past artistic creations ("sees with feeling eye, feels with a seeing hand"), by looking at a cultivated nature embedded in a city that has renewed itself, the elegies project the picture of an individual who is capable of true development.

In *Wilhelm Meister,* the landscape representations are thematically aligned with Meister's journeys and his spiritual and intellectual development to understanding the comprehensive social reforms that serve as preparation for a new, viable community. Travel provides the opportunity for the exploration of the world. But travel is more than a way station to serene contemplation of either troubled life or social unrest. It is a primary experience etched indelibly on Wilhelm's mind emerging from his perception that the journey symbolizes individual development across the life span. Wanderers and journey, exodus and return, loss of direction and search for orientation identify the human condition. When Wilhelm sets out on the journey he hopes for fulfillment of his dreams; when he continues the travel he envisions the full development of his potential; when he accepts the mandate of the " Tower Society" neither to remain in any place longer than three nights nor to return to it within the same year he consciously affirms the quest for understanding of the world. The instruction from the society compels him to observe, reflect, learn, and only thereafter, to offer advice. The journey covers successive phases in Wilhelm's growth, junctures where he is forced to decide on the right course of action, and stages of increasing self-insight. The journey is highlighted in the title of the narratives that comprise the years of Wilhelm's deliberate study of the social scene. Thematically, travel integrates multiple narrative strands. In signification it is both lucid and open-ended. The phases of the journey mark a distinct progression toward intellectual clarity and the endorsement of a life dedicated to the service in the community. However, the metaphoric field of the existentially exposed individual invests the theme with an unlimited dimension. The dominant pattern of life in an organically evolving community includes as an important element the recognition and acceptance of a physical life cycle. Individuals grow, mature, age, and face death. They have the potential to develop intellectually and contribute innovative thought to the accumulated knowledge in the group. They should be capable of spiritual regeneration but must renounce the dream of eternal youth (JA 19: 195-263). They merge into the reform circle. Their insights contribute to a conceptual spiral pattern assigned to communal aspirations.

The narrative design of the journey integrates three levels of representation. (1) It relates phases of Wilhelm's travel with stations of significant encounters and repeated decisions at crossroads. Wilhelm feels free from restraint, follows sudden inclinations, lingers, and hesitates but pursues the great adventure of fulfilling his ambition. (2) It conveys the conception that human individuation progresses in stages of increasing awareness throughout life. The conscious acquisition of knowledge succeeds undetermined experiments with diverse possibilities. The creation of a new community gives direction to aspirations. The spirit of reverence has mastered the dark powers of the subconscious and the violent temper of conquest that is an essential element of the Western mind in *Faust*. (3) Throughout the novels, the theme has contrapuntal function. Individual sensibility is reorganized during the journey in reflection. Supra-personal conceptualizations affect reflection which is subsequently converted into renewed individual sensibility. Moreover, the process of clarification that accompanies

Wilhelm's growth to the time when he accepts his role in the community as a physician is disrupted by exclamations or observations that
indicate an unabated yearning for unrestricted development of all capacities. Such junctures create ambiguity. They signal the possibility
of recurring error and disturbance. They also point to the fact that
the dynamic potential of collective ideational patterns is continuously
enriched by individual perception.

Meister's travels convey recurring impressions of agricultural land
utilization, the methodical management of estates, the careful calculation of the return on investment, and the attitudes of landholders to
workers. The administration of the estates indicates an all-inclusive
process of introducing efficient methods to agriculture. The trend is
clearly evident in competently administered estates, in the breeding of
livestock, especially horses, and the far-flung economic interests of the
"Pedagogic Province," and in the sales organization established by
Hersilie's uncle. The economic agrarian interests are paralleled by the
efforts of merchants, businessmen, and even the traveling actors to
raise the productivity of their ventures. Significant differences exist.
Within the utilitarian orientation of society, the diverse groups reflect
the same emphasis on the planning and setting of goals. All spatial
motifs in *Wilhelm Meister* that are linked to the foundation of a new
community elucidate concrete possibilities of social reform. They
show a high correlation in structure and signification. The agrarian
use of the land is accepted. The cultivated landscape neither gives rise
to lament nor awakens the desire to return to a state of nature untouched by civilization.

The panorama of the countryside, the farmland, and the buildings
is evaluated positively through the adverb and prefix "well." The
land is well-inhabited, -cared for, -ordered, fertile, and planned.
Lothario's estate, for example, presents a picture of meaningful order
(JA 18: 180 ff.). Odoard's farm and the large land holdings of
Hersilie's uncle in particular show the total transformation of nature
into cultivated tracts. Pastures, fields, orchards, vegetable and herbal
gardens give clear evidence of careful planning (JA 20: 47 ff.).
Makarie's estate and the wide domain of the "Pedagogic Province"
indicate that nature has been completely transformed by human activity (JA 19: 131-47; 20: 3-20). All work is purposeful. The landscape
becomes a symbol for human efficiency and productivity. The pre-

technological perspective of nature vanishes because society has imposed its patterns on the land. Development is inevitable but demands a thorough reorientation in socially derived attitudes. The view most consistently expressed in *Wilhelm Meister* is that of a possible beneficial symbiosis between society and nature. The prerequisites for this life-sustaining relationship are respect, even reverence, for all manifestations of nature, rejection of attempts to exploit the environment, insight into sociohistorical change, and dedication to a communal spirit that embraces nature and the other (JA 19: 10-28, 41 ff., 72 ff., 173 ff., 180-81; 20: 46 ff., 212). The principles guiding both the education of the youth in the "Pedagogic Province" and the preparation for emigration to America together with the overall perspective that includes arable land, mining, and industry suggest a fusion of the agrarian with the cultural-civilized landscape.

Goethe's own report of the "Sankt Rochus—Fest zu Bingen" concentrates in a series of observations the structural-ideational pattern of the classical landscape. The narrator seeks to establish a sensitive balance between the individual, nature, and society by reconciling changes in the landscape that may have evolved over decades or centuries with the perception of nature as an organic entity, new trends of thought with older traditions, and shifts in the condition of life with individual aspirations. While retaining the perspective of a travelogue, the work captures the continuous process of seeing - reflecting - learning - observing - renewed reflection. The landscape of villages, fertile, cultivated fields, vineyards, and fruit trees clearly shows the stamp of human activity. The observer notes the soil condition and considers its advantage or disadvantage for specific plants. He views the old gate at Bingen, recognizes the chapel, the church, and immediately muses over the fact that the French occupation prevented the St. Rochus celebration during the previous decades. Then he discerns stones and minerals, begins to analyze them while almost simultaneously noting a structure that recalls the Roman settlement of the area. The dialogue with the past is interrupted by a glance across bridges, gates, houses, hedges, and flowers that, perceived as an ensemble, give the impression of organic growth (JA 29: 193). The movement of the procession toward the church initiates renewed historical considerations that are followed by observations and judgments of different persons. As joyous eating and drinking alternates with serious reflection, as the legend of

St. Rochus succeeds the anecdote of the vigorous wine-swilling priest, and the sermon is joined by a critical appraisal of architecture, the sacred and the secular merge in a broad vista of the history embedded in the landscape. The observer's horizon of experience widens. He understands that he cannot escape the changes wrought by society. He accepts the cultivated landscape and, aware of the forces that shaped it, affirms the possibility of future growth and transformation.

Goethe's last narrative, the *Novelle*, consolidates the classical conception of cultivated land. Free from nostalgic yearning for primeval forests, the fascination with ruins or picturesque settings, and the feeling of futility in the face of elemental forces that seem to defy human power, the *Novelle* incorporates landscape descriptions into a strong sense of the affirmation of life, the capacity for love, the affirmative dialogue, and self-restraint as constructive principles that guide the individual toward self-realization. To portray the phenomenal occurrence that an escaped wild lion can be subdued without violence by a young boy who sings softly and plays his flute, the novella employs a series of contrast patterns (civilized / wild, hunt / peaceful life, tamed / untamed, fire – violence / prevention – self-control, self-assertion / renunciation). The narrative points to an exemplary form of existence by resolving potentially destructive conflicts through self-knowledge. By juxtaposing unrestrained growth, elemental forces, and subjective passions with the cultivated land, order, and self-control, and by showing the individual's ability to act reasonably, the work captures the substance of civilized society.

The description of the landscape focuses on habitation and creates an atmosphere of purposeful activity. Residence and town, a regional commercial center, are centrally located. The Prince supports all commercial activities. Small river boats transport merchandise. The market square bustles with traders, artisans, farmers, and shoppers. Farmers tend the fields; meadows have been mowed for the second time; a broad expanse of fertile land is readied for tilling. Liberally applying the prefix "well," the narrator points to the cultivation of nature. Villages, houses, fields, and gardens are characterized as well-founded, -ordered, -cultivated, -improved, -built, and -inhabited. As in *Wilhelm Meister*, the comprehensive picture is one of harnessed energy and organic growth. The factors that could disrupt the equilibrium and impede development are metaphorically described as wild

growth, fierce power of animals, unrestrained passion, and the out-
break of fire. The novella's action shows that the dangers besetting the
civilized community are essentially threefold: society can lose sight of
the basic principles that govern life; it could ignore nature's elemental
power; it could suffocate creativity through convention.

Since nature, fire, and human emotions can unleash destructive
forces, society is asked to develop the means to guard its achievements
and the well-being of its citizens. This judgment is reflected throughout the novella in the stress on cooperation, restraint, foresight, and the
ability to renounce selfish interests. The prince and the princess, tolerant and restrained, are characterized as persons who seek a consensus
of opinion. The young boy's father is not overwhelmed by the extraordinary events but seeks an acceptable solution. Honorio, who not
only admires but loves the princess, matures by witnessing the lion's
taming. The reader understands that the individual can master instinctive behavior. Just as fire may erupt at any moment but can be controlled by the precaution of having fire-fighting equipment ready, so
powerful passions may engulf the individual but can be subdued by
self-restraint. The boy's song, a fusion of aesthetic and ethical concerns, of strong faith expressed in the biblical allusion to Daniel in the
lions' den and a deep reverence for the capacity of all persons to develop their potential, presents a final synthesis of the constructive
forces shaping civilization. As the gentle hymns cast a spell over the
onlookers, the reader becomes aware that the world has achieved a delicate balance of conflicting forces. The dynamic energy of wild
growth is harnessed without violence. Landscape and civilization have
become one. The child "looked like a victorious conqueror." Yet,
the lion, the "tyrant of the forest," appeared "not as one who was
conquered," because his power remained in him but "nevertheless
like one under the control of his own peaceful volition" (JA 16: 359).
This observation is as important as the comment made by the animal
exhibitor's wife to Honorio who looks westward into the setting sun.
She calls out to him: "Do not hesitate. You will conquer. But first
conquer yourself!" (357)

A comparison of the spatial relations portrayed in Goethe's narratives with those in his poems "Willkommen und Abschied,"
"Wandrers Sturmlied," "Der Wandrer," "Seefahrt," "Meeresstille,"
and "Glückliche Fahrt" and such varied plays as *Satyros, Prome-*

theus, and *Faust* substantiates the conclusion that landscape representations consistently serve as subtle commentary on individual development and understanding of historical change. Moreover, such a comparison shows that Goethe consistently assigns symbolic significance to the correlation between observers or figures in a text and their perspective of space. The technique is complex, since space is not only seen optically and simultaneously stylized, but also portrayed as an element that identifies human cognition or misconception. The open landscape corresponds to an expansive vision that holds the promise of potential development. The ironically modulated vista of a landscape represented by diminutive detail, picturesque elaboration, disrupted horizontal lines and landscapes that are colored by preconceived literary or philosophical ideas reveals restrictive forces in a person's perception of nature.

The upward thrust on a vertical plane captures the yearning for liberation, the desire to be close to God, and the hope to fathom the cosmic principle of creation. The axis of the vertical plane seems to connect the observer with a moment of cosmic consciousness residing in an indeterminate point of space. Yet, a straight ascent appears to be as impossible as the direct penetration of nature's mystery. Ganymed's longing must be met by grace descending from above; Euphorion's soaring flight in the sky ends in a deadly plunge to earth; and Faust, awakening at dawn, cannot look into the rising sun and only symbolically ascends through a progression of stages after his "physical" life has ended. The vision of a solemn, mute landscape that appears to dwarf the sailor in "Meeresstille," the observer in "Weltschöpfung" and "Mächtiges Überraschen," and Ottilie immediately after the child's death, accords a prominence to nature that underscores human frailty. In relation to the figures, the landscape appears massive. The perspective conveys the impression that nature is inert, immovable, or fossilized and impedes individual progress. Sharply focused images of enclosure, as for instance, Werther's room, Faust's study, and the circular path in *Die Wahlverwandtschaften* highlight individual restrictions, the limitations of individual efforts, and the inability to comprehend the effect of historical change on nature.[29]

In contrast, Goethe's classical landscapes invite the observer to move into the cultivated space. Like La Fontaine's or Pope's civilized settings, they appear expansive because they open the perspective to a movement along a plane that extends from detail to considerations of archetypal forms and socio-historical questions. From the perspective of the classical landscape, it is evident that human activity has inexorably transformed nature. Faust's cultivation of land and his recourse to Mephisto's helpers disclose the ever-present danger of abuse and attendant guilt. The "Metamorphose der Pflanzen," *Römische Elegien,* and *Geschichte meines botanischen Studiums* point to a stance of heightened consciousness that permits the observer to enter into a productive dialogue with nature. The successive landscape representations identify different levels of individual awareness and distinctive stages of self-knowledge. They capture attitudes ranging from powerful emotional identification and sentimental yearning to alienation and finally to a real dialogue with nature's forces. To identify the stage of individual awareness, Goethe advances the literary technique of interpreting it in terms of landscape patterns. Since the interrelationship between landscape and figures is portrayed as a significant formative influence, it is apparent that the shift in accent from introspection to outward orientation, from the hymn to nature to the cultivated, civilized landscape highlights a process of individuation that stresses the active participation in life and recognition of historical forces.

Dynamic Contrast Patterns in the Civilized Landscape: Schiller

In contrast to Goethe, Schiller tends to relate landscape metaphors and natural phenomena such as mountain, valley, storm, or sunlight primarily to a terrain of vertical and horizontal dimensions that underscore counterpositions. Moreover, he illustrates conflicting views of social change and stages of historical awareness through spatial relations and the unique perception of space by the observer or figures in plays. Frequently, the landscape accentuates a broad space that embodies visions of tranquil country and shapes that appear to be wrested from the ground and thrust upward by a powerful will. The pattern of the cultivated land conveys impressions of peaceful coexistence between nature and inhabitants. Society has established a partnership that fosters organic growth. The forces of intellect and feeling that

constantly attract and repel one another, as well as the dynamic interplay of progressive and conservative tendencies, seem to have merged
into a morphologically conceived chain of existence. The glimpses at
landscapes in "Die Herrlichkeit der Schöpfung," "Der Spaziergang," *Die Piccolomini* I. iv., and *Wilhelm Tell* hold the promise of a
balanced existence that is rooted in innocence, simplicity, and an unconscious inner unity. Such scenes are reminiscent of contemporary
views of Arcadia and even the picturesque detail of Albrecht Haller's
Die Alpen. Yet, they differ fundamentally. Schiller's landscape of coexistence emerges from a struggle for dominance between a teleological vision of peace and the somber appraisal of a land that is transformed by history, convention, human pride, and the will to power.
Indeed, social and historical considerations seem to color especially
those symbolically charged landscape representations that establish a
direct relationship to the onlooker's feelings or thoughts.

Schiller's critical observations concerning the development of social and political institutions indicate that, like many of his contemporaries, he greatly admired classical antiquity. His evaluation indicates,
however, that he shared neither the widespread acceptance of
Rousseau's social contract theory nor the enthusiasm for the notion of
an original state of nature characterized by all those positive attributes
missing in modern civilization. Historical evidence, he argued, supports the conclusion that cultural patterns constitute a dynamic, inter-
dependent complex. Over time, they have promoted progressive technological advances, encouraged great artistic achievements, and also
institutionalized the ever-increasing specialization in human activities.
Schiller attributes the feeling of discontent with civilization to the antagonism of forces that simultaneously sustained cultural progress and
hampered the full development of individual potential. But he considered cultural change as inevitable, had no inclination for a Utopia
patterned after the Greek model, and smiled at the notion that humans
could return to the much-lauded golden ages of Alexander or
Augustus.[30] Society could only benefit by accepting a process that
had led from an original natural condition, in which individuals were
chained by customs and traditions, to a state characterized by the rational maturity of self-imposed laws.[31]

At times, Schiller charges landscape metaphors with an ideational
signification that corresponds to distinctive attributes assigned to na-

ture in the typology established in *Über naive und sentimentalische Dichtung*.   Hence, it is possible either to ascertain parallels between spatial representations in creative works and philosophic considerations of nature as an ideal that encompasses beauty, moral grace, and morality or to point to the fact that Schiller received impulses for his definitions from Shaftesbury, Ferguson, Montesquieu and Kant.[32] However, the spatial motif serves primarily specific textual functions. It may highlight views of history or society strongly criticized in Schiller's essays.   It may also contribute to or establish a design that contrasts the imperfection of civilization and human failure with a model of possible historical and human development espoused by Schiller.

Schiller's landscape representations range from tableaux capturing a naive, harmonious coexistence of people and cultivated land to the symbolic universe of a countryside that contains the dialectic of antithetical forces and embraces polar dimension. In "Der Spaziergang," for instance, the glance of the wanderer-observer shifts from the serene countryside of fields and houses covered with vines (ll. 51 ff.) to the towering city ruled by the indomitable will to achieve greatness. He surveys the harbor, the sails hoisted to set forth into the unknown, the continuous struggle with the elements, the present, the past, and the forces that shaped the spirit of the nation. The wanderer does not remain a detached observer but enters into a dialogue with the land. Yet, his disposition differs from the conciliatory stance that characterizes the developmental observer-learner figures in Goethe's writings. The voice is authoritative; it challenges, admonishes, and asserts the necessity for judicial principles and regulations governing human relations. As a result, the poem moves from organic evolution to revolutionary thrust and culminates in a view of history as a liberating force. Yet, the poem's intellectual momentum is disturbed by the sudden fear that historical processes may be cyclical and not cumulative. The wanderer suddenly awakens and is confronted by wilderness: "behind me lies every trace of human activity . . . only towering matter . . . wild, frightful, and desolate" (ll. 176-178). He resolves his doubts by reaffirming the possibility of a productive partnership between individual and nature: the world is "waiting for the creative hand."

The dialectic in Schiller's landscape representations is apparent in the contrastive relationship between nature and historical forces.

According to Schiller, any presumption that a "naive" unity with nature could provide an acceptable basis for existence fails to consider the important role of history in shaping social development. While individuals partake of a natural cycle of growth and decay, they can be guided by a principle of optimum development. They can cultivate the intellect, can reason, observe, articulate, and consciously contribute to historical processes. In the distich "Das Höchste," Schiller expresses the idea of optimum human development through a comparison between individuals and plants: "You search for the highest, the greatest? Let the plant be your guide. / Achieve through your will what it is by design—that is it!" By linking human volition to the perfection of a living organism, Schiller also places a subtle restraint on the will. The potential for unfettered self-assertion, as well as the quest for absolute freedom, are held in check by the principles governing organic growth.

It is evident that Schiller consistently uses the civilized landscape as both a model for peaceful coexistence and a real or postulated contrast element to other landscape representations. The perspective of the civilized, classical landscape establishes a dynamic balance between the observer who accepts nature's transformation by society but simultaneously rejects the thoughtless exploitation of the earth and looks toward a future in which social stability harmonizes with the vitality of the land. The contrasting landscape of simple, rural coexistence depicts naive dreams of a peaceful, bucolic existence that are shattered by the intrusion of hostilities (*Die Jungfrau von Orleans*) or the arbitrary actions of oppressive rulers (*Wilhelm Tell*). While Schiller arranges spatial motifs more systematically than Dryden, he clearly advances the classical stance expressed, for instance, in Dryden's *Aureng-Zebe*. In Schiller's plays the landscape frequently identifies the success or failure of individuals and the community. The land ravished by insurrection and warfare bears witness to individual arrogance, the powerful but destructive assertion of individual wills, erroneous judgments of the state's interest, and historically derived misconceptions of the common weal.

The garden motif's unique features in the spatial contrast pattern are especially evident when its peaceful setting is disrupted by everpresent strife and the antagonism of conflicting forces that not only wreak havoc but also propel individuals to a new plane of self-knowledge. The successive garden scenes in *Don Carlos* provide settings in which Posa's devotion to Queen Elisabeth and the expressions of friendship between Posa and Don Carlos dominate. Yet, their peace is also marred by undercurrents of political intrigue and misunderstanding occasioned by Posa's reluctance to share his plans with his friends. This transformation from harmony to aggression culminates in the queen's isolation, the arrest of Don Carlos, and Posa's death. Similarly, the garden's tranquility proves illusory when Maria in *Maria Stuart* is guided outdoors by the warden (III. i.). Released from the oppressive atmosphere of her confinement and tempted by open space, Maria exultingly envisions herself as a free person. Aroused by the experience, she fails to control her emotions in the meeting with Elizabeth which evolves into a bitter confrontation. Even before she is returned to jail, the conspirators who have failed in their attempt to assassinate Queen Elizabeth flee across the scene. Their leader Mortimer enters in wild agitation, declares his love for Maria, and seeks to embrace her. Confronted by a distorted reflection of her own emotional outburst, Maria perceives the effect of uncontrolled passion and flees to her cell which in contrast to the garden's turmoil suddenly seems to offer peace.

The contrast between the garden as peaceful setting and as location of violent conflict is especially pronounced in *Die Braut von Messina.* When Don Manuel first encounters Beatrice, he pursues a hind that seeks protection in a convent's garden at her feet. Lowering his spear, he is immediately attracted to Beatrice. Subsequently, as their love blossoms, he meets her in the sheltered garden (I. vii.) and upon instigating her escape from the convent, begs her to wait for him in a secluded garden within the city of Messina. However, instead of offering peace, this garden becomes a place of terror. Beatrice, listening as the city's resonance contends with the rustling leaves, is overcome by deep existential anguish. Unprotected by the garden as sanctuary, she feels dwarfed by the "immense, fearfully unknown" world storming toward her: "Cast away like a leaf from a tree, / I lose myself in infinite space" (II. i.). Her terror is further intensified by Don Cesar's violent intrusion and murder of his brother (III. iv.). By displaying the disruption of the sanctuary, the motif imparts to the audience or reader the recognition that unchecked personal violence may at any moment destroy human control over nature. The obvious similarities between Schiller's recourse to the garden as a sanctuary that is violated and the function of violated space in the works of Corneille and Dryden or Goethe's *Tasso* underscore the literary constant in a pronounced stylistic feature in classical writing. The unexpected, yet ever-present invasion of the civilized world of the palace or park by wild, untamed passion has a direct parallel in the disruption of carefully sheltered life in any sanctuary.

Just as the vehemence of individual aggression obliterates tranquil gardens in these plays, so the fury of war overwhelms the peacefully settled land in *Wallenstein*. Upon his return from Vienna to the army's camp, Max Piccolomini relates to his father the experience of traveling through the country untouched by war. Comparing the soldiers to buccaneers who swiftly sail the ocean trapped in a dim, oppressive boat and only land ashore to plunder without ever seeing the beauty of the countryside, Max contrasts the continuous discord and turmoil of such life with a meaningful form of existence. He sets forth the picture of a landscape in which human activity blends into nature. Fields, meadows, villages, and cities are populated by a society that has renounced violent strife (*Piccolomini* I. iv. 534- 558). Octavio's response shows that he agrees with Max: Peace must be restored so that civilization can flourish. However, father and son cannot agree on a common course of action to end the war.

Schiller illustrates their conflicting philosophical considerations, as well as those of other figures in the trilogy, by linking the motifs of the crossroads and the path with the play's spatial organization. Max articulates his vision of an ideal society in which all aspire to personal perfection, a society in which absolute honesty, love, and dedication to the common interest have replaced deception, hate, and egotistical designs by means of the metaphor of the straight path. In his unwavering pursuit of the direct, uncharted and innovative path, Max represents the classical expectations of a true order governing human conduct. Octavio expresses his dissenting belief by sketching a verbal tableau of life following the meandering course of a river that either avoids or slowly erodes serious obstacles (I. iv. 473-478). True to his conviction, Octavio demands that individuals adjust to the ever-changing demands of society, make compromises, seek accommodation, reject claims to absolute truth, and accept traditional political systems. Octavio's decisions are dictated by political expediency. Octavio, bound to the old hierarchal order of the empire, fails to comprehend his son's faith in a straight path to truth. His own vision extends from the battlefield to the court in Vienna. His decisions are dictated by mistrust of others and purely political considerations.

Wallenstein plays with the idea of launching a new order that is to bring peace to the land. He appears to repudiate time-honored, firmly implanted modes of thinking but is unwilling to accept the vision of Max. He stands at the crossroads of diverging paths and at the point of spatial intersection between vertical and horizontal orientation. He is directly aligned with vertical space through his blind faith in astrology and the reliance on planetary constellations for determining the opportune moment of action. But he looks upon the planets as harbingers of success, not as symbols of a viable order. Through the army that is supposed to guarantee the success of his plans, Wallenstein is firmly linked with the horizontal spatial dimension of the conquest of the land. His plan to impose peace upon the warring parties is marred by political intrigue. His longing for a better world is blurred by personal ambition. His search for honesty is tainted by deceit. Caught in the cross-currents of shifting political alignments, unreliable personal allegiances, and military actions that have developed an uncontrollable momentum, Wallenstein hesitates and is ultimately forced to pursue a strategy not chosen freely but dictated by circumstances. In the end he searches in vain for stars in a sky covered by dark clouds (V .iii. 3410-13). As he rejects his astrologer's desperate warning of impending disaster (V. v. 3608-19) and prepares for the final struggle, he can only see the turmoil before him: "Earth belongs to the evil spirit, not to the good. The Gods above send only general gifts; their light is pleasing but does not bring wealth to individuals" (II. ii. 799-802). But his new order is tainted by decisions based on political considerations and personal desires. The contrast between disorder, order, and real reform corresponds not only to the spatial configuration of setting, action, and expression that identifies the figures but also to their unique perception of space.

The panoramic scenes of *Wallenstein's Lager* (campfires, tents, sheds of peddlers) form the frame for a great diversity of figures who are affected by war, participate in it, and await from Wallenstein a decision that will determine their future. The setting, the activities of the soldiers (waiting, drinking, gambling), and the topic of conversations (to gain riches in the war, plunder, rob, rape, and kill) highlight the restricted view of life. While the mercenaries appear to look up to Wallenstein, their true point of orientation is the goddess Fortuna. He is but a "vessel" for their journey and quest. The setting matches their view that existence is a gamble and should be risked for a throw of the dice. The deadly essence of the circular confinement penetrates both horizontal and vertical space. In the end Fortuna abandons the army and Wallenstein. The open space becomes a graveyard when the battalion's galloping horses race over the fallen Max.

The identification of groups and individual characters with a spatial dimension that reveals their inner demon is framed by the suprapersonal panorama of war. War, the magnet captivating the inner circle surrounding Wallenstein as well as the distant emperor and the Swedish forces, is the prominent manifestation of historical change. The individual orientation in space informs the audience of personal hopes and ambitions. The attitudes toward war show a general inability to comprehend historical forces. Those who suffer and those who believe that they control war can only express limited personal opinions. The multiple voices alternating between clamor for plunder and hope for a peaceful future, between protest and accommodation, blend into a chorus of misconceptions. Even Max, whose ideal of a true order of existence embraces the vision of a classical landscape, remains bound to his soldiers and is swept away by a tide of destruction. The stage setting of enclosed tents, rooms, and halls mirrors the caged existence of the participants whose personal and political strategies have suffocated the honesty that is essential for the foundation of lasting reform. The play's final tableau underscores this conclusion. When Octavio looks upward as if to profess his innocence, his glance actually breaks on the ceiling of the hall that has become a place of death. The vertical axis merges with the horizontal in a centripetal movement. The individual stands in isolation at the center of a universe that eludes comprehension.

The intense action in *Die Jungfrau von Orleans* pervades all landscape metaphors. They are aligned with the figures' contrasting opinions concerning the effect of political turmoil on the kingdom and the reaction of all participants to Johanna's claim to be chosen by God to free France. The attitudes are rooted in unacknowledged, therefore easily overlooked, views of history that embody distinct spatial orientations. Johanna's father, Thibaut d'Arc, anticipates quietly the possible destruction of the land and the villages. But he also asserts that the earth endures; spring will bring forth new growth; and farmers will rebuild their huts (Prologue 4. 377-382). He avows the same blind trust in the continuity of the patriarchal order, will accept as ruler whoever is crowned in Reims, rejects his daughter's vision, accuses her of witchcraft (IV. vii., xi) and, in condemning her, denies the possibility of any miraculous or providential intervention in the course of history. Trapped by his convictions, Thibaut cannot look beyond the narrow confines of the most immediate sphere.

The beliefs articulated by the archbishop of Reims are linked to a deeply troubling, uncertain spatial and temporal cycle. He accepts a providential view of history and a divine plan for France. Yet, as he listens to Thibaut's accusation and the simultaneously occurring portentous thunder from heaven, he is overcome by suspicion and demands visible, convincing proof for Johanna's mission. After Johanna has been banned from the court and the enemies once again attack victoriously, he feels remorse but cannot resolve his doubts. He is willing to grant that the girl was chosen by God but insists on a clear sign from heaven that can be understood by mortals (V. vii). His response, similar to Isabella's lament in *Die Braut von Messina*, expresses the uncertainty of individuals in a secular world who cannot discern truth in the commitment to an ideal by others and seek guidance from Gods whose voices fail to reach earth. For the archbishop the ultimate destiny of the world has been communicated through Revelation while the immediate course of history remains shrouded in darkness. The ever-changing demands of living suffuse his polar spatial orientation.

King Charles VII, whose vision of the state is embedded in a poetic pastoral landscape, is represented in the "romantic tragedy" as an enlightened ruler who seeks peace and considers it his duty to serve the people of his state. Consonant with his visionary landscape, he abhors force and regards the political struggle as a stage in historical evolution that precedes a just government for the entire population. He identifies with the poet's dream of an ennobled world and spiritualized existence: " Poet and king should together stride; both live on humanity's lofty height!" (I. ii. 483-484) He has faith in Johanna's vision, accepts her help, remains true to his convictions when he is crowned, shows mercy toward his enemies (V. x), never falters yet

bows to public opinion after Johanna fails to answer her father's accusation. The state he expects to rule in the future is embedded in a poetic pastoral landscape and populated by persons who are rejuvenated
because they are blessed by the continuous renewal of the earth and
the grace of illuminating light.

The play's spatial horizontal and vertical orientation is most pronounced in Johanna's sense of her calling. Her feats, either performed
on stage or reported by couriers, link her to the military campaign.
She carries the banner, leads the troops, slays enemies, is captured,
breaks the iron chains, frees the king, and dies on the battlefield. This
horizontal movement in space is balanced by the vertically oriented
scenes that focus on her self-perception, bond to God, and relation to
others. Intuiting this dimension, she hears voices from above, feels inspired by heavenly glory, sees herself as the virgin chosen to free the
country, experiences doubt when touched by the love of men, cannot
respond to her father's indictment, and finally sees heaven's golden
gates opening for her welcome (V. xiv. 3537-40). The duality in her
nature and the tension between vertical and horizontal planes is captured succinctly in the motif contrast of the white dove and the iron
helmet and breastplate. Johanna yearns to fly; even her advance on
the battlefield is frequently characterized as flight. But she is bound
by iron necessity to war, to the ravaged land. Only the moment of
death resolves the conflict: "The heavy armor becomes a winged
gown. Upward – upward – the earth recedes" (V. xiv. 3542-43). As
Johanna envisions herself soaring into the sky, the vertical plane expands and encompasses the earthly panorama.

The ahistorical, direct intervention of providence on behalf of one
warring party and the allegorical identification of Johanna with the individual's yearning for freedom would justify the play's subtitle "A
Romantic Tragedy." Yet, a comparison with "Das Ideal und das
Leben" shows a direct parallel in the spatial structure that, though distinctly different from Goethe's delineation of the classical landscape,
has the salient features of classical space. Contrasting the panoramic
perspective of worldly aspirations, strife, extraordinary deeds, and inevitable death with an eternal realm of light, beauty, and truth and
considering the conflict between the individual's sensuous nature and
godlike yearning for purity, Schiller resolves the polar tension
through a transfiguration of the human entelechy. By contemplating

and finally completely identifying with the serene regions of pure forms (ll. 121-22) the individual is changed into ideal potential. The divine form, divested of mortal manifestations, soars blazingly into the sky. Leaving the oppressive world of illusions, the individual ascends and enters the region of light, harmony, and freedom (ll. 141-50).

The shifting locations in *Wilhelm Tell* are anchored in a common spatial pattern. Mountains frame a tranquil setting of cultivated fields, pastures, and forests. The intrusion of a tyrannical political regime, accompanied by violent acts of oppression and the construction of a stronghold for the bailiff, disturbs the peaceful coexistence of population and nature. The political unrest is paralleled by tumultuous storms. A vertical thrust replaces the horizontal perspective as individuals attempt to defend their rights, look to heaven, contemplate the sun, the planets, and the stars, and seek guidance from an immutable universal order. The restoration of social harmony is reflected in a dynamic balance of the vertical and horizontal spatial dimension. Tell, justifying his tyrannicide as just and necessary since it lays the foundation for a free society, raises his hands to heaven. Simultaneously, bright sunlight floods the open landscape.

Systematic developments of horizontal and vertical dimensions, of sun and storm, vision and loss of sight, fugitive and shelter, open space and imprisonment not only form the background of the play but also serve as contrastive pictorial representations of justice and injustice. By capturing the disparity between organic growth and willful disruption of life by authoritarian rule, between communal living and social unrest, the landscape motif underscores the organization of the play's central theme and reinforces its resolution. The population portrayed in *Wilhelm Tell* has developed social and political institutions that benefit communal living. Shepherds, farmers, and hunters exist in harmony with nature. Settlements and cultivated land blend into the environment. The people and the landscape convey the appearance of a living organism. The disruption of the balance of nature and communal interest is countered by the group's resistance, Tell's resolute action, and the recognition that any lasting reform, even if it is initiated by an individual, requires the shared, collective vision of a free society founded on mutual respect, helpfulness, and common concern.

The play presents a unique resolution to the thematic cluster of conquering injustice, individual self-realization, and collective will.

The people's concerted struggle for freedom fosters unity, and united action begets freedom. Immediate personal and exemplary but unreflected conduct may serve others in times of need. Still, action based on conscious reflection will enhance the supra-personal volition and thereby serve the community best (IV. iii. 2568 ff.; V. ii. 3181 ff.). This philosophic consideration determines the artistic modulation of spatial motif patterns. Freedom is supported by images and metaphors of light; the loss of freedom is linked with vanishing light (I. iv. 585, 607, 744; III. iii. 2066; IV. i. 2220-21; IV. ii. 2358-60); tyranny is consistently symbolized by thunderstorms; unity is associated with fertility; and as the play advances the vertical axis and the horizontal plane are fused into a dynamic spiral.

In Schiller's works the successful vertical ascent to mountain tops and the ensuing critical survey of the land's broad panorama generally signify achieving self-mastery and control over adverse circumstances, whereas raging water, fog, and mist identify the loss of vision and control. However, in *Wilhelm Tell* the idea is extended to incorporate changing social and historical circumstances. Initially, Tell mentions his delight in climbing apparently impenetrable paths, hunting the gemsbok, and scanning the far-flung lowlands. He clearly identifies his achievement with self-control. However, after his imprisonment, escape from the boat, and the pivotal monologue in which he reflects upon his previous existence and reaches the decision to destroy the tyrant (IV. iii.), the spatial relations shift almost imperceptively. As all individuals join others in building a new society based on freedom, unity, and common efforts, the vertical and the horizontal merge in a complex perspective of the landscape that entwines earth and sky. The confidence in apparently unlimited individual potential is supplanted by the recognition that the individual has to accept the restrictions inherent in a communal existence. The vertical and the horizontal intersect. In the vision of a civilized landscape that balances the individual and the universal Schiller has created the equivalent of the Chinese hexagram for peace: earth and heaven unite.

The examination of selections from Schiller's poetry and tragedies discloses a precise technique in spatial organization. Schiller establishes metaphoric fields that capture the disorder of human relations in the light of an ideal order and also clarify essential character traits of figures through their unique perception of space. Some works such as *Wallenstein* and *Die Jungfrau von Orleans* focus on irreconcilable views that contribute to pronounced contrast patterns. Others like *Wilhelm Tell* highlight a consensus of opinions which is reflected in the resolution of conflicts. By establishing parallels between landscapes, historical development, and human nature, Schiller creates reciprocal relations among phenomena usually considered distinct in essence. Attributes of nature and characteristics of thought, the semblance of reality and visionary landscapes, form poles in a dialectic process of increasing awareness. In addition, the simultaneously occurring complex interactions between the poetic voice and the observations of figures form the basis for horizontal and vertical alignments that contour the textual structure. Although the movement in a journey or the action in plays conveys the impression of linear progression, the existential commitment of figures, their success and failure, foster internal dynamics that shape configurations ranging from centripetal movement to centrifugal spiral. The confluence of historical continuity in individual failure to comprehend the forces that govern social transformation and the panoramic vision of devastated land, of unchanging human nature and accommodation to political expediency, results in a circular matrix. *Wallenstein's Lager* introduces all those who participate in a moment of historical change, but fail to discern the nature of the conflict. *Wallenstein's Tod* concludes with a tableau of a survivor who gained neither self-insight nor understanding of the world. With the exception of Max and Thekla, individuals remain trapped in the narrow confinement of a circle in which they continuously confront imponderable events emanating from their own unreflective actions.

The vertical ascent in *Die Jungfrau von Orleans* presents a striking contrast to this circular confinement that arrests regeneration. Yet, Schiller portrays the visionary experience and simultaneous transcendence of human limitations as a spiritualized consummation. Johanna is inspired by prophetic spirit but remains naive. She does not mature intellectually, never gains self-knowledge, and does not comprehend the forces struggling for dominance. Wilhelm Tell, neither visionary nor slave to permanence, gains a critical understanding of the individual's role in society and shows a growing historical awareness. Similar to Schiller's other plays, *Wilhelm Tell* has a historical antecedent and presents the convergence of a personal life with history while simultaneously elevating it to a supra-historical continuum. Tell's development from a person who acts quickly without deliberation to one who carefully considers the right course of action for the community conveys the impression of a developmental personality. He matures and moves along stages of increasing awareness on an upward spiral. This classical conception of individuation is paralleled by a spatial representation that coalesces in a classical landscape.

The thematic examination of space in classical drama, poetry, and narrative provides convincing evidence that:

(1) the spatial coordination along a vertical or horizontal axis determines thematic alignments. Spatial motifs like sky, open expanse, palace, room, wilderness, sea, garden, fields, mountains, and valleys can serve as primary focus for orientation and highlight classical constellations. Introduced as contrast patterns, the motifs can either augment, enhance, and sustain classical figure conceptions and themes or support highly critical, yet distinctly realistic visions of individual disorientation and confinement;

(2) physical travel becomes a mental journey leading to encounters with nature that has been transformed in the course of history by human activity. Encounters with the agrarian landscape (well-defined vistas of paths, villages blending into the countryside, cultivated fields and gardens) or the "civilized landscape" of the palace and city initiate in the observer a process of continued reflection on possibilities of individual and social reform;

(3) the classical landscape includes both horizontal and vertical planes. The horizontal plane occurring alone accentuates circular patterns of restriction. The reciprocal relation between the horizontal-panoramic and the vertical dimension initiates the centrifugal movement forward, outward, and upward on stages of increasing understanding of the world.

CHAPTER 5

Renunciation: Self-Fulfillment and Ideal. From Self-Interest to Concern for Others

The theme of renunciation holds a unique position in classical constellations. It is frequently introduced in representations of human development at a moment when figures begin to understand that self-regard and communal concerns must be balanced in the interest of society. The theme necessitates that figures are conceived as developmental and capable of either discerning rationally or grasping intuitively that the egocentric sense of self, based on the satisfaction derived from fulfilling personal goals, must be brought into a sensitive, dynamic equilibrium with the needs of the community. By giving direction to the crossroads decision for the affirmation of either exemplary personal conduct or social reform, the theme often merges with other dominant themes while retaining the double perspective on empirical needs and spiritual aspirations of both individual and community. As a primary theme, renunciation highlights unique individual achievements and establishes stark contrasts to personal failure and communal deficiencies. The representative works examined in this chapter were selected because renunciation seems to hold the key to understanding the figures both as individually developmental and as exemplary for others. Because renunciation occurs in many other classical works besides those discussed, the theme will form part of the discussion of the themes of models of excellence and of the reform circle, as well as the centrifugal spiral. Conversely, the representative works for renunciation also use the themes of exemplary conduct and the reform circle as organizing principles.

Renunciation as Key to Self-Insight and Building of Community in Classical Drama

The crossroads decision of the protagonists of Racine's *Bérénice, Iphigénie,* and *Phèdre* leads them to a renunciation of the self, of their interests or desires, and, in the case of Phèdre, of life itself. In these plays, the act of renouncing has three consequences. It represents a quantum leap in the protagonists' self-development and -insight. However, it also isolates them from others. Ultimately, with the exception of Phèdre, it lifts them up as models to be imitated by others. Because it serves as a transition between the themes of self-insight and exemplary conduct, the signification of renunciation differs in classical literature and in the literature of romance. Although Racine and Dryden admired and imitated the treatment of passion and honor in the pastoral romances of Honoré D'Urfé and Gauthier Coste de La Calprenède, they both chose to make the renunciation of passion and possession of the loved one a culminating point in their heroic tragedies. In Corneille's *Cinna,* Racine's *Mithridate* and *Esther,* Dryden's *The Indian Queen* and *The Indian Emperour* and Addison's *Cato,* renunciation as a theme links together self-insight, concern for others, and a radical reordering of priorities. The traditional concepts of love and honor are given new meanings. Although the concept of the crossroads is missing and the right / wrong path motif sequence plays a negligible role, the decision to sacrifice possession of another's love or one's own life is always a conscious one that entails leaving old patterns behind and embracing new ones. Like the crossroads decision, then, the theme of renunciation represents a break with the past and a decision for the future. As in the crossroads decision, the motif sequences heart / hand and enlightened dialogue / confrontation – silence assist in linking self-insight with concern for others.

Because the alignment between the two motif sequences and renunciation is unique in *Phèdre,* this tragedy stands thematically apart from the others.[1] Instead of associating heart with genuine concern for others and enlightened, constructive dialogue and hand with violent acts, aggressive discourse, or silence, the play's exposition of Phèdre's incestuous love for her stepson Hippolyte reveals that the heart and its passions are the aggressors, while the hands remain innocent: "Thanks to heaven, my hands are not criminal. / Would to the gods that my heart were as innocent as they!" (I. iii. 221-22). The tragedy inverts the motif's traditional signification. Letting the heart speak is the equivalent of the acts of the violent or possessive hand in Racine's other tragedies. Consistently portrayed as "burning" or "flaming," the passionate heart is not the consequence of a consciously made decision but fated by a potent divine will against which even the most assiduous human efforts are futile: "I recognized Venus and her fearful fires, / The inevitable torments of a blood[line] that she pursues . . . / In vain did my hand burn the incense on [her] altars . . ." (277-78, 284). At the midpoint of the tragedy, Phèdre avows that all control of her heart and of both her and Hippolyte's fate lies in divine hands: "Your triumph is perfect" (III. ii. 816). The only possibility to challenge divinely ordained fate and to quench the violence of the burning heart is to accept full responsibility for her words and the acts of her hands. By commanding Oenone, "Go, leave me the care of my deplorable fate" (IV. vi. 1318) and stating to Thésée, "I must break an unjust silence: / I must give back to your son his innocence" (V. vii. 1617), she effectively breaks out of her fated role and takes control of the future. To implement her decision to renounce her life, she uses her "innocent" hands to administer the cold poison that stills the fated fires of her heart. In renouncing fate and life, she opens to those whom she leaves behind a future world of restored purity and unity.

In contrast to the predominant focus on the protagonist's self-conflict and -development in *Phèdre*, Racine's *Mithridate* integrates the motif sequences in the movement from self-interest to concern for others. This movement can be traced through the association of the recurring nucleus word "interest" with the motif of the heart and the motif sequence dialogue / silence. When "interest" first occurs to express Xipharès' love for Monime (I. i. 31), it serves to alienate him from his father and condemns him to silence. The association of a

love-interest with silence is reaffirmed by Monime, who adds the perspective of the grieving heart (II. i. 410).   In Pharnace's and
Mithridate's declarations, in contrast, the love interest is associated with
a demanding heart and verbal confrontation: PHARNACE: "Our
common interests and my heart demand [marriage]" (I. ii. 239);
MITHRIDATE [to Monime]: "Remember that your heart is a property which is due me" (IV. iv. 1281).[2] Mithridate has already assigned Xipharès the task of pressing his "interest" on Monime (II.
v.). The alignment of the love interest with either the grieving, silenced heart (Xipharès, Monime) or the demanding, confrontational
heart (Pharnace, Mithridate) determines the characterizations of the
figures and their actions.   The actions of Mithridate and Pharnace
dominate.   Their aggressiveness in battle is continued in their antago-
nistic relations with each other and their demands on Xipharès and
Monime. They use discourse as a weapon to attack, insinuate, and destroy: MITHRIDATE: "My will, Prince, ought to suffice. / Obey . . .
/ Prince, you've heard me, / And you are lost if you answer." PHAR-
NACE: "But Xipharès, sir, hasn't told you everything; / He has told
you only the least part of the secret" (III. i. 959-60, 965-66; ii. 994-
95). Likewise, Mithridate commands Monime to "cease to be interested in Pharnace" and to accept instead Xipharès: "You vainly resist, and I anticipate your flight" (III. vi. 1051, 1095).

   While Pharnace's and Mithridate's verbal confrontations dominate
the dramatic action leading to the climactic battle between their forces,
the silence to which Xipharès' and Monime's interests seem consigned
shrinks to a secondary role. When they succeed in announcing to
each other their carefully hidden love interests, they learn simultaneously to renounce them. This alignment of renunciation with the motifs of open dialogue and the grieving heart becomes apparent in
Xipharès' early avowal of his love for Monime, dutifully hidden out
of respect to his father: " . . . I run to defend you / Without asking
anything of you, without daring to expect anything" (I. iii. 211-12).
Monime's later announcement of her concealed love and her renunciation of it parallels Xipharès': "My grief has too much energy to be
silenced any longer? . . . But I must indeed, despite [a rigorous duty] /
Speak for the first and last time. My heart responded to all your same
speeches . . . / I flee. Remember, Prince, to avoid me . . ." (II. vi. 675,
677-78, 690, 745). In renouncing possession of each other, Monime

and Xipharès acquire the capacity for shared sympathy and respect for the other that contradicts the aggressive possessiveness of those around them.

Furthermore, Monime's and Xipharès' relationship with Pharnace and Mithridate exhibits the same pattern of renunciation. Monime describes herself as an obedient "victim" (III. vi. 1078) to Mithridate's desire, and Xipharès risks his life repeatedly to defend his father from the Romans. Finally, Monime communicates their conduct directly to Mithridate: "And despite my inclination and my first designs / For a son, the greatest of humans after you . . . / I renounced, sir, this prince . . . / Both of us agreed to sacrifice each other, . . ." (IV. v. 1329-33). In their placing of loyalty to Mithridate and openness with him above self-interest and intrigue, Xipharès and Monime trigger an unexpected growth of insight. Inspired by their generosity, Mithridate shifts the emphasis of his struggle with the Romans from self-aggrandizement to self-effacement. He recognizes that he is but one among other "famous names" who fight for liberation of the oppressed. He offers Xipharès his last possession: Monime. In direct contrast to previous patterns of conduct, he forbids the two lovers from risking their lives to glorify him in funeral rites.[3] The movement from self-interest to concern for others is summarized in the play's last line: "And throughout the universe let us search for him avengers" (V. v. 1698). Renunciation of self-interest has resulted in Mithridate's recognition and acceptance of his place in a larger chain of being that will be continued by Monime and Xipharès.

In Dryden's heroic plays *The Indian Queen* and *The Indian Emperour,* renunciation of a loved one or of one's life marks the model figures who, having gained insight into their true place in society, sacrifice self-interest to the general good as well to principles of honor and virtue. Their act motivates those around them to alter their conduct and attitudes from past patterns of vengeance and passion toward a future of reconciliation and mutual trust. As in *Mithridate,* the act of renunciation forms the climax of each play. It is carefully prepared through the alteration between confrontation and reconciliation, which structures the basic rhythm of both plays.[4] The opening scene of *The Indian Queen* demonstrates the relationship between two potential patterns of conduct. While Montezuma's passionate decision to kill the Ynca because the latter refuses to yield him his daughter begins the scene, Acacis' plea for moderation and reason ("No, I must your Rage prevent, / From doing what your reason wou'd prevent . . . Thy virtue seems but thy revenges slave . . ." I. i. 59-69, 107) wins over revenge. Moreover, Acacis' renunciation of personal freedom in favor of honor persuades Ynca to respond with a trust that begins the movement toward reconciliation: "Come, then, we are alike to honor just / Thou to be trusted thus, and I to trust" (151-52). Though Acacis is generally represented as the voice of moderation, generosity, and honor, he also speaks the language of passion and violence when he demands that Montezuma give him Orazia "as my Mistress" (IV. ii. 16) and insists on a duel despite Montezuma's pleas for friendship. Yet, even this scene closes with a projection of reconciliation as a result of freely chosen renunciation: "Now Montezuma since Orazia dyes, / I'le fall before thee, the first Sacrifice; . . ." (112-13). His role as mediator through renunciation reaches a climax in the great sacrifice scene (V. i.). His freely chosen course of suicide to remove himself from the scene of contention paves the way for his final reconciliation with both Montezuma and Orazia and inspires Montezuma to pardon Zempoalla ("Acacis lives in me, and cease to grieve" V. i. 385). The chiasms in the final verse, "Love crowns the dead, and death Crowns him that lives, / Each gains the Conquest which the other gives" (309-10), integrate personal renunciation of life into a renewed life of the community.

Consonant with the relative independence of the theme of renunciation from character development in *The Indian Queen* is its association with the abstract concepts of "Honor," "Virtue," and above all, "Death," as well as its antithesis to "Revenge," "Passion," and of course, "Life."[5] These concepts weave the fabric of the dialogue. They communicate each character's momentary attitude and conduct in an ever-shifting action in which characters do not always behave according to expectation. While interweaving these abstractions into motif patterns, the dialogue of Dryden's *The Indian Emperour* also makes use of the "heart" motif to indicate a greater consistency of characterization. Montezuma's "Lyon-heart" (I. ii. 180), and Cortez's "noble heart" and "generous heart" (IV. ii. 48; V. i. 103) communicate a certain mode of behavior that includes honor, generosity, and even the ability to listen to and respect an adversary within certain well-defined limits. These limits are revealed as external in the first exchange between the two leaders. It is significant that Vasquez, not Cortez, announces the Spaniards' conditions for peace, while Cortez insists on "peace," "clemency," and "friendship." By repeatedly renouncing force, postponing battles, and setting prisoners free, Cortez develops from his initial inclination to abduct Cydaria by force into a figure concerned with building a harmonious future based on love and mutual concern. Montezuma, in contrast, develops his trait of "Lyon-heart" into an unflinching devotion to his kingdom and religious traditions. He represents the past to which he clings despite defeat, captivity, and torture, and renounces any part of the future by freely choosing to take his life.[6] Renunciation shapes each of these characters differently: Cortez grows from past confinement to future expansiveness, while Montezuma shrinks from past domination into the void of death.

The theme also functions to highlight the antithesis between the two brothers Odmar and Guyomar. In the first confrontation over Alibech (I. ii.), they appear differentiated only in that Odmar's love reaches further into the past than Guyomar's, which is "of a fresher date" (166). This differentiation is significant, however, because it serves to link the two brothers to the two patterns of expansive future and shrinking past established by the antithetical attitudes and behavior of Cortez and Montezuma. Odmar's and Guyomar's subsequent development into villain and hero, as reflected in their recurrent antithetical choices of action, clearly aligns renunciation of aggression and possessiveness with the future of their community, while the decision for aggressiveness and forceful possessiveness leads to death and exclusion from the future. Thus, Guyomar's conduct consists of arguing for peace rather than battling the Spaniards (III. i.), offering to risk his life defending his father (II. ii.; V. i.), refusing to commit a "dishonorable deed" even to please Alibech (IV. ii.), warning Cortez of Orbellan's treachery (III. i.), and finally of renouncing his right to Alibech rather than to see her harmed (V. i.). Odmar, in contrast, argues for war but deserts rather than risking his life in battle, and is willing, though reluctant, to fulfill Alibech's plea to beg Cortez for release from the siege. When frustrated by Montezuma's awarding of Alibech to his brother, he plots revenge: "I by Revenge and Love am wholly led" (IV. iii. 58.) and even threatens to kill first Alibech ("Death shall enjoy what is to thee deny'd" V. i. 24.), then Guyomar

("But in his death, I some Advantage see" 43.). His obsession to possess Alibech leads to his mortal conflict with the equally possessive Vasquez ("This Lady I did for my self design; / Dare you attempt her Honour who is mine? . . . It rests we two our claim in Combat try, / And that with this fair prize, the Victor flye" 85-86, 105-06). The result of this reciprocal aggression and possessiveness, death for both participants, contrasts sharply with the triumph of the renunciation of those behavior patterns which closes the play with the words of Guyomar: "We to our selves will all our wishes grant; / And nothing coveting, can nothing want" (V. ii. 3745).

In Corneille's *Cinna,* Racine's *Esther,* and Addison's *Cato,* the theme of renunciation is directly linked with the self-insight of the protagonist. Confronted with the conspiracy of his closest friends and his feelings of anger and despair, Auguste in *Le Cid* renounces the temptation to take a justified revenge and to abdicate a detestable throne. In so doing, he discovers that he can master his feelings as well as determine the feelings of others: "I am master of myself as [well as of] the universe" (V. iii. 1696). Esther learns to sacrifice the silence dictated by self-preservation to the well-being of her people, and Cato realizes that the only way to save both his honor and his friends is through suicide. While Auguste's monologue focuses on a crossroads decision, *Esther* and *Cato* are structured around the protagonists' realization that certain developments in the situation of those around them require an assumption of a responsibility beyond that of self-preservation. The assumption of this responsibility will lead to a departure from past patterns of behavior and will initiate a radically different future. For Esther, this change occurs when she breaks with the past pattern of silence about her origin that was dictated by Mardochée ("The one by whom Heaven directs my destiny / Still keeps my tongue tied on this secret" I. i. 91-92) to plead for her people. For Cato, the transformation comes in abandoning a past course of moderation between extremes that is no longer applicable in the present situation governed by Caesar: " . . . the conquered world / Is Caesar's. Cato has no business in it" (IV. ii.). Both become obedient victims to further the interests of their community rather than their own concerns.

Esther's consuming interest in preserving her people contrasts with the prevailing pattern of self-interest as expressed particularly by the antithetical figure Aman. Their language reflects this antithesis: ES-THER: "What was in secret my shame and my sorrow . . . / . . . in Jerusalem grass covers the walls!" (I. i. 82, 85); AMAN: "But, believe me, in the rank I've been elevated to, / My soul, attached entirely to my own grandeur, / Is feebly touched by interests of blood" (II. i. 488-90). His wife Zarès identifies his goal: "This care to surrender all to his [the King's] supreme power, / Between us, did it have any other aim but yourself?" (III. i. 876-77). The two antithetical perceptions of interest meet in Esther's audiences with the king.

> ASSUERUS: What interest, what cares agitate you, press you?
> ESTHER: A pressing interest impels me to implore you.
> ASSUERUS: All your desires, Esther, will be accorded you
> Should you. . . . .
> Demand half of this powerful empire.
> ESTHER: I dare to implore you, both for my own life,
> And for those of an unfortunate people .
> . . . .
> But I ask . . . that . . . you hear me speak.
> (II. vii. 681, 686; III. iv. 1023-24, 1029-30; 1041-42)

The King's action of according Esther the privilege of open dialogue and condemning Aman to silence ("Keep quiet! Dare you speak without the order of your king?" 1090-91) paves the way for the triumph of Esther's renunciation of self in favor of the security of her people.[7]

The polarity of open dialogue and silence also assists in sharpening the contrast between renunciation and aggression in Addison's *Cato*. The chief aggressor Caesar, whose increasing military power threatens to overthrow Roman liberty and civilization, speaks only indirectly through Decius, whose "dazzled eye / Beholds this man in a false, glaring light, / Which conquest and success have thrown upon him; . . ." (II. i.). The plot hatched between Syphax and Sempronius to abduct Marcia requires secrecy (silence) and surprise ("Rush in and seize your prey" IV. i), to support aggression. In contrast, the chief voice disavowing military aggressiveness belongs to Cato. Although its power has shrunk from the once "thundering" oratory

in the Roman senate to the quiet, low tones heard only by a few remaining friends, it communicates his values throughout the play. Not
only does Cato publicly extol moderation, virtue, and liberty ("Let us
appear nor rash nor diffident . . . A day, an hour, of virtuous liberty,/
Is worth a whole eternity in bondage" (II. i.), but he also recognizes
that constructive communication is based on others' comprehension
and response: "Fathers, pronounce your thoughts . . . Sempronius,
speak. . . . Lucius, we next would know what's your opinion. . . ." (II.
i.). That Cato has at least partially succeeded in this aim is testified by
the Numidian Juba's identification of Cato as a "noble soul, bent on
higher views," raised to "god-like height" (I. i.). Two developments
interrupt the mutual understanding envisioned in the first two acts:
Cato's refusal to listen to Juba's suit for the hand of his daughter
("Adieu, young prince, I would not hear a word" II. i.) and the
mutiny of his disaffected followers that results in the death of his son.
The effect of both is to isolate Cato from even his friends and family
and ultimately from life itself: " . . . the conquer'd world / Is Caesar's!
Cato has no business in it" (IV. ii.). Faced with the expanding influence of aggression into his own camp and his inability to counter it
with mere allegiance to the old Roman values, Cato chooses a radical
reorientation of his role. Previously proudly self-sufficient and assured in his self-assigned role as upholder of Roman virtue, Cato recognizes that the present situation calls for self-sacrifice. In voluntarily
reducing his own status to that of a corpse, he nevertheless upholds a
subtle open dialogue, one which, according to Lucius' words closing
the play, communicates with the enemy: "[His body] A fence betwixt
us and the victor's wrath: / Cato, though dead, still protects his
friends" (V. i.). The play ends with a vision of the profound future
effect of renunciation on expanding aggression: to preserve lives.[8]
Renunciation as the individual's direct response to the needs of others
becomes the basis for building a new community.

Stylized Renunciation: Friendship

The theme of idealized renunciation structures the flourishing literature of sentiment throughout the eighteenth century. The striking
resemblance in tone, supporting motifs (heart – soul / mind – intel-

lect), and thematic confluence with love in the poetry of Edward Young, Thomas Gray, Barthold Brockes, Johann Christian Günther and Friedrich Matthisson and in novels by Pierre Carlet Marivaux, Abbé Prévost, Samuel Richardson, Oliver Goldsmith, Johann Thimotheus Hermes, Sophie Schubert, and Sophie La Roche show that renunciation has become an edifying theme. As a counterpoint to the rising utilitarianism in middle-class attitudes, it was often the convenient medium for expressing noble, ethical, or religious sentiments. Of interest to the study of classical and realistic patterns are: (1) the transposition of the theme to a timeless or historical setting that conveys psychological probability to chivalric attitudes; (2) the correlation with the fairytale motif of trial by endurance to prove love; (3) the fusion with transcendence of personal desires and hopes in the face of death; (4) the tendency to saturate the theme with philosophical considerations; (5) and a shift in emphasis toward resignation that foreshadows the thematic focus in the works of Stifter, Raabe, and Fontane during the nineteenth century. Works by Wieland, Heinrich von Kleist, and Friedrich Heinrich Jacobi illustrate the general thematic pattern of the period. Specific resolutions and constellations in Schiller's and Goethe's writing offer insights into compositional possibilities and restrictions inherent in the theme.

The central motif of a test of faithful love connects the theme of renunciation with love in Wieland's verse epic *Oberon*. The verse epic blends fairytale elements, characteristics of the chivalric tradition, and the narrative action sequence of adventurous journeys. Indebted to Pope's point of view in *The Rape of the Lock* and reminiscent of Wieland's "Geron der Adelige," the epic is narrated with discreet humor and a gentle amusement that tempers the excitement of action-packed scenes and the serious, at times sententious observations on love. Its thematic axis is love, portrayed and observed as tempting, passionate, deceptive, covetous, jealous, faithful, and exemplary. Love motivates the conduct and thinking of all primary figures; it unifies the adventures; it sustains the interest through travel, abductions, shipwreck, and separation of lovers. All motifs and secondary themes emanate from and converge again in love. The crucial event, the equivalent of the "pregnant moment" suggested by Lessing in *Laokoon* (Chap. 3, 16) and *Hamburgische Dramaturgie* (Chap. 30, 34, 46) that produces an extraordinary ordeal for two lovers occurs when Oberon observes an act of adultery among mortals. When his wife Titania makes allowances for human weakness, Oberon leaves and vows not to see her again until he has found two persons who can remain faithful throughout severe afflictions and temptations.[9]

Renouncing a blissful life at the side of his queen, Oberon imposes upon himself a painful separation and watches with mounting apprehension the trials of the lovers Hüon and Rezio. He helps at moments of danger but also adds to their suffering when Hüon is overwhelmed by passion and breaks his pledge not to consummate their love until they are married. The lovers experience the abduction, shipwreck, separation, and slavery common to pastoral romances. But they prove their steadfastness and withstand even the offer to save their lives by compromising their love. Hüon resists the advances by the alluring queen Almansaris; Rezio rejects Sultan Almansor's proposals. Finally, the "noble pair" stands at the stake "espousing death in the flames rather than becoming unfaithful for a throne!" (Canto 12: stanza 77). At that moment Oberon is convinced that fidelity exists and saves the lovers. The harmony of sensuous emotions and spiritual love that beckoned in the dreams of Hüon and Rezia (Canto 4: stanzas 46-49; canto 5: stanzas 2-5) triumphs at the conclusion of the epic. The gentle admonition that a reorientation of personal conduct is desirable for everyone in society indicates that the renunciation of individual desires is viewed as the basis for general social reform. By mirroring human sentiments in the fairyland, the epic elevates renunciation to a plane of timeless persistence that excludes the stark consequence of the theme's periphery: loss of self-identity or death.

Heinrich von Kleist penetrates the dark recesses of complete self-abnegation in *Das Käthchen von Heilbronn*. Calling the play a "spectacle of knights errant" did not diminish its unfavorable reception. Yet, the frequently voiced criticism that the figure conception is improbable and that Käthchen's sentiments are inconceivable points to the difficulties inherent in portraying renunciation of personal self-interest as an all-consuming passion. In order to create the semblance of psychological probability for a renunciation that culminates in utter self-abnegation, Kleist resorts to the dream motif.[10] Dreams in which the lovers Käthchen and Wetter vom Strahl intuit the perfect "heart-mate" motivate their indissoluble attachment. The function of the dreams is identical in *Oberon* and Kleist's play. But Kleist probes in the dreams a subconscious level of intuitive empathy and also superimposes on them a social aspect. Käthchen experiences the world, home, the class system, the conventions of society, and the rigid moral codes in a trance. She is a sleepwalker who lives a dream of fulfillment that is impossible in the existing social structure. In contrast to Egmont who actively affirms every moment of existence, she renounces personal volition. She suffers, endures mortification, and even seeks humiliation. Life appears as a continuous ordeal forever demanding abnegation. She is prepared to sacrifice herself for an unshakable inner certainty. Because her conviction precludes doubt and uncertainty, it also inhibits reflection. The essence of such renunciation differs fundamentally from the capacity for renunciation that is acquired by the figures in Goethe's *Wilhelm Meister* during their journey through life. By correlating the appropriate motif of the search for the bride – sojourn home – installation with the fairy-tale motif of the true / false bride and with the action, the play offers a conclusion that redeems Käthchen's faith in the validity of her dream (ll. 2081-2229). The outcome underscores the limitations in Kleist's vision compared with the classical temper. Renunciation and love solely based on inner conviction transcend the sphere of potential social reform. Käthchen's allegiance to intuition culminates in self-fulfillment but does not reach out for a response from society.

Similarly, in Friedrich Heinrich Jacobi's *Eduard Allwills Papiere* and *Woldemar*, the representation of the attempt to resolve the clash between individual aspirations and those of the community by renouncing self-interest focuses on the personal sphere of an inconclusive struggle for inner certainty. It therefore offers no concrete proposals for social reform. Instead, the works project the ideal of an absolutely chaste friendship that can be attained by rejecting all feelings that impair pure sentiments. The letters in *Eduard Allwills Papiere* examine from the perspective of several writers the mental state induced by the perception that all traditional proposals including eudemonic ethics and the imperative to obey the primacy of reason have led society into an impasse. Sylli von Wallberg extols the sensibility inspired by unselfish friendships that can alleviate if not cure the experience of utter confinement in life. She sees human activities as mechanical movements on a treadmill moving forever in a circle.[11]

Clerdon feels deep despair after brief moments of identification with nature (32). He yearns for release and full development of his potential (68 f.) but reconciles himself to the more modest goal of improving life in a small community. Amalie seeks fulfillment in love for husband and children and attempts to create the illusion of perfection in the enclave of a family. Clärchen and Leonore aspire to an ideal friendship. But Eduard Allwill experiences the incongruity between the sentient heart and the unfeeling world to such a degree that the conflict dominates every thought. He trusts his "glowing, valiant heart" (35), laments the inherent deception in all social relations, searches almost incessantly for individuals whose conduct would lend credence to his belief that a divine spark can be ignited in mortals (243-44), and seeks love and friendship but experiences bitter disillusion over his lost innocence that compels him to ponder the cause of the general social disorientation. Eduard elevates friendship to a plane of an absolute ideal by synthesizing all qualities assigned to it in the epistolary novels of the period. Friendship is expansive. It transcends the barrier between classes; it posits equality among lovers or husband and wife; it sanctions the exalted "soul-brother and soul-sister" relationships among friends because it sublimates sensuous desires. Friendship encourages constructive dialogues and gives the heart a mate for common altruistic devotion.

The ideal requires the unconditional renunciation of all personal desires and self-centered intentions (245-62). Yet, aspiring to the ideal, Eduard feels the need for powerful emotions and passion: "I will obey only the voice of my heart" (238). As a consequence, Eduard cannot reconcile his innermost thirst for spontaneous expression with the longing for friendship. He cannot renounce the passion in his heart and can only resign himself to continued emotional and spiritual turbulence. Thus, the letters represent a circle of confinement dominated by resignation, not renunciation.

In *Woldemar*, two friends reach a level of self-knowledge that enables them to renounce all confining sentiments and establish an idealized friendship. In his review of the novel, Friedrich Schlegel censured the exclusive focus on love-friendship that inhibits the real development of either figures or ideas.[12] Yet, an extensive examination of factors that encourage or impede friendship reveals the signification attributed to renunciation more clearly than other narratives de-

voted to the cultivation of sensibility during the period. Jacobi scruti-
nizes the reciprocal relations of love and friendship, the inception,
growth, disruptions triggered by misunderstanding and the influence
of dominant conventional attitudes, perseverance, and successful renunciation of personal wishes. The novel introduces into the action a
series of events designed to show a slowly maturing friendship that
must prove its feasibility under adverse conditions. The sequence
suggests a further refinement of ideas presented in *Eduard Allwills
Papiere*. Friendship is the expression of an innate disposition that can
be cultivated under favorable circumstances. The disposition manifests itself in naive and spontaneous affections that reach out toward
the other. The undifferentiated affection grows into focused love
when it encounters the same sentiment. Such love is characterized by
a confluence of emotions and spirit, freed from all physical desires
and untroubled by convention.

The narrative traces first the unfolding of such a friendship between Henriette and Woldemar. They embrace, kiss, caress, and fondle
each other like children while discussing sublime ideas. Family and
friends misunderstand the relationship. Rumors of secretive passions
abound, and Henriette's father demands before his death a vow from
his daughter never to marry Woldemar. Henriette resolves the social
tension by persuading her friend to marry Allwina. She reasons that
marriage would remove all suspicion from the friendship. Instead, the
marriage gives rise to a new phase in the relationship, as Henriette and
Woldemar discover that they are physically attracted to each other.
They question the sincerity of sensibility and the essence of their
ideal. They experience confusion, error, and guilt. To withstand
temptation, they must renounce all selfish desires. Woldemar masters
his "horrible egotism"; Henriette finds guidance in pietism and
Aristotelian ethics. After losing their innocence and suffering a total
disruption of their lives, they aspire to a friendship reborn after conscious reflection and the acquired capacity for renunciation. Hence,
renunciation becomes integrated into the stages of a friendship that
advances from naiveté through temptation and reflection to a plane on
which pure emotions and ideas coincide. Every dialogue in the narrative points to the fact that the envisioned friendship will give balance
to individual existence. However, whether it will encourage social reorientation remains unclear.

Renunciation as Allegiance to the Unconditional

From the perspective of an unqualified identification with an absolute ideal, all temporal values including love, friendship, and political reform appear transitory. Schiller recognized this fact. While he devoted careful consideration to the role played by love and friendship in human development in "Tugend, Liebe, Freundschaft," "Philosophische Briefe," and *Über die ästhetische Erziehung des Menschen,* he centered all interest in his plays on one question: How does the individual meet the challenge of a situation that demands the total allegiance to an ideal? Posa (*Don Carlos*) subordinates his friendship with Don Carlos to his ideal of political freedom. He renounces and even betrays the friendship offered by King Philipp because he misjudges Philipp whom he considers incapable of effecting sweeping political reforms. Ultimately he identifies the basis of his feelings for Don Carlos with the foundation of liberty and sacrifices his life for the dream of freedom (V. iii). Max Piccolomini is torn in conflict between his admiration, respect, and love for Wallenstein and his uncompromising allegiance to truth. His torment in reaching the right decision is further intensified by his love for Thekla who will be lost forever if he abandons Wallenstein. He pleads and offers to share Wallenstein's fate under the condition that the general renounce his plan to commit treason. Wallenstein refuses. Max turns to Thekla who reaffirms his conviction: "As you remain true to yourself, you remain true to me. Destiny separates us, our hearts remain united" (*Wallensteins Tod* III. xxi. 2348-49). Both renounce the fulfillment of love but preserve their integrity and vision of truth. When Max dies, Thekla leaves home in search of his grave (IV. xii.). Wallenstein is left to contemplate the meaning of Max's life, "transparent and radiating, without a single dark spot" (V. iii. 3424-26). Despite his death, the ideal he embodied and articulated endures and points to the future.

The critical significance of renunciation for the thematic constellation in Schiller's *Maria Stuart* remains concealed in veiled allusions until the explosive resolution of conflicts. The play opens with the death sentence read to Maria and ends with her death. Her adversary Elisabeth stands at center stage as the curtain falls. To create and sustain suspense in the events between verdict rendered and judgment ex-ecuted, Schiller uses the effective technique of raising and subsequent-ly destroying hope for Maria's rescue. Hope opens the spectrum to conflicting personal ambitions, political considerations, intrigue, and the interest of the state. As a result, questions of legality, justice, truth, and freedom overshadow the fine thread of renunciation interwoven with the will to power. The clash between the two wills can only be re-solved by either renunciation or death. The renunciation envisioned in the play is oriented toward an ideal human perfection. The individ-ual is challenged to renounce all passion, frivolous, irresponsible be-havior, fear, and false hope (I. iv. 296 ff; 586-690; 671-80; II. iv. 1541-42; III. iii., iv.; IV. v.), all personal ambition and pride (I. i. 64 ff.; II. vi. 1160-61, viii. 1775-93; III. iv. 2242 ff.; 2447 f.; IV. x.), de-ceptive love (II. ii. 1055 ff.; II. ix. 1952 ff.; IV. vi. 2910 ff.), and all political intrigues, lies, deception, and self-serving objectives (I. i. 98-115; vii. 828 ff., 961 ff.; viii. 1033-37; II. iii. 1294, 1302 ff., 1323 ff., 1440 ff., v. 1509 ff., vi. 1652 ff.; IV. iv., xi). The individual, then, is asked to renounce all designs associated with the will to power in favor of a sphere of unconditional values, morality, and law. The figures in the play are held accountable for their conduct and judged by abso-lute ethical standards. Maria attains a state of grace when she under-stands herself, forgives Elisabeth, and renounces life (V. vi.-ix.). Elisabeth prevails, but her triumph is hollow. Lord Shrewsbury, the faithful servant of the state, returns his seal: "This straight hand is too stiff / To seal your new deeds. / . . . I could not save your nobler part" (V. xi. 1025-29). The end reverses Burleigh's prophecy: Maria's death does not assure Elisabeth's life. It promises death in the arena of political confinement.

In Goethe's *Wilhelm Meister*, political and social considerations in-fluence the representation of the renunciation of personal ambition in the interest of common welfare. Renunciation coupled with the growth of self-insight in Goethe's *Die natürliche Tochter* and *Pandora* appears to owe its inception not to the interrelation of fig-ures or their character traits but to an archetypal design. In *Die natürliche Tochter,* individual characteristics fade into stylized func-tions or offices (pastor, king, duke, judge, secretary). Attitudes and convictions correspond to changing circumstances. As the figures blend into such conflicting forces as the will to power, political intrigue, accommodation, and crime that vie for dominance, the call for renunciation identified with Eugenie becomes a primary condition for any reform. Similarly, in *Pandora*,[13] the mythic figures are agents who together stand for a general human situation. Prometheus rejects Pandora's gift which, contrary to tradition, offers fragile, immaterial apparitions of beauty, that is, the artistically enhanced semblance of life. Epimetheus welcomes Pandora. But when they live together, he begins to confuse semblance with reality. He seeks to possess Pandora's spirit and fails to master his desire to control inspiration and grace. She retreats to her ethereal home and leaves Epimetheus in a semi-conscious dreamlike existence between sleep and wakefulness. He is awakened from his anguished longing for her return and the lament over lost possibilities only when the gods intervene and unite his daughter Epimelia with Phileros, the son of Prometheus (ll. 784 ff., 1046 ff.). The offspring of inspiration and purposeful activity join in a vision that promises a new stage of human development (ll. 1055-58) attained after the renunciation of both the confining urge to tame and possess the world and the self-inhibiting intoxication with a vision of fantasy.[14]

In *Stella*, Goethe centers the theme in the traditional situation of a love triangle that is laden with potential conflict. Fernando, driven by a feeling of confinement, abandons his wife Cäcilie and their daughter Lucie. During his restless wanderings, he meets Stella and lives with her in blissful harmony on an isolated country estate. Overcome by renewed restiveness and a longing for his family, Fernando forsakes Stella. Returning to the estate three years later, he finds that the two women have consecrated their lives to the remembrance of their love. The reunion precipitates a test of their convictions. Whereas Fernando vacillates, both women renounce all purely personal desires. Cäcilie, deeply touched by Stella's love for Fernando, renounces her conjugal rights: "Your presence gives me new life, new strength . . . my love for you is not self-serving, is not the passion of a woman who would sacrifice everything to possess the desired object. Fernando, my heart is filled with tender emotions; they spring from the feeling of a wife who can renounce her love because she loves" (V. "Saal"; JA 11: 187). But Stella renounces not only her love but, like Phèdre in Racine's tragedy, sacrifices her life for the happiness of others. She blesses Fernando and Cäcilie and takes poison "everything for love,

and therefore now death!" (192).   With a final gesture of renunciation, she bids Lucie to go to her father and dies "alone" while
Fernando commits suicide. The thematic exposition, restatement, and
conclusion unfold in a series of love scenes designed for the fleeting
gestures and graceful movements normally associated with dance or
ballet. The dance of life and death sustains a brings an abstract idea to
life. Renunciation augments love. A new ethereal essence becomes
briefly apparent at the moment of death as figures transcend all personal aspirations.[15]

Representations of renunciation as the ultimate expression of allegiance are governed by a dual orientation. Individuals are challenged
to renounce their personal desires for an absolute. Ideals can range
from clearly attainable social reforms to the elusive vision of a just
government controlled by pure reason, and from personal reorientation to self-sacrifice. An objective can be concrete and as clearly
specified as Demeter's command to mortals to relinquish barbaric customs for the respect of all life in Schiller's "Das eleusische Fest" (ll.
61 ff., 201 ff.). The ideal can be hidden in the categorical imperative
"Conquer yourself!"[16] that crystallizes the reflections prompted by
the examination of a turbulent life: "our physical existence and our
social life, customs, habits, good sense and knowledge of the world,
philosophy, religion, indeed serendipitous events, everything calls out
to us that we must renounce."[17] To convey the spirit of renunciation,
authors resort to different techniques. Racine and Schiller tend to
crystallize the theme in specific scenes. Dryden, Wieland, and Goethe
seek to substantiate the elusive quality of renunciation through a development that probes and verifies the credibility of the decision to renounce personal aspirations. But whereas the ironic tone in Wieland's
Oberon undercuts the illusion of probability and the philosophical
discourse in Jacobi's writings strains its limits, the other authors either
locate the thematic resolution in the moments preceding death or integrate it into an outlook on social regeneration. Indeed, the classical
stance gravitates toward representations that align renunciation with
the thematic clusters surrounding models of excellence and the reform circle.

CHAPTER 6
Models of Excellence

Like the other themes in classical literature, the affirmation of life through exemplary conduct is rooted in the perception that individuals can freely develop their potential, can master their destiny, and are capable of striking a sensitive balance between self-interest and the concern of the community. As in other themes, the representation of exemplary conduct also raises serious questions. Can one individual's choice become a model for other figures or when filtered through the semblance of art, for the audience? What motivates other figures to accept or reject the model? The theme's intersection with renunciation and the reform circle provides an answer. When the model of excellence is central to the dynamic development of a dramatic or narrative structure, it forms the core of a future community of like-minded individuals, that is, of those figures who admire the exemplary act or figure and freely decide to model their conduct on the example. When the model of excellence is secondary or subordinate to other themes, especially those associated with possessive passion or violence, the exemplary behavior is assigned a secondary, subordinate, or even antithetical role in the dramatic or narrative structure.

The recurrence of the word "example" in classical literature signals the belief that both the crossroads decision and the act of renunciation of self-interest are not to be understood as isolated acts of the individual in the quest for self-insight and -development. Instead, they are to attract both the admiration and emulation of others. As others are drawn to the exemplary act, they join together in a circle composed of recipients, admirers, and participants. This circle may be small and closed, consisting of a few intimate associates. Or it may be expansive and open, reaching out to include an entire people, empire, or ideally, the whole human race. Whether the circle is intimate or expansive depends not so much on the individuals who respond to the exemplary deed or attitude as on the power of the exemplary individual to influence predominant patterns of conduct in society. The ability of the model to shape others' thoughts and actions extends from the limited range of such secondary figures as Curiace in Corneille's *Horace* or Junie in Racine's *Britannicus* to the potential to free a whole people, as Tell does in Schiller's *Wilhelm Tell* or to shape the course of an empire or a people given to Auguste in Corneille's *Cinna*, Titus in Racine's *Bérénice,* Iphigenie in Goethe's *Iphigenie auf Taurus,* and Tell in Schiller's *Wilhelm Tell.* Yet, other models like Racine's Iphigénie or Addison's Cato find themselves isolated from the main action at the end or voluntarily withdraw with their circle of associates as Guyomar does in Dryden's *The Indian Emperour.* In contrast, Goethe's Iphigenie in *Iphigenie auf Tauris* has a central function in forming and leading the circle of men around her into renouncing past patterns of violence and embracing a future focused on human potential and reconciliation.

The two motifs most frequently linked with the concept of "example" are the heart and open dialogue. Exemplary conduct depends upon the opportunity and ability of the "heart" to speak and to listen in order to be communicated from one individual to the next. An early instance occurs in Corneille's *Le Cid:*

> RODRIGUE: You know how a fistblow to the face
>   touches a man of heart.
> CHIMENE: Yes, I know what honor after such an
>   outrage . . .
> But also, in fulfilling [duty], you have taught me mine
> . . . .
> I will follow your example . . . .(III. iv. 875, 911-12)

The association between the heart, communication in the form of teaching, and exemplary conduct becomes more explicit in Livie's apotheosis of Auguste at the end of *Cinna:* " You have found the art of being master of hearts . . . / Your royal virtues will teach Rome too well . . . / And posterity, in all provinces,/ Will give your example to the most generous princes" (V. iii. 1764, 1767, 1773-74).[1] In *Polyeucte,* Corneille adds the element of surprise to the association of the two motifs with exemplary conduct.[2] Sévère confesses that he has heard "in amazement" with ears that he "can hardly trust," that when Polyeucte is about to die, in an act of supreme sacrifice of self-interest, he freely relinquishes his wife to Sévère, her former lover. Polyeucte's act is unique: "His resolution has so few equals . . ." (IV. v. 1315). Yet, despite Polyeucte's singular conduct, Pauline voices the demand that Sévère follow his example by appealing to Sévère's "great heart" (1362). By fulfilling Pauline's wish, Sévère sets himself apart from "any common soul" (IV. iv. 1403). Corneille thereby carefully prepares for the communication between hearts which will lead to the others' acceptance of Polyeucte as exemplary: "And I'll show you all . . . how one must live, / If you have a good enough heart to follow me" (V. ii. 1519-20). The successive conversions of Pauline and Félix and Sévère's conciliatory attitude toward the new sect testify to the ability of those with "listening hearts" to follow the example of a unique model. In doing so, they form a small admiring circle around Polyeucte's example which has the potential of expanding outward to include an ever-growing number of those embracing the new faith.

In Racine's tragedies, exemplary conduct connects with both the crossroads decision and renunciation of self-interest. Exemplary conduct has two significations: a negative one recalling heroic conduct extolled in the past that upon reflection appears tyrannical, possessive, and brutal (actions associated with the hand motif) and a positive one projecting a rupture with past patterns of behavior to embrace new, untried conduct.[3] Recurring at focal points in the dramatic structure, the "example" acts as a motivating force in determining the future course of action. The negative function of continuing past patterns of behavior is evident in Oreste's use of the concept in *Andromaque* to explain the soldiers' ferocious slaughter of Pyrrhus to Hermione: "But it was I whose ardor served them as an example" (V. iii. 1529), as well as to point out his peculiar role as the gods' object of fury: "I was born to serve as an example of your anger / To be an accomplished model of misfortune" (V. v. 1618-19). Oreste's crossroads decision to carry out Hermione's command to assassinate Pyrrhus has resulted in his transformation into a double example of both the initiator and victim of brutality. Through his actions and sufferings, the cruelty of the past Trojan War is guaranteed a continued future role.[4] In *Bajazet,* "example" is connected with power and the motif of the strong hand. Troops will continue the past mode of "[t]he example of a blind and base obedience" (I. i. 62) as long as Amurat remains victorious on the battlefield. Bajazet can find, according to Roxane, a "common example" in the history of the Sultans for repelling a "murderous hand" and thereby gaining the power of the throne (II. i. 443). Acomat adds that he would only be following "those most respected / By their example. . ." (II. iii. 624). When Roxane announces that the seraglio would become an "example" of obedience, once Bajazet has assumed power, it becomes clear that in this play the model of excellence consistently evokes both past modes of conduct and aggression – victimization patterns. No future circle of human relationships is built.[5]

Two past patterns of heroic and exemplary conduct confront the figures of Racine's *Britannicus:* that exhibited by the Domilius tyrants and that carried out by the "virtuous" Augustus. For the powerless Britannicus, only one course of action is feasible: the one based on virtue. "I believe that in accordance with my example [being] incapable of betrayal, / He [Néron] either hates with an open heart, or stops hating" (V. i. 1517-18). This limited vision of choices in conduct, synonymous with Britannicus' lack of self-development and -insight, reinforces his status as victim of Néron's aggression. For Néron, in contrast, the choice between the two models is crucial both for his self-development and for the dramatic structure. He can, according to Agrippine, "leave one day the model of a long-term virtue" (I. i. 44), or he can "end where Augustus began" (34). His immediate model is his own past "three years of virtue" (II. ii. 461-62). In turning away from this immediate past and adopting the brutality of the pre-Augustan past, Néron makes the conscious decision to break with the exemplary conduct of Augustus and to become instead, as Agrippine declares at the end of the play, a model for the conduct of tyrants: "And your name will appear, in the future race, / A cruel insult to the cruelest tyrants" (V. vi. 1691-92).[6] Exemplary conduct functions most positively in the development of the character

of Junie. Though powerless as an object retained and soon to be possessed by Néron, she not only remains as dedicated to sincerity and
the "open heart" as Britannicus, but also willing to use the deception
of "removed paths" to escape her potential possessor and embrace
Augustus' exemplary conduct. Like him, she will devote herself to the
gods[7] and the people and create the potential for a large circle of relationships based on service.

While the play's concluding focus on Néron's future aggressiveness makes clear that Junie's exemplary behavior is of minor importance structurally, the theme's positive motivating force moves into
center position in *Bérénice*. The theme's prominence is apparent in
Bérénice's final admonition to Antiochus: "Regulate your conduct
according to Titus' and mine. / . . . Farewell: let all three of us serve as
an example to the universe . . ." (V. vii. 1499, 1502). Likewise,
Antiochus opens the play's exposition by proclaiming himself an
"unfortunate example of a long constancy" in unrequited love (I. i.
44). Between these two examples, the first of a publicly announced
decision for renunciation, the second of personal pain, lies the transformation of the two lovers Bérénice and Titus from private individuals who have learned to speak and listen to their hearts (325-26) to
models whom "the universe is to imitate" in renouncing the private
sphere in favor of public interest.[8] Titus' crossroads decision to obey
the laws of Rome and send away Bérénice not only severs him from
the foreign queen but also makes him incomprehensible to her. For,
unlike her counterpart in Corneille's *Tite et Bérénice*, she has had no
other desire but "[a] sigh, a look, a word from your mouth . . ." (II.
iv. 576). From this perspective, Titus' exemplary resolution seems improbable and unworthy: "You count Bérénice's tears for nothing . . . /
Rome has its rights, Sir: don't you have yours? / Are its interests more
sacred than ours?" (IV. v. 1147, 1151-52). Titus' answer in the form
of the question, "do you think me unworthy / Of leaving an example
to posterity / Which can't be imitated without great effort?" (IV. v.
1172-74) heightens the distance between the two lovers, because it sets
him far above her. This distance is closed only through the recognition that the two hearts can continue to communicate with each other
in the very act of renouncing each other. Bérénice's declaration just
before the final appeal to Antiochus to join in their decision incorporates the heart motif before moving on to the exemplary deed: "My

heart is known to you . . . / You love me always. Your heart is troubled" (V. vii. 1475, 1482-83). The inclusion of Antiochus in her call for exemplary conduct provides structurally the basis for an expansive circle which actively contrasts with and substitutes for Antiochus' reference to his exemplary misfortune that began the play. By ending the play on the positive message of shaping not only their own but others' and perhaps all humanity's future, the exemplary deed has assumed a significant role in *Bérénice*. Titus' question during his earlier self-examination: "Has the universe seen its course changed?" (IV. iv. 1035) has the potential of being answered through the inherent expansiveness of exemplary behavior.

The expansive quality of a model renunciation of self-interest in favor of the community forms a central focus in Racine's *Mithridate*. Exhibiting and following exemplary behavior or ignoring it becomes a contrastive indicator of character. Thus Mithridate's two sons define their love for Monime according to whether they place their self-interest or her aspirations first:

> XIPHARES: I don't know the secret sentiments of her
> heart
> But I would submit to them without hoping anything .
> . . . .
> PHARNACE: Your example is not a rule for me.
> XIPHARES: Nevertheless in this place I know no one
> Who should not imitate the example that I give.
>   (I. v. 318-19; 322-24)

These words become prophetic: Xipharès' example moves Mithridate from initial self-aggrandizement to self-sacrifice in order to liberate others. As he becomes aware that Xipharès "[t]o all other interests [prefers] his duty" to risk his life in order to protect his father (II. iii. 470), Mithridate grows not only in admiration of his son but also in imitating him. Battling Rome now becomes a means of service to the oppressed as well as his path to glory: "I have avenged the universe as best as I could" (V. v. 1653). This realignment, together with Mithridate's surrender of Monime to Xipharès, establishes the basis for the model conduct to be imitated by his survivors: "Let's unite our sorrows / And throughout the universe let us search for him avengers" (1697-98).[9]

The final appeal to a universe that incorporates the pure essence of an exemplary act recurs in Racine's *Iphigénie* and Addison's *Cato*. In agreeing to become the "obedient victim" of the gods, Iphigénie has, according to Agamemnon, the opportunity to exemplify the full human potential in contrast to the brutality of the gods: "Show, in expiring, whose child you are:/ Make those gods blush who have condemned you" (IV. iv. 1245-46). Though it is Eriphile who actually fulfills Agamemnon's command in her bold self-execution that sheds "[t]he blood of those heroes from whom you [Calchas] would have me descend," Iphigénie alone recognizes the exemplary deed of Eriphile's defiance by mourning her.[10] Because of this shift in focus from Agamemnon to Iphigénie to Eriphile in carrying out the exemplary act, the circle built by it is less definite and more restricted than in *Bérénice*. For although the Greeks are its beneficiaries, the joy with which they hasten to their ships leaves no time for acknowledging the sacrifice that made their departure possible. Only Iphigénie possesses the insight to make the connection between the sacrifice and the future of the Greek community. Phrased in the terms of the fertility – sterility motif sequence, her analysis relates the renunciation of her individual life with the building of the community's future.[11]

> Think, Sir, think of these harvests of glory
> Which victory presents to your brave hands.
> This so glorious field to which you all aspire,
> If my blood doesn't bedew it, is sterile for you.
> . . . .
> I hope that at least a happy future
> Will join my memory with your immortal deeds.
> (V. ii. 1541-44; 1559-60)

In Addison's *Cato,* in addition to linking self-renunciation with the communal well-being, the exemplary personality also serves to define character. Cato's decision for suicide parallels Iphigénie's willingness to become the sacrificial victim. Like her, he grows from initial horror to acceptance and defense of the exemplary deed: "This world was made for Caesar. / I'm weary of conjectures:—this must end them. . . . / The righteous gods . . . / Will succor Cato and preserve his children" (V. i.). But whereas the Greeks in Racine's *Iphigénie* take no time to acknowledge the human sacrifice for them, Cato's beneficiaries form a circle ready to follow his directive of using his corpse for their preservation:

> But let us bear this awful corpse to Caesar
> And lay it in his sight, that it may stand
> A fence betwixt us and the victor's wrath:
> Cato, though dead, shall still protect his friends.
>
> (V. i.)[12]

Moreover, just as Iphigénie's acceptance of her sacrifice divides the figures into two camps of proponents and opponents of her sacrifice, so Cato's model of true Roman virtues attracts some and repels others among his followers. Thus, while Syphax argues against the "civilizing arts" as exemplified by Cato as unnatural, Juba praises Cato's model of the Roman soul "bent on higher views / To civilize the rude, unpolish'd world . . . / To make men mild, and sociable to man . . ." (I. i.). Syphax's subsequent meeting and attempted abduction of Cato's daughter form the antithesis of Juba's careful modelling of his behavior on Cato's: "With how much care he forms himself to glory,/ And breaks the fierceness of his native temper, / To copy out our father's bright example" (I. i.).

In addition to linking self-development with the future of the community, the model of excellence can serve to divide the present community into those who reject self-renunciation and those who emulate it. If the dramatic interest focuses on the former group, the model links the present with the past patterns of aggressiveness and possessiveness and limits the potential of character development to repetition of past patterns of aggression and brutality. If, instead, the focus is on the circle of admirers and imitators of the exemplary act of self-sacrifice, the present becomes linked with a future that promises a more humane form of existence than the past could offer.

References to the exemplary in Goethe's writings strongly suggest that he distinguishes between the conception of an abstract essence and its manifestation in existence. The exemplary is dependent on the idea of perfection which can be objectified in the semblance of artistic creations. The exemplary in any style can only be attained if a work appears free from all external designations or functions such as to elucidate values or create the semblance of historical truth. Moreover, it should appear to be free from artificially imposed rules or formal restrictions passed on by tradition and transcend the purely individualistic manner of an artist. Freed from all heterogenous restrictions, the work of art conveys the idea of freedom to the observer.[13] The representation of human perfection, however, is contingent on the concrete immediacy of figures whose character traits, attitudes, and actions resemble those encountered among individuals in real life and their horizon of expectations. In addition, exemplary conduct in individuals is rarely disinterested but motivated instead by concern for others.

Goethe's view of individuals and the sociopolitical institutions that they have created during the course of history is governed partially by his scientific studies and partially by his desire for reform. It is based on the premise that individuals are simultaneously free and restricted. They can develop their potential or fall victim to enslavement. They live in imperfection and yearn for perfection. They are tied to earth by their sensuous nature and reflect upon ideals of pure essence. This apparent contradiction is an essential element of existence and a manifestation of the dynamic interrelation of polar forces that hold sway over nature.[14] Nature continuously builds and destroys. But the unremitting action between opposing forces not only shapes, reshapes, and retains basic substances but also brings forth a progressive augmentation and change of forms. Individuals partake of the dynamic interplay. They experience stasis and change, the finite and infinite. But the rhythm of action, reflection, and renewed action enhances the process of thinking itself. Hence, polarity and enhancement are principles that coexist and complement each other. The exemplary can therefore only be grasped as an approximation in the process of action and continuous reflection. "The exemplary in its unique existence must transcend it, it must become something else, something incomparable."[15] What appears separable in contemplation is inseparable in existence. The pure essence can only be represented in approximations on stages of development that mirror human potential.

Two plays, Goethe's *Iphigenie auf Tauris* and Schiller's *Wilhelm Tell*, capture succinctly the characteristics of development and the often elusive, subtle changes that identify an augmented level of self-perception and knowledge of the world. Both plays counter the call for revolutionary political reform that reverberates throughout the period with an appeal to reason and a vision of radical change through spiritual rebirth. Both are parable plays that center on moral dilemmas: Can individuals remain true to themselves, preserve their personal integrity and aspire toward exemplary action when they initiate sociopolitical change, or will they be forced to accept compromise, renounce their ideals, and seek accommodation in a world of strife, corruption, and deception?

By focusing on Iphigenie's development from doubt to inner certainty and from faith in her vision of a peaceful world to bold action, Goethe's play seems to crystallize a deceptively simple story. Iphigenie's humanity triumphs in a potentially deadly conflict. King Thoas is persuaded by her conduct to accept a new standard for human relations. Thematic analysis indicates that the conciliatory resolution is embedded in a dual perspective that affirms basic contradictions in life. Individual resolution and the desire for truth coexist with weakness, error, and changing reorientation. By juxtaposing an ideal of human potential and a factual assessment of historically and self-imposed restrictions, the play solidifies the intuition of Iphigenie and the destiny of Orest. With Iphigenie, it looks ahead to salvation; with Orest it sustains the endurance of confusion.[16]

Goethe intensifies Racine's attention to essential individual reorientation that is associated with the development of human potential. As a result, the familiar motif patterns are charged with additional signification through new thematic alignments. The motifs in *Iphigenie auf Tauris* initiate a series of contrasting and complementary relations that recur at critical moments in the sequence of events and establish a grid of references that clarify the thematic constellation. The setting, the sacred grove before Diana's temple, links the earth to a vertical dimension through the symbolic presence of the goddess whose commands are experienced as real. The reports of past and present conflicts introduce a panoramic, horizontal view of a world torn by personal and collective strife. The monologues and dialogues reveal conflicting patterns in the orientation of the figures who seek to justify their actions by invoking the commands of the gods and also by appealing to the "inexorable demands" of life.

A series of symmetrically arranged motifs, principally heart / hand, dialogue / monologue / silence, and order / disorder, contrast the divine and the secular. The motifs figure prominently in the thematic constellation of freedom / confinement – cooperation / aggression that serves as outer parameter for the representation of self-realization.

When the play opens, Iphigenie seems to stand at the periphery of human activity. She has been uprooted from her family and country, has dedicated herself to the service of Diana, but longs to return home. The ensuing scenes propel her to the center of action, reveal that her perception of physical and spiritual isolation was mistaken, and show her development from a person capable of love to one who commits her affection to the effort of inspiring others with her vision of a purified society. First, Iphigenie is stunned by the marriage proposal of King Thoas who seeks to enforce his will by threatening to resume human sacrifice, thereby invalidating Iphigenie's peaceful dominance over brutal Taurian customs. Next, she is overwhelmed by the arrival of Pylades and her brother. Orest seeks delivery from the Furies who have pursued him relentlessly since his matricide. Charged by Apollo to return his sister to Greece, Orest fails to discern the command's ambivalence. He looks for the sacred statue of Apollo's sister Diana and is prepared to risk everything for the success of his quest. Suddenly, Iphigenie is confronted by choices that appear sensible and reasonable under the circumstances but are unfeasible because each course of action threatens to destroy her personal integrity. The necessity to save her brother's life coupled with the unexpected prospect of returning home and the king's unreasonable demand encourage the escape from Tauris. The desire for truth deters a betrayal of Thoas. Similarly, Orest and Pylades must choose between persuading Iphigenie of the need to deceive Thoas or relinquishing their mission when success is immanent. And Thoas can either enforce his will or renounce all personal desires.

The figures' initial decisions, reconsiderations, and subsequent resolve highlight two contradictory assessments of existence. Life could be determined by custom, environment, and history. Individuals are shaped by foreordained patterns. Since the whims of the gods, chance, or fate control the outcome of all endeavors, existence is fated, and individuals may suffer but are absolved from the responsibility of their actions. The alternate view of life insists that persons are fully accountable for all decisions. They should therefore not resort to the rationalization that the gods or fate decree afflictions or punish generations for the offenses of ancestors. Individuals can master their own destiny. The conflicting views are brought into sharp focus through Iphigenie's perception of the gods, her self-awareness, and her stance toward others. She had been saved by divine intervention at the moment she was to be sacrificed and has dedicated her service as priestess to the purification of Diana's image among the Taurians. Still, she is deeply troubled: she "submits to a high will," does "not argue with the gods," but feels that she is held "in sacred bonds of slavery," and has not "consigned her life freely" to the service of Diana (I. i. 8, 23, 34, 38). She serves with mute reluctance. The king's message, conveyed by Arkas, deepens her apprehension and doubt. Again, circumstances beyond her control seem to dictate her decisions. Arkas reminds her of the duty and mission to guide the Taurians toward a higher plane of civilization. The Taurians stand at the threshold between barbaric customs and a new social order. Iphigenie's gentle influence and "soft persuasion" have brightened the king's somber mind, halted the tradition of human sacrifice, and prepared the people for a humane form of existence. To yield to the king's wish guarantees the successful continuation of efforts on behalf of the people but also entails the loss of personal freedom. To refuse will precipitate the community's relapse into mythic beliefs and savage customs.

When Thoas confronts Iphigenie directly, she seeks to persuade him to renounce his desires in favor of communal interests. She opens her heart, speaks truthfully, but fails to move him. The dialogue breaks down. When she speaks with him, he only hears the "No." However, Iphigenie also asserts her independence, rejects his attempts to force her into submission, and proudly insists on equality by revealing that she is Agamemnon's daughter. The account of her ancestors has multiple functions. Iphigenie sees herself at that moment as a descendant in the noble lineage from the house of Atreus. She recounts the archetypal story of fated existence. Thereupon Thoas can raise the critical objection that perhaps the descendants of Tantalus were not cursed but guilty of their own transgressions (I. iii. 327). The history of the house of Atreus chronicles a recurring pattern of aggression, arrogant self-assertion, passion, hubris, transgression of moral codes, and destruction. Everyone in the chain feels that the events were foreordained by the gods. All share in the spirit of denouncing the gods and holding them responsible for their own conduct. Moreover, as the play unfolds, Orest likewise concludes that the gods have "chosen him as butcher, as murderer" of his "revered mother" (II. i. 707-08). The conspicuous combination of self-assertion and rejection of responsibility is highlighted again when Iphigenie recalls the ancient "Song of the Parcae" at the moment of gravest doubt in her vision of a new order of life (IV. v. 1726-66). However, after chanting the song she trusts the purified divine "image in her soul" and repudiates the fatalistic, malignant ancestral spirit. Her subsequent action proves that she rejects any allegiance to the communal creation of a myth that justifies human weakness by defining the conditions of life through a distorted picture of the gods.

The horizon of a new humane order becomes perceptible through the awareness of a higher reality and the attitudes toward others expressed by Thoas, Pylades, and Orest. Thoas is ready to learn, to develop, and to revise his views. Lost in his affection for Iphigenie, he resorts to traditional patterns of behavior. But Iphigenie's extraordinary truthfulness and truly exemplary conduct now convince him that her vision is viable. He renounces his personal desires and embraces the new order of cooperation (V. vi. 2174). Pylades, astute and cunning, ready for compromise when it serves his plans, seeks to steer a steady course in the cross-currents of "fate." He seizes opportune moments, counsels Iphigenie that personal escape and rescue cancel other obligations and that gratitude and the desire to retain a "pure heart" are emotions ill suited for worldly success. "Life teaches us to be less strict with ourselves and others . . . / Humanity is formed so wondrously; / So various are its knots and interweavings / That no one can remain pure and forthright" (IV. vi. 1653-59). His perception of the gods corresponds to his assessment of reality. The divine will can be turned to one's own advantage. The gods bless those who succeed; they ignore those who fail (II. i. 713-17; IV. iv. 1604-06). Identified with the hand reaching for success, Pylades is tethered by deception and bows to the "iron hand of necessity" that remains inscrutable.

The motif of the bloody hand that exposes the destructive tendencies in society is firmly linked with Orest, haunted by the Furies since he murdered his mother. His quest for Diana's statue is essentially a search for purification. Yet, he still believes that the matricide was destined and blindly trusts a promise of redemption that appears to demand courage but no change in his beliefs. He is healed from his tormenting visions by the presence of his sister. He also seems to reach a new plane of self-insight when he falls into a trance that transports him to the realm of his dead ancestors. He has a vision of purified humanity. Reconciliation, love, and peaceful coexistence have obliterated aggression, hate, and strife. The scene is tempered, however, by the continued torment of Tantalus, whose presence serves as a warning to human hubris (III. ii. 1258-1309). Orest awakens refreshed. The Furies have left. His outlook on life has changed. His appearance indicates that he has been rejuvenated by the presence of his sister and the visionary experience in his dream. But has he intuitively reached a new plane of self-insight? Orest's subsequent actions, especially his recourse to armed battle and the wish to prove his nobility in combat (V. v., vi.) suggest that the dream's vision has receded into his subconsciousness. Orest has reached a stage that promises future development. Conscious reflection, renewed error, and dedication to continued efforts to make Iphigenie's conduct the basis for lasting reform still lie before him.

Iphigenie achieves the breakthrough to a new formulation of human interrelations and the individual's appreciation of the divine. She struggles with a revolutionary change of attitudes that demands the obliteration of the old self. The play translates this willingness to speed toward a new light by answering the summons to depart from the permanence of past and present into acknowledging Iphigenie's decision to remain true to her vision at the risk of her freedom and her brother's life. She rejects the horrors of the past and the discord of the day as temporary way-stations on the road to an enlightened existence. She realizes that both the deceptive power play of the hand and the accommodation with changing circumstances in life enslave the individual. She trusts her understanding of the gods. They embody visions of society and are therefore in a process of continuous becoming. They are anchored in time and eternity. They mirror the expansion and contraction on earth but also reflect the hope for absolute purity. Convinced that all can hear the voice of truth in their heart, Iphigenie casts off the yoke of necessity and appeals to Thoas not only to accept her ideal but also to incorporate it into his action. Thoas hears "the voice of truth and humanity." He frees himself from personal limitations: his "farewell" confirms that he is prepared to enter into a constructive dialogue with the other. His stance bears witness to the classical view that the relations of individuals to the environment are continuous, reciprocal, and indissoluble. Moreover, self-knowledge gained through self-development can initiate social change.

The play's organization, the interrelations of motifs, and the diversity of individual responses and solutions to the central conflict are consistent with this view. However, despite its clarity in organization, the play conceals information in a complex system of allusions that permits Goethe to affirm contradictions. Allusions to the basic crisis indicate that it is precipitated by a clash between divergent perceptions of individual freedom and social responsibility. The chain of existence represented in the tales of the house of Atreus recounted by Iphigenie and Orest at critical junctures displays several recurring characteristics. Tantalus and the gods live together peacefully. He is admired for his knowledge that is unsurpassed on earth. The gods seek his advice. To test the limits of this capacity to know, Tantalus has his son killed and served at a banquet in their honor. Crime, punishment, and the ensuing view of the world suggest a pattern that is glossed and expanded in the play. To be free and godlike, Tantalus asserts his autonomy. His plan serves three purposes. By testing the gods he hopes to prove their ignorance and depose them through the power of his mind. By destroying his son, he removes a possible future challenge to his rule. By sacrificing what should be closest to his heart, he includes in his design a ritual of appeasement that might save him if he miscalculated the chances for success. Tantalus is punished and forced into obedience.

The motifs in the play assigned to the myth are: will to power / failure; self-assertion – illusory freedom / enslavement; heart / bloody hand. The descendants interpret personal guilt as a curse of the gods, hence unavoidable. The immortals are viewed as capricious. They "destine manifold confusion," "use power as they may see fit," exalt some, destroy others. The ritual of sacrifice is intended to pacify them, but the "clouds rising" from below drift away like "thin odor." Some communities continue to offer their own blood relations (Iphigenie); others like the Taurians sacrifice strangers. The bloody hand triumphs over the heart. As the gods recede further into the distance, fate begins to dominate the thinking on earth. The belief in a foreordained existence absolves individuals from responsibility for their actions. The immortals no longer represent visions of order but reflect the human disorder. The original prohibition of killing is misunderstood. Instead, aggression is institutionalized in continued warfare that annihilates the youth of the land (I. ii. 131-32, 157; V. vi. 2069-75). Minstrels remain silent about "the tears shed in a thousand days and nights when a silent soul consumes itself in vain" (V. vi. 2071-74).

In *Iphigenie*, this pattern collides with the perception of a new mode of existence. By aligning personality structure and social awareness, Goethe focuses on the consciousness of the developing self and the individual who perceives the self as embodiment of timeless human emotions. The developmental personality evolves, is in a process of change, listens to the faint voice of the immortals, trusts in the vision of reform, seeks cooperation, and confronts violence with a new truth perceived by the heart. All experience is cumulative and provides for new insights. The mental state of those who perceive their character traits and social attitudes as timeless is governed by the adherence to recurring patterns. Historically developed customs become laws not to be broken. The old disorder becomes permanent and is the order of the day. A chain of recurring events creates the illusion that experience is repetitive.

The play alludes to three solutions to the crisis in conflicting values. They are associated with the development of Orest, Thoas, and Iphigenie herself. Orest escapes into a dream, receives the vision of potential human relations as a gift from the healing power of nature, accepts Iphigenie's blessing and purification, and rationalizes the events by reinterpreting Apollo's command. By substituting Iphigenie for Diana's statue, he persists in the old pattern. By replacing the artistic symbolic form with the living form, he transfers value into life but remains bound to the world. The hand, though purified, reaches for success. Thoas learns and redefines the situation. He renounces his passion, accepts friendship as a sign of love, and is persuaded by Iphigenie's truthfulness to adopt her view of social order.

Iphigenie completely repudiates the traditional pattern. Placed into an incomparable situation, she masters existential anxiety, adheres to absolute truth, becomes free, and through her action, exemplary. "What is called great? / What lifts to awe the soul of the narrator? What is told forever? / Only what the bravest dared though success seemed inconceivable" (V. iii. 1895-98). Iphigenie clarifies the human perception of the immortals and through a dialogue breathes new life into their substance. In her view, truth becomes the very essence of any constructive dialogue. The gods become dynamic and believable when individual action begins to approximate what humanity sees in them. Goethe articulates the same belief in "Das Göttliche": "We honor / The immortals / As if they were human. / Achieve in the wide realm/ What the best among us/ Accomplishes or aspires to do." To live up to this expectation, Iphigenie renounces deception and violence and raises cooperation and truth to universal categories. By holding out the promise that a chiliastic vision can be attained through action and by simultaneously enunciating conflicting solutions to the crisis, the play sustains contradictions in life. It affirms a dynamic process of becoming that advances from a circular pattern through stages of hesitation, doubt, and faith on to a spiral toward spiritual rebirth.

The state of emergency represented in *Wilhelm Tell* is identical to the crisis that demands a decision from Iphigenie. However, by linking a concrete political situation with the issue of individual development, Schiller's play interweaves two primary thematic considerations. The theme of righting political injustice and the theme of self-realization are connected through the common struggle for freedom, the reciprocal relations between Tell and the Swiss people, and a sharply defined central figure of oppression, the burgrave Geßler.[17] Both themes call forth complex associations, require different justifications for action, and influence the selection and organization of motifs. In addition, the juxtaposition of tyrannicide and exemplary conduct raises questions of the right to resistance, the recourse to violent action, and the essence of any exemplary behavior. Motifs and secondary themes are positioned in contrast patterns. Some that serve as attributes of figures are reversed during the play's sequential action which opens with moves by the bailiffs who hold the power in their hand and closes with a vision of peaceful coexistence achieved through efforts of the "helping hand."

By reducing a wide range of emotions and a maze of social, political, and economic conditions to lucid contrasts, the motifs advance the action and aid in representing tyranny's effect upon the community. Successive restatement, development, and inversion of motifs accompany the continuous evaluation of the condition that would legitimize not only the right to resistance but also the use of force in the struggle against oppression. The dominant motif clusters and their alignment focus on the extraordinary crisis affecting single individuals and the population as a whole. The thematic structure is supported by primary patterns that include both abstract concepts and concrete images: order – heaven, natural order / disorder on earth; freedom / suppression; justice / injustice; aggression / cooperation; tyrannicide – (Tell eliminates Geßler) / murder – (Johannes von Schwaben kills the emperor); violent hand – aggression by bailiffs, soldiers, servants / helping hand – communal effort: hands raised to the stars while swearing the new oath of allegiance to the land; individual struggle: Tell; hunter – bailiffs / hunted – population; fugitive / shelter. The raising of the "hat of Austria" in the market square that is designed to destroy the dignity of the people precipitates Tell's arrest and hastens the end of Austrian rule. The recurring pictorial contrasts of sunlit landscapes and storms or rising fog underscore the clash between population and oppressors. References to storm and fire show the concern for uncontrollable forces unleashed by a rebellion. The most significant reversals and realignments of motifs that add new signification address the conflict's resolution: legality - power / obedience of the people – passive suffering; revolution / adherence to new order; helping hand resorts to violence but seeks to retain purity; Geßler pursues and traps Tell who escapes, then stalks and kills him. The sentient heart and the helping hand become indivisible when Tell strikes down the tyrant after careful consideration.

In a series of fast-paced opening scenes, Schiller portrays the oppression of the land. Imperial governors try to impose Austrian rule upon the Swiss people who recognize the emperor as ruler but refuse to be incorporated in the Austrian monarchy. To crush the freedom-loving spirit, the bailiffs resort to terror. No one is safe from their arbitrary interpretation of the laws and their brutality. The curtain opens on a sunny alpine scene, filled with melodic sound of cowbells and the songs of a fisher boy, a shepherd, and a hunter. The tranquility is short-lived. The threat of a thunderstorm appears and is immediately related by Ruodi to the menacing political situation (I. i. 37, 41). While the animals and their keepers seek shelter from the coming storm, the hunted fugitive Baumgarten enters and pleads to be ferried over the story lake in order to escape certain death from the pursuing horsemen. He has defended his wife and the sanctity of his home by killing the provincial governor Wolfenschießen with an axe (I. i. 81-

97). As Ruodi asserts that it is impossible to cross the lake, Tell, armed with his bow, enters and extends his "helping hand." He steers the boat in the raging elements to safety whereas Seppi loses his herd and Kuoni his shelter when the furious horsemen attack the animals and burn down the hut (I. i. 175-84). The ensuing scenes show the ruthless suppression of workers who must construct a fortress, capture the moment when the hat is raised on a pole in the town square with the proclamation that all men must salute it with bent knee and bowed head or forfeit home and life (I. iii.), and inform the audience that Melchthal's father has been blinded as reprisal for his son's refusal to surrender his oxen (I. iv.).

By the end of the first act, it is obvious that mutual assistance, self-defense, and the use of arms will be the only way for the Swiss to free themselves. Calls for action are interspersed by frequent appeals to heaven and counsel for moderation (ll. 87, 190-95, 302-11, 400, 469-72, 660 ff., 704, 2095). The apprehension that armed resistance could be construed as insurgence against the principles of law that form the basis of all government is allayed after the conspirators ascertain beyond doubt that the despotic dominion of the bailiffs has perverted the state. The tyrannical acts are designed to destroy the community's foundation and constitute a direct attack against the natural order. They are in essence the exact opposite of visions of exemplary conduct. Indeed, obeisance to the hat is paramount to a transgression of Christian morality: only God is supreme; an absolute obedience to worldly rulers does not exist. After reflecting upon their former peaceful existence and the present state of emergency, the people raise their hands to the stars and swear in the presence of God in "truth, in judgment, and in righteousness" (Jer. 4:2; II. iii.) an oath of communal cooperation. They will defend their "inalienable human rights." They renounce their allegiance to the regime since even passive acquiescence in its rule supports injustice and harms the community. With sword in hand, they will restrain themselves, forego any thought of revenge, but only secure their freedom and restore justice.

The decision of the people aligns restraint thematically with the exemplary. Tell's personal struggle, his recognition that it reflects a common concern, and his judgment that he must act on behalf of communal interest links the stages of his growing insight to the possibility of transforming resistance into exemplary action. In accordance with the thematic focus Geßler is represented as the archetype of forces denying the possibility of individual perfection. Though Tell is immediately introduced as a person ready to assist anyone in need, he remains aloof from the common planning. Despite his ever-present crossbow, he opposes the use of weapons as a means of revolt. "Now the only course of action is patience and silence . . . / Whoever is peaceful will be left in peace" (I. iii. 420, 427). He dislikes deliberations, relies on his own strength—the "strong is most powerful *alone*"(I. iii. 437)—but will serve when the time is ready: "I can neither reflect nor slowly choose, / I will come if you need me for definite action" (442-3). Courageous yet gentle, Tell like Egmont intuitively affirms the freedom of existence. In Geßler's eyes he typifies the spirit of the people. To defeat the population, Geßler must subdue Tell. Moreover, to humble him in public will guarantee the surrender of the land. Hence, the confrontation of Geßler with Tell that culminates in the apparently capricious order that Tell shoot an apple from his son's head is firmly grounded in Geßler's planned strategy to eradicate any vision of individual or social perfection.

The encounter pits the statesman who only recognizes his autonomous will against the dreamer whose vision of freedom is embedded in respect for the dignity of life. Two irreconcilable modes of existence vie for dominance. Geßler claims to serve his monarch but similar to Alba in Goethe's *Egmont* places himself above all principles of government. He recognizes only the dictates of his own will and by abrogating the right to peaceful existence, becomes the enemy of life. He is struck by Tell's arrow while threatening to ride over a pleading woman and in the midst of announcing the future order: "I am still much too lenient ruling these people . . . I pledge, / I will break the unyielding attitudes, / That brazen spirit of freedom / I will proclaim a new law—I will—" (IV. iii. 2778-85).

Geßler's incommensurable demand, truly staggering through the juxtaposition of Tell's inner turmoil and his son's childish confidence, initiates the process in Tell's coming of age that culminates in an exemplary action on behalf of society. Confronted with Geßler's command to shoot the apple from Walter's head, Tell is suddenly defenseless and overwhelmed by emotions. Geßler's statements that accompany Tell's turmoil reveal his delight in using unchecked power. More importantly, they illuminate the process of reorientation that changes

Tell's view of life, his self-perception, and subsequent conduct. He is uprooted and forced to reflect consciously upon the challenge to master his destiny. Tell apologizes for his failure to salute the hat, pleads for lenience, and finally offers his life. Geßler rejects the appeals and declares that Walter will also die if his father refuses to shoot. He studies Tell:

> You are suddenly so thoughtful,
> I was told you are a dreamer,
> Detached from the ways of others.
> . . . .
> Another person would reflect—*You* close your eyes
> And risk courageously the bold venture.
>
> (III. iii. 1902-08)

Rejecting the appeals from the assembled people and his own entourage, he continues by asserting that he can easily kill Tell but is really offering him self-determination:

> The person forced to master his destiny
> Cannot rail against a harsh sentence.
> . . . .
> The true master
> Is sure of his art at anytime.
> His heart does not intrude on the hand
> Nor interfere with the eye. (III. iii. 1933-41)

Emphatically he declares that Tell's "fate" is in his own "hand" and finally gives a clue to the essence of his plan:

> I don't seek your life,
> I demand the shot.
> You can do everything, Tell, you never despair,
> You handle the boat's rudder as well as the bow,
> You don't fear storms when it is time to save someone,
> Now, rescuer, rescue yourself—you rescue everyone.
>
> (III. iii. 1985-89)

In obeying Geßler's command, Tell acts, saves his son's life, but forfeits his freedom. Once he has regained his freedom by escaping the boat taking him to prison, Tell reaches his crossroads decision, as he awaits Geßler on the road leading to the fortress. When Tell accounts at this moment for his life and considers the future of his community, he knows that neither nature nor God will directly intervene in human affairs (IV. i. 2170 ff.). He reflects on the communal life of the past, considers his decision to kill the tyrant, sits down and looks at the path that he now sees as the great highway of life traveled by the wanderer, merchant, pilgrim, monk, robber, and minstrel (IV. iii. 2560-2650). He realizes "every road leads to the end of the world," leads to the marker of the universe. He matures and understands that civilized existence cannot endure unless the evil threatening its foundation is eliminated by force. The cornerstone of the universe is not death but a deep respect for life that forms the basis of all social organization. This insight governs his action. Mind, heart, and hand become indivisible. Tell, who obeyed throughout the life the "hunter's rule"—stalk carefully, never kill for pleasure, never in anger—shoots Geßler without hesitation, skillfully, and unheroically. Returning home, he reassures his wife, who momentarily hesitates to take his hand, that he "may raise it freely to heaven" (V. ii. 3145). The Parricide scenes that immediately follow and contrast Tell's action with a regicide prompted by a personally experienced injustice, reinforce the view that Tell's resistance was exemplary because it restored nature's order (V. ii. 3181-84).

The play's resolution fuses the theme of righting injustice and the theme of individual self-development. The common effort not only restores the communal organization, perceived as the natural order, but also gives direction to the search for freedom. The lands' nobility is accepted in the alliance; Attinghausen envisions a new society of equals; and Rudenz frees his serfs. Unity prevails. Tell's accomplishment becomes a measure of possible exemplary conduct. He reaches a plane of consciousness that permits responsible action in the interest of the community. Thus, the play balances individual rights and the prerogatives of society. The true order of the future will be based on institutions that guarantee basic rights and thereby enable individuals to develop their potential freely. The individual must be worthy of this trust, respect the dignity of life, and recognize an obligation toward the community.

The theme of exemplary conduct provides the connecting link between the individual and others. It is based on the classical view that all humans have both the capability and freedom to determine their development and the desire to emulate those who have freely decided to reject traditional patterns of behavior for a vision that augments and expands the freedom of others and the community at large.

CHAPTER 7

The Reform Circle: The Limited Spiral. Individual and Community

Forming a Circle of Friends Within Social Limitations

Besides varying the position of the models of excellence from central to subordinate, and from protagonist to antagonist, classical texts also show variations in the social environment in which the exemplary conduct takes place. If the figure embodying the model of excellence is an emperor who begins a new reign like Titus in Racine's *Bérénice,* it is clear that this figure has the power to shape the sociopolitical environment. If the exemplary conduct of a less powerful figure can persuade the dominant figures who set the agenda for their society, they can influence the sociopolitical environment indirectly, as in Goethe's *Iphigenie auf Tauris.* But if those in power either reject or are ignorant of the model of excellence, then its influence on the sociopolitical environment remains much more limited.

Thus, the grand centrifugal spiral envisioned by Corneille, Racine, and Addison that begins with an individual's exemplary deed and ends with the universe offers only one pattern for structuring classical themes and motifs. Other classical writers sought to place the themes and motifs within the limitations set by the reality of a society that values individual growth and insight far less than the assertion of power, prestige, and possessiveness. In such a world, the building of an expansive circle of like-minded individuals is restricted to the less assertive characters whose ability to let their hearts speak and listen contrasts with the dominant characters who embody the social values of power and possessiveness. The motif sequences of sentient heart / aggressive hand and constructive dialogue / verbal confrontation serve to distinguish textually between the two types of characters. Those building true relationships that move forward and outward reflect the sentient heart and open dialogue in their discourse, while those interested in acquiring riches and power over others practice the actions of the aggressive hand and confrontational discourse.

That the figures valuing power and possessiveness dominate those who long to build a mutually supportive community is reflected in the explicit negation of exemplary conduct in Dryden's heroic tragedies and Molière's comedies.[1] Though Acacis's gentleness and concern for others are recognized as exemplary by the dominant figures in Dryden's *The Indian Queen* (YNCA: "I must myself thy Honors Rival make" I. i. 143; MONTEZUMA: "How great a proof of virtue have you shown" II. iii. 36), his revelation of his longing to possess Orazia suddenly restricts his ensuing renunciation of life to a non-exemplary, individualistic framework. When Almeria in *The Indian Emperour* declares that exemplary conduct would require that Cydaria die to honor her deceased father, Cydaria responds: "Do you dye first, and shew me then the way" (V. ii. 296). Although Almeria fulfills this request by fatally stabbing herself after she has wounded Cydaria, Cydaria rejects the model in favor of love and life. The ensuing community founded by her union with Cortez is thus based on a rejection of exemplary self-sacrifice, which contrasts with Guyomar's renunciation of possessiveness. While Aureng-Zebe's devotion to his father at first fulfills Indamora's demand that he "Lose not the Honour, / But stand the blameless pattern of a son" (*Aureng-Zebe* I. i.), he soon manifests a quite unexemplary hostility toward his father's possessive attitude toward Indamora and a stubborn possessiveness of his own. The one behavior that could be termed exemplary, Melesinda's self-sacrifice, is rejected as absurd by the majority of the community.

The rejection of exemplary behavior also forms a consistent textual pattern in Molière's comedies. In *L'Ecole des maris*, for example,

Isabelle concedes to Léonor that "Your example condemns such an outburst" (III. ix. 1081) but defends her "shameful strategy" of plotting to deceive her old mentor and suitor Sganarelle as her only recourse as Sganarelle's virtual prisoner. Although Arnolphe in *L'Ecole des femmes* (II. iv. 450) recalls the "example" of the ancient Greeks to repeat the alphabet in order to calm one's anger, he is unable to follow their model to control his rage. Don Elvire warns Don Juan in vain in *Don Juan ou le festin de Pierre* (IV. ix.) against becoming a "grievous example for the justice of Heaven." Likewise futile is Cléante's attempt in *Le Tartuffe* (I. iv. 384-86) to persuade Oronte of Tartuffe's hypocrisy by citing "glorious examples" of true piety. The false "reconciliation" between Jupiter and Alcmène prompts Amphitryon's confused valet Sosie to ask his wife "that according to their example / We make a bit of peace between us" (*Amphitryon* II. vii. 1429-30). In *Les Femmes savantes* (I. i. 77-80), Henriette rejects Armande's demand that she aspire to their mother's "exemplary" cultivation of the intellectual life. The negativeness of Clitandre's argument that "famous examples [of science making fools] are not lacking" is continued by Trissotin's double negation: "You could cite some that are hardly conclusive . . . / As for me, I don't see these famous examples" (IV. iii. 1291, 1295-96).[2] Argan in *Le Malade imaginaire* (II. v.) characterizes Cléante's "impertinent" pastoral song as a "very bad example."

Instead of profiling the exemplary deed initiating a grand centrifugal spiral, these plays by Dryden and Molière focus on the regenerative force initiated by the loving couple who despite all obstacles have learned to let their hearts speak. Their union is opposed by authoritative forces that reflect the socially accepted values of exerting power over others, sometimes in the disguise of love or passion. In their struggle against these dominant forces, the couple is aided by a circle of friends, relatives, and servants. And by demonstrating the capacity to build a relationship based on mutual understanding and concern within a society devoted to possessiveness and intrigue, the couple and their circle can become exemplary for the audience if it accepts the challenge to imitate the staged action in their relationships.

Dryden's *The Indian Queen, The Indian Emperour,* and *Aureng-Zebe* focus on the struggles of a central couple to achieve union despite the obstacles of others' passions and possessiveness. To win

Orazia, Montezuma must successfully counter her father's resistance, Traxalla's and even his friend Acacis's passion, and a number of threats to his life. Each obstacle tests the lovers' constancy to each other. They learn to value their love for each other above their lives, as Orazia declares to Montezuma: " . . . I had rather see / You dead, than kind to any thing but me" (IV. i. 64-65). But they also learn to respect the passions of others. In pardoning Zempoalla and urging her to live, as well as in acknowledging the renunciation of Acacis, they exhibit an understanding that the basis of a true community lies not in exclusion but inclusion of others.

The challenge to overcome passionate possessiveness, unquestioned devotion to the past, and divisive traditions in order to build the community of the future plays a significant role in Dryden's *The Indian Emperour*. In the first act, both obstacles prevail. On the one hand, Cortez and Montezuma confront each other with menacing statements reflecting the values of their cultures. On the other, both Cortez and Montezuma, along with the two Inca brothers Odmar and Guyomar, express passionate possessiveness for the objects of their love:

> CORTEZ: I will turn ravisher to keep you here.
>   (I. ii. 388)
> MONTEZUMA: In vain I strive.—
>   My Lyon-heart is with Loves toyls beset. (180)
> ODMAR: My claim to her by Eldership I prove.
>   (139)
> GUYOMAR: It seems my soul then mov'd the quicker
>   pace,
>   Yours first set out, mine reach'd her in the race.
>   (147-48)

Interestingly, it is the conflict of values engendered by these two patterns of behavior that is responsible for the movement away from both devotion to past cultural values and possessiveness. Though Cydaria exhibits the former when she exclaims to Cortez: "Strange ways you practice there [in Spain] to win a Heart" (II. iii. 67), her love for him impels her to reject loyalty to her nation that requires her to demand Cortez's death and later to die as an act of respect for her deceased father. Cortez's love for Cydaria leads him to attempt postponement of the battle with her father. Recognizing the imprisoned

Guyomar as a kindred lover, Cortez responds with an act of generosity transcending loyalty to Spain's cause by releasing Guyomar. This deed establishes a reciprocal pattern continued by Guyomar's warning Cortez of Orbellan's treachery, Cortez's release of Montezuma from torture, and Guyomar's relinquishing of his bride to protect her life. Those who do not participate in the transcendence of national loyalty or passionate possessiveness die (Orbellan, Odmar, Vasquez, and even Montezuma, who is unwilling to desert Inca traditions). The triumph of generosity over national and religious loyalties clears the way for the union of the two couples based on mutual understanding rather than convention. Their union signals reconciliation between the Spaniard and the Inca. Though Guyomar's rejection of Cortez's offer to share the kingdom with him reflects the limitations of reform, the play ends on reconciliation and dialogue as the course of action for the future.

The intense passion and violence exhibited by the figures of Dryden's *Aureng-Zebe* seem not to leave any room for a reform circle. With the exception of Melesinda, the characters are intentionally non-idealistic. Because most are passionately possessive, ready to seize others by force in order to satisfy their longing for power or possession of another, they see deceit even in self-sacrifice and love. As in *The Indian Emperour*, however, the source for reform lies paradoxically in passion itself. Its violence literally destroys Morot and Nourmahal, though not before they have been at least partially enlightened. Thus, Morot's desire for Indamora impels him to listen to her, as she shows him "the distant prospect of a shore / Doubtful in mists" (V.). Under the influence of her words he reconsiders momentarily his pursuit of fame as "vain," and using the pilot-ship metaphor, declares that he has "[s]ailed farther than the coast, but missed my way / Now you have given me virtue for my guide" (V.). Most significantly, the Emperor repents of his possessiveness and permits the union of the young couple as a signal that the future will be one of reconciliation and understanding among the three remaining characters, who have learned to transcend their past shortcomings.

Molière underscores the domination of aggressive and possessive figures by placing the motifs of the violent hand and confrontational dialogue in prominent positions in his comedies. The tendency of the dominant figures to seek, to acquire, even to purchase, to trade, play with, mold, or confine other figures provides a common basis for many of Molière's most powerful character portrayals, diverse as their other traits are, and shapes to a large extent the action of his plays.[3] Indeed, as both *Ecoles* illustrate, many of Molière's plots, reduced to their simplest level, can be summarized as the struggle of two hands for the possession of a woman who is treated as an object to be bought, confined, or stolen.[4]   Thus, the dominant Sganarelle in *L'Ecole des maris* declares his "full power" over his young charge Isabelle, bequeathed to him by her dead father, by imprisoning her in his house and planning to acquire her in marriage without regard for her wishes.   In *L'Ecole des femmes*, Arnolphe has purchased Agnès from a peasant and proudly states that he has molded her like soft wax "to give her the form that I like" (III. iii. 811) as his wife. Sganarelle's and Arnolphe's possessiveness of their young charges is challenged by the would-be possessors Valère and Horace.   While Valère plays the part of the pupil who must be instructed in the strategy of outwitting Sganarelle by the contriving Isabelle, Horace more clearly expresses his possessive urge by calling Agnès "a young object," "a pretty jewel," that he wants to own at any cost.   When it becomes apparent that he cannot purchase her with the money he has borrowed from Arnolphe, he steals her.   Thus, his initial attitude does not differ from Arnolphe's.

The collusion between the two dominating figures of Tartuffe and Orgon leads to a doubling of the power of possessiveness and confrontation in *Le Tartuffe*.   Though it seems at first that the impostor's hand has gained ascendancy in the family through the blindness of its head, Orgon's yearning for complete control over his family, as well as for Heaven's favors, impels him to trade away his property, access to his wife, his daughter, and his friend's confidential papers to the hypocrite Tartuffe.   Orgon's words as he contracts his daughter to Tartuffe reveal his choice of "hand" over "heart," of personal advantage over concern for another: "Come now, firm my heart, absolutely no human weakness" (IV. iii. 1293).   Yet, the stronger, more malicious hand belongs to Tartuffe.   Were it not for the direct intervention of the Prince at the end, his grasping "hands" would have destroyed the family completely.[5]

In his opening dialogue, Alceste, the dominating figure of *Le Misanthrope*, in contrast, appears to advocate the need for sincerity, a

prerequisite for building a community, by linking constructive dialogue to the heart: no word should be spoken "that does not come
from the heart" (I. i. 36). Similarly, the socialite Célimène who dominates her circle of admirers would seem to be the central focus of society. In the course of his conversation with Philinte, it becomes evident, however, that for Alceste, sincerity is a tool to humiliate others
by revealing to them their weaknesses and vices.[6] Instead of forming
the basis for improved relationships with others, the practice of honesty leads Alceste to an arrogant view of himself above and outside society. If he cannot dictate to others, he will separate himself from society (I. i. 95-96). Though his appeal to Célimène that she commit
herself to him exclusively would appear to form the basis for a lasting
relationship, his final demand that she follow him "in my desert
where I have vowed to live" (V. vi. 1763) points to an utter disregard
for Célimène's character, attitude, and feelings. Unable to find a part-
ner to share his design, Alceste is finally alienated from society.
Célimène, despite her apparent sociability, does not fare differently.
Her propensity to play with the affection of all her various suitors as
objects of her pleasure, as well as her "acute embarrassment" in
"speaking openly" of her feelings when questioned, make it equally
impossible for her to establish a mutual relationship with any one of
her admirers. Their desertion after the reading of the "secret" letter
leaves Célimène as isolated as the other domineering and possessive
figures.[7]

Featured with increasing complexity and power in Molière's later
comedies are the alienation and even destruction of other characters
through the actions and attitudes of the dominant figures. Don Juan's
defiantly playful hand destroys the trust and lives of those he touches
in *Don Juan ou le festin de Pierre*. Jupiter's divine playfulness in
Amphitryon and Harpagon's insidious greediness in *L'Avare* threaten
to destroy the trusting relationship of a loving couple and thereby the
basis for the human community. Under the absolute dominion of
these authority figures, those subordinate to them are reduced to either ineffective pleading or silent suffering. Some of the most amusing dialogues in these plays are structured around the breakdown of
communication as participants pursuing their goals without regard to
others talk past or misconstrue others. While the audience is enter-
tained, however, it is also offered the message that the result of this

misunderstanding is an alienation so permanent that no basis for the establishment of a community is possible. Thus, it remains questionable whether Jupiter's promise of an enviable future to the couple whose conjugal trust he shattered or Harpagon's reconciliation on his materialistic terms with the goals of Valère and Elise can eradicate the painful distrust with which they afflicted their subjects earlier.

Molière's last two plays, *Les Femmes savantes* and *Le Malade imaginaire* expand on the doubling of aggression and confrontation already developed in *Le Tartuffe*. Repeatedly insisting upon compliance with her desires ("I don't want any obstacle to the desires that I show" II. vi. 440; "And this man is the gentleman that I have determined / By my choice to be destined to be your husband" III. iv. 1073-74; "I absolutely must have my desire carried out" V. iii. 1674), Philaminte, the assertive wife and mother of *Les Femmes savantes*, is seconded in her pseudo-intellectual goals by her elder daughter Armande, her eccentric sister-in-law Bélise, and the pedant Trissotin. Although diverse in their pursuits, they are united in regarding "the heart" of another as an object to be conquered (Armande), played with (Bélise), or traded (Trissotin: "The gift of your hand . . . / Will deliver to me the heart possessed by Clitandre" V. i. 1489-90). Their discourse and conduct provide the play's entertainment.[8] Similarly, the ironic position of the dominating figure Argan in *Le Malade imaginaire* lends itself to many amusing scenes. While tyrannizing his family with his egocentric hypochondria ("I will force her . . . I will absolutely command her to be prepared to take the husband I tell her to" I.v.), Argan exhibits blindness to the manipulations of his doctor who, as Béralde states, "holds in his hand the thread of your life which he with supreme authority lengthens or shortens as he wishes" (III. vi.) and his wife Béline. His contracting of his daughter's hand to the insipid Thomas Diafoirus on the ground that "this one is most suitable for me" (III. iii.) is seconded by Thomas's eagerness to accept the unwilling Angélique "from the hands of your distinguished father" (II. vii.). Like Orgon of *Le Tartuffe*, Argan falls into the unscrupulous hands of those who would profit financially from his weakness (Bélise: "There are papers, there is money that I want to seize" III. xii.) and unwittingly joins a team of controlling forces that contradict any meaningful establishment of positive relationships.

The most direct use of force by the dominating figures in Molière's comedies is that of the stick.[9] It intensifies the violence of the hand and signifies the antithesis of enlightened communication. Wielded liberally by the dominant figures, the stick "speaks," and its victims listen and learn. As the stricken Sosie says to the striking Mercure in *Amphitryon* (I. ii. 386-87; 389, 91): "I keep silent. / The dispute is too unequal between us . . . . / I am what you want [me to be] . . . / Your arm makes you master." Beating his servant Maître Jacques for telling him the truth, Harpagon in *L'Avare* (III. i.) says bluntly: "Learn to speak." With a stick Argan forces his young daughter Louison to recount the clandestine meeting she has witnessed between Angélique and Cléante in *Le Malade imaginaire*. It is a tactic repeatedly used by Arnolphe in *L'Ecole des femmes*. The threat of the stick even keeps Sganarelle in conformity with the heretical ideas of Don Juan. Attempts by others to discuss differences calmly are nearly always thwarted by rude interruptions by the dominating figures. Once they have clearly ascertained their goal, they choose the swiftest and most direct path toward its fulfillment. As they hasten toward it, others become either obstacles to be overcome or objects to be used or possessed. As long as their spirit of possessiveness prevails, these figures are unwilling to listen or learn from others. In this role, they are basically unfit to be members of the community. By exaggerating their possessive traits and by showing their treatment of others as antisocial, the playwright offers these characters to his audience as somewhat less than human objects of ridicule to which the audience responds with laughter.[10] Laughter both distances the spectators from the deeds and attitudes shown on stage and unites them into a listening and learning community.

Molière's spectators are helped by the example of a few characters who learn to listen to their hearts and to others. These individuals, frequently subordinate, suppressed, and less colorful than the dominant protagonists, point the way toward learning to communicate, to exhibit the characteristics of generosity, self-sacrifice, freedom of choice, and concern for the feelings of others, and thus to establish the true basis for the community even within a society dominated by the characteristics and action of the possessive, confining, grasping, playing, or trading hand. Their persistence and success, while limited by their need to adopt temporarily tactics abhorrent to their goals, bring harmony and joy at the end of a tension-filled play. They provide a glimpse of a truly humane existence, not yet fully realized but potentially conceivable.

Perhaps the most remarkable example of the courage, compassion, and generosity needed for a genuine relationship is found in *L'Ecole des femmes.* Though later seconded by an ever-widening circle, it is the confined and unschooled Agnès who discovers and develops the attitudes that are basic to shaping a sense of community. Her instinctive opening of the door to Horace, despite Arnolphe's interdiction, the sentiment "that in order to help him, I would have given [him] everything" (II. vi. 586), the direct aim of her letter with her plea for open dialogue: "I am so moved by your words that I cannot believe them to be lies. Tell me frankly if they are, for as I am without malice, you would commit the greatest wrong in the world if you deceive me . . ." (III. iv.) contrast sharply with the grasping nature of the other characters' actions. In setting her apart from the dominant patterns of buying, trading, confining, and confronting others, Molière establishes her compassion ("heart") and need for sincerity (open dialogue) as the pattern for a genuine relationship. Unschooled in the ways of the dominant figures, she is to become the focal point of a small circle of imitators (Enrique, Oronte, Chrysalde, Horace) that excludes those unwilling to listen and learn such as Arnolphe.[11]

More common in the structure of Molière's comedies, however, is the introduction of the secondary couple whose relationship provides the antithesis of the dominant figures' patterns of behavior. By slowly, even imperceptibly, building this quiet, subordinate union until it reaches a focal point of interest at the end of the play, Molière points to the mutual trust and concern of these couples, seconded at times by a circle of faithful friends, relatives, and even maids, as the configuration of a future, genuine community. In *L'Ecole des maris,* for example, the relationship of the secondary figures Ariste and Léonor forms a quiet, even dull, contrast with the colorful strategies of the dominant Sganarelle and Isabelle. Ariste's granting of full freedom to his charge Léonor to decide her course of action gives him anxious moments when he is temporarily led to believe that Léonor has betrayed his trust. But his generosity is rewarded when Léonor openly declares her desire to marry him. Their partnership, founded on freedom and trust, not only contrasts with Sganarelle's isolation, as signified by his silence in the final scene, and Isabelle's admittedly "shameful strategy" to escape her confinement, but more importantly, forms a model for a genuine relationship for the audience.

The same antithesis between a dominant confrontational, and consequently alienated pair and a subordinate couple of lovers who practice together trust, generosity, and free choice determines the configuration of *Le Misanthrope.* In contrast to Alceste's passionate possessiveness and Célimène's playfulness, both Philinte and Eliante seek first the well-being of each other. Placing Eliante's interest above his own, Philinte is even willing to risk his relationship with her by intimating to Alceste that "the sincere Eliante has a liking for you" (I. i. 215) and later repeating the suggestion to Eliante herself as well as imputing to Alceste his own feelings (IV. i. 1186-90). Eliante responds by appealing to the heart as arbiter: "I don't oppose his affection / To the contrary, my heart is interested" (1193-94). Nevertheless, she accords Alceste the same freedom of choice that Philinte has accorded her. She is not offended when Alceste withdraws his suit in favor of Célimène. Philinte's and Eliante's reciprocal generosity draws them into a close partnership which they acknowledge and celebrate by their engagement. Their efforts to include the alienated Alceste in their joyous circle testify to their relationship's centrality for the establishment of an inclusive future community at the close of the play.[12]

The couples practicing mutual trust and esteem in Molière's last two comedies are subservient to the wishes of strong parental figures who dispose of their daughters' hands without regard for their feelings. In their struggle against this denigration to mere objects, the pairs turn to loyal supporters whose goal is to unite the lovers despite the formidable obstacles. Like their opponents, they represent a motley group: the lovers Henriette and Clitandre, seconded by her father Chrysale and uncle Ariste in *Les Femmes savantes*; the lovers Angélique and Cléante supported by the maid Toinette in *Le Malade imaginaire.* Their insistence on their own values of sincerity, freedom of choice, and respect for the feelings of others is expressed by the motifs of the heart and open dialogue, often combined:

CLITANDRE to ARMANDE: No, madam, my heart

that disguises little,
Feels no constraint in making an open avowal . . .
                                                    (I. ii. 129-30)
CLITANDRE to HENRIETTE: My most solid hope is
your heart . . .   (V. i. 1450)
ANGELIQUE to her father: Give us at least some
time to become acquainted and to watch grow in us
the inclination for each other, so necessary for a
perfect union. (II. vi.)
ANGELIQUE to TOINETTE: . . . my heart warmly
profits from every moment it can open itself to you.
                                                    (I. iv.)

CLEANTE [indicating the reason for his disguise as
Angélique's music teacher]: To know my destiny, to
speak to the charming Angélique, and ask her for her
decision . . .   (II. i.)

Even his fabricated musical duet with Angélique becomes a medium
through which their hearts can secretly communicate with each other.

But the heart-based decision cannot be realized without a cun-
ningly devised strategy. Belonging to the sphere of the hand motif
(plotting, scheming, executing a lie), this temporary abandonment of
sincerity is the only means by which the subordinate figures who listen to their hearts can counter their opponents.[13] For, unlike the figures in the tragedies of Corneille and Racine, the dominant figures in
Molière's comedies never stand at a crossroads decision, gain self-insight, or renounce their self-interest. Only after they have been outwitted can they be persuaded to consider joining the circle supporting
the lovers. Except for *Le Tartuffe* and the last two plays, the dominant
figures are unwilling to give up their egotistical goals and thus remain
outside the reform circle. Their alienation is expressed by the inex-
pressive (Sganarelle's silence, Arnolphe's "ouf!", Jupiter's withdrawal
to Olympian heights) or the desire for isolation (Alceste's longing for
a "secret place"; Harpagon's wish to "see my dear strong-box"
rather than to join in bringing the joyous news of the young couple's
union to other family members in *L'Avare*). In contrast, once they
have been forced to concede that they have been outmaneuvered,
Orgon in *Le Tartuffe*, Philaminte in *Les Femmes savantes* and Argan
in *Le Malade imaginaire* are persuaded to join the circle of figures
dedicated to furthering the mutual sincerity, trust, and esteem of the
loving couple. They indicate this transformation from egotism to

concern for a larger circle in their final words: ORGON: "Let's fall at his [the Prince's] feet with joy / To praise the kindness his heart has granted us; . . ." (V. vii. 1957-58); PHILAMINTE: "To see with a content eye their love crowned" (V. v. 1773).[14]

While the dominant figures are persuaded to surrender at least a portion of their would-be power over others, the subordinate characters under their power find themselves forced to adopt temporarily the behavior patterns of disguise, confrontation, and dissimulation in order to escape. The use of these strategies often leads to misunderstandings and conflicts that threaten the couple's love and trust. But they also test their sincerity and ability to see the truth beneath the lies. When finally triumphant, their union will provide firmer ground for the new human community to grow. In *L'Ecole des maris,* for example, the unschooled Valère has tried the direct way of letting his eyes speak for his heart, but "who can inform me, / If their language has finally been understood?" (I. iv. 351-52). As Sganarelle's "pupil," Isabelle has comprehended that their only means of communication is indirect double talk ("two hearts that love each other ought to understand half-truths"). She teaches Valère how to communicate by using Sganarelle as their intermediary. Though he remains clumsy, Valère learns to imitate her ambiguity, and together, they build a partnership based on a complex mutual understanding and deception of their opponent. In learning to communicate under the most oppressive circumstances, as well as to trust each other in a risky strategy, the lovers establish a firm relationship on which to build their future.[15]

The doubling of domination in the conspiracy between Orgon and Tartuffe in *Le Tartuffe* either silences both tongue and heart in the subordinate family members or forces them to adopt uncharacteristic schemes to combat the liaison.[16] Thus, Damis's angry confrontation is punished by his being banned from the family. Mariane's denigration to an object of barter in her father's hand results in her silence which she signals by a cold "I don't know," not only before her father but also before her lover Valère. Instead of mutual understanding, the lovers speak of "the plot that my mind conceives" and "how he has handled me" (II. iv. 746, 774). While the lovers question their hearts (VALERE: " . . . and your heart has never had true feeling for me" 716), Tartuffe readily uses "heart" to approach his benefactor's wife

Elmire: "My breast doesn't enclose a heart of stone"; "It is, I confess, very great audacity / For me to dare to offer you my heart"; "And when it sees your heavenly figure, / A heart is moved and cannot reason" (III. iii. 930, 953-54, 967-68).

Ironically, it is precisely Elmire's temporary adoption of this strategy of using the heart motif to unmask the grasping hand that breaks the conspiracy of alienation and silence that threatens the family. By opening her second interview with Tartuffe with repeated references to the heart ("How little you know a woman's heart"; "We make known well enough that our heart is ready"; "Would I have, I beg you, with so much gentleness / Listened all along to the offer of your heart . . ." (IV. v. 1412, 1420, 1427-28), she cleverly manipulates him so that he reveals his true grasping nature to her hidden husband. The strategy succeeds in reconciling the family. United along with the devoted Valère in the single goal of combating Tartuffe's stranglehold on them, the family now forms a circle dedicated to honesty, generosity, and the union of the lovers as well as praise of the Prince who has saved them.

In *L'Avare,* Harpagon's avarice overshadows any attempts to listen to the heart.[16] In reaction, the lovers either try to express their feelings in materialistic terms (Cléante's stealing of his father's ring for Mariane) or withdraw confidence from each other, as Elise states to Valère, because of "the anger of a father, the reproaches of a family, the censure of society, but above all, Valère, the change in your heart" (I. i.). This "change of heart" becomes most clearly perceptible in Valère's choice of words to appease Harpagon. He assures Harpagon that he "is right" to marry off Elise to Anselme because the latter will take her "without dowry": "that closes the mouth to everything" (I. v.). Later in the scene, Valère abruptly changes the tone and meaning of his words to Elise when he suddenly views Harpagon: "if your love, Elise, is capable of firmness . . . Yes, a daughter must obey her father. "

In order to counter the tyranny of this "least human of all humans," the lovers are forced into strategies disruptive to the building of a genuine relationship. Chief among these designs is the use of double-talk, simultaneously to hide their true feelings from Harpagon and yet to communicate them to each other. This complex game requires mutual trust and skill. Upon learning that Mariane is to become his mother-in-law, Cléante explains his strong outburst of repugnance to Mariane: "This discourse will appear brutal to the eyes of some; but I am certain that you will be the person who will take it as it should be taken . . ." Mariane's reply to Harpagon's excuse of his son as "a young fool who does not know yet the consequence of the words that he speaks" indicates that she is equal to playing this game of words: " . . . he has given me the pleasure of explaining his true feelings to me . . ." (III. vii.). Outwitted in double-talk by Harpagon, the lovers must turn to the strategy directly connected to the hand by seizing Harpagon's true love, his strong-box, in order to exchange it for his acquiescence to their union. Supported by the revelation that previously unknown family ties already unite them, the two pairs of lovers, together with Anselme and his wife, form a large family circle centered around "this double wedding" of the two pairs. Mutual affection and confidence conquer only because the tyranny of avarice has been temporarily muted by the generosity of a giving father.

The power of generosity, connected semantically in the text with the heart, over greed, expressed by actions of the grasping hand, also propels the conclusion of Molière's final two comedies. Clitandre's offer to the "stricken" family of "What means fortune gives me" (*Les Femmes savantes* V. iv. 1732) and Agnès's and Cléante's spontaneous grief over the "death" of her father (*Le Malade imaginaire* III. xxi) win out over the "mercantile interests" of their opponents. But in order to be heard and seen, they require elaborate strategies that test the true intentions of all concerned. Thus Ariste explains his adoption of the "false news" of the family's bankruptcy: "And this is a strategy, a surprising aid, / That I wanted to try in order to serve your love . . ." (V. iv. 1761-62). Those whose interests were centered in the family's money suddenly withdraw when tested, while those whose affections have tied them with the family suddenly find that they can express them, be listened to, and become the uniting factor of a circle built around their relationship.[18]

It is interesting to note that even in those plays of Molière in which the reform circle expands to include the outmaneuvered authoritarian figures (as in *Le Tartuffe, Les Femmes savantes,* and *Le Malade imaginaire*), they are not truly reformed. Rather, the members forming the circle learn to accommodate and respect each other's wishes and values. An easy exchange, assisted by the addition of humor, takes place. In *L'Avare*, Harpagon gives his permission for the two marriages in exchange for Anselme's footing the bills. Philaminte in *Les Femmes savantes* hopes to punish the "base avarice" of the unmasked Trissotin by means of the lovers' "brilliant" wedding, while Bélise contents herself with the warning that Clitandre could "repent of it all his life." In *Le Malade imaginaire*, Argan conditions his consent to Angélique's and Cléante's union upon the latter becoming a physician but accepts with good humor Béralde's proposal to be "inducted" into the profession. Béralde's response to Angélique's protest that he is making "a bit too much fun of my father" indicates the adaptability of the reform circle in Molière's comedies: ". . . it's not to make fun of him but to accommodate his fantasy . . . we can perform the comedy for each other" (III. xiv.). Not in fundamentally transforming society but in learning to listen and respond to each member's wishes and needs does the reform circle perform its task as a fundamental building unit of society.

The pattern of building a flexible reform circle, expansive and attentive to each member's needs, does not shape all of Molière's plays. Rather, it seems restricted to those plays in which the union of the loving couple is a future rather than a past event. In *Amphitryon* and *George Dandin*, both of which portray the married rather than the to-be-married couple, the central relationship on which the reform circle is based is destroyed by mistrust, insincerity, and strategies that cannot be outmaneuvered. The divine Jupiter's use of "a hundred ingenious tricks," foremost the "strategy" of disguising himself as Amphitryon in order to possess Alcmène, so seriously disrupts communication and sentiment between husband and wife that even his final revelation as god and promise of future glory cannot repair the damage. Sosie's final emphasis on silence and withdrawal signals the fracture of the relationship:

> But now, let's cut short the talk,
> And let everyone quietly retire.
> On such affairs, always
> The best is to say nothing. (III. x. 1940-43)[19]

In *George Dandin* by contrast, the couple's relationship is destroyed through their own actions and attitudes.[20] Having been married without regard for each other's feelings, each feels used by the other. Angélique, whose marriage to the wealthy but lower-class George Dandin was arranged by her parents for financial reasons, expresses this lack of mutual understanding in terms of the heart and dialogue motifs: "I didn't give [my consent] with a willing heart; you forced it out of me. Did you, before the wedding, ask my consent and if I really wanted you?" (II. ii.). She explains to her lover: "We take [husbands] because we can't get out of it and because we depend on parents who have eyes only for [their] property" (III. vi.). George has a similar explanation for the "arranged" match: "The marriages that [nobles] make have little to do with our persons; it is only our property that they marry" (I. i.). Even when challenged to develop the ability to listen to the heart (as when Angélique pleads: "Show yourself generous . . . I beg you with all my heart" III. vi.), the couple is incapable of developing an open dialogue. Indeed, George's response, "Ah! crocodile that flatters people in order to strangle them!" signals their relationship at the end of the play as one of specifically less-than-human dimensions. It is supported by an authoritarian tyranny which eliminates genuine dialogue, as reflected by Angélique's final acquiescence to her father's command that she remain married: "That word closes my mouth; and you have an absolute power over me" (III. vii.). The only divergence from this movement toward strangulation in relationships is the brief exchange between the servants Lubin and Claudine. Claudine's definition of the desirable husband as "one so full of confidence and so sure of my virtue that he would see me surrounded by thirty men without being upset" and Lubin's response: "I will give you the liberty to do everything you want" (II. i.) point the way to a true, open relationship based on trust. By assigning this positive building of a relationship to a powerless couple who never reappear together after this brief scene, Molière consigns it to a vague future outside the framework of the present dramatic reality of the play.

Limited Reform

In the theater, traditional forms and themes continue to coexist with formal experiments and shifting trends in the theme of social protest well into the eighteenth century. At the same time, in the literary debates of the period, several prominent critics like Gotthold

Ephraim Lessing, Edward Young, and Thomas Thorild pave the way
for new aesthetic considerations. Others, as for instance, Samuel
Johnson and Johann Christoph Gottsched, affirm the classical principles of composition outlined by Nicolas Boileau in *L'Art poétique* and
accept the optimistic view of history as the hallmark of human
progress advanced by Jacques-Bénique Bossuet in his *Discours sur
l'histoire universelle*. Thematic innovations are most pronounced in
the eighteenth-century novels of Richardson, Goldsmith, Sterne,
Fielding, and Smollett that are animated by the spirit of social change.
But even while a flourishing new tradition generates a gradual reorientation in themes and motifs, it also motivates the classical temper to
renew the theme of social reform and to broaden its scope.
Therefore, the thematic constellation of social change is evident not
only in novels that display distinctly realistic patterns but also in the
romances, epic poems, and novels that extend the classical tradition.
At times, these texts make fervent appeals to moderation and balance;
at other times, they expound maxims derived from Charles-Louis
Montesquieu, John Locke, Voltaire, or Jean-Jacques Rousseau. Some
narratives develop a propensity toward moralizing; others seek to project visions of exemplary action. Despite the diversity, they share one
feature in the representation of reform proposals. Their focus narrows thematically to specific educational goals of the rising middle
class and concrete agrarian improvements. The limited perspective is
important for thematic analysis because it shows the effect of stratification on figure conceptions. It accentuates thematic elements to be
expanded by Goethe and other authors of the nineteenth century. It
also permits comparisons of a cross section of novels in order to trace
the specific thematic configuration.

From a genre-oriented historical point of view, the dominant features of eighteenth-century narratives have been classified under formal aspects (epistolary, dialogue, panoramic), narrative disposition
(sentiment, satire), and focus (education, development, social criticism).[21] From a thematic perspective, the novels show recurring patterns that are characterized at times by the careful compositional integration of action sequences and figure development, crossroads decision, and social reform. At other times, they appear to blend
panoramic descriptions of the social climate with criticism of manners. But they also present unresolved contradictions that occur when

the description of an oppressive social milieu raises doubts or even negates the narrative's optimistic resolution. The structural patterns evolving during the period show a striking correspondence in figure conception, narrative point of view, design of the journey, thematic focus on love / friendship, fulfillment / renunciation, and didactic explications of crucial arguments. This pattern is evident in Johann Timotheus Hermes's *Sophiens Reise von Memel nach Sachsen,* Marie Sophie La Roche's *Geschichte des Fräuleins von Sternheim,* Friedrich Heinrich Jacobi's *Woldemar,* Johann Karl Wezel's *Herrmann und Ulrike,* Adolph Knigge's *Reise nach Braunschweig,* and Knigge's *Geschichte des Amtraths Gutmann.*

The fictive biographies, autobiographies, and narrations of formative influences in a person's life vie for a comprehensive representation of the social climate through a multiple perspective. Careful, often minute, descriptions of figures, behavior, and milieu create the impression of immediacy. The action sequence of the journeys is punctuated by incidents that heighten the traveler's awareness. The ensuing reflection lends itself to a critical assessment of the existing conditions, the exploration of ideals, and the evaluation of pedagogic principles. The novels endeavor to survey the intellectual climate of the time by including vignettes of figures from a cross section of society. They interpolate accounts of the lives of others, as for instance the "Story of the Spiritual Growth of Pastor Karl Gros" in *Sophiens Reise,* the story of Schwinger's development in *Herrmann und Ulrike,* or the narration of Carl von Fürstenruf's experiences in *Geschichte des Amtraths Gutmann.* They intersperse the narration freely with maxims concerning manners, ethical conduct, and the education of children.[22] While they resemble and sometimes appear to be modeled after the English novelistic tradition of Richardson, Fielding, and Smollett, they draw their strength from the unique atmosphere of the German scene. They capture the ceremonial of tiny principalities and duchies. They breathe the spirit of the small town, even if the setting is Leipzig instead of the tiny Mehlbach. They portray the conventions of the aristocracy and the class of government officials, merchants, tutors, and landholders. Above all, they reveal the peculiar blend of high aspirations and accommodation with the existing conditions, of the yearning for free personal development and the desire for success strengthened by moral sentiments that are defined by pragmatic concerns.

Themes and motifs are set in metaphoric fields that abridge and stratify linguistic features informing the philosophic discourse during the period. Self-realization is linked to ethical perfectibility, the *Sittengesetz* examined by Kant and Schiller. The voice of the heart is aligned with the capacity to express sincere emotions that are not colored by the ambivalence of linguistic expressions. The constructive dialogue is associated with the genteel atmosphere of a social setting that becomes the center for the civilized exchage of ideas.

The figures are conceived as travelers seeking orientation in life. A series of adventures and encounters with persons representing a cross section of society familiarize them with the existing social climate. For instance, Sophie von Sternheim's accounts cover her life at home, her education, the experiences at the house of her aunt, at court, with Derby, the period when she assumes the name Madam Leidens and founds a school, her abduction and rescue in Scotland. Herrmann observes the attitudes of noblemen, servants, artisans, students, beggars, and prostitutes. Gutmann encounters government officials, farmers, aristocrats, and representative figures from the middle class. The main figures suffer hardship, fall prey to temptation, and are led astray. But they are either rescued from impending ruin by persons of good will or freed from spiritual confinement by trustworthy friends. The motif of the mentor-guardian is not as systematically developed in these novels as in *Wilhelm Meister* or in the novels of the nineteenth century where it is linked to social enclaves. Nevertheless, such figures as Karl Gros, Widow E., Schwinger, Mrs. Hill, and Westerberg provide formative influences similar to those imparted by the members of the "Tower Society" to Meister.

All major figures experience love and seek friendship. The action sequence frequently follows the patterns of the romance: love occasions confusion, intrigue, pursuit, and reunion. As a primary factor in individual development, the action initiates self-analysis and reflection on human interrelations. Friendship as an expression of an unselfish impulse, high personal esteem, and the desire to offer oneself freely to another person is portrayed in these novels as an indispensable virtue to be acquired during the self-development. Both Mr. Less** and Cornellis Puf van Vlieten are generous, prove to be true friends of Sophie von Sternheim, and renounce their personal desires. Sophie constantly wonders whether love can endure and views the affection of friendship as a superior emotion. When she reflects upon her capacity for love and her desire to help others, it becomes apparent that she considers the shared experience of friendship an essential element in her love and self-improvement. Both Herrmann and Gutmann realize that friendship transcends class distinctions. It permits the honest exchange of ideas that is otherwise stifled by convention and courtly etiquette. Friendships between reform-minded aristocrats and bourgeois, administrators and farmers lay the foundation for actions that benefit the community. Friendship, then, advances a person's own perfection and provides an impetus for social reform.

As the stories unfold, it becomes evident that limited social reform is directly linked to travel. The journey is designed both as a trial of individual perseverance and as an educational experience. The travelers endure successive tests that threaten their lives or personal integrity. Both misfortune and fortuitous encounters serve as learning experiences that could lead to an understanding of the inner self, the social climate, and the forces that shape the period. This intention is undeniable. However, since the action arises from a conflict between ideal conceptions of social organization or individual self-development and concrete tendencies of middle-class thought, the central figure may mature and gain a measure of self-insight without attaining a genuine knowledge of the forces governing the thinking of the period. The novels rarely address the problem directly. Nevertheless, the thematic resolutions reveal contentment with a rational criticism of the cult of sentiment, acceptance of modest reforms, and satisfaction with life in a family circle. Education seeks to instill in children a spirit of cooperation and attempts to develop specific aptitudes instead of exploring the full human potential.[23] Similarly, proposals for social reform are pragmatic and focus on specific improvements in the management of estates and the administration of small communities. To achieve desirable but limited goals, the figures make concessions to the existing order. Indeed, one of the most striking features of the novels is the spirit of accommodation. In *Herrmann und Ulrike*, for example, Wezel's chronicle of the social scene indicates that the willingness of the rising middle class to compromise with social conditions impedes comprehensive reforms.

The travelers become representative primarily through their increased intellectual awareness of the significance of their experiences. They are defined to a considerable degree through their response to ideas and ideologies. Despite their focus on primary figures, the subject matter of the novels gravitates therefore toward the impersonal. The perspective shifts from specific individuals to a general, desirable mode of individuation. The figures advance on a horizontal plane through space. The journey provides for encounters that shed light on the class structure and show how social barriers can be bridged. But the effect of the encounters, potentially unlimited for a person's expanding intellectual horizon, remains firmly restricted by moral imperatives. Hence, the vertical progression through stages of increased awareness and crystallization of thought is negated. The absence of satirical humor and ironic detachment in the narrative voice that mark the narrative voice in eighteenth-century French and English novels and Goethe's narratives further restricts playful manipulation of the themes of social reform and accommodation that would encourage a continuum of reflection. When humor is interjected, as for instance in Knigge's *Reise nach Braunschweig*, it is anchored in a series of farcical situations.

The succession of adventures creates the appearance of dynamic development. But the movement is essentially circular and centripetal. The journey leads into the world but ends in a familiar setting. An atmosphere of quiet resignation parallels the limited reform proposals. As a consequence, the thematic constellation is closely related to the restricted reform circle in realism. Either accommodation or peaceful happiness triumphs over the cosmopolitan spirit. Sophie whose exalted vision of friendship and love prevents her from choosing one of two equally forthright men loses both Mr. Less** and Cornellis Puf van Vlieten. She remains ensnared by her obsession with absolute virtue, love, and honor. She is despondent, nevertheless fears that any emotion may be misinterpreted, fails to see that she is not a victim of life but of the ideology of sentimentalism, and asks for asylum on the estate of her friend Henriette. That she offers her services as tutor for Henriette's children confirms her lack of self-insight. She has traveled, was abducted and freed, listened to the admonitions of Pastor Gros, but did not mature. She appears ill prepared to educate children. Sophie von Sternheim is rewarded for her unswerving ethical commitment and truthfulness. She marries Lord Seymour and lives in the small family circle as model wife, mother, and overseer of the estate.[24] Herrmann endures hardship and frequently changing fortunes for eight years. He succeeds because he is steadfast and able to accommodate himself to conventional expectations. He marries Ulrike. The narrator, righteous and humorless, concludes: "Love creates heaven in their home . . . love awakens them in the morning and closes their eyes at night; love glides with extended wings above their heads and distributes from its inexhaustible horn the reward for faithfulness and steadfastness."[25] Gutmann is reunited with his son, finds his brother whom he has not seen for thirty years, is able to aid his old friend von Fürstenruf, and looks forward to the management of an estate in Mehlbach.[26] Such conclusions increase in frequency in the popular literature of the second half of the nineteenth century. In several works of Berthold Auerbach, Otto Glaubrecht, and Karl August Wildenhahn, for instance, they are superimposed on a narrative exposition that belies the possibility of an idyllic resolution of the coming-of-age theme. They clash with the conflicting countercurrents in the description of a social environment that seems to impede the free development of human potential.

The various themes that had been linked in the literary tradition of the eighteenth century with individual education and social reform are modified, expanded, transformed and fused into an essential pattern in Goethe's *Wilhelm Meister*. For his novel, Goethe not only draws upon the existing tradition but also retains several prominent features in the design of the journey, the emphasis on renunciation, and pragmatic pedagogic considerations. But he changes the figure conception to one of a person endowed with unlimited potential that is developed in stages to a level where the acquired knowledge serves the best interest of society. He also shifts the focus from the private sphere of a purely individualistic dimension to typical constellations. Essential issues and possible solutions move to the center of interest. The process of problem-solving becomes a subject of narrative exploration. As a result, individual characteristics are subsumed under distinctive attributes. Persons are introduced as Abbé, the Man of Fifty Years, the Hazelnut Colored Girl, or the Sojourning Simpleton. Significant stages of the journey and major learning experiences are identified as the "Flight to Egypt" or "Confessions of a Sensitive Soul." The artistic expression no longer adheres to a familiar mode of perceiving and representing figures in action in an environment to which the reader can relate. The concentration on ideational constructs, on problems and possible solutions is a pronounced feature in *Wilhelm Meister, Pandora, Die natürliche Tochter,* and " Das Märchen." In addition to the decrease of individual characteristics, a common element in the representation of typical constellations, including the symbolic delineation of historical forces, lies in the apparently unmotivated alternations in a figure's perspective or even surprising changes in attitudes. The narrative stance shifts toward a rigorous anti-realism.

The difference between Goethe's technique and the narratives of his contemporaries is apparent in the point of view and the structure of the novels. Hermes, La Roche, Wezel, and Knigge animate the journey with descriptive detail. The encounters with diverse individuals give a panoramic view of society. The successive adventures, though filtered in the reflection of the major figures, are distributed on a single plane of consciousness. Goethe's narration is configuration-oriented. As a result, *Wilhelm Meister* incorporates in a paradigmatic form the principles, themes, and motifs that characterize the reform circle's fusion of individual development and social improvement.

Reciprocal Relations Between Individual and Community in Goethe's *Wilhelm Meister*

Narrative Technique. Since the publication of the novels *Wilhelm Meisters Lehrjahre* and *Wilhelm Meisters Wanderjahre oder Die Entsagenden,* critical attention has focused on Wilhelm's individuation and the pronounced stylistic innovation that characterizes especially the *Wanderjahre.*[27] In tracing the action sequence of Wilhelm's adventures, the novels assign major importance to his personality. But thematic analysis points to a constellation which, while not diminishing the prominence of a specific personality formation, balances individual development and social change and highlights the reciprocal responsibilities of individual and society. The thematic constellation of the novels consolidates ideas about individual growth and communal cooperation (love, renunciation, transcendence, metamorphosis) that govern the colorful events in "Das Märchen" (*Unterhaltungen deutscher Ausgewanderten*). The configuration encompasses: (1) the journey which yields encounters that simultaneously serve as stations on the road toward self-development and stages of increasing social awareness; (2) the inception of a new community and preparations for emigration; (3) primary and secondary learning experiences of love, friendship, and renunciation; (4) the education for the new community in the "Pedagogic Province." Throughout the novels the attention alternates between human potential and entelechy, individual development and characteristics of the community.

The apparently amorphous structure of the *Wanderjahre* can be attributed to the technique of repeated mirroring that enables the narrator to elucidate basic culturally derived modes of thought. The novels trace the growth of a young man from preoccupation with himself to an understanding and acceptance of his place in the community. While the narration focuses on Wilhelm, it accords equal importance to the other prominent organizational units of the design: social structure and social interaction. The atmosphere, milieu, and human relations are conveyed through a technique of continuous digressions and narrative detours. Observations of minute detail, apparently purely individualistic traits, and unique incidents combine with representations of group characteristics to create the sense of a typical pattern. The technique enables Goethe to highlight the chance occurrences and fragmentary aspects attached to individual lives while subordinating them to an overall constellation. The spirit of the different classes is objectified in sketches of the aspirations, traits, and behavior of a wide range of figures who reveal both positive and negative tendencies.

The minute observations, vivid description of scenes, accounts of distant events, and abrupt interjections with admonitions that outline general rules of conduct are embedded in a continuous, seemingly unending flow of conversation. Instead of relating the course of lives consecutively, the narration meanders into remote recesses. Unexpectedly it picks up an apparently forgotten thread only to submerge it in renewed conversations. The analysis of this narrative technique establishes that it differs from the conventional patterns of dialogues in novels of the period. It is designed to capture the spiritual presence of social interaction in conversations. Conversations show order and disorder, the capacity and the inability to think, stagnation and progress. In conversations, Wilhelm encounters the multiplicity of society and the social character of the generalized other. Conversations acquaint him with the social disorientation and the appeal to reform.

Furthermore, the narrative continuity of Wilhelm's journey is interrupted from the onset by events and intricate stories whose true significance is revealed much later. Some appear to be episodic at first glance, others are carefully developed tableaux that are meaningful in themselves. All are arranged in parallels distributed throughout the novels. They identify primary experiences, formative influences, and shed light on the process of individuation. Above all, they draw attention to an inner struggle in Wilhelm that is repressed but evident in gestures and not articulated until it is resolved at the end of the novels: Wilhelm seeks to protect himself from insights that disturb his self-perception and the allegiance to his own self. Two examples are: (1) Wilhelm's uncertain, emotional relationship with Mignon is mirrored and illuminated in two apparently unrelated, yet parallel stories: "The Man of Fifty Years" (19: 195-263) and "The New Melusine" (20: 100-27). Both narratives converge in events testing the inner certainty, the permanence of emotions, and the ability to sustain commitment to the other. The barber-surgeon recounts how his passion for Melusine ensnared him until he lost his social identity. Transformed by the ring on his finger into a dwarf, he experiences the pain of utter enslavement and breaks out from the confining circle to resume his former life characterized by social distractions. Hilarie's resolute proposal to marry her aging uncle in "The Man of Fifty Years" sets events into motion that force all participants to examine the nature of their attachments. Hilarie realizes that she was attracted by a deceptive picture of familial stability and discovers her love for the major's son Flavio. Flavio becomes aware that his devotion to the beautiful but older widow was not strong enough to withstand the sudden onslaught of conflicting emotions. The major, first tempted by the promise of youthful regeneration, resigns himself to graceful aging. Reflecting on the loss of a front tooth auguring others to follow (19: 256) he voices "painful satisfaction" with his decision to let reason prevail. (2) The intricate interweaving of love – androgyne – friendship – death in Wilhelm's complex relationship with Mignon is furthermore filtered in the "Story of the Drowned Boy" (20: 33-44). Significantly, the information is withheld from the reader until Wilhelm has transfigured Mignon in his memory. The story relates a crucial childhood experience. A young boy, deeply stirred by still undifferentiated emotional affection, beholds physical beauty and spiritual perfection in the other boy. He gains a fundamental sense of self in the encounter that concludes with the other's sudden death.

The technique of setting up multiple narratives that mirror the same learning experiences and interweaving them with numerous observations in regard to their significance indicates clearly that the entire process of human individuation is designed for the audience. The phases in the coming of age of an average yet extraordinary figure, the love story, the experience of homelessness, the search for direction, and the foundation of a new community coalesce in a sphere of continuous reflection that includes not only the figures in the text but also the reader. The *Meister* novels explore two types of social interaction and group formation: society and community.[28] Society was derived from communal associations over the course of history. Juridical, political, and economic considerations determine its organization. Administrative systems have a rational design; moral imperatives are replaced by situational ethics; and religious expression shows increasing rationality. The opposition of material interests, the pursuit of wealth, the division of property, a clearly defined class system, and a hierarchical power structure dominate social interaction. But competition and the antagonism of conflicting forces stimulate progress. The dominant view of history sets forth that historical forces move toward the unknown but always present new challenges, new signification, and new insights. Individual human relations become increasingly impersonal. Finally, individuals are viewed in terms of the functions they perform. The resulting experience of confinement increases social disorientation, and individual volition begins to clash with the collective will. The opposition of interests and the antagonism of social forces call for reform.

The Larger Circumference: A Society in Transition. The narrative setting of the *Wilhelm Meister* novels portrays panoramically a society in transition from an agrarian community to the beginning of the institutionalization of impersonal relations through the rise of the middle class of merchants, tradesmen, and industrialists. The accumulation of capital, the conflict of interests, competition, the division of labor, and specialization are considered constructive stimuli for individual advance and social progress. Wilhelm is introduced as an ordinary but talented youth in a setting breathing the spirit of the wealthy merchant class. The tradition (grandfather, father, his friend Werner and Werner's father) is characterized by rational self-interested behavior and the acquisition of wealth. It is perceived as legitimate order. The exchange of commodities, commerce, strict accounting, and the motivation for profit, that is, economic rationalizations, control human relations. The trust in the mercantilistic system, confidence in the success of hard-working individuals, and faith in progress color sentiments. They determine the attitudes toward education and the arts.

Brief accounts of Wilhelm's father and grandfather describe the adaptation to economic interests. Economic gains permitted the grandfather to acquire a fine art collection. It is sold by Wilhelm's father who invests the money wisely in a business venture. He displays his social status in his home. Massive furniture, luxuriant wall covering, decorative rugs, and ornamental objects evoke the impression of stability that is further underscored by the merchants' deliberate movements. Both enjoy their wealth and combine the motivation for personal profit with a paternalistic attitude in their outlook toward society. The critical portrait of Werner exemplifies the salient features of the group's ideology. Wilhelm's brother-in-law is intelligent, rational, active, capable of sincere emotions, and proves his friendship with Wilhelm throughout the years. He accepts the existing class structure, loves order, works hard, lives austerely and counts on a calm existence untroubled by bursts of sentiments. He is interested in increasing his wealth by seizing new business opportunities. But for Werner the accumulation of capital has already become an end in itself. As a youth he gains "profit" by supplying Wilhelm with the attire for puppets (17: 36) and when he marries Wilhelm's sister he sells the large house so that the proceeds can bring "a hundredfold interest" (18: 9, 265f.) The sequence of acquiring wealth but collecting art—selling the collection in order to enlarge the business – selling the house to invest in speculative ventures—shows the shift in thinking toward the exclusive preoccupation with capital. The possession of art, expensive furniture, and even real estate diverts money from its primary function. When Wilhelm sees Werner after years of separation, he is shocked by his appearance. Werner has completely surrendered to the commercial "ethic," looks unhealthy, and is obsessed with the pursuit of profit (18: 263). By focusing on the entrepreneurial spirit of commerce, the novels establish that the class does not create wealth that is of direct benefit to society. But by showing that Werner can be educated and by detailing Wilhelm's growth, the narrative points to the possibility of a reform that is set into motion on the individual level within the larger sphere of a society about to enter the age of commercialization.

The recurring contrast motifs of the dysfunctional and exemplary family accentuate the family's role as an interactive system in the process of individuation. The motif of the dysfunctional family, which becomes prominent throughout the nineteenth century, subsumes in *Wilhelm Meister* vulnerable children and adolescents reared in a bleak environment, incestuous love (harpist), orphans (Mignon, Susanne, Sophronie), half-orphans (Felix), family conflicts among parents and children, brother and sister, husband and wife (Melina, Serlo, Aurelie), and disruptions caused by abandonment, illness, and death (Mariane, Adolf, Friedrich). Dissociation in the family threatens the social fabric. For these reasons, the "Tower Society" seeks to provide a stable, ethical model of education and guardian-mentors for children from dysfunctional families. The exemplary love, mutual respect, cooperation, and profound reverence for the creative forces in the universe illustrated by the family life chronicled in "Sankt Joseph der Zweite" (19: 10-28) contrast with the images of abused children in the larger social setting.

The broad panorama of artisans, tradesman, miners, barbers, workers, and especially the weavers (Lenardo's diary in *Wanderjahre*) acquaints Wilhelm directly through observations or indirectly through reports of members of the "Tower Society" with society at the moment when technological innovation gives rise to social change. At this juncture traditional views, uncertainty, worry, fear of the future, and hopeful expectations coexist. Spinners and weavers fear the unemployment caused by mechanization (20: 85). The yarn trader is convinced that he will find suitable work, the repairman (*Geschirrfasser*) who has mastered the technique of weaving and the principles of constructing looms strongly supports technological innovations. (20: 92 ff.) He foresees an increase in productivity and has no inclination to join the emigrants (20: 98). Susanne who oversees the operations of a small weaving mill anticipates moral dilemmas and ethical compromise. She fears the impending mechanization—"it rolls toward us like a thunderstorm, every so slowly; but it has found its direction, it will come and strike" (20: 190)—because the industrialization will destroy the reciprocal interaction of the small self-sufficient community. Lenardo has an abiding interest in technology and studies the varied application of science to commercial crafts and machines throughout his travels. He studies and understands the history of technology. He realizes how the modification and innovation of all implements influence economic systems and cultural attitudes. Still, his spiritual preference is for the work which enables the craftsman to retain a sense of direct involvement with the product of labor (20: 81f). He favors almost instinctively the integration of work in a community association that encourages direct interaction and cooperation of everyone.

The chorus of conflicting voices conveys an impression of society in transition. Artisans and workers face an uncharted course. The best that can be expected is the acceptance of change and the affirmation of the future. That spirit is expressed by Baron Jarno who becomes the geologist Montan and works with miners before joining the emigrants. He tells Wilhelm twice that neither the introspective cultivation of the self nor the quest for the complete development of a person's full potential is meaningful without unwavering dedication to service for the common interest and the unflinching acceptance of continuous transformation of the self (19: 41-44; 20: 46-47). Appropriately, he conveys his conviction through a metaphor based on his observation of workers stoking a charcoal-kiln: "I consider myself an old coal basket of beech coal" and have "the idiosyncrasy to burn myself on behalf of the self"(19: 42).[29]

The detailed portraits of the life, manners, and attitudes of figures from the aristocracy also express the temper of a class in transition. This is significant. The aristocracy is the privileged class and others look toward it for orientation. Especially Wilhelm believes initially that only aristocrats have the advantage of unimpeded individual development. However, instead of a concern for the political events affecting the country's future, he encounters an atmosphere of indulgent waiting for history to take its course. The accounts of preparations for receptions, dinners, and theatrical performances establish the loss of historical perspective. In addition, they contour the essential features of a daily routine that permits the in-depth diagnosis of a serious social problem. The class has lost the ethos of service to society. The aristocrats who are farsighted and prepared to encourage social reform either stand apart from the group or participate actively in preparing the socioeconomic structure of the new community. The others are trapped in a circle of "busy indolence." The daily routine consumes all available time and leaves no room for serious reflection. Meetings are governed by etiquette (17: 170f.) Conversations are disrupted by the hair stylist, by the demand to serve a cup of chocolate, and by the interjection of unrelated personal proposals or requests (17: 188 ff.).The inability to listen indicates the absence of a constructive dialogue. The boredom is relieved by visits, theatrical performances, and travel. But the duke looks at the theater as a medium that can enhance the status of the nobility; the baron sees in it an outlet for his amateurish playwriting; and travel fails to to open new horizons. The narrator mentions that landowners are concerned with the sound management of their estates but frequently refers almost in passing to a recurring preoccupation with business transactions, settling accounts, and arranging the transfer of wealth to heirs. The story of "The Man of Fifty Years," for instance, focuses on love, error, and renunciation but also captures the atmosphere of self-complacency, the habitual display of wealth, the daily routine of overseeing the estate, and the compelling desire to keep the wealth in the family (19: 195-263). In their relation with members of other classes the aristocrats are paternalistic, friendly, if slightly condescending. The duke and duchess express sincere interest in Wilhelm's plans and care for the comfort of the actors. However, the appearance is deceptive. The servants on the estate display utter contempt for the troupe (17:180-84). Similarly, army officers (17: 225-26) small merchants, innkeeper, the pastor and his wife (20: 36) and suppliers dependent on the good will of the aristocrats have internalized attitudes that are characteristic of a rigid social structure.

Small Circles That Have the Potential for Reform. Within the large circumference of this complex society about to enter the age of industrialization, mercantilism and impersonal forces, the narrative establishes several smaller, personal circles which both relate to and contrast with the large circumference. These include: (1) the company of traveling actors and entertainers that Wilhelm joins and later finances; (2) the estates of Odoard and of Hersilie's, Julietta's, and Lenardo's uncle; (3) the "Tower Society"; and (4) the "Pedagogic Province." Each offers the wandering Wilhelm a different opportunity to learn and experience relationships with others that ultimately leads to his gradual development and reform. The group of entertainers (dancers, jugglers, tightrope walkers) and traveling actors that Wilhelm joins form an association characterized by a relatively open class system. They are not a subculture. On the contrary, the group is represented as a class that displays all the symptoms of social strain and intellectual disorientation present in society. In addition, the actors have three primary functions in the novels. They advance the action. By joining troupes, Wilhelm continues a journey that acquaints him with a cross section from society, with social stratification, and with unresolved social issues; the function is transferred to travel by and with members of the "Tower Society" when the actors recede into the background. The actors provide the setting for Wilhelm's desire to free himself from conventional restraint. He experiences love, seeks friendships, and forms lasting attachments. The association with the actors also forces Wilhelm to prove his abilities, clarify his objectives, and recognize his limitations.

The social prestige accorded to the actors varies widely among other classes and individuals. However, the group has an internal hierarchical structure that mirrors the societal system. The relative status, prominence, and power of street dancers, actors playing incidental roles, minor parts, or leading character, and director are determined to some extent by professional competence but to a large measure by alliances with those who finance the production. Next to professional envy, intrigues, and flirtatious affairs, economic considerations determine the group's interaction. For instance, Melina is a petty bourgeois who constantly worries about money, flatters the rich, takes advantage of his actors, and not only deceives but bilks them (17: 121,150,175). Serlo encourages Wilhelm's aspirations but is motivated by his own interest (18: 7). Philine imitates the mannerism of aristocrats by enjoys shocking others with impetuous behavior. Rehearsals deteriorate into contentious altercations or bouts of drinking (17: 142). In general the atmosphere is charged with erotic overtones and a latent, all-pervasive anxiety.

The administration, lifestyle, and social relations on the estates of

Odoard, the "Pedagogic Province," and Hersilie's, Julietta's, and Lenardo's uncle contrast sharply with the established order. They should be considered as operative prototypes of collective efforts that point in the direction of the system envisioned for the new community. The nature surrounding the estates has all the characteristics of the cultivated cultural landscape. Well-maintained buildings, attractive villages, and cultivated fields blend into the landscape. Trading centers attract persons from far and wide. In addition, the estates send their products directly to those who live in the region. Ownership imposes the responsibility to assure the well-being of all employees. All workers from field labor to overseers and from craftsmen to teachers understand the reasons for their activity and are encouraged to introduce modifications or innovations to the process. As a result they feel that they control their actions and attain self-respect. But self-reliance is tempered by the spirit of cooperation. Capital is not solely employed to enlarge the existing agricultural-commercial combines but to support the community. The shift from personal interest to public benefit is evident in the uncle's stance toward the world. Born in Philadelphia, he has returned to Europe to launch the pioneering reforms that the " Tower Society" intends to introduce in its settlements in America. He has faith in reason, is tolerant, believes in human equality, and trusts that everyone can be inspired to seek perfection in a chosen profession. The numerous inscriptions decorating the walls of his estate underscore his confidence in the cumulative increase in knowledge. The epigraph " From the utilitarian through truth to beauty" (19: 72) serves as a reminder that the final goal of all activity is the creation of a value benefiting the entire community (19: 47-94; 20: 3-9; 152 ff.).

The new community envisioned by the "Tower Society" is impractical and unfeasible in a modern global economic environment. In spirit, it corresponds precisely to the hopes for reorientation expressed by many thinkers in the Western world during the last decades of the twentieth century. It has utopian characteristics. Nevertheless, it incorporates the essential elements that guarantee the development of healthy individuals in a healthy environment. The principles governing the membership, organization, and spirit of the community permit organic growth. They assure the adaptation to a new environment expected in America. They also permit the initiation of social reform at home (18: 18f.; 19: 91f; 20: 144). Members are chosen from every existing social class. Many were endangered by the milieu (Philine), swayed by emotions (Friedrich), or had acquired bad habits (the barber). Some like Lothario change and renounce their feudal privileges. Others like Odoard assume responsibilities that crystallize their lifelong efforts. All members learn from error, are willing to serve, and become capable of instructing others. In fact, they mature into servant-teachers. Hence, the novels clearly show that while many are shaped by their environment, the individual has the freedom to shake off the yoke of social determinism. The new community includes persons from all vocations: farming, crafts, management-planning, industrial arts, public service, and artists. They are chosen for their skill and dedication.

The communal organization is based upon a set of principles that seek to balance the crucial relation between individual autonomy and necessary social regulation. The constructive thought given to the preparation for emigration, that is, the foundation of the community, centers on two comprehensive objectives: the reorganization of the economic and social relations that exist in society and the establishment of a system that ensures peaceful cooperation. To achieve the goal, all individuals must exercise voluntary self-control over the unrestrained expression of emotions that endanger the communal order. They learn to govern themselves.[30] They join freely in an association that emphasizes equality. Members who have demonstrated organizational skills are chosen as supervisors who may be recalled. The new community will have a police force and a judiciary with a jury system but hopes to promote a spirit that minimizes deviation from the general effort on behalf of the commonwealth (20: 160-71).

That spirit is best expressed in the intrinsic principles that govern the education of children in the "Pedagogic Province." When Wilhelm entrusts his son to the educators he is puzzled by the ceremonial salutations practiced among the children. He is told that nature has endowed everyone with much that can and will be developed. However, the most important quality that determines the essence of a person—"that guarantees that a human being becomes truly human"—has to be acquired: it is an abiding respect for all manifestations of life. It is a profound reverence that springs from the reverence for above, below, and the other (19: 180-81). The reverence for above expresses respect for the cosmic creation, the recognition of principles of order, and the awareness that humans seek to clarify their image of the gods. The reverence for the earth shows an understanding not only of fertility and growth but also of the dark forces residing in an individual's antaean nature. Mortals experience "extraordinary bliss" and "disproportionate sorrow." They voice the joyous affirmation of life (Philine's song 18: 45-46) and chant the lament communicating the grief of all those who feel overwhelmed by dark demonic powers (Harpist's dirge 17: 155-57). Mortals are exposed. They seek orientation during their journey through life in the shelter of a home, the cradle of origin. While not stated as a pedagogic principle, the education for life seeks to strengthen the will to prevail over the latent death wish present in the desire to return to the primal source of awakening (Mignon 17: 165). Individuals yearn for communion with others (18: 92) and begin to understand that unselfish friendship offers hope for ethical self-mastery.

The reverence for the friend, instilled in all pupils, frees persons from the preoccupation with the self. They encounter and share with the generalized other. They interact on a personal and symbolic level. They become aware of social concerns. All travelers in the novels encounter the aspirations, values, and norms of a viable community acclaimed in Schiller's "Das Lied von der Glocke." But in contrast to the affirmation of permanence of a social structure that is anchored in middle class virtues, the wanderers in *Wilhelm Meister* are exposed to the idea that the new community may not endure. All plans are open to revision. Therefore, they meet during the journey a vast array of unique problems that call for specific solutions, such as the management of Odoard's estate (20: 152 ff.), and receive conflicting advice that often leaves them confused (18: 7). They experience existential anxiety but stand apart from a society that is spiritually disinherited because they share the spirit of reverence. Reverence for the creative spirit, for the source of life, and for the other is the root of all knowledge. Reverence is the basis of cognition, socialization, and social reform. The timeless concern for individual perfection and the specific need for social, economic, and political reorientation intersect in the recognition that the individual must be worthy of life (*lebenswürdig*) and capable of translating thinking into action. This perception becomes a communal mode of reasoning and thereby a basic cultural disposition of thought.[31]

   Individual Development: Small and Expansive Circles. Wilhelm's development illustrates the general process of preparation for service in the community. His growth has a unique personal and a supra-personal dimension. His learning adventures, errors, disappointments, reversals, and accomplishments mirror those of others. They are also played out before his eyes when Felix, Hersilie, Hilarie, and Therese blunder into mistakes. Their recurrence galvanizes renewed reflection that provides the basis for enhanced learning experiences. As Wilhelm's development advances to the point where it corresponds to the group's communal objective he sheds the cloak of the wanderer-surveyor and becomes the archetype of the physician who cured himself and is prepared to heal others.
   The course of the action exposes Wilhelm to formative influences that enhance and objectify early impressions from childhood and youth revolving around love – friendship – death, the tradition of his class, the arts, and social interaction. The initial phases of his journey, narrated in detail, reveal his preoccupation with himself. He is immersed in emotions, lured by dreams of success in the theater, an almost feverish search for reorientation, and above all in half-awareness of the forces that govern his life. The tentative nature of his slowly forming convictions is illustrated by his sensitivity to individuals and the response to stories that mark important lessons.
   Throughout the early phases of his journey, Wilhelm relives the general cultural disorientation. He has absorbed the spirit of "order and cleanliness," of his class and has inherited a good measure of his father's "love for luxury" (17: 62), but dreams of accomplishments that transcend the confines of the existing conditions. Wilhelm creates for himself a world of fantasy. He is performer, stage designer, and director of his puppet theater. He writes poetry, memorizes literature, adopts epics for his theater, and imagines future roles he will play in life as hunter, soldier, horseman, and director (17: 9 ff, 22, 33 ff.). Awakened by his love for the actress Mariane, he envisions not only a life of bliss on her side but also feels called to found a German national theater. He overlooks the disorder of the theater's milieu, remains ignorant that Mariane has another lover who supports her financially, stands lovestruck behind the stage, and is ready to escape

the pressures to conform to life at home when his father asks him to embark on a journey to collect debts from customers. Wilhelm regards the journey as first step in his liberation, not as the socially accepted sojourn that familiarizes businessmen with trading centers, commerce, and new opportunities (17: 38-40).

The initial exploration of the world offers additional insights into the attitudes of the middle class and opens a new perspective on the life of actors (Melina's escape with his fiance, arrest and release). Wilhelm sees the daily routine, hears complaints about debts, witnesses personal intrigues. He also perceives that the actors are not drawn to the stage by an affinity to literature but consider acting as a tedious profession. Wilhelm, overcome by "apprehensive uneasiness" (17: 65) returns home but prepares to leave again to join another theater company (Serlo). He writes a moving letter to Mariane outlining his plans only to be completely disillusioned by the discovery that she has had another lover. The narration passes over several years during which "our bruised friend" (17: 83) concentrates actively on business activities. He becomes reliable and successful, apparently understands the incompatibility of his dreams with reality, renounces his love, and burns all mementos of Mariane. As a final gesture he repudiates his poetic aspirations because he failed to achieve perfection and reduces the folders containing his poems to ashes (17: 90).

The essence of Wilhelm's experiences at the initial moment of his coming of age is formed by elements drawn from the personal and social realm. He encounters the conflict between a legitimate, conventional bourgeois order and the mode of existence of entertainers. He recognizes the limitations of both. He is troubled by the tension between his yearning for affective relations and the prevalent associations dictated by material interests. He loves and forms friendships, but is disappointed. He seeks a new professional orientation but fails. He suffers, feels dejected, and reproaches himself. The narrative succeeds in transforming this common experience of dissatisfaction with convention, first love, and dejection into an extraordinary event through innovative thematic alignments, the focus on typical patterns, and the introduction of philosophic considerations that are further explored in Wilhelm's ensuing travels. The initial phase of the journey functions as a prologue to a process of successive thematic enhancement, the crystallization of thoughts, and the examination of interrelated questions. Some issues originate in the action sequence (individual – community, love – friendship), some are injected by the narrator (self-sufficiency of love, monologue instead of dialogue 17:61; success / failure 17: 83); others are addressed abruptly by a figure suddenly introduced in the novel for the purpose of raising a question of recurring concern. For instance, Wilhelm meets a stranger who is later in the novels identified as a member of the "Tower Society" just before the discovery of Mariane's double life leaves him utterly dejected and helpless. During their conversation, the stranger clarifies the difference between a spectator's emotive identification with a painting's motif and the critical understanding of its execution, the distinction between a painter's style and artistic perfection (17: 76-77). Moreover, the stranger states views on chance and fate that anticipate Wilhelm's subsequent effort to free himself from the idea that fate determines self-fulfillment. Wilhelm hears for the first time that all individuals have the potential to shape their destiny. Success, however, depends on a person's capacity to learn and to mature (17: 78-79). Wilhelm's decision to burn his poetry and then renew his travel appears to be a direct consequence of the conversation.

When Wilhelm ventures forth again, the narration begins to alternate between highlighting his experiences and representing the conduct of persons who are representative of the social scene. The bipolar focus permits an account of Wilhelm's unfolding life and the simultaneous characterization of formal social structures. During the early phases of the journey Wilhelm remains introspective. He cannot forget Mariane, is deeply touched when he hears that she gave birth to a child (17: 129), becomes entangled with Philine, and forms an intensive emotional bond with Mignon by sharing with her the love of an adoptive father for his daughter. The preoccupation with himself is interrupted by moments of reflection and the acquaintance with strangers who unknown to him are members of the Tower Society (Abbé, Jarno-Montan). Alternating between inwardness and reflection, Wilhelm reaches a point where he can neither commit himself without reservations to the theater nor completely reject his aspirations. He finances Melina's traveling troupe, joins the actors, becomes a member of Serlo's company, writes, designs, and directs a performance of *Hamlet*. Yet, he remains intellectually aloof. He tarries when he should leave, becomes snarled in situations, participates in daily routines of the actors, and is absorbed in the lives of others. Over time, the phases of Wilhelm's growth blend affective and cognitive experiences. He keeps a careful diary. His observations of the business climate (manufacture of linen) are as penetrating as those of aristocratic conventions (17: 176 ff.) or Philine's nature. The meeting with Felix gives rise to concern for the care and education of his son. Werner's letter informing Wilhelm of his father's death impels him to reconsider his plans. Still, while Wilhelm's affective behavior is enhanced, his conative impulse lacks direction and is diffused.

He writes to Werner that his desire is the "complete development" of himself, the "harmonious growth" of his full potential (18: 13, 15). He argues that the stage is ideally suited to such pursuit because it assimilates the currents of the time and transcends the traditional class structure. His reasoning is spurious and serves to justify his decision at one of the many "crossroads" (18: 8) to join Serlo's troupe. Writing, acting, and directing plays will hone his native empathy. Wilhelm adopts roles and shows the capacity for extremely diverse orientations in life. His existence is and remains extravagant throughout the early phases of his journey. The fact that the motif sequence heart / hand is notably absent from the narrative underscores Wilhelm's immersion in emotions. His conduct is prompted by emotions but he does not experience a strong conflict between feeling and action. His love is expansive and leads him to others, but it is also restrictive because he cultivates his own sentiments. Until he leaves the theater his heart is filled with overflowing emotions, pain, joy, sadness, love, and affliction. Wilhelm's affective impulses are only tempered by careful reflection after he becomes the conscious wanderer-surveyor of the world. He can then decide upon a course of action that best serves the interest of the community. The technique of comparing affection with reflection extends to the counsel Wilhelm receives from members of the "Tower Society" and has a double function: it exposes Wilhelm's inner hesitation and the difficulties of absorbing conflicting advice and also shows a continuous process of clarification.

The parallels, including similarities of salient characteristics in figures, are linked thematically and profile Wilhelm's indecision and growth. They extend from the *Lehrjahre* to the *Wanderjahre*. Encounters capture the essence of previous experiences. Their significance is examined, verified, and augmented in the light of previous observation. Hence, all perception is enhanced and projected onto a higher plane of cognition. This process becomes apparent in the changing perceptions of love and friendship, in the revaluation of formative influences and ideas of educational reform, and the ongoing debate over social reorientation.

He is deeply troubled by an education that requires the full commitment to the community, a commitment that presupposes reverence for the other. Hence, he is portrayed as a precarious individual, a *Sorgenkind des Lebens*, whose resolution has to be proved during the years of travel. He experiences continuous emotional upheaval, finds his son, falls in love, realizes that his engagement was a mistake, and meets his bride. He wavers at every crossroads. Intellectually, he absorbs a continuous flow of impressions but remains initially uncommitted. He reads for instance the "Bekenntnisse einer schönen Seele" (18: 93-168) to Aurelie to comfort her as she lies dying, but the confessions submerge in his subconscious. Their essence, the effect of the exclusive, excessive cultivation of refined, exalted sentiments of love and friendship on an individual, becomes a source of serious reflection only after Wilhelm meets Natalie and Makarie. Similarly, Wilhelm is passionately attached to Mariane, feels rejected by her infidelity, falls ill as a result, and grieves over her loss. But the news of her death, the discovery that Felix is their offspring, and the attraction of other women begin to color his memory, and as a result, he remembers Mariane as an individual who experienced profound sorrow, was capable of personal sacrifice, and loved her son and him. Later, Wilhelm is tempted by the countess (17: 227 ff.) and Philine. But he is most deeply affected by the fleeting encounter of an amazon on a white horse immediately after the traveling actors were attacked by robbers and he is wounded on the head and chest (17: 260-75). Although a physician from the group bandages Wilhelm, the amazon appears as the true healer: she removes her coat and covers Wilhelm who drinks in a vision of a beautiful woman whose head is "surrounded by rays as a shining light spread slowly over her picture" (17: 266). As he faints, the "saint" disappears from sight.

The encounter leaves an indelible mark. Love expands in the vision to embrace the power to heal and to give life, even when Wilhelm remains confused and uncommitted. Love overwhelms Wilhelm again when Therese freely expresses her desire to become his wife (18: 316-

17). The engagement leads to inner confusion. The love cannot be sustained since Wilhelm proves incapable of accepting her without reservations. He transfers to the relationship not only his past experience with Mariane and affection for Mignon but also the memory of his vision.

Mirroring the experiences of the protagonists in the two interwoven stories "The Man of Fifty Years" (19: 195-263) and "The New Melusine" (20: 100-27), Wilhelm and Therese learn to clarify their emotions and thereby succeed in establishing a meaningful friendship. When Wilhelm, upon meeting Natalie, discovers that she is the amazon, he can reconcile his vision with reality. At this moment, he is ready for marriage and a relationship based on respect for each other. Wilhelm has matured and proves his steadfastness during the years of absence from Natalie. Their letters give evidence of mutual respect and common concern for the welfare of others. The narratives indicate that Wilhelm reaches this stage of self-knowledge that permits him to share his life fully with Natalie and his son only after understanding his deep affinity to Mignon and after observing Makarie. On a symbolic plane, these encounters parallel Faust's sensitivity to Knabe Lenker-Euporion and his journey to the realm of the mothers.

Mignon and Makarie typify the two poles, indeed the proto-phenomena, in the continuous process of perceiving and reflecting that determines the growth of self-insight. Mignon's life captures the essence of the impulse toward self-fulfillment and inner harmony attained by merging with the source of life. She yearns to return home, longs for the caressing touch of night, and embraces death while nourishing Wilhelm's capacity for love through her own consummate affection. She ministers to Wilhelm's physical and emotional wounds. She stills his bleeding with her hair when he lies on the field and urges him to affirm life when she dies. Makarie embodies the spirit of dynamic expansion. Her imagination, mind, and soul have become one with the creative spirit of the universe. She is moving with the constellations. "She circles the sun since childhood, however, as is no established, in a spiral receding more and more from the center circling toward the outer regions" (20: 214). Mignon and Makarie's stance toward the world reflects two unique, yet entirely different forces of individuation that also personify cultural patterns. Mignon consumes herself in the process of yearning for the ever-distant objective: union with home and Wilhelm. But she finds fulfillment in her romantic longing. Makarie has attained the serene outlook on the human conditions that springs from the integration of her desires in a classical supra-personal norm. As representatives of the micro- and macrocosmic perspective, as moon and sun, they become guiding lights on Wilhelm's spiritual firmament.

The ambivalence of Wilhelm's relationship with Mignon whom he has rescued from a debasing subsistence as street dancer, who is mysteriously related to the harpist, who combines deep longing for her homeland Italy with religious devotion in her songs, but who grows increasingly attached to him and his son, leads Wilhelm away from the communal life of the reform circle. Mignon's only "holds on life" are her longing for Italy and her desire to be with Wilhelm which she also extends to his son. Her consummate devotion is expressed in her salute of arms folded over her breast (17: 123) and the ability to divine his needs. Her songs calm his restless striving for some indistinct self-fulfillment; they also beckon him to follow into a realm far removed from the concern for the community. He dreams and hears: "Only those who know longing / know how I suffer!"(17: 280). Mignon's dancing expresses Wilhelm's strong conviction that spectator, performer, and spirit of of art should become one during a performance. At the moment when Wilhelm prepares to leave, Mignon has a epileptic seizure. Wilhelm, utterly distressed, clasps her to his heart. His tears cover her face. Clasping and kissing "the child," Mignon becomes his daughter: "You are mine, I will keep you and not leave you! My father! I am your child" (17: 164).

Wilhelm keeps his resolution and proves his compassion for Mignon. Nevertheless, the encounter, veiled in sexual undercurrents, gives rise to a prolonged struggle marked by strong ambiguities between love and friendship, the desire to embrace the demonic and the call to action, art, and life that is only resolved after Wilhelm attains a level of insight that enables him to view Mignon as the spiritual essence of inwardness.[32] The narrative anticipates the transfiguration through allusions to Mignon's affect on Wilhelm. He is not only moved by compassion but attracted by the aura of the arts. He feels a deep, perplexing affinity with the dispossessed and the outsider-artist. He thinks about Mignon and the arts, Mignon and the disorderly lifestyle, Mignon and the androgyne, but quickly suppresses his thoughts. The narratives detail two occasions when Mignon dances before Wilhelm. For the first dance she has carefully practiced the fandango and adapted the fast paced steps to the "egg-dance" she performed in the troupe. Swirling between the raw eggs on the carpet and clapping the castanets, Mignon appears wild and unrestrained yet "serious and austere" as she moves like "clockwork." The dance becomes a festive-somber ritual that induces Wilhelm "to forget his worries" and stirs his desire to keep Mignon (17: 130-31). The second dance, a frenzied, even savage, rhythmic outburst of emotions takes place immediately after Wilhelm's successful *Hamlet* performance and prior to Mignon's attempt to visit him at night. Mignon strikes the tambourine; her hair flies, her head is thrown back; she looks "like a maenad" (18: 56). Her sensuous performance excites the whole group of actors and actresses. It creates the atmosphere for the night in which Wilhelm abandons himself to a woman whose identity he does not know. He is ready to follow the allure of the extravagant life when the still mysterious guardians intervene with the warming: "For the first and last time! Flee! Youth, flee!" (18: 58).

Mignon's performances crystallize many of Wilhelm's previous experiences in the world of theater. They leave their imprint and enhance his awareness of the theater's Janus face. Mignon remains pure, is henceforth move reserved, changes physically into a young woman, but sheds the interim appearance to assume her true form in death. Dressed as an angel distributing gifts to children at Christmas, she expresses the wish to leave the world. Her song apotheosizes the metamorphosis into the timeless entelechy: "let me radiate appearance until I become" (18: 283). Subsequently, after witnessing Wilhelm's engagement (18: 316-17), her "heart" can no longer endure the pain experienced in feeling the beloved and home removed to "infinite distance." The death mass celebrated by the Abbé challenges the participants to venerate the creative force that inspires all existence (18: 353-55). Extolling life, the choir restates, modulates, and affirms the admonition in the inscription on the sarcophagus of Natalie's uncle: "Remember to live" (18: 312). As the spirit of everything Wilhelm sought in the arts departs, he loosens the bond to the deep-seated composite picture of love and death. The affection for Mignon is transformed into the remembrance of friendship between kindred spirits. Finally, as life summons him to a new stage, Mignon becomes a symbol for a basic human disposition that animates a cultural thought pattern (19: 266-68) which he renounced but never disavowed. Clearly, the spirit of renunciation that permeates the representation of individual development in the *Wanderjahre* is grounded in profound respect and understanding of conflicting forces.

The contrasting figure of Makarie is introduced as an extraordinary, dignified (*wunderwürdig*) lady who gives spiritual direction to the teachers guiding the education of young girls. The setting, an ancient yet perfectly modern estate surrounded by towering oaks and beeches, corresponds to the atmosphere of learning in the charitable institution. The wisdom of the past is nourished as wellspring of modern thought. History moves neither in cyclical patterns nor in a linear progression but evolves toward the unknown. The study of history, complemented by a continuous dialogue with the present, raises life in all its manifestations to intellectual consciousness. A perception becomes part of the collective thinking. Insights from artists and philosophers are collected in folios in Makarie's archives.[33] They comprise concentrated abstracts, aphorisms, and maxims that illuminate humanity's unbroken effort to understand life. Ranging in scope from Hipprocrates and Plotinus to Cousin and modern scientific thinkers, the writings give impetus to an continuing discourse with the world. They provide orientation and give direction but also raise questions by pointing to the difficulties encountered in the search for truth.

Makarie is described as a wise person venerated by those living with her (20: 212), as a healing influence in the life of others (19: 263), as a sibyl whose unique vision merits the lifelong study by her friend, the astronomer, mathematician, and physician (19: 145 ff.; 20: 215 ff.), and as an individual who radiates a quality of essential being that calls forth the best in everyone she meets. Wilhelm, for instance, acclaims after speaking to her: "we should pray to God for great thoughts and a pure heart" (19: 136). Makarie has studied astronomy, biology, mathematics, and philosophy. She has obviously also devoted her life to examining human relations, and discovered that the observed data failed to corroborate her intuitive vision. In the light of everything related about Makarie (dialogue with the world, renunciation of selfish interests, concern for the common good), this observation indicates that the narrative has approached the outermost limit of any representation of development, that is, existence in the process of becoming. Makarie herself passes beyond the studies of thought as historically concrete evidence of existence to concentrate on the cognitive process. She also sets out to verify the truth of being. As a result, she is transformed in the narrative into a symbolic conception of a being that circles in a spiral toward infinity while it continuously absorbs and emanates light. Thus, Makarie becomes the essence of thought structures. She moves into a direction "where imagination cannot follow" (20: 217). In contrast to the unique individuations represented in Mignon, the physical and spiritual substance that finds unity in the center, Makarie advances toward the unexplored periphery. Wilhelm is profoundly affected by both the grace of inner self-sufficiency and the creative spirit of dynamic expansion. They form as much a part of his expanding spiritual horizon as the impulses he receives from the triumvirate Abbé, Jarno-Montan, and Hersilie's uncle. Ultimately, Wilhelm finds it impossible to distinguish what he learned from each. He clearly absorbs the prevailing atmosphere of faith in human integrity, worth, and dignity. He begins to understand the need for renunciation, respects the allegiance to communal cooperation, and accepts the view that life is not dominated by chance.

The astronomer outlines the results of his observation of Makarie's nature immediately before the novels end with a picture of Wilhelm saving his son's life. Thus, the sequence of the final events juxtaposes for the last time a fundamental conflict that is sustained throughout *Wilhelm Meister.* The education for social reform requires the cultivation of skills and interests benefiting the community. Individuals are called upon to aid a fragile human association. They must renounce the dream of unrestrained, unlimited development of human potential in favor of the view that the total potential resides in the group. The actualization and progressive refinement of the primary themes of education for life, preparation for a new community, and renunciation create the impression that the conflict is resolved in the firm allegiance to the communal spirit. Nothing could be further from the truth. The conflict is only stabilized among individuals who accept the idea that the individual will should be subordinated to a collective value. It continues in the next generation.

Felix carries within him the seeds of Wilhelm's dreams: "You are always created new, magnificent image of God! and immediately you are wounded, wounded from within and without" (20: 226). The exclamation affirms a fundamental contradiction inherent in the polar forces that propel the human spirit. The thematic juxtapositions as well as the disruptions of a continuous narration verify this observation. The themes linked to social reform are explored, restated, and augmented. They are distributed on an arc leading from society to community. The theme of the journey is open-ended. When themes intersect the journey, they are developed in a process that establishes connections with successively higher planes of possible signification. They are stacked on a spiral. The educational principles, the Abbé's observations, and Jarno-Montan's lessons are followed by explanations that clarify and prevent any misunderstanding. The encounter with the "Schöne Seele," Mignon, the harpist, Makarie, and the astronomer-physician call for continued reflection.

The Reform Circle. Contradictions – Polarities – Dynamic Balance. The parallel design of successive explications of educational principles and junctures during the travel that call for reorientation confirms the tight interlocking of one set of themes with the exploration of potential throughout the journey. The pedagogic principles that govern the instruction in the "Pedagogic Province" and guide the counsel given by the Abbé, Jarno-Montan, Natalie, Therese and the Antiquarian are flexible and pragmatic. Reiterated throughout the novels, they set standards for an education that benefits both individual and community.

1. The mentors encourage natural inclinations in young pupils. They strengthen and improve aptitudes as rapidly as possible to provide for an evaluation that permits reorientation in the event that the chosen direction proves to be a mistake (18: 167). Any skill, craft, or profession is taught with careful attention to detail. In the process students are prepared for excellence in work and learn that perfection is attainable. As they progress, they are introduced to the liberal arts, the cultural heritage, and the intellectual tradition. However, the attention to detail, careful observation, and the perfection of abilities remains the core of all instruction. Students learn that the arts, philosophy, the sciences, and technology may posit unique axioms and profit from different approaches to problem solving. They discover that poetry requires attention to rhyme, that the painter must master per-

spective before modifying it, that musical compositions obey their own law, and that mining technology requires in addition to knowledge of geology the mastery of mathematical calculations (19: 38 ff.). They "understand that art is called art because it is not nature" (20: 10) and that the liberating arts fail to free the spirit if they are regarded as a source of diversion for amateurish interests. All students and wanderers alike are discouraged from dilettantism.[34] They should seek knowledge and use it constructively by serving the community (18: 393; 19: 168, 171).

2. The historical orientation in governmental-institutional arrangements singles out aspects that illustrate consent, tolerance, moderation, and a continuous search for enlightenment. Government is essential, but all authority is limited by laws that are open to revision. Supervisors are selected for demonstrated abilities and can be recalled. Individuals are bound by a social contract for safe and peaceful living. Many of the observations are reminiscent of Locke's theories and Rousseau's ideas. They stress reason and denounce the artificiality of rigid conversations (17:137; 18: 60). They consider the creation of a stable consensus in society and the reconciliation of individual liberty with necessary regulations. However, the members of the "Tower Society" never contemplate a return to a state of nature, never express notions of a general will residing in the community, and never overvalue personal economic interests. Instead they expect individuals to reach a level of self-insight that permits the renunciation of those personal ambitions that impede social stability. The management of the resources of the pedagogic province and the uncle's estate points in the direction of future communal growth. The group has shed social prejudice. The uncle manages the estate so that his private advantage coincides with the general interest.

3. The standards governing the conduct of everyone in the new community seek to assure that a wide range of values is organized into a combination that permits everyone to experience self-worth in freely accepting the ethics of reverence. Conduct is judged by its total value for human living. Mutual trust, constructive dialogues, respect for the other, and friendship foster confidence. Individuals appreciate the reasons of organizational structures and communal action. By contemplating the paintings in the octagonal hall, the pupils in the pedagogic province recognize that faith reaches for an ideal of strength

and wisdom that is beyond individual attainment (19: 184-92). They also learn that phases in religious thought (ethnic, philosophic, Christian 19: 182-83) reveal humanity's persistent endeavor to free itself from the bonds to the demonic power of the abyss. In stressing Christ's mediating role and his dual nature as divine and human, the mentors prepare the youth for the spirit of humanistic reverence for the above, below, and the other that ultimately erases the distinctions between religion and ethics.

The humanistic spirit is nourished by respect for all efforts to understand the physical order and all attempts to explain the values that ennoble existence. Hence, the narrative gives more prominence to the motivation for the collection of art and the preservation of historical documents than to the collections themselves. When Wilhelm rediscovers his grandfather's collection, it broadens his understanding of perfection within styles of different periods (18: 313). When he looks at the portraits in the gallery of Hersilie's uncle, he sees how individual self-reliance progresses toward communal cooperation while retaining the spirit of dedication to activity. Meeting the Antiquarian, he becomes acquainted with the incentive for preserving functional artifacts as evidence for persistence, continuity, and advance in the materials and methods used in fashioning implements for social needs (19: 167-71).

Divergent in nature and specific significance, the various collections ranging from books to firethongs have intrinsic value as testimony to the reciprocal interrelations between individuals and the group. The dominant view that influences all educational principles is articulated in Jarno-Montan's assessment of the Abbé's convictions (18: 326). The Abbé refuses to posit absolute evil. He accepts polar tensions as constructive forces for social development. He encourages the development of individuals and seeks to guide them toward perfection in a chosen field, but discourages the unfocused straining for a achievement inspired by vague hopes of self-fulfillment. He concludes that Wilhelm's enchantment with inspiration is a desirable characteristic but determines that his desire for an artistic career is doomed. He observes that Wilhelm is at the moment incapable of gaining critical detachment from his emotions and therefore will fail to develop his unique abilities (18: 321-25). The Abbé dedicates his life to the education of individuals and believes that all talents and ca-

pacities should be developed—"but in many, never in a single individual" (18: 327). The total potential of humanity resides in the
group and can only advance fully as individuals contribute their
unique achievements. It is consistent with his view that the design for
communal association excludes national aspirations and envisions the
cooperation of nations in a world community.[35]

This paradigm also provides for a dynamic interchange between
developing self and a changing world. However, the constructive integration of the individual in society always entails the renunciation of
apparently unattainable objectives, of dreams, and conceivably the
sparks of intuition. The reciprocal relation between individual and
community safeguards a generative reception of formative influences
and sustains the prospect of social change through individual action.
But any renunciation that is based on the complete identification with
concepts of morality, conceived as timeless, restrains the erratic spark
of genius and reduces the possibility of sudden change, unexpected
breakthroughs, or chance occurrences. The dominant cultural imprint
tends to reinforce the disposition toward organic change. Thought
can stagnate or exhaust itself in the search for communal equilibrium.
All classical representations of individual self-realization struggle with
a basic paradox: there can be no compromise between the vision of
absolute ethical commitment and the existing social reality. When
texts outline social reconstruction through individual-communal interaction and adaptation, they either incline toward resolutions reaffirming general cosmopolitan principles or highlight specific educational
goals. Goethe absorbs and stylizes the contemporary literary current
of social-educational novels in *Wilhelm Meister*. He also frees himself
from the limitations imposed by the theme of social reform. The novels explore and affirm contradictions. They also face resolutely the
incompatibility of a desirable, practical orientation in life with the
ideal of perfect human development.

Goethe succeeds in representing the permanent process of becoming that is inherent in contradictions and polarities by amplifying the
theme of the journey. In contrast to the novels by Hermes, Jacobi,
Knigge, La Roche, and Wezel, travel in *Wilhelm Meister* does not merely motivate a series of sequential events but integrates multiple narrative strands. The journey is the nucleus of the narrative, the catalyst
for change, and the medium for sustaining paradoxes. It accommo-

dates all themes related to individuation. It provides the matrix for the action sequence, the crossroads, and the stations that identify stages of the process of intellectual and spiritual growth. Travel is a primary experience etched indelibly on Wilhelm's mind emerging from his perception that the journey symbolizes individual development across the life span. Wandering and journey, exodus and return, loss of direction and search for orientation identify the human condition. The successive phases of Wilhelm's journey commence with his search for self-fulfillment, extend over years of learning, and conclude with his decision to live an active life in a small circle. The primary stations single out preliminary stages of progress, stasis, sudden spurts, and relapses that precede the end-state of ultimate self-realization. Some extend on long periods; others highlight moments of self-discovery. They identify prominent aspects of the self in social interaction: (1) Self: undifferentiated self, primary impulse, Adolf; Mignon; (2) Self: self-sufficiency and mirroring, Mariane; the theater as alter ego; (3) Self: potential self, Werner; Mignon; the image of the artist-actor; (4) Self: shared experience, Mariane; Therese; Natalie; (5) Self: significant other, Schöne Seele; Sankt Joseph; Makarie; Abbé; Jarno-Montan; Hersilie's uncle; (6) Self: constellations of love / friendship, fulfillment / renunciation, society / community; (7) Self: self-insight, from introspection to critical observation of the self in the interrelationship with others. The years of Wilhelm's conscious travel enhance the theme by adding the dimension that the journey is a survey of the human condition and the unrealized potential of the community.

Important junctures occur when the dominant theme of the reciprocity between individual and community intersects with the theme of the journey. The themes are then no longer simply developed but raise questions, are contradicted by future events or pose a problem that could be resolved by different solutions. To be sure, the intersections initiate a process of continued reflection in the reader by creating ambivalence and by defamiliarizing the action. However, they also coincide with moments when it becomes apparent that *Wilhelm Meister* is more than a narrative of individual development. The novels trace basic categories of thought that characterize the intellectual history of a society. They describe a persistent mode of thinking that holds sway in a culture and shapes individual perception. Above all, they contour an innovative pattern that is designed to change the prevailing categories. Established thought and elements of new perceptions converge in parallels, juxtapositions, and antithesis that center on education, fate, art, travel, and self-insight. The pattern highlights:

Education. Education should encourage the complete and free development of all capacities in an individual and disregard specific objectives (Wilhelm 18: 13). "Your general education ("Bildung") and all the preparation for it is foolishness." Achieve excellence in one field. "That counts in the community" (Jarno-Montan 20: 47). Persons are endowed with general capacities and specific abilities. Some are awakened and developed as a result of experiences at home and social contact. Others remain undeveloped (Wilhelm 20: 31-32). All education instills the desire for perfection in a chosen craft or profession (Goal of the Pedagogic Province and the Tower Society). The true potential of humanity lives in the community. Individuals expand it through unique achievements resulting from their dedication to perfection (Abbé).

Fated and free existence. An individual's life is determined by birth, family, class, and environment. Chance occurrences exert a decisive influence (the prevailing view in society, initially expressed by Wilhelm). Individuals have the power the shape their destiny (exemplified by everyone who joins the new community). Chance can be controlled by reason (the Abbé's observations; 17: 137 passim). But the Abbé wavers in his convictions and fears that Wilhelm will fall prey to the atmosphere of the theater. He warns him and outlines the program for Wilhelm's journey which controls unforeseen encounters by imposing rules of conduct that prevent Wilhelm from pursuing a trail offered by chance.

Theater Arts. Art is the spontaneous expression of inspiration and emotion. The artist is an inspired minstrel. The performance evokes emotions that unite actors and audience with the spirit of the artistic creation. They surrender to emotions (Wilhelm 17: 90-92; his expectations for the *Hamlet* performance). Art is not emotion but creates the semblance of emotions after a process of careful reflection. The theater should not inspire the complete emotional identification of the audience with the performance. It should appeal to emotions and the mind (20: 18). The artist is above all a highly skilled craftsman (17: 136-39; 20: 10-13, 46).

Journey. The narrative design of the journey integrates different levels of representation. It relates phases of Wilhelm's travel with stations of significant encounters and repeated decisions at crossroads. The narration proceeds along stations that form the basis for a growing understanding of the world. Wilhelm's journey is disrupted repeatedly. He hesitates, looks for a new beginning, sets out in different directions, and is completely confused by the conflicting advice (18: 7, 169, 184, 225, 324), yet pursues the great adventure of fulfilling his ambition. The Abbé informs Wilhelm: "Hail young man. Your years of apprenticeship are over" (20: 261), but the sustained process of learning, of observation and reflection begins at that point. Travel conveys the conception that human individuation progresses on stages of increasing awareness throughout life. The conscious acquisition of knowledge succeeds undetermined experiments with diverse possibilities. The creation of a new community gives direction to aspirations. The spirit of reverence has mastered the dark powers of the subconscious and the violent temper of conquest that is an essential element of the Western mind in *Faust*. Throughout the novels, the journey functions contrapuntally. Individual sensibility is reorganized during the journey in reflection. Supra-personal conceptualizations affect reflection which is subsequently converted into renewed individual sensibility. Moreover, the process of clarification that accompanies Wilhelm's growth to the time when he accepts his role in the community as a physician is disrupted by exclamations or observations that indicate an unabated yearning for unrestricted development of all capacities. For instance, while observing his son at play, Wilhelm decides to give structure to the game, "to prepare it for him better, more orderly, more purposefully." At the very instant, the child loses all interest. Wilhelm exclaims: "You are a true human being! . . . Come my son! Come my brother, let us play in the world without purpose" (20: 347). Rephrasing Schiller's observation that the purposeless activity of play enables individuals to experience true freedom, Wilhelm envisions himself as *homo ludens* on a journey to freedom. Hence, the journey signals the possibility of recurring error and disturbance. It also affirms polarities and contradictions that are at the core of civilization and continuously enrich collective ideational patterns.

Self-insight. Introspection opens the door to self-knowledge

(Wilhelm). Individuals can feel the cosmic order in their hearts (Astronomer-Physician 19: 137). Individuals are not happy until they limit their impulse toward the acquisition of absolute knowledge and their desire for the development of all capacities (Abbé, Jarno-Montan 18: 328). A person gains insight by cultivating the anticipatory perception that initiates a process in which every observation is reorganized in the light of subconsciously absorbed cultural patterns ("Tower Society"; see "Anschauende Urteilskraft"; JA 39: 30). "A person who has great potential gains self-insight and understanding of the world late in life" (Instruction to Wilhelm 18: 324). Any attempt to understand the self must begin by seeing the self through the eyes of others (Wilhelm reading his biography 18: 270 ff.). Real self-insight is elusive but can be attained by observing the world (the lesson of Wilhelm's education for life).

Community. The historical cultural tradition gives Meister and the " Tower Society" the awareness of continuity and a strong sense of purpose for the present. The understanding of the past requires conscious reflection, insight, and self-knowledge gained in active life. From the reflection springs the desire for reform. But the foundation of a model community is represented in its inception and the continuous process of preparation. The novel does not address the question whether the new community in America will prove viable in the future. The thematic resolutions offer a realistic and appraisal of all structured, institutionalized social regeneration. One group emigrates to America. The others will uphold the virtues of common efforts in an enclave at home. This pragmatic, yet restricted outlook points in the direction of the narrowing focus in representations of human development and social reform throughout the nineteenth and twentieth centuries. In Adalbert Stifter's *Der Nachsommer*, Wilhelm Raabe's *Der Hungerpastor*, and Gottfried Keller's *Der grüne Heinrich* reform is initiated in a small group and does not reach outward to society. In many of Raabe's novels, a circle of friends sharing common ideal form enclaves in the threatening environment of impersonal cities. In Thomas Mann's *Der Zauberberg,* the development of the individual is all-encompassing, but the novel's conclusion shows that the community is not ready for reform. However, the dynamic potential of the thematic cluster comes to full efflorescence again in Thomas Mann's *Joseph and seine Brüder,* and Hermann Hesse's *Das Glasperlenspiel.*

In *Wilhelm Meister,* journey, quest for self-development, renunciation, and social reform merge in the prospect of an exodus from existing society that is characterized by outward emigration and inner concentration. Possible expansion and contraction appear momentarily in equilibrium. The full thrust towards ever-new horizons requires the full affirmation of a permanent revolution of change.

Wilhelm Meister integrates the diverse features that are associated with the thematic constellation of the reform circle in the classical tradition. The representations of the theme in the dramas and narratives of seventeenth-century France and eighteenth-century England and Germany range from proposals to rectify specific conditions identified as detrimental to personal, economic, and social security to calls for a complete reorientation in individual behavior by forswearing the aggressive tendencies of the will to power. The reform circle gives direction to the individual's crossroads decision by balancing individual interests with the concerns of the community. The metaphoric field supporting the theme consistently includes allusions to the existing "order" in which individuals give free rein to the desire for personal, economic, and political power. In contrast, the new community, be it the small circle of like-minded individuals or a domain within the state, is built on a solidarity of values (noble sentiments - heart, constructive dialogue, respect for the other, sensible distribution of wealth) that guarantee healthy social relations. The representations all express the view that cooperation must replace the antagonism of self-centered interests, and that all persons from courtiers to kings and from servants and workers to heads of households, agrarian, or industrial organizations must renounce personal advantage to achieve a common end. Hence, the theme and supporting motifs advance a paradigm of common effort, respect, and cooperation. The distinction between society and community transcends the contrast between artificial conventions and natural life because the new communities are grounded in the freedom of individual decision-making that promises continued renewal.

CHAPTER 8
CENTRIFUGAL SPIRAL: EXPANDING HORIZONS – SELF-INSIGHT

The action of building a community based upon the exemplary decision of a pivotal individual, group, or pair that forms the structure and dramatic or narrative interest of many classical texts requires a more dynamic figure than a concentric series of circles can convey. Far more descriptive is the concept of the centrifugal spiral. Its expansive movement forward, upward, and outward is as limitless as the future and as the universe. We propose that the figure of the endlessly expanding centrifugal spiral elucidates most clearly the vitality and appeal to universality in classical texts. By reaching forward toward the future, upward to a divine order or a principle that gives direction to human aspirations, and outward ultimately to the audience, the centrifugal spiral points beyond the framework of the text, as illustrated by the verbal picture drawn by Pope's *Essay on Man:*

> As the small pebble stirs the peaceful lake:
> The centre moved, a circle straight succeeds,
> Another still, and still another spreads;
> Friend, parent, neighbour, first it will embrace;
> His country next; and all the human race;
> Wide and more wide, th'overflowings of the mind
> Take every creature in, of every kind;
> Earth smiles around, with boundless bounty blest,

And Heaven beholds its image in his breast.
(IV. 364-72)

Starting with the "center moved," that is, the individual's commitment
to virtue, Pope's spiral traces consecutive concentric circles outward
that link together ever larger segments of the "human race," until
eventually all are encompassed. After it has run its course outward to
embrace "every creature . . . of every kind," the spiral turns upward
to link the earth with "Heaven" in a continual mutual reciprocity.
Since the spiral's movement never ceases, the verbal picture is one of
boundless energy moving into the indefinite future. Because it seeks
to encompass all, it ultimately binds all individual manifestations into
Pope's vision of the "Grand Design" of the universe.[1]

Other classical authors describe the encompassing energy of the
centrifugal spiral less visually than Pope. Instead, they use its ever-
upward, -outward, and -forward movement as a device to structure
their focus on the progression from individual exemplary conduct to
community, from a restrictive past to a liberating future, or from
human chaos to divine order. In classical dramas written for the entertainment and instruction of audiences, the centrifugal spiral reaches
out beyond the borders of the text to include spectators. For example,
at the end of Molière's *L'Ecole des maris* Lisette addresses the theater-
goers: "As for you, if you know of any werewolf husbands, / Send
them at least to our school" (V. x.). The play's "school" has taught
two chief lessons: that a human being cannot tolerate being treated as
an object, and that the foundation of true love is predicated on communication. Though presenting these simple rules for human behavior in the form of an entertaining comedy filled with amusing plots
and deceits, the playwright nevertheless offers the "lessons" as models. The centrifugal reformative movement away from Sganarelle's
isolated and isolating possessiveness opening the play toward the couple's mutual dialogue and trust at the end reaches out to the audience
through Lisette's final words.[2] While in *L'Ecole des maris*, Sganarelle
excludes himself from the joy shared by the other figures in the
young couple's coming union, in other comedies by Molière, the authoritarian figures (Arnolphe in *L'Ecole des femmes*, Orgon in *Le
Tartuffe*, Harpagon in *L'Avare*, Philaminte in *Les Femmes savantes*,
and Argan in *Le Malade imaginaire*) are persuaded to join the sup-

porting figures in the coming celebration of the young couple's marriage. This reconciliation that, according to Frye, typifies the ending of the conventional romantic comedy,[3] underscores the centrifugal movement of these comedies as reaching outward to include as many figures as possible and forward to the future continuation and regeneration of society in the form of potential offspring.

Contemporary critics were among the earliest to perceive and note the centrifugal outreach of classical dramas that relates a figure's choice of exemplary conduct on stage with the audience. Guez de Balzac wrote Corneille: "Your *Cinna* cures the sick."[4] Pope stated in a letter to Caryll in February of either 1712 or 1713 that Addison's *Cato* fills the audience with "so warm a love of virtue" that it unifies its audience by popularizing virtue.[5] The drama also succeeds in linking each individual spectator with the exemplary conduct of its protagonist:

> To wake the soul by tender strokes of art,
> To raise the genius, and to mend the heart;
> To make mankind in conscious virtue bold,
> Live o'er each scene, and be what they behold; . . .
> (Pope, "Prologue" to *Cato* 1-4)

In praising *Cato,* John Eusden traces the centrifugal movement begun on stage that sweeps the public upward: "'Tis nobly done thus to enrich the stage / And raise the thoughts of a degen'rate age . . . / See how your lays the British youth inflame."[6] In lauding the play's appeal to the audience, Pope and Eusden have identified its salient feature. For without the transcending centrifugal spiral that moves simultaneously upward and outward, the play would be of limited interest. Its action of conspiracy, stubborn resistance, murder, and suicide is hardly uplifting. Military force and subterfuge threaten increasingly to conquer and render futile any hope for freedom and self-determination. But the upward and outward movement that begins with Cato's determination to incorporate and thus preserve for the future the original Roman virtues into his person, attitude, and decisions conquers the general atmosphere of hopelessness. The spiral moves from Cato to Juba, who in modelling himself on Cato, has changed from the "licentious savage" to one of Cato's "reformed men." It encompasses all those who will benefit from the "god-like height" reached by Cato's self-sacrifice for family and friends, including vicariously the audience, if it too will imitate Cato's decision.[7]

The outward-, upward-, and forward-moving centrifugal spiral provides both the energy and the structure for Corneille's *Cinna* and *Polyeucte.* In both plays, the spiral's motion commences when an individual decides to strike out on a new, unexplored path of action that represents the rupture with a constrictive past and points to a liberating future. By emphasizing the forward thrust of Auguste's decision for magnanimity and Polyeucte's conversion to Christianity, Corneille sets the centrifugal spiral in motion. Its direction differs in the two plays. In *Cinna,* Auguste's resolution to pardon the conspirators first embraces Cinna ("Let's be friends, Cinna" V. iii. 1701), then Emilie, Maxime, and by implication, the entire circle of conspirators. Through Livie's prophetic words, the spiral continues its outward movement to include all future would-be conspirators, all of Rome and its provinces in the future as well as in the present. Simultaneously, the spiral propels Auguste upward to "a place among the immortals." Upward, outward, and forward propulsions of the spiral become united in Auguste's final anticipation of the future communal sacrifice to the gods.

In *Polyeucte,* in contrast, the spiral's movement upward precedes and at first interdicts any movement outward. Polyeucte's haste to flee his new wife, home, and worldly position and pleasures for an assured entrance into heaven through baptism and martyrdom at first excludes all others. Indeed, his decision to substitute a precipitous upward-bound movement for the calm immobility of a continual earthbound existence even threatens to alienate him from his baptismal sponsor Néarque:

>
> NEARQUE: But in this temple death is certain.
> POLYEUCTE: But in heaven the palm is already pre-
>   pared.
> NEARQUE: You should merit that by a holy life. . . .
> POLYEUCTE: Why leave to chance what death assures?
>   When it opens heaven, can it appear hard?
>   . . . .
> NEARQUE: Live to protect Christians in these parts.
> POLYEUCTE: The example of my death will fortify
>   them better.   (II. vi. 661-72)[8]

Only the recognition that the impulse to martyrdom is based on an immediate response to divine grace convinces Néarque to join Polyeucte in the self-sacrifice that promises a straight and upward path to heaven. As Albin informs Félix after Polyeucte's witness of Néarque's martyrdom: "Far from being beaten down, his heart is [set] even higher / . . . you are indeed far from reducing him" (III. v. 999, 1002). The alienation effect of the upward moving spiral reaches a climax in Polyeucte's exaltation that no wifely charms will draw his heart away from its heavenly aspirations toward "[a]n assured happiness without measusre and without end / Above desire, above destiny" (IV. iii. 1193-94).

When confronted by Pauline's appeal to their former conjugal union, however, Polyeucte responds by setting into motion the outward movement of the spiral: "She has too many virtues not to be a Christian" (1276). His martyrdom will no long merely guarantee his own place in heaven but will also "purchase" Pauline. Once Pauline has been "baptized by this blessed blood" and stands ready to join her husband in martyrdom, the spiral of conversions accelerates outward to include even Félix:

> I give in to unknown feelings
> And by a movement that I don't understand
> From my fury I have been transformed to my son-in-
> law's zeal.
> . . . .
> His love shed on the whole family
> Draws after him the father as well as the daughter.
> (V. vi. 1770-72; 1775-76)

Confessing that Christians "[h]ave something within them that surpasses the human," Sévère, like Auguste in *Cinna,* gives this centrifugal movement its last direction: forward to a future reconciliation.

While *Cinna* and *Polyeucte* are structurally aligned with complete centrifugal spiral movements, Corneille's *Horace* provides an example for the technique of developing the spiral as a potential structural device. The potential development of the spiral occurs at two separate points. Each time it replaces a menacing isolating stalemate with a dynamic outward and upward movement. At the end of Act I, it takes the guise of the longed-for truce that dramatically breaks the stalemate of battle, suspicion, and despair that has characterized the figures' interaction thus far. The realization that "We are your neighbors, our daughters are your wives / And marriage has joined us by so many ties / That there are few of our sons who aren't your nephews" (I. iii. 288-90) leads to an abrupt renunciation of a "parricidal" war. This dynamic reversal unleashes a movement first outward to others ("Rome is in our camp, and our camp is in Rome . . . / Each is going to renew [association] with his old friends" 332, 334) and then upward to the gods, as Julie hastens outside the isolation of the palace to "our altars" to render thanks. This outward and upward momentum is immediately crushed, however, with the announcement of the opposing duelists. The return to hostility and alienation causes much of the play's dialogue and action to be devoted to an exaltation of heroism on the one hand (Horace) and a centripetal movement centered on fear, anger, grief, and despair on the other (Curiace, Sabine, Camille). The isolation, suspicion, and self-pity dominate the relationships between the figures and culminate in Horace's assassination of his sister. Having reached an extreme ambiguity (glory in fratricide), the momentum shifts again to form the beginning of a new, now uncontested centrifugal spiral when instead of continuing the cycle of blood-letting, King Tulle pardons Horace on condition "[t]hat neither hate nor anger remains between you [and Valère]" (V. iii. 1764).[9] In his reconciliation of the two rivals with Sabine, the King includes those who have died. Thus, the circle expands outward to comprise all who have sacrificed their lives in defense of their community: "It is in drying your tears that you show yourself / The true sister of those you mourn" (V. iii. 1769-70). Once more, the spiral reaches upward and forward in Tulle's final plan of a sacrifice to the gods that will cleanse Horace and bring all together in a communal celebration.

Tulle's vision of the unity of the community both at peace with itself and with divine order in the future is echoed by the voices of many other authority figures in Corneille's plays. These include not only Don Fernand in *Le Cid,* Auguste in *Cinna,* and Félix in *Polyeucte,* but also Pridamante in *L'Illusion comique,* the chief protagonists of *Heraclius* and *Agésilas,* and the community itself in *Andromède* which as a chorus invites the lovers to participate in the food, drink, and abode of the gods. The location of this emphasis on a dynamic movement outward, upward, and forward, often expressed in forms of the verb *go*, at the conclusion of the action testifies to the persistence of the centrifugal spiral as a structuring device of Corneille's plays.

In contrast to the dynamic impulse of exemplary action that forms the dramatic structure of Corneille's *Cinna* or *Polyeucte,* the centrifugal movement outward, upward, and forward in Racine's tragedies often depends on a pivotal character's renunciation of possessiveness or even life. The most decisive example is *Phèdre.* In choosing to remove herself from society through suicide, Phèdre opens the way not only for reconciliation but also for purification ("And death, concealing the light from my eyes, / Returns to the sun what they soiled [of] all its purity" (V. vii. 1643-44) and a future of hope for those left behind. With Phèdre gone, Thésée can reverse his previous direction toward isolation ("Let me, far from you and far from this shore / Flee the bloody image of my torn son" 1605-06) to form a new family circle with a future: "Let's go, enlightened all too much about my error, . . . / Let's go to embrace the remains of my dear son / . . . His beloved shall be my daughter henceforth" (1647, 1649, 1654).[10]

The identification of the triple centrifugal movement outward, upward, and forward with the moment of renunciation forms a recurrent pattern in Racine's *Britannicus, Bérénice, Mithridate, Iphigénie,* and *Esther.*[11] *Britannicus* differs from the others, because neither the title character nor the figure of authority initiates the centrifugal spiral. Rather, it is the imprisoned Junie who escapes the confinement of Néron's palace and passion, gives herself to the gods as a Vestal Virgin, and is carried triumphantly to the temple by the protective Roman crowd whom she will henceforth serve in devoting herself to the gods. Because her reach upward and outward separates her "forever" from Néron, whose future course will be quite different, the play's projection of the future does not include the centrifugal spiral, as Burrhus' final words testify: "May it please the gods that it is his last crime" (V. viii. 1768).[12] Nevertheless, Junie's acts of separating herself from the arms of Néron and uniting herself with the Roman people and gods presage a recurrent pattern in Racine's tragedies. For the female protagonists of *Bérénice, Iphigénie,* and *Esther* also willingly flee the arms of loved ones to offer their lives or union with their loved ones in order to fulfill the needs of the larger community. In subordinating their desires to communal requirements or divine commands, they set in motion a centrifugal spiral that stretches outward, forward, and upward. As in Corneille, the verbs expressing going or fleeing form the clearest signs of this spiral. Together with their opposite of staying, going and fleeing express a radical rupture with the confining past or preoccupation with the self. Titus's words are prophetic when he asks in his decisive monologue in *Bérénice*: "Has the universe seen its course changed? / Let's delay no longer . . ." (IV. iv. 1035, 1038). Likewise, Bérénice expresses her rejection of the possibility of continuing past patterns of "disturbance, horrors and blood ready to flow" in favor of a conciliatory future with the words: "I love him. I flee from him; Titus loves me; he leaves me" (V. vii. 1500) and then directs Antiochus to do the same (1504). Functioning like Phèdre's suicide, her voluntary departure guarantees Titus' future reconciliation with his people. Unlike Phèdre, however, her exemplary renunciation impels a centrifugal movement that reaches out beyond the Roman people "to the universe."[13]

Iphigénie's willingness to obey her father's and the gods' apparent demand for sacrifice would at first seem to isolate her from others, especially from her mother and Achille who struggle to preserve her life. As she combats Achille's possessiveness, she seeks orientation from above: "Alas! It seemed to me that a beautiful flame / Lifted me above the fate of a mortal" (III. vi. 1045-46). But, as Agamemnon suggests, this vision extends beyond the historically grounded perception of the gods: "Make the gods who have condemned you blush" (IV. iv. 1246). In demonstrating with absolute certainty the superior strength of human attachment and devotion in contrast to divine cruelty, Iphigénie's projected rise to a status beyond the gods becomes a movement toward the Greek community: "Go: and let the Greeks who are going to kill you / Recognize my blood in seeing it outpoured" (1248). It is, of course, not Iphigénie but Ériphile who, by choosing the path to Calchas and eventual sacrifice, finds her place and role in the community that had rejected her. But it is Iphigénie who interprets the sacrifice as a fertility rite for the community and thus initiates the movement forward into the future: "And one day, my death, source of your glory / Will open the recital of such a beautiful tale" (V. ii. 1561-62).[14] The three movements of the spiral become coordinated in Ulysse's final verbal picture of the

Greeks' witness of Eriphile's precipitous sacrifice, the thunder of the gods' acceptance, the descent of Diana to receive the Greeks' incense and prayers, and the immediate departure of the Greeks into a glorious future. The energy of the centrifugal spiral, presaged in visions of communal festivities in other classical works, becomes dynamically explicit in *Iphigénie*.

In *Esther*, the title character's renunciation of self and possibly of life begins a centrifugal spiral that unites two opposing communities with each other and with both the divine and the future. Because Esther, despite her elevation as queen of Persia, unequivocably identifies herself as belonging to Israel and its God, she willingly accepts the Israelites' lot: "To perish for his [God's] name and his heritage" (I. iii. 217). In doing so, she moves forward into the future, outward toward her people, and upward toward God in prayer:

> Tomorrow, when the sun illuminates the day again,
> Willing to perish, if it is necessary that I perish,
> I will go offer myself as a sacrifice for my country.
> . . . .
> It is for you [God] that I march.
> (I. iii. 244-47; iv. 287)

But the final words of her prayer, "Turn finally his [the King's] anger against our enemies" (292) indicate the hope that Assuérus can be persuaded to join the initiated centrifugal spiral, a hope that is fulfilled when he listens to her explanation of her people's heritage and beliefs. By including Assuérus' predecessor Cyrus in her exposition of the divine plan, as well as by announcing the Jews' inclusion of the King in their prayers, Esther extends the threefold movement outward, forward, and upward to Assuérus. His response of guaranteeing future protection for the Israelites and acknowledgment of their God sets into motion a mutual reciprocity in which the two peoples will honor each other and God:

> I want them [the Israelites] to be honored equally as
> the Persians
> And may all fear the name of the God whom Esther
> worships.
> Rebuild his temple and populate your cities.
> May your happy children in their solemn feasts

> Consecrate the triumph and glory of this day,
> And may my name live forever in their memory.
> > (III. iv. 1184-89)

Reciprocity in renunciation forms the crux of the centrifugal spiral in *Mithridate*. Begun by Xipharès' subordination of his own desire for possessiveness to the as yet unknown feelings of Monime (I. iii. 318) and continued by Monime's willingness to open her heart to Xipharès "for the first and the last time" (678) despite the danger to do so, the movement outward at first includes only the two lovers. Once sure of Monime's love, Xipharès extends the denial of self-interest to his father when he first proposes going on his father's misiion and later valiently defends Mithridate against Pharnace's and Roman troops. Nevertheless, the spiral movement forward and outward of self-denial does not proceed unimpeded. Recurring self-interest in both Xipharès and Mithridate threatens to estrange each from the other. The last words of Mithridates' monologue: "how should I get out? . . . where should I leave?" (IV. v. 1421) indicate that the centrifugal movement has been stopped by possessiveness and accusatory jealousy. Just as his self-willed death threatens a final alienation, however, Xipharès' generous espousal of his father's cause opens the way to the expansive movement outward and forward in Mithridate's reassessment of himself as avenger of the universe against the tyranny of Rome, his gift of Monime to Xipharès, his concern for the lovers' security and dismissal of funereal honors. The centrifugal spiral assumes its widest spatial dimensions in Xipharès' final words: " . . . let us unite our sorrows, / And throughout the universe let us find him avengers" (V. v. 1596-97).[15]

Like Corneille's *Horace*, Goethe's *Faust* contains integrational units that relate and sustain both centripetal and centrifugal configurations. *Faust* exemplifies the parallelism of ideational construct and textual patterns.[16] Charting the interrelations between thematic clusters and figures, we can observe a dominant centrifugal spiral and a subordinate centripetal circle established within a figure resembling the hourglass. The figure of the hourglass is composed of two cones, one upright, one inverted; the vertexes of each intersect on a horizontal coordinate:

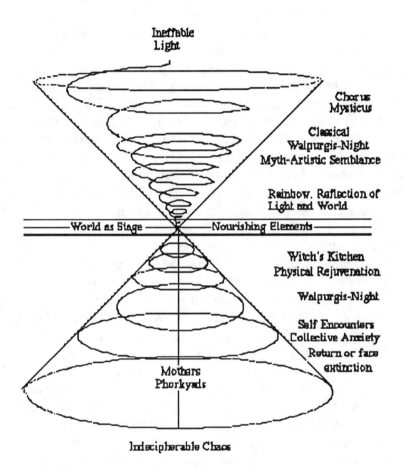

Ineffable
Light

Chorus
Mysticus

Classical
Walpurgis-Night
Myth-Artistic Semblance

Rainbow. Reflection of
Light and World

World as Stage —— Nourishing Elements ——

Witch's Kitchen
Physical Rejuvenation

Walpurgis-Night

Self Encounters
Collective Anxiety
Return or face
extinction

Mothers
Phorkyads

Indecipherable Chaos

Helixes designating human thought move within the upper mirror-cone in ever-widening curves toward increased understanding of the macrocosm. The top opens to an as yet ineffable order. The advance in the lower cone is restricted by philosophical materialism, determinism, and introspection. The vertexes intersect in the matrix of human life and history. Individual life forms grow, mature, and die. The sand in the hourglass falls steadily down. Collective thought persists in history. Hence, the horizontal line is not stationary. History is dynamic and moves toward the unknown. The human spirit can either expand toward the infinite or explore the finite. The will to know is positive. But understanding the word becomes impossible if the self moves in a confining circle of self-reflection. The diagram indicates that up or down depends on the perspective. In the free realm of thoughts that are shaped by human imagination, archetypal figures and newly created forms change positions (Earth Spirit) or metamorphose into a new essence (Homunculus). "Descend! I could as well say: rise! / All's one" (6275-76). The textual dynamics issue from the polar structures, contrast figures, thematic recurrence on different planes of signification, the juxtaposition of centrifugal and centripetal forces, and the disruption of action by distancing effects.

The parameters of polar forces, the possible centrifugal or centripetal movement, and the action are set in "Dedication," "Prelude in the Theater," and "Prologue in Heaven." The axis above – existence below corresponds to the orientation indicated in the salute of reverence practiced by the pupils in the pedagogical province of *Wilhelm Meister*. The dynamic macrocosm of light and darkness is a reflection of the creative energy that is to be venerated but cannot be fathomed even by the archangels (268). The Lord is distant but draws near from time to time (271). His clearly defined role in human events is to express confidence that mortals will find truth through constant ferment, error, and effort. To authenticate his conviction, he surrenders the life span of his "servant" Faust to Mephistopheles who is equally convinced that he can "guide Faust cautiously" along his own path (314). The conversation specifies Mephisto's assignment. He is to prevent mortals from becoming complacent (340-41). He will enter into the action, arouse, foment unrest, and galvanize error and guilt. In the process, he will attempt to substantiate his view that creation is imperfect. He sees mortals moving up and down in circles. They resemble crickets taking "flying leaps" only to fall back into the "grass to chant the same old song" (288-90).

As Mephisto enters the action, he plays different roles as illusionist, rogue, jester, seducer, and forthright commentator.[17] But he always points to the spuriousness of good intentions, creates awareness of unresolved contradictions, and holds forth the promise of peace in the acceptance of finite existence (1354-58). Mephisto's field of activity is the world. His function is to move Faust on a centripetal path toward self-fullfilment (stasis) within a confining world. His sphere, however, extends to protomorphic matter. He partakes of the beginning, the darkness "that gave birth to light" (1351), the force of chaos. Elemental and demonic, he has access to the source of "formation and transformation." He hands Faust the key to the realm of the Mothers, the spring of eternal recreation (6287-88). Yet, he cannot penetrate the floating "wavering appearance" of the pure spirit.

The action centers on the sphere of human activity. The world is the stage for a performance of the tragedy and comedy of life. Poet, director, and comedian consider the artistic limitations imposed on any recreation of the labyrinthine confusion of an "unformed" process of becoming. The poet seeks to create a pinpoint of eternity in the crystalline perfection (72) of art. He hesitates; his thoughts return to his youth (6-8, 184-85) when the spark of genius was untroubled by reflection. The director advises against the unity of the composition: "You offer a piece, give it in pieces then! / A rich ragout, you will succeed" (99-100). The comedian insists on incorporating the spirit of humor because it concentrates on the present and strengthens the will to persevere by playing with all serious issues (88, 164 ff.). A slice of life, a light touch, and the boards will come to life (234-40). The technique of direct representation in units that capture typical aspects of existence is complemented by a system of allusions, symbolic interrelations, thematic correspondences, and a carefully aligned spatial design.

The centrifugal and centripetal movements of expansion and contraction form a pattern of spirals, circles, and circles within spirals. The tension in the comprehensive pattern is especially pronounced in the metaphoric field that sustains the action-thought sequence of the theme of human development on a road leading to understanding the

world. Expansion is succeeded by restriction which gives rise to a renewed, augmented exploration of the world. The forces interpene-
trate each other since the spiritual dimension of culture informs the
physical or symbolic presence of all figures. Hence, the text shows
distinct junctures, discontinuity in the sequence, and stations that are
designed to enhance the interplay of conflicting tendencies. Junctures are frequently highlighted by transposing spatial and temporal
locations, changing roles, shifts in the narrative point of view, and the
objectification of emotional-mental states. The technique creates aesthetic distance to the immediacy of the action and calls for reflection
upon the immense diversity of human efforts in the historical span
captured in the semblance of art. The distancing technique ranges
from literary or political satire ("Auerbach's Cellar," "Walpurgis
Night," "Walpurgis Night's Dream," "Spacious Hall") and the disruption of theatrical illusion (Faust and Mephisto step out of their assigned role: 6501, 9048-49) to descriptions of Mephisto's all-too-
human nature (2513, 3004-05, 3149 ff., 7760 ff., 11780-11800,
11838-39) and interjections when characters question the reality of
events or their own existence (1248, 1527-28, 2333, 7271 ff., 7819-
20, 8075-81, 8347-52, 8719-22, 8838-40, 8874-75, 9411-16, 9594-
95).

The chain of development displays a series of functional and integrational units. Thematically they range from accommodation to
transformation of the self.

Accommodation and Revolt. Visions of a new society and calls
for reform contrast throughout the play with the acceptance of traditional modes of behavior, religious practice, a limited perspective of
life, social conventions, and the pursuit of political power. Faust embodies the spirit of revolt. Yet, he lapses into established patterns
whenever Mephisto succeeds in diverting his attention from absolutes
to easily attainable goals or when his actions are dictated by the will to
power. Faust expresses trust in God's love and the human capacity for
love (1184-85, 3431-58). But he rejects the basis of Christian
ethics—love, grace, faith, hope, patience (1604-05)—and rages that
Christ's suffering did not succeed in atoning for the sins of all other
sufferers ("Desolate Day – Field" 25 ff.). Faust denounces humanism, the traditional philosophical and scientific inquiries, and the accumulated knowledge of the past. He cultivates intuition and tries to

establish relations among phenomena that are not grouped together in order to reach new insights. But he resorts to force to actualize his vision (6553-63), transcends limits of perception (9949-53), and compromises his efforts by the unwillingness to tolerate different views of life (11233-42). Faust rebels against seemingly intractable conventions and the oppressive social system. He scorns war (10235) but condones violence as the necessary means to achieve reform.[18] However, Faust rebuffs all attempts by Mephisto to accept the accommodation with life as a precondition for contentment. Convinced that his view will prevail, Faust disavows existenctial anxiety when the ghost of worry enters to blind him: "Clear light within my inner substance shines still" (11500).

Confinement – Freedom. The contrasts extend from descriptive detail of scenes to symbolic representations of emotions and thoughts. Enclosed, oppressive spatial features coincide with instinctive behavior and feelings of despair, guilt, or nausea induced by knowledge ("Faust's Study," "Auerbach's Cellar," "Witches' Kitchen," "Nightscene Before Gretchen's House," "Prison," "Imperial Palace," "Baronial Hall," "Rival Emperor's Tent," "Faust's Palace," "Burial"). The sense of confinement energizes the thirst for freedom and immediate, direct breakthroughs to new planes of existence (magic, suicide as a step toward unexplored horizons: 690-712; dreams and visions of beauty or harmony: 1447-1505, 2429-40, 4183-4205; physical transformation by alchemy: 2577-86; the metamorphosis of Homunculus when the test tube breaks: 4869-73). Garden scenes, open landscapes, and the vertical orientation correspond to experience of freedom (walking outside the city gate and with Gretchen, "Garden," "Summer House," Gretchen's resurrection, "Pleasing Landscape," "Ageaen Sea," "Arcadia," "Mountain Heights," the open country before the hunt of Philemon and Baucis, Faust's ascent).

Motion and rest. The motif clusters wanderer: uncharted course / hut and love: respect for the other / self-seeking pleasure sustain the recurring tension between expansion and constriction. Faust is the typical wanderer on the road toward the unknown. His companion and at times alter ego Mephisto is the typical macrocosmic surveyor who is certain that all paths merge into a predictable design. The familiar characteristics of the figures are intensified and enhanced since they mirror distinctive tendencies in Western thought. Moreover, the figure conception of Faust consolidates all primary features of the developmental personality. Mephisto, despite his multi-functional complexity, concretizes all sentiments and judgments that thwart growth. He is forced to admit his miscalculation of foreordained, predictable events when Faust's essence disappears in the sky: "Fooled in old age / You deserved it . . . / You, the intelligent experienced master" (11834-41).

Faust affirms the vitality of action and accepts error as a constituant aspect of life. He resists the temptations offered by Mephisto, disdains all diversions by superficial pleasures, and is as dissatisfied with Mephisto's insights as with Wagner's erudition. This stance blinds him when Mephisto castigates his immorality or arrogant self-assertion and self-deception (3283-3300; Desolate Day 1 ff.); it also prevents him from recognizing the potential in an established tradition to achieve scientific breakthroughs of momentous importance and possible changes to society. Faust does not witness the creation of artificial life. He dreams and thereby inspires Homunculus and gives direction to his true becoming but remains disinterested in the peril of research that is divorced from values. Faust adores Gretchen's pure spirit, respects and even achieves her pious devotion (2695 ff., 3205 ff.), and is tempted to seek fulfillment in love. Still, the tension remains (3240-50). Lust overpowers love; compassion conquers lust but not the yearning for new experiences. Faust recognizes the disorientation in society and constructs a safe port for the realm he arrested from the ocean (11100-06, 11149-50). Yet, he rages against the shelter, the innocence, hospitality, love, and pure sentiments of Philemon and Baucis because their grove obstructs his view of the vast expanse of untamed nature. To accept their presence would require Faust to acknowledge the viability of a tradition he has denounced. Faust dreams of paradisiacal perfection, harmonious confluence, and peace (1447-1504, 6902-20); his mind is at rest when he relives the dream of Arcadia; and he even admonishes Euphorion to restrain his boundless striving (9819-20, 9877-83, 9891-92); he is momentarily content when he gains an overview of creation that appears to unfold organically (10095-104); and he accempts, if only conditionally, the possibility that a "free life in a free society" (11580) would crown his aspirations. Thus he dies while he envisions a distant future.

Self-development as process of becoming. The journey through life and history, the tension between motion and rest, aggression and cooperation, the motif of metamorphosis, and the contrast motifs of ascent / descent and light / darkness reinforce the process of individuation. In contrast to *Wilhelm Meister,* where aggressive tendencies are curtailed, healed, or converted into beneficial communal action, aggression in *Faust* persists unabated until the burial scene. It is clearly an indication of the energy unleashed by the will to power. It furthers change but also mirrors the continuity of a circular pattern:

> Behold the world:
> It rises and falls
> And rolls ceaselessy;
> It sounds like glass —
> Soon it breaks!
> . . . .
> It is made of clay,
> It will burst. (2402-15)

Aggression dominates the interplay of historical forces. Representative figures from emperor to soldiers (emperor, rival emperor, courtiers, bishop, Valentine, soldiers 844 ff.) seek to advance only their personal interests at the cost of the community. Collectives (ants, pygmies, dactyls, smite-all, brag-all, keep-all) strive for dominance. Social customs enforce conformity ("At the Well," "Night," "Cathedral"). Coexistence and cooperation are pictured in the water realm of Thales among the nereids, tritons, sirens, and dorids; they are alive in Philemon and Baucis; and they are central in Faust's vision of a future society.

Water, rising vapors, and light are sources of regeneration.[19] Water and fire, elements of boundless energy, generate the constant flow and ebb of life. They enter into the substance of the Earth Spirit (501-12); they give rise to upheaval (Seismos: 7503 ff.) and gradual transformation (Nereus: 8034 ff.). Faust yearns to share in the dynamic energy that he encounters on the surface of earth not only in raging storms, cascading waterfalls, and bizarre rock formations but also the turmoil of war and historical change. Although Faust's longing for direct access to nature's wellspring is initially governed by emotions (488, 5ll), he follows a path that leads to increased intellectual clarity.

The stages on the spiral toward light and understanding are marked by contrasts between darkening haze or fog and ascending mists colored by light.[20] Faust loses his vision when he is surrounded by haze or smoke (1142-43; 1310-13; 3938 ff.; 11380-83); he compares himself to a waterfall plunging toward the abyss (3350) when emotions overpower him. But dew regenerates his spirit (397, 4629-33), and the rainbow confers solace when he realizes that he cannot penetrate the source of light directly (4702-03, 4715-27). Faust reaches a new plane of insight when he contemplates the rainbow rising from the waterfall. "Mirrored hues" created by light and vapor point to the possible integration of the spiritual and physical nature of existence. The rainbow bridges the gulf between clarity and darkness. Its role as mirror and mediator points to Faust's experience of Helena's beauty in a historical setting and the miarriage of intellect and beauty in the timeless atmpsohere of Arcadia. Fog rising from Eurota's "sacred stream" envelope Helena and her maidens as they rise form the past (9087 ff.). A veil, semblance of Helena, remains in Faust's hands and lifts him swiftly above "everything common into the ether" (9951-52).

The yearning to soar into the sky toward absolute ideals (703-05, 1075 ff., Knabe Lenker, 5990-96), most vividly expressed in Euphorion's headlong heavenward rush (9897-9900), is tempered in Faust's disposition by the equally strong urge to affirm life through action. Successive action indicates the impact of previous learning experiences. It also reveals a continuous struggle with existential anxiety in moments of despair and worry that are succeeded by renewed dedication to the quest for clarity. Faust like Egmont experiences the agony of spiritual doubt moments before his death.[21] The scene in which Worry blinds Faust crystallizes all previous instances of uncertainty, irresolution, and suffering from which he emerged after lapsing into darkness or unconsciousness. The existential anxiety has three roots: paralyzing fear that the inner demon will overwhelm the individual, the doubt that spiritual love is unattainable, and the apprehension that the vision of a new society is doomed to repeat the cycle of rise and decline. Just before Worry enters, Faust rages against the "accursed *here*," and the chiming bells which, as Mephisto reminds him, signal that life is but "an empty dream" (11233, 11258, 11268). By blinding him, Worry asserts her place in life. But she fails to extinguish the inner light. As Faust has risen from previous confusion, he now looks to new transformation (11500-10).

While many figures are transformed in the play to articulate changing historical perceptions and dormant possibilities, Mephisto, Faust, and Homunculus pass through true metamorphosis. Mephisto's multiple roles dictate a changed appearance and stance. He beocmes totlaly absorbed by his roles which include the demon of negation, illusionist, devil, moralist, an alter ego figure, and even Phorkyas after experiencing complete disorientation in the past. But he seems to retain an unchanging inner essence. This appearance is deceptive. Slowly but steadily Mephisto is transformed into the midwife-assistant-agent who transmits the knowledge of contradictions. To be sure, he defines himself as spirit of contradiction (4743-50). Yet, he conveys the dialectic process of thinking by living, not acting, irreconcilable roles. Therefore, Mephisto moves down and up but does not descend to Manto who is: "I abide, time circles around me" (7488) and cannot penetrate the essence of the Lord who calls for the "joyous" contemplation of life which he "enfolds in love" (345-47). Homunculus remains chrysalid in his test tube until he sacrifices himself in a living embrace with the elements. As the chrysalis breaks, new life springs forth and transfigures the "waves with fire-laden wonder" (8473). Intellect and senses unite: "Glowing forms" spurt along a new path. Faust, like Euphorion (9654-61), is identified as entelechy in a chrysalid stage (11981-88). During his journey he experiences physical rejuvenation in dreams, in art, from the contact with earth ("spring-rain of petals" 4613 ff.), by contemplating the rainbow, and through spiritual rebirth in his encounter with antiquity. As he ascends from stage to stage, the chorus of blessed youths removes the "flakes" of the chrysalis and the "Penitent, once called Gretchen" prepares "to teach and guide him" (12092). The Chorus Mysticus reaffirms: the "insufficient / has been actualized; the indescribable / Here it is achieved" (12106-09). What has transpired? The eternal feminine earth has absorbed Homunculus and moved on the spiral upward to unexplained regions to form a new base for continued spirals. By introducing into the centrifugal movement the potential for continuous renewal, the spiral becomes an ideogram for the myth of youth.

The classical conception of a developmental personality posits stages on a spiral of continued emotional and mental change. Such change is not necessarily organic, uninterrupted, or directly linked to the preceding phase. But each successive stage involves integration of new experiences in the accumulated reservoir of knowledge. Figures reflect and compare new impressions in the light of previous experiences. Individuals are perceived as capable of developing their full potential. The measure of such growth is an ideal of social organization: individuals and community exist in reciprocal relations that foster respect for the dignity of life and for universal ethical principles. Since such principles are augmented and clarified during the process of historical evolution, the quest for full self-realization in active life and thought is never complete.

Hence, the literary works from Corneille to Goethe represent in one form or another figures at various moments of an identity crisis. The crisis calls for (1) the revaluation of the previous stance toward life; (2) a decisive shift in attitudes; (3) the recognition of a possible order in human interrelations that is more desirable than the existing relations; (4) the decision to act. Proposals for reform range from pleas for moderation and personal restraint[22] to calls for an unqualified commitment to ideals. They center on a constructive dialogue, the renunciation of selfish desires, and the willingness to reach out to the other and consider one's own interests in the light of what others think. In the process, the figures develop the capacity to affirm the polar forces and contradictions of life. At times, the counterpoints are veiled by the search for balance and the adherence to "classical" forms. But they are sustained in the short, balanced, clear expression of similarities and contrasts between past and present in Pope's couplets to the symbolic juxtapositions of apparent paradoxes in Goethe's octaves. They are fused in the spiritual essence of Rome's cultural landscape (*Römische Elegien*). Goethe considers the dynamic interplay between the attraction and counteraction of polar forces a powerful factor in individuation. The understanding of polarities contributes not only to the knowledge of the world but also to individual self-insight ("Gingo biloba," "Eins und Alles," "Elegie," and "Aussöhnung").

The developmental curve that posits stages of increasing understanding of the world raises the question whether such knowledge imparts true self-insight. Of the authors considered in our study who wrote before psychoanalysis left its imprint on literature, Goethe was perhaps most troubled by the challenge to attain self-insight. His observations indicate a deep skepticism toward introspection. Goethe's thinking was informed by a mode of observation and systematization that is outlined in "Der Versuch als Vermittler von Objekt und Subjekt," *Zur Farbenlehre,* "Anschauende Urteilskraft," "Analyse und Synthese," and "Geschichte meines botanischen Studiums." The investigator observes concrete phenomena, notes functional relations, reflects, makes a renewed, more focused observation, compares it with other available evidence, and arranges all the data. The process of observation, reflection, renewed observation, and systematization is impossible without constant verification. The verification requires comparison with data collected by others and also the ability to understand others and their methods. Whenever Goethe reflected upon the possibility to gain self-insight, he called for a clearing of a person's mental vision through a learning process gained by actively participating in the world.

> Know yourself—I admit that I was always suspicious of this important and profound obligation. It seemed like a cunning device of secretly allied priests who confuse persons by making unattainable demands and lure them from active participation in life to a false, inner contemplation. Individuals know themselves only if they know the world: the world reflected within and the self reflected in the world. Every new entity, carefully considered, unlocks a new capacity in us.[23]

Thoughtful observation gives rise to a better understanding of phenomena and increases the observer's self-awareness. With this awareness comes the recognition that each individual has the "duty" to understand the world. "How can one gain self-insight? / Never through introspection but through action. Try to do your duty and you know immediately what you are.—What is your duty? The obligation of the day."[24] The demands of the day impose on everyone the responsibility to discover the vital links between the present and the past in history, culture, and technology. Goethe certainly realized that the demand for the continued acquisition of knowledge seemed overwhelming: "Know yourself, what reward? / If I succeed, I must depart" (JA 4: 29). Yet he insisted that everyone aspire toward self-insight, because it alone can bridge the distance between self and others. "The highest that can be attained is insight into one's own motivation and thoughts, the knowledge of the self, which enables persons to understand the sentiment of others."[25] By including the dimension of the other, self-insight is expansive and, by extending the individual's intellectual horizon,[26] becomes a primary force that propels figures toward stages of critical knowledge.

NOTES

Full references to all primary texts are cited in the notes. Thereafter, all volume and page references in the *text* refer to the initial citations. Unless otherwise noted, all translations are our own. For easy access, all dates of publication or stage performance for primary literature are located in the *index* immediately following titles. Because the Bibliography focuses primarily on studies of interest to thematic research, subsequent references give the *volume, chapter, and note number* (I.1. n.1) of the first citation for complete information.

Chapter 1

[1]See Michel Bouty. *Dictionnaire des oeuvres et des thèmes de la littérature française.* 2 vols. Paris: Hachette, 1972; Elisabeth Frenzel. *Stoffe der Weltliteratur. Ein Lexikon dichtungsgeschichtlicher Längsschnitte.* Stuttgart: Kröner, 1962; —. *Stoff-, Motiv- und Symbolforschung.* Stuttgart: Metzler, 1966; —. *Motive der Weltliteratur. Ein Lexikon dichtungsgeschichtlicher Längsschnitte.* Stuttgart: Kröner, 1976; Franz Anselm Schmitt. *Stoff- und Motivgeschichte der deutschen Literatur.* Berlin: de Gruyter, 1976; and representative for "thematic anthologies," Albert Raasch (Ed.). *Thèmes et variations dans la poésie française du XVe au XXe siècle.* Frankfurt: Diesterweg, 1970. For a brief history of the concept of *Stoff,* as well its relationship to other liter-

ary elements, see: Manfred Beller. "Von der Stoffgeschichte zur Thematologie. Ein Beitrag zur komparatistischen Methodenlehre." *Arcadia* 5 (1970): 1-38; Adam John Bisanz. "Zwischen Stoffgeschichte und Thematologie: Betrachtungen zu einem literaturtheoretischen Dilemma." *Deutsche Vierteljahrsschrift* 47 (1973): 148-66; Horst S. and Ingrid Daemmrich. *Wiederholte Spiegelungen. Themen und Motive in der Literatur.* Bern, München: Francke, 1978: 6-10; and Raymond Trousson. "Plaidoyer pour la Stoffgeschichte." *Revue de Littérature Comparée* 38 (1964): 101-14. Recently, the study of themes has been included in surveys of comparative literary studies. However, most scholars remain indebted to either *Stoffgeschichte* or intellectual history. See among others Manfried Beller. "Thematologie." In Manfred Schmeling (Ed.). *Vergleichende Literaturwissenschaft.* Wiesbaden: Harrassowitz, 1981: 73-93; —. "Stoff, Motiv, Thema." In Helmut Brackert, Jörn Stückrath (Eds.). *Literaturwissenschaft. Ein Grundkurs.* Reinbek bei Hamburg: Rowohlt, 1992: 30-39; and Claudio Guillén. *The Challenge of Comparative Literature.* Trans. Cola Franzen. Cambridge, MA: Harvard UP, 1993: 191-239. While Beller takes cognizance of recent research devoted to the structural and functional dimensions of themes, Guillén outlines an approach that was already developed during the late nineteenth and early twentieth centuries. Two examples of the exploration of the relationship of *Stoff* to other literary components of individual works are: Mireille Frauenrath's study, *Le Fils assassiné. L'Influence d'un sujet donné sur la structure dramatique.* München: Fink, 1974 and Volker Klotz. *Die erzählte Stadt. Ein Sujet als Herausforderung des Romans von Lesage bis Döblin.* München: Hanser, 1969.

[2]The research is cited in Horst S. and Ingrid Daemmrich. *Themes and Motifs in Western Literature. A Handbook.* Tübingen: Francke, 1987; of specific interest to the present study are: Robert Martin Adams. *Nil: Episodes in the Literary Conquest of Void during the Nineteenth Century* . New York: Oxford UP, 1966; Gaston Bachelard. *L'Eau et les rêves.* Paris: Corti, 1942; Victor Brombert. "Esquisse de la prison heureuse." *Revue d'Histoire Littéraire* 71 (1971): 241-61; Robert T. Denommé. "The Theme of Disintegration in Flaubert's *Education sentimentale.*" *Kentucky Romance Quarterly* 20 (1973): 163-71; Laura G. Durand. "Thematic Counterpoint in *L'Exil et le Royaume.*"

French Review 47 (1947): 110-22; Marie-Madeleine Fontaine. *L'Homme et la machine. (Thèmes et parcours littéraires)*. Paris: Hachette, 1973; Enrico Garzilli. *Circles Without Center: Paths to the Discovery and Creation of Self in Modern Literature.* Cambridge, Mass.: Harvard UP, 1972; Sander Gilman. "The Uncontrollable Steed: A Study of the Metamorphosis of a Literary Image." *Euphorion* 66 (1972): 32-54; Charles I. Glicksberg. *The Self in Modern Literature.* University Park, PA: Pennsylvania State UP, 1963; R.W.B. Lewis. *The American Adam. Innocence, Tragedy and Tradition in the Nineteenth Century.* Chicago: U of Chicago P, 1955. 6th printing, 1966; Herman Meyer. *Der Sonderling in der deutschen Dichtung.* München: Hanser, 1963; Renate Mohrmann. *Der vereinsamte Mensch: Studien zum Wandel des Einsamkeitsmotivs im Roman von Raabe bis Musil.* Bonn: Bouvier, 1974; Richard M. Müller. *Das Strom-Motiv und die deutsche Klassik. Eine Untersuchung zur Dichtung der "Deutschen Bewegung" unter besonderer Berücksichtigung Hölderlins.* Bonn: Bouvier, 1955; Tzvetan Todorov. *Introduction à la littérature fantastique.* Paris: Editions du Seuil, 1970; Kurt K.T. Wais. *Das Vater-Sohn-Motiv in der Dichtung. I. Bis 1880. II. 1880-1930.* Berlin and Leipzig: de Gruyter, 1931; Theodore Ziolkowski. *Varieties of Literary Thematics.* Princeton: UP, 1983; Alexander Zholkovsky. *Themes and Texts. Toward a Poetics of Expressiveness.* Ithaca: Cornell UP, 1984.

[3]See Hellmuth Petriconi. *Metamorphosen der Träume. Fünf Beispiele zu einer Literaturgeschichte als Themengeschichte.* Frankfurt/M.: Athenäum, 1971; Margot Kruse. "Literaturgeschichte als Themengeschichte." In Petriconi: 195-208; and Joachim Schulze's criticism of Petriconi in "Geschichte oder Systematik? Zu einem Problem der Themen- und Motivgeschichte." *Arcadia* 10 (1975): 76-82.

[4]Beller 35.

[5]Georges Poulet. *Les Métamorphoses du cercle.* Paris: Plon, 1961.

[6]Jean-Pierre Richard. *Littérature et sensation.* Paris: Editions du Seuil,

1954: 13 ff.

⁷Jean-Paul Weber. *Domaines thématiques*. Paris: Gallimard, 1963.

⁸Harry Levin. "Thematics and Criticism." *Grounds for Comparison*. Cambridge, MA: Harvard UP, 1972: 91-109.

⁹Raymond Trousson. *Un Problème de littérature comparée: les études de thèmes*. Paris: Minard, 1965: 9 ff.

¹⁰Klotz; see also Philip Noss. "The Cruel City." *Revue de Littérature Comparée* 48 (1974): 462-76, who traces the theme of the "cruel city" in African short stories.

¹¹See Trousson *Un Problème* 63 ff.

¹²Todorov 112, 146 ff.

¹³Z. Czerny. "Contribution à une théorie comparée du motif dans les arts." In Paul Böckmann (Ed.). *Stil- und Formprobleme in der Literatur*. Heidelberg: Winter, 1959: 38-50.

¹⁴Johann Wolfgang Goethe. *Sämtliche Werke. Jubiläumsausgabe.* 40 vols. Ed. Eduard von der Hellen. Stuttgart: Cotta, 1902-1912. 38: 286; unless otherwise noted, all references are to this edition cited as JA.

¹⁵See Max Lüthi. *Das europäische Volksmärchen. Form und Wesen.* Bern: Francke, 1947 and "Motiv, Zug, Thema aus der Sicht der Volkserzählung." In A.J. Bisanz, R. Trousson (Eds.) *Elemente der Literatur*. Stuttgart: Kröner, 1980: 1:11-24. Many literary critics have used the folklorists' concept as a basis for their own definition. See, for example, Joseph Körner. "Erlebnis – Motiv –

Stoff." In Julius Wahle (Ed.). *Vom Geiste neuer Literaturforschung* . Wildpark-Potsdam: Athenaion, 1924: 80-90; Willy Krogmann. "Motiv." In W.A. Kohlschmidt, W. Mohr (Eds.). *Reallexikon der deutschen Literaturgeschichte.* 2nd ed. Berlin: de Gruyter, 1965: 2: 427-32; Harry Levin. "Motif." In *Dictionary of the History of Ideas* 235; Wilhelm Scherer. *Poetik.* 1888, new ed. München: DTV, 1977; and René Wellek and Austin Warren. *Theory of Literature.* New York: Harcourt, Brace, 1956: 207. Recent trends are succinctly evaluated by Dan Ben-Amos. "The Concept of Motif in Folklore." In V.J. Nevell (Ed.). *Folklore Studies in the Twentieth Century.* Totowa, N.J.: Rowman & Littlefield, 1980: 17-36.

[16]Frenzel *Motive* vi ff.

[17]Goethe. "Bedeutendes Fördernis durch ein einziges geistreiches Wort" (1823); JA 39: 49-50.

[18]Willy Krogmann. "Das Friederikenmotiv in den Dichtungen Goethes. Eine Motivanalyse." (*Germanische Studien* 113). Berlin: Matthiesen, 1932: 115 ff. See also Krogmann. "Motivübertragung und ihre Bedeutung für die literaturhistorische Forschung." *Neophilologus* 17 (1932): 17 ff.

[19]Robert Petsch. "Motif, Formel und Stoff." (*Germanische Studien* 222). Berlin: Matthiesen, 1940: 129-40.

[20]For a detailed analysis of the motif's functional characteristics as opposed to its visual quality, see Ingrid G. Daemmrich. "The Ruins Motif as Artistic Device in French Literature." *Journal of Aesthetics and Art Criticism* 30 (1972): 449-57.

[21]Eugene H. Falk. *Types of Thematic Structure.* Chicago: UP, 1969: 2, 3, 17, 23, and Ernst Robert Curtius. *Kritische Essays zur europäischen Literatur.* 2nd ed. Bern: Francke, 1954: 165-66.

[22]Czerny 47.

[23]See Herman Meyer. "Hütte und Palast: Vom Leben eines literarischen Topos." *Doitsubungaku-Ronkô* (*Forschungsberichte zur Germanistik*)5 (1963): 1-19; and Hans Bänzinger. *Schloß, Haus, Bau. Studien zu einem literarischen Motivkomplex von der deutschen Klassik bis zur Moderne.* Bern: Francke, 1983.

[24]See Horst S. Daemmrich. "Fertility - Sterility: A Sequence of Motifs in Thomas Mann's Joseph Novels." *Modern Language Quarterly* 31 (1970): 461-73. These patterns recall Todorov's two clusters of themes. See also Efraim Sicher. "Binary Oppositions and Spatial Representations: Toward an Applied Semiotics." *Semiotica* 60 (1986): 211-14, for the role of binary oppositions in thematic decoding.

[25]For problems encountered in periodization, see Wilfried Barner. "Tradition als Kategorie der Literaturgeschichtsschreibung." In Reinhard Lauer, Horst Turk (Eds.). *Prinzipien der Literaturgeschichtsschreibung.* Wiesbaden: Harrassowitz, 1988: 27-45; Herbert Cysarz. "Das Periodenprinzip in der Literaturwissenschaft." *Philosophie der Literaturwissenschaft.* Berlin: Junker & Dünnhaupt, 1930: 92-129; Claudio Guillén. "Second Thoughts on Currents and Periods." In Peter Demetz (Ed.). *The Disciplines of Criticism.* New Haven: Yale UP, 1968: 477-509; Jost Hermand. "Über Nutzen und Nachteil literarischer Epochenbegriffe." *Monatshefte* 58 (1966): 289-309; René Wellek. "Periods and Movements in Literary History." *English Inst. Annual 1940* (1941): 73-93; —. "Periodization in Literary History." In Philip Wiener (Ed.). *Dictionary of the History of Ideas*. New York: Scribners, 1973: 481-86; Benno von Wiese. "Zur Kritik des geisteswissenschaftlichen Periodenbegriffs." *Deutsche Vierteljahrsschrift* 11 (1933): 130-44.

[26]Cf. Heinrich Henel. *Goethezeit. Ausgewählte Aufsätze.* Frankfurt/M.: Insel, 1980; Alexander Heussler. *Klassik und Klassizismus in der deutschen Literatur.* Neudeln: Krauss, 1970; Franz Schultz. *Klassik und Romantik der*

Deutschen. 2 vols. Stuttgart: Metzler, 1952; Gerhard Storz. *Klassik und Romantik.* Mannheim: Bibl. Institut, 1972.

[27]See Ehrhard Bahr. "Revolutionary Realism in Goethe's *Wanderjahre.*" In William Lillyman (Ed.). *Goethe's Narrative Fiction. The Irvine Goethe Symposium.* Berlin, New York: de Gruyter, 1983: 161-75; Alan P. Cottrell. *Goethe's View of Evil and the Search for a New Image of Man in Our Time.* Edinburgh: Floris, 1982.

[28]The presentation is based on our previously published theoretical considerations in *Themes and Motifs in Western Literature:* 189-90, 240-41.

[29]Ernst Robert Curtius. *Europäische Literatur und lateinisches Mittelalter.* Bern: Francke, 1948: 185-86.

[30]See Heinrich Lausberg. *Handbuch der literarischen Rhetorik.* München: Hueber, 1960: 1: 571-83; Werner Mittenzwei. *Gestaltung und Gestalten im modernen Drama.* Berlin: Aufbau, 1965: 197 ff.; Robert Petsch. *Wesen und Form des Dramas.* Halle: Niemeyer, 1945; —. *Wesen und Form der Erzählkunst.* Halle: Niemeyer, 1942; Georges Polti. *Les Trente-six Situations dramatiques.* Paris: Mercure de France, 1885; tr. *The Thirty-six Dramatic Situations.* Boston: The Writer, 1945; Etienne Souriau, *Les deux cent mille situations dramatiques.* Paris: Flammarion, 1950; —. *Les Structures de l'oeuvre d'art.* Paris: Centre de Doc. Univ., 1956.

[31]See Roland Barthes. *Image. Music. Text.* New York: Hill and Wang, 1977: 79-141; Umberto Eco. *Einführung in die Semiotik.* München: Fink, 1972; Michel Foucault. *Les Mots et les choses.* Paris: Gallimard, 1966; — (Ed.). *Théorie d'ensemble.* Paris: Ed. du Seuil, 1968; Algirdas J. Greimas. *Du sens.* Paris: Ed. du Seuil, 1970/1983; —. *Sémantique structurale.* Paris: Larousse, 1971; — and Joseph Courtes. *Sémiotique.* Paris: Hachette, 1979; — (Ed.). *Sign, Language, Culture.* The Hague: Mouton, 1972.

[32]The specific linking of figures and themes is outlined in Horst S. and Ingrid Daemmrich. *Themen und Motive in der Literatur.* Tübingen: Francke, 1987.

[33]Joseph Addison. *Cato: A Tragedy.* In *Eighteenth-Century Plays.* Ed. Ricardo Quintana. New York: Modern Library, 1952. All references in the text are to this edition.

[34]René Wellek. "Classicism in Literature." In *Dictionary of the History of Ideas* 1: 451. See also "classical" in *Oxford English Dictionary* (1989); Frank Kermode. *The Classic: Literary Images of Permanence and Change.* 2nd ed. Cambridge, MA: Harvard UP, 1983: 15; Harry Levin. *Contexts of Criticism.* Cambridge, MA: Harvard UP, 1957: 38; and Pierre Moreau. *Le Classicisme des romantiques.* Paris: Plon, 1932:1. Earlier critics connecting Aulus Gellius' quote with classicism include Diderot and d'Albembert in *Dictionnaire raisonné des sciences et des arts* (1778-79) and Sainte-Beuve in "Qu'est-ce qu'un classique?" *Causeries de lundi,* 3, 21 octobre 1850.

[35]Wolfgang Bernhard Fleischmann. "Classicism." In *Princeton Encyclopedia of Poetry and Poetics.* Ed. Alex Preminger et al. Princeton: Princeton UP, 1965: 137.

[36]Wellek 454.

[37]Wellek 451; *Oxford English Dictionary*; Fleischmann 137; Emile Littré (*Dictionnaire de la langue française:* 2: 379) lists this meaning first for *classique.* See also Moreau 2; Diderot and d'Alembert. *Encyclopédie ou dictionnaire raisonnée des sciences et des arts* in Jules Brody. *French Classicism. A Critical Miscellany.* Englewood Cliffs: Prentice Hall, 1966: 2; also quoted by Levin 41.

[38]Fleischmann 137. Joseph M. Levine (*The Battle of the Books. History*

and Literature in the Augustan Age. Ithaca: Cornell UP, 1991: 5) points out that from the sixteenth to the eighteenth centuries, the classics of antiquity were the only reading assigned in schools preparing students for government positions.

[39]Georg Luck. "Scriptor classicus." *Comparative Literature* 10 (1950): 151-52.

[40]The *Dictionnaire de l'Académie Française* of 1694 defines "auteur classique" as "auteur ancien fort approuvé." See also Brody v. Dr. Johnson's Dictionary defines "classick" as pertaining to antique authors. For this and other references to early English usage of classical to mean "antique" see James William Johnson. *The Formation of English Neoclassical Thought.* Princeton: Princeton UP,1967: 8 ff. See also: Littré, third meaning of *classique*; *Oxford English Dictionary,* second meaning of "classical"; Levin 42.

[41]Raymond Bray, *La Formation de la doctrine classique en France.* Lausanne: Payot, 1931: 49-61. See also Fleischmann 137-39 for a brief summary of the influence of these treatises on Italian, English, and German critics from the Renaissance through the eighteenth century; Bruno Markwardt. *Geschichte der deutschen Poetik.* Berlin: de Gruyter, 1956-58: 1:188 ff; 2: 25-130.

[42]The works that had a lasting impact on the subsequent evaluations of literary compositions are: Giovambattista Giraldi Cinthio. *Discorsi intorno al comporre de i romanzi . . .* (1554); Jacopo Mazzioni. *Discorso i difesa della 'Commedia' del . . . Dante* (1572); Torquato Tasso. *"Discourses" on the Heroic Poem* (1594); Nicolas Boileau. *L'Art Poétique* (1674); Dominique Bonhours. *La Manière de bien penser dans les ouvrages de l'esprit* (1687); Charles Perrault. *Parallèle des Anciens et des Modernes* (1688/96); Anne Dacier. *Des causes de la corruption du gout* (1714); Antoine La Motte. *L'Iliade, poème, avec un discours sur Homère* (1724); Edward Gibbon. *Essai sur l'étude de la littérature* (1761); John Dryden. *An Essay of Dramatic Poesy* (1668/84); Hugo Blair.

Lectures on Rhetoric and Belles Lettres (1783); the "Querelle des Anciens et des Modernes" in Germany is carefully documented by Peter K. Kapitza. *Ein bürg-erlicher Krieg in der gelehrten Welt.* München: Fink, 1981. As Victor Giraud. "Qu'est-ce qu'un classique?" *Revue des Deux Mondes* NS I (jan.-fév. 1931):119 points out, some ancient works have always been considered more classical than others. For example, Virgil and Horace were characterized as more classical than Ennius and Plautus. See also John L. Mahoney. "The Problem of Imitation in Neoclassical and Romantic Aesthetics and Criticism." *Proceedings of the Xth Congress of the International Comparative Literature Association.* New York: Garland, 1985: 135-45.

[43]See, for instance, Joachim Du Bellay. *Défense et illustration de la langue française* (1549); Antonio Minturno. *L'Arte poetica. Della toscana poesia* (1564); Martin Opitz. *Buch von der Deutschen Poeterey* (1624); Saint-Evremond. *Des tragédies. Des comédies* (1672); Johann C. Gottsched. *Versuch einer kritischen Dichtkunst vor die Deutschen* (1730); Johann J. Breitinger. *Kritische Dicht Kunst* (1740); Christian F. Gellert. "Von den Ursachen des Vorzugs der Alten vor den Neuen in den schönen Wissenschaften" (1767).

[44]Madame de Staël. *De l'Allemagne, seconde partie* Ch. 11. Paris: Didot Frères, 1845: 145.

[45]J.C. Maxwell. "Classic." *Notes and Queries* 208 (1963): 220 has noted its earliest use in a preface by George Sewall to Pope's *Shakespeare* (1725). It is conveniently used by publishers in the series of "World Classics" and the "Klassiker-Ausgaben" that include masterworks from all periods.

[46]T.S. Eliot. "What Is a Classic?" *Selected Prose of T.S. Eliot.* Ed. Frank Kermode. London: Faber and Faber, 1975: 116.

[47]Sainte-Beuve. "Qu'est-ce qu'un classique?" in Brody 29. In "What Is a Classic?" (116), T.S. Eliot states: "A classic can only occur when a civilization

is mature; when a language and a literature are mature; and it must be the work of a mature mind. . . . It is the importance of that civilization and of that language, as well as the comprehensiveness of the mind of the individual poet which gives universality."

[48]Levin 41.

[49]For this reason, both Littré and OED give "opposed to the romantic," or "the opposite of romantic" as one of the meanings of "classical." See also: Wellek 450; Fleischmann 140; Levin 39; Brody v; Léon Emery. *L'Age classique.* Lyon: Les Cahiers Libres, 1967: 7.

[50]Most critics point to Madame de Staël's *De l'Allemagne* and Stendhal's *Racine et Shakespeare* as the most important critical works of the period defining classicism as the antithesis of romanticism. Madame Necker de Saussure is credited with assisting in the change of the term "classical" from the valuation to a stylistic trend in her preface to Schlegel's *Vorlesungen über die dramatische Kunst und Literatur.* Stendhal picked many of the ideas up from Ermes Visconti's series of articles "Idee elementari sulla poesia romantica" (1818); see Wellek 450; also Wellek. "The Term and Concept of Classicism in Literary History." *Documentations. Further Concepts of Criticism.* New Haven: Yale UP, 1970: 66. Moreau (7) also mentions an article by Chateaubriand in *Mercure* on March 2, 1805, in which he calls "classical books" those of the school of Boileau and Racine. Diderot and d'Alembert in their article on "classique" in the *Encyclopédie* define *classiques français* as "good authors of the century of Louis XIV"; see Brody v.

[51]See Clemens Heselhaus. "Die Romantische Gruppe in Deutschland." In Ernst Behler (Ed.). *Die europäische Romantik.* Frankfurt/M: Athenäum, 1972: 58-81; Wellek, "Periodization" in *Dictionary of the History of Ideas* 450, 483; *Discriminations* 81.

[52]See A.F.B. Clark. *Boileau and French Classical Critics in England.*

Paris: Champion, 1925, but also the sharply critical rebuttal by Louis L.
Bredvold. "The Rise of English Classicism: A Study in Methodology."
Comparative Literature 2 (1950): 253-68.

[53]See Wellek, *Discriminations* 57-58. In the *Dictionary of the History of
Ideas,* Wellek credits Louis Cazamian's *Histoire de la littérature anglaise* (1925)
which was widely read in translation with the application of "classicism" to the
age of Pope and Dryden (450). Fleischmann refuses to identify a clear-cut period
of "classicism" in English literary history. For a discussion of the usefulness of
these various terms by two more recent English critics who come to different
conclusions, see James William Johnson. *The Formation of English
Neoclassical Thought.* Princeton: Princeton UP, 1967: 3-30; or Pat Rogers.
The Augustan Vision. London: Weidenfeld & Nicolson, 1974: 2 ff.

[54]See W.L. Renwick. "English Literature 1789-1815" and Ian Jack.
"English Literature 1815-1832." In *Oxford History of English Literature.*
Oxford: Clarendon, 1963; Gerhart Hoffmeister. *Deutsche und europäische
Romantik.* Stuttgart: Metzler, 1978: 38-43.

[55]Heinz Otto Burger (Ed.). *Begriffsbestimmung der Klassik und des
Klassischen.* Darmstadt: Wiss. Buchges. 1972.

[56]See Luigi Foscolo Benedetto. "Legend of French Classicism." In Brody
145.

[57]See the remark by P. Rapin in *Réflexions sur la poétique* (1674) in Henri
Bénac. *Le Classicisme. La Doctrine par les textes.* Paris: Hachette, 1969: 82
and Paul Bénichou. *Les Moralistes du grand siècle.* 3rd edition. Paris:
Gallimard, 1948: 45 ff.

[58]See Maurice Magendie. *La Politesse mondaine et les théories de l'honnêteté en France de 1600 à 1660.* 2 vols. Paris: Félix Alcan, n.d.

[59]See Henri Peyre. *Le Classicisme français*. New York: Editions. de la Maison Française, 1942: 45-47, but also Bénichou (59); Pierre Goubert. *L'Ancien Régime*. Paris: Colin, 1973; Ingrid Heyndels. "Le Lecteur implicite du texte racinien." *Cahiers de Littérature du XVIIe siècle* 10 (1988): 32; Bernard Magné. *Crise de la littérature française sous Louis XIV: humanisme et naturalisme*. Paris: Champion, 1976; Will G. Moore. *French Classical Literature*. Oxford: UP, 1961: 14-15; and Hartmut Stenzel. "Essor culturel et conscience de crise. Remarques comparatistes sur la genèse du classicisme louis-quatorzien." In Stéphane Michaud (Ed.). *L'Impossible Semblable*. Paris: SEDES, 1991: 25-40, all of whom emphasize the period's crises and conflicts in economics, politics, and morals and even portray it as wavering in its pursuit of centralization.

[60]Giraud (137) states that the classical movement fits the French "character" of clarity, precision, elegance, and sociability, although these traits best characterized a very small segment of French society.

[61]See Brody vi, 130; Louise K. Horowitz. *Love and Language. A Study of the Classical French Moralist Writers*. Columbus: Ohio State UP, 1977: 18; Moore 170; Stenzel 36.

[62] Giraud (138) credits the "exaggerated recourse by their successors to reason as the arbiter of everything" with the destruction of French classicism.

[63]See Fleischmann 140; Johnson 3-30; Roger Lonsdale. "Introduction" to *History of Literature in the English Language*. Vol 4: *Dryden to Johnson*. London: Barrie & Jenkins, 1971: 9.

[64]Bredvold argues for the continuity and genuineness of English classicism. However, B.H. Bronson. "When Was Neoclassicism?" In Howard Anderson, John S. Shea (Eds.). *Studies in Criticism and Aesthetics, 1660-1800. Essays in Honor of Samuel Holt Monk*. Minneapolis: U of Minnesota P, 1967: 13-35

views the role of classicism as introducing in an unstable period a steady refinement of values and lofty visions of beauty. Johnson 15 asserts that after the ex-
travagance and individualism of the Renaissance, English writers felt a need for
decorum, order, authority, and tradition, an idea seconded by Lonsdale in his
essay on Alexander Pope in *History of Literature in the English Language* 4:
101.

[65]Johnson 19 traces the first use of the term "Augustan" to the preface to
The Second Part of Mr. Waller's Poems (1690), commonly attributed to Francis
Atterbury. See also: Maximillian E. Novak. "Shaping the Augustan Myth.
John Dryden and the Politics of Restoration Augustanism." In Paul J. Korshin,
Robert R. Allen (Eds.). *Greene Centennial Studies.* Charlottesville: UP of
Virginia, 1984: 1-21; and Howard Erskine-Hill. "John Dryden: The Poet and
the Critic" 25-44; Lonsdale. "Alexander Pope" 113; and Charles Peake. "Poetry
1700-1740" 166, all in *History of Literature in the English Language.*

[66]Thus, Dr. Johnson in his *Lives of the English Poets* characterizes
Addison's *Cato* as "rather a succession of just sentiments in elegant language
than a representation of natural affections." See Johnson 165-92, who points
out that the anti-tragic philosophy of English classicism as well as the insistence on historical accuracy in literary works doomed attempts to create genuine
classical tragedies in England, but also Pope's implication in his *Discourse on
Pastoral Poetry* (1709) that by refining earlier models, each imitator could create
a more perfect work.

[67]See Dieter Borchmeyer. *Die Weimarer Klassik.* Königstein/Ts.:
Athenäum, 1980; Walter H. Bruford. *Culture and Society in Classical Weimar
1775–1806.* London: Cambridge UP, 1962; Hermann August Korff. *Geist der
Goethezeit.* 5 vols. (specifically 2, 4). Leipzig: Koehler & Amelung, 1954-
1964; Terence J Reed. *The Classical Center. Goethe and Weimar.* New York:
Barnes & Noble, 1980; and Franz Schultz. *Klassik und Romantik der
Deutschen.* 2 vols. Stuttgart: Metzler, 1952.

[68]See Goethe's letters to Buchholtz (February 14, 1814), to Schubarth (July 8, 1818), to Boisserée (August 19, 1825), to Zelter (June 6, 1825 and November 13, 1829), the important letter to Carlyle (July 20, 1827), and also his remarks to Reimer (November 18, 1806), to Müller (April 7, 1830), and to Eckermann (March 11, 1832).

[69]A similar sentiment was expressed in 1869 by Matthew Arnold, who greatly admired Goethe: ". . . culture being a pursuit of our total perfection by means of getting to know, on all matters which most concern us, the best which has been thought and said in the world; and through this knowledge, turning a stream of fresh and free thought upon our stock notions and habits, which we now follow staunchly and mechanically . . ." *Culture and Anarchy.* Cambridge: Cambridge UP, 1935: 6; see also 27 ff., 44 f.

[70]This view, clearly expressed in "Was heißt und zu welchem Ende studiert man Universalgeschichte?" (1789), provides for unintentional change in the pattern of culture. Any action undertaken for an immediate end may bring about in the future some unforeseen pattern. Friedrich Schiller. *Sämtliche Werke.* Säkularausgabe in 16 Bänden. Ed. Eduard von der Hellen. Stuttgart: Cotta, 1904-1905 (hereafter cited as SA): 12: 9-10.

[71]"Die Gesetzgebung des Lykurgus und Solon." SA 13: 79.

[72]Letter to Augustenburg, July 13, 1793; *Schillers Briefe.* Kritische Gesamtausgabe. Ed. Fritz Jonas. Stuttgart: Cotta, 1892-86: 3: 335-36.

[73]Bray 64-65 traces the dictum *docere cum delectatione* to Scaliger who borrowed it from Castelvetro. Bernard Tocanne ("L'Efflorescence classique" in *Précis de la littérature française du XVIIe siècle.* Paris: PUF, 1990: 229 ff.) points out that the public addressed by classical writers was exceedingly diverse. Peyre (106) views the prefaces of classical dramatists as stratagems or convenient propaganda by the authors to insist on the utlity of their works. Giraud (126)

observes that in classical works, man is always judged "according to a high and precise moral standard" which is insinuated, not preached. According to Bronson (17) this moral standard is seen as part of human nature. It is also viewed as the determining factor in aesthetic considerations; what is beautiful must be also good. See Walter Jackson Bate. *From Classic to Romantic: Premises of Taste in Eighteenth-Century England.* Cambridge, Mass.: Harvard UP, 1949: 4.

[74]See Jean Racine. *Théâtre complet.* Paris: Garnier, 1980: 304. All references to Racine are to this edition. Bronson (17) states that to the classical writers, the Ancients were models. Giraud (124) observes that though undisputed masters, the Ancients were also looked upon as rivals to be imitated and surpassed. Kathleen Williams ("Jonathan Swift" in Lonsdale 79) points out that Swift sides with the Ancients in his *Battle of the Books* because of their civilized humane approach to art. Ernst Merian-Genast ("Das Problem der Form in der französischen und deutschen Klassik." *Germanisch-Romanische Monatsschrift* 27 [1939]:101) sees the classical genius as renewing the old rather than creating the new. In doing so, the classical writer will, according to Robert Kilburn Root (*The Poetical Career of Alexander Pope.* Princeton: Princeton UP, 1938: 13) "in humility of heart invoke [the Ancients'] intercession and hope that he may have the grace to follow their good example."

[75]Alexander Pope. *An Essay on Man.* II: 713. As Peyre (89) points out, the realism of the classical writers lies precisely in their attention to the "innermost and true 'surreality' of consciousness" or as Charles Peak in "Poetry 1700-1740" (Lonsdale 166) states, in their portrayal of the fundamental and permanent aspects of human nature and experience. Horowitz observed recently (4): "It is somewhat of a cliché to state that the preoccupation, the obsession even with the passions dominated the classical experience."

[76]Jean Racine. "Preface" to *Bérénice. Théâtre complet* 324; *Phèdre. Théâtre complet* 578.

[77]Literary historians have until recently generally agreed upon the pivotal

position of reason in classical doctrine. Reason, according to Bray (126-29) transcends individual customs and points to the universally human. In contrast, Daniel Mornet (*Histoire de la littérature française classique 1660-1700*. Paris: Colin, 1940: 54 ff.) defines reason as the natural judgment of a man of taste who selects the natural and plausible and rejects the monstrous and accidental. Peyre (68) prefers to call it "intellectuality," that is, the pleasure of analyzing the passions. Giraud (129) sees reason as an ordering principle, while Johnson (177) observes that for the classical writer all emotions are to be submitted to reason, to which Root (18) would add taste.

[78]For a discussion of the rules governing classical style and structure, see: Bate 8; Bray 191-288; Giraud 121; Peake 166; Peyre 72, 96 ff., 104, 141-44; Root 16-17; Geoffrey Tillotson. *Augustan Studies*. London: Athlone Press, 1961: 14-17; *On the Poetry of Pope*. Oxford: UP, 1938: 2, 112 ff.

[79]For the classical writers' propensity for self-analysis, judgment, and reflection, see: Ramon Fernandez. "De l'esprit classique." *Nouvelle Revue Française* 32 (1920): 44; Giraud 124; Peyre 72; Root 27-28. Pope in his *Essay on Criticism* II: 204 ff. emphasizes the critic's need for "true" judgment.

[80]See Johnson 175 ff.

[81]Thus Corneille wrote in his dedication of *Horace* to Richelieu that by reading on the prelate's face what was pleasing or displeasing to him, "we instruct ourselves with certainty concerning what is good and what is bad and draw from that infallible rules of what to follow." Pierre Corneille. *Oeuvres complètes*. Paris: Gallimard, 1980: 1: 834. For a thorough presentation of author intent and audience expectation, see Dieter Borchmeyer. *Höfische Gesellschaft und französische Revolution. Adliges und bürgerliches Wertsystem im Urteil der Weimarer Klassik*. Kronberg: Athenäum,1977; Klaus Berghahn, Beate Pinkerneil. *Am Beispiel Wilhelm Meister. Einführung in die Wissenschaftsgeschichte der Germanistik*. Königstein/Ts.: Athenäum, 1980. For a limited conception of classical humanism, see, for example, Horowitz's analysis of the

Chevalier de Méré (17-26) and Tillotson, *Augustan Studies* 14. Recent studies by Lennard J. Davis ("Conversation and Dialogue." *The Age of Johnson* 1 [1987]: 347-73), Dustin Griffin ("Augustan Collaboration." *Essays in Criticism* 37 [1987]: 1-10), and Robin Grove ("Nature Methodiz'd." *The Critical Review* 26 [1984]: 52-68) focus on literature as a social activity.

[82]For the emphasis on experiment and reaction to contemporary questions, see: Bénichou 8-9; Moore 15, 71, 74; Erskine-Hill 23-48; Lonsdale 121 ff.; F.W. Bateson. "Addison, Steele and the Periodical Essay" in Lonsdale 144; for a revaluation of the rules see especially Corneille's *Discours de la tragédie* and Moore 64; for the classical portrayal of the predominance of the passions, see Horowitz's analysis of Madame de Lafayette's novels (51-71); for an emphasis on tension as the outstanding characteristic of classical tragedy, see Moore 65-66 and Roland Barthes. *Sur Racine*. Paris: Editions du Seuil, 1963: 34 ff. who sees the conflict for power, violence and combat between tyrant and victim as the motivating forces in Racine's theater. See also Charles Mauron. *L'Inconscient dans l'oeuvre et la vie de Racine*. Gap: Orphrys, 1957: 333 ff. and Moore 58, 72-73.

[83]Jean Rousset. *La Littérature de l'âge baroque en France: Circé et le paon*. Paris: José Corti, 1953, particularly ch. 9; *L'Intérieur et l'extérieur. Essais sur la poésie et sur le théâtre au XVIIe siècle*. Paris: Corti, 1968: 243-56. Jules Brody in his introduction to *French Classicism. A Critical Miscellany* (viii) states that what classical writers have in common is as yet unknown and that today the notion of baroque threatens to swallow up the concept of classicism. Emery (10) declares that there is no true classical age, only emerging "zones." Fleischmann (140) questions "whether the term continues to be useful as a description of periods of literary history" in the light of its many contradictory meanings.

[84]See for example Peyre (187-90). Other critics, as for example Stenzel (37-40), in accord with the current trend to stress the geographic distance of Weimar from the French Revolution, emphasize "idyllic" aspects in Goethe's and

Schiller's works. As a consequence, they underestimate the revolutionary thinking of German classicism.

[85]Addison. *Cato* I. In his essay "De l'expérience" (III. Ch. 13), Montaigne quotes from Aymot's translation of Plutarch's *Life of Pompey* : "Insofar are you God as / You recognize yourself as human." ["D'autant es-tu Dieu comme / Tu te reconnais homme."]

[86] In a letter to P. Caffaro in 1694, quoted by H. Bénac. *Le Classicisme: La Doctrine par les textes.* Paris: Hachette, 1969: 70, Bossuet defines the art of the tragedian as inducing the spectator to be moved by beautiful persons, to serve them as divinities.

[87]See Pope's letter to Caryll, February 1712/13, quoted by Johnson (99), as testimony to the popularity of Cato as a model of virtue.

[88]See Horst S. Daemmrich. "Classicism." In Daemmrich and Diether Haenicke. *The Challenge of German Literature.* Detroit: Wayne State UP, 1971: 143-82; Eric A. Blackall. *Goethe and the Novel.* Ithaca: Cornell UP, 1976: 15, 40; Peter Boerner. "Die deutsche Klassik im Urteil des Auslands." In R. Grimm, J. Hermand (Eds.). *Die Klassik-Legende.* Frankfurt: Athenäum, 1971: 79-107.

[89]Honoré de Balzac. "Préface" to *La Comédie humaine.* Paris: Gallimard, 1977: 1: xix.

[90]Theodore Dreiser. *Hey Rub-a-Dub-Dub.* New York: Boni and Liveright, 1920: 242-43.

[91]Littré, vol. 6: 936; OED, vol. 8; René Wellek. "Realism in Literature." *Dictionary of the History of Ideas* 4: 51; George J. Becker. "Introduction" to *Documents of Modern Literary Realism.* Princeton: Princeton UP, 1963: 36.

[92]See Ulrich Weisstein. "Realism." *Princeton Encyclopedia of Poetry and Poetics:* 685 and "Realism: An Essay in Definition." *Modern Language Quarterly* 10 (1949): 184 ff.; OED; Becker, "Introduction" 6; Elbert B.O. Borgerhoff. "*Réalisme* and Kindred Words: Their Use as Terms of Literary Criticism in the First Half of the Nineteenth Century." *PMLA* 53 (1938): 840; Ian Watt. *The Rise of the Novel. Studies in Defoe, Richardson and Fielding.* Berkeley: U of California P, 1964: 10. An interesting counter-argument to mimesis theories is presented by proponents of a "possible worlds" theory, for example, by Lubimír Dolezel. "Mimesis and Possible Worlds." *Poetics Today* 9 (1988): 475-96; and Thomas G. Pavel. "The Borders of Fiction." *Poetics Today* 4 (1983): 83-88.

[93]Wellek 51; Borgerhoff 838-39, who quotes the passage from David Sauvageot's study, *The Age of Realism.* Ed. F.W.J. Hemmings. Middlesex: Penguin, 1974: 9; and Harry Levin. *The Gates of Horn.* New York: Oxford UP, 1963: 68. Stephan Kohl (*Realismus: Theorie und Geschichte.* München: Fink, 1977: 75-111) locates the beginning of a debate about realism in eighteenth-century comparisons between romance and the novel by Christoph M. Wieland, Friedrich Blanckenburg, and Clara Reeve.

[94]René Dumesnil. *Le Réalisme et le naturalisme.* Paris: Editions Mondiales–De Gigord, 1955: 19. See also: Levin 68; Harold H. Kolb, Jr. *The Illusion of Life. American Realism as a Literary Form.* Charlottesville: U of Virginia P, 1969: 21. Arthur McDowall (*A Study in Art and Thought* in *Documents of Modern Literary Realism* 572) makes a distinction between "ancient realism," which was pictorial and modern realism, which is critical and analytical. Ioan Williams (*The Realist Novel in England: A Study in Development.* Pittsburgh: U of Pittsburgh P, 1974: x) characterizes the movement's view as "a naive confidence that Reality consisted in the material and social world around them." Watt (12) defines "modern realism" as the position that truth can be discovered by the individual through his senses. According to Gustav Regnier (*Les Origines du roman réaliste.* Paris: Hachette, 1912: viii), the desire to restrict creativity to the faithful imitation of reality came much later

than the literary preoccupation with beauty, glory, love, adventure, and illusion.

[95]See Hartmut Steinecke. *Romantheorie und Romankritik in Deutschland. 2: Quellen.* Stuttgart: Metzler, 1976.

[96]Theodor Fontane. *Sämtliche Werke. Aufsätze, Kritiken, Erinnerungen.* München: Hanser, 1969: 1: 538.

[97]The strong moral stance of English and American mid-nineteenth-century writers has led critics to exclude them from realism. See especially: F.W.J. Hemmings. "Introduction" to *The Age of Realism* 11; Williams 130, 174; also Howells's call for an optimistic, "smiling" realism in Jane Benardete (Ed.). *American Realism.* New York: Putnam, 1972: 103, which, according to Parrington, evoked the criticism that Howells avoided the "more tragic aspects of life" and made his work seem trivial. See Vernon Louis Parrington. "The Beginnings of Critical Realism in America." *Main Currents in American Thought.* New York: Harcourt Brace, 1930: 3: 249.

[98]As Becker, "Introduction" and "Realism: An Essay in Definition" 189-91 and Dumesnil (23), among others, point out, realism from its beginnings exhibited the tendency "to drift downward." It often offended "good taste," propriety, and decorum by espousing descriptions of dirty, crowded rooms and streets, vulgar situations and language, and "animal-like" or "underground" human behavior.

[99]*Realismus und Gründerzeit. Manifeste und Dokumente zur deutschen Literatur 1848-1880.* Ed. Max Bucher, Werner Hahl, Georg Jäger and Reinhard Wittmann. Stuttgart: Metzler, 1975: 2: 117-21.

[100]See Dumesnil 35; Watts 6; Diana Spearman. *The Novel and Society.* London: Rouledge and Kagan Paul, 1966: 20 ff.; Regnier 14, who traces the realism of such medieval works as the *Roman de Renart* and *fabliaux* to their being addressed to a bourgeois rather than an aristocratic audience; Levin (*Gates*

of Horn 70-71, 81), who characterizes the period of bourgeois capitalism in France, 1789 to 1939 as the "heyday of the realistic novel"; and Parrington 3: 3-17, who traces the roots of American literature after the Civil War to the predominant expansionist attitude, the "welling-up of pagan desires after long repressions—to grow rich, to grasp power, to be strong and masterful and lay the world at its feet." (11)

[101]Levin (*Gates of Horn* 70-71) points to the "ambivalence" of the realist novel which was a product of the middle class and yet critical of it; see also Watt 14, 32; Spearman 19.

[102]See Hermann Broch. "Dichten und Erkennen." *Essays I.* Zürich: Atlantis, 1955: 345; Peter Demetz. "Der historische Roman. Skizze eines Modells." *Formen des Realismus. Theodor Fontane.* Frankfurt/M: Ullstein, 1973: 13-43; Georg Lukács. *Der historische Roman.* Berlin: Aufbau, 1955.

[103]Clemens Heselhaus. "Das Realismusproblem." In Richard Brinkmann (Ed.). *Begriffsbestimmung des literarischen Realismus.* Darmstadt: Wissenschaftliche Buchgesellschaft, 1969: 337-64; Richard Brinkmann. *Wirklichkeit und Illusion.* 2nd ed. Tübingen: Niemeyer, 1966.

[104]See Mikhail M. Bakhtin. *The Dialogic Imagination.* Ed. Michael Holquist. Trans. Caryl Emerson and Michael Holquist. Austin: U of Texas P, 1981: 263. Bakhtin aligns the realistic novel with a centrifugal structure, because it incorporates a number of "sublanguages," while the classical insistence on a unitary, "correct" language is centripetal. Cf. Rosemary Clark-Beattie. "*Middlemarch's* Dialogic Style." *Journal of Narrative Technique* 15 (1985): 199-218; Peter K. Garrett. *The Victorian Multiplot Novel. Studies in Dialogical Form.* New Haven: Yale UP, 1980; John Kucich. "Dickens' Fantastic Rhetoric: The Semantics of Reality and Unreality in *Our Mutual Friend.*" *Dickens Studies Annual* 14 (1985): 167-89; Henri Mitterand, "Sémiologie flaubertienne: Le Club de l'Intelligence." *La Revue des Lettres Modernes* 703-06 (1984): 61-77; Laurence Rothfield. "Discursive

Intertextuality." *Novel* 19 (1985): 57-81. Other critics have used the concepts "centrifugal" and "centripetal" to denote antithetical patterns in certain novels. H.M. Daleski (*Dickens and the Art of Analogy.* New York: Schocken Books, 1970: 270-72) identifies the movement in *Bleak House* from Esther and Jarndyce outward toward others as centrifugal and the movement of Esther and Lady Dedlock into each other's world as centripetal. Similarly, he calls the movement in *Our Mutual Friend* from Gaffer's discovery of the body in the river to the distant horizon at the end, expansive and the centering of the novel on images of money, dust, death, and resurrection, contractive. Garrett traces the dialogic relationship in George Eliot's *Middlemarch* between the centripetal organization around the protagonist and the simultaneous centrifugal development of relationships between all figures in the novel. Poulet traces two spheres of energy at work in Balzac's novels: a center within each individual figure and a circumference comprising total society. Energy moving from the circumference to the center is centripetal; energy moving from the center to the circumference is centrifugal.

[105]See, among others: Michel Butor. *Répertoire* II. Paris: Minuit, 1964: 54-55: "To describe furniture and objects is a way to describe figures . . ."; Claude Duchet. "Roman et objets." *Travail de Flaubert.* Paris: Editions du Seuil, 1983: 11-43 (rpt. from *Europe,* sept.-nov. 1969); and Roland Le Huenen and Paul Perron. "Le Système des objets dans *Eugénie Grandet.*" *Littérature* 26 (1977): 94-ll9. Many critics have applied to literature A.A. Moles's sociological study *Théorie des objets.* Paris: Ed. Universelles, 1972.

[106]Karl Eibl. "Das Realismus-Argument. Zur literaturpolitschen Funktion eines fragwürdigen Begriffs." *Poetica* 15 (1983): 314-28; Ulf Eisele. *Realismus und Ideologie.* Stuttgart: Metzler, 1976; Christoph Miething. "'Realienklassifikation' oder 'Wirklichkeit'? Einige Anmerkungen zum logischen Status des Realismus-Begriffs." *Germanisch-Romanische Monatsschrift* 65 (1984): 1-7; Helmuth Widhammer. *Die Literaturtheorie des deutschen Realismus (1848-1860).* Stuttgart: Metzler, 1977; see also Françoise Gaillard. "The Great Illusion of Realism, or the Real as Representation." *Poetics Today* 5 (1984): 756.

[107]Guy de Maupassant. "Le Roman" (1887) in *Pierre et Jean.* Fribourg: Ed. du Lac, 1976: 4-16; Richard Brinkmann. " Zum Begriff des Realismus für die erzählende Dichtung des neunzehnten Jahrhunderts." In Brinkmann (Ed.) *Begriffsbestimmung des literarischen Realismus* . Darmstadt: Wiss. Buchges., 1969: 222-235; See also Françoise Gaillard (753-63), who traces in Flaubert's *Bouvard et Péchuchet* the protagonists' discovery that reality is best approached through a master of fiction like Scott who can make the reader see, feel, hear, and touch the objects described.

[108]*Documents of Modern Literary Realism* 497; see also 29, 95, 175; W.B. Carnochan. *Confinement and Flight. An Essay on English Literature of the Eighteenth Century.* Berkeley: U of California P, 1977); Parrington 248; Watt 11.

[109]See Philip Rahv. "Notes on the Deline of Naturalism." In *Documents of Modern Realism* 579; also Erich Heller. "The Realistic Fallacy: A Discussion of Realism in Literature." *The Listener* 53 (1955): 888-89.

[110]For the origin and definition of the concept of naturalism, see Wellek 53-54; Dumesnil 336 ff.; Levin. *Gates of Horn* 71-72; Becker. "Introduction" to *Documents of Modern Realism* 35; Parrington 323-26.

[111]A. A. Zhdanov. "Address at the First Soviet Congress of Writers," August 7, 1934. *Documents of Modern Realism* 487. Thus, Engels considers Balzac a far greater realist than Zola in portraying the collapse of the aristocratic order and the rise of the bourgeois, materialistic society. See his letter to Margaret Harkness, April 1888 in *Documents of Modern Realism* 484-85. The question whether socialist realism is truly realism perturbs critics. See Becker, "Introduction" to *Documents of Modern Realism* 21-22; Wellek 55; Karl Eibl 314-28.

[112]Becker. "Introduction" to *Documents of Modern Realism* 9, 28.

[113]See, for example, Belinsky. "On Realistic Poetry." *Documents of Modern Realism* : 42; also Becker's "Introduction" 29; Kolb 97-101; Williams 116 ff.; Watt 15-19.

[114]Levin. *Gates of Horn* 182; Regnier 33. For Flaubert's use of film techniques, see: Pierre Danger. *Sensations et objets dans le roman de Flaubert.* Paris: Colin, 1973: 186 ff.

[115]See Becker. "Introduction" to *Documents of Modern Realism* 29-20; Kolb 58-89; Levin, *Gates of Horn* 156; Rahv 583-85; Weisstein 685.

[116]See Levin. *Gates of Horn* 84 ff.; also Parrington's notes on naturalism 325 ff., who points out that naturalistic works are "inevitably tragic," not in the Aristotelian definition but rather closer to Nietzsche's use of the term.

[117]Kolb 58; see also Heller 888-89. Spearman (58-63) points to the realists' desire to rival, imitate, or repudiate earlier works as an important formative influence on realistic techniques, while Regnier traces these techniques as at least partially present in late Latin and medieval literature.

Chapter 2

[1]See also Friedrich Schiller. *Über naive und sentimentalische Dichtung* (1796) and Immanuel Kant. *Kritik der reinen Vernunft* (1791). *Sämtliche Werke.* (Ed.). Theodor Valentiner. Leipzig: Meiner, 1919: 263, 479; — *Prolegoma zu einer jeden künftigen Metaphysik* (1783): #14, 17, 36; and Heinrich Ratke. *Systematisches Handlexikon zu Kants Kritik der Reinen Vernunft.* Leipzig: Meiner, 1929: 119-21, 151-56.

[2]Cf. Erik H. Erikson. *Dimensions of a New Identity.* New York: Norton,

1974; Howard Gardner. *Developmental Psychology.* Boston: Little, Brown, 1982; Jane Loevinger. *Ego Development: Conception and Theories.* San Francisco: Jossey-Bass, 1976; Abraham Maslov. *Toward a Psychology of Being.* Princeton: Princeton UP, 1962; —. *Farther Reaches of Human Nature.* New York: Viking, 1971; M. E. Spiro. "Culture and Personality: The History of a False Dichotomy." *Psychiatry* 14 (1951): 19-46. On the role of readers in organizing figures, see, among others: Mieke Bal. *Narratology. Introduction to the Theory of Narrative.* Trans. Christine van Boheemen. Toronto: U of Toronto P, 1985; James Garvey. "Characterization in Narrative." *Poetics* 71 (1978): 63-78; Uri Margolin. "Structuralist Approaches to Character in Narrative: the State of the Art." *Semiotica* 75 (1989): 1-24; and James Phelan. *Reading People. Reading Plots.* Chicago: U of Chicago P, 1989.

[3]See Jerome H. Buckley. *Season of Youth. The Bildungsroman from Dickens to Golding.* Cambridge: Harvard UP, 1974; Francois Jost. "The Bildungsroman in Germany, England, and France." *Introduction to Comparative Literature.* Indianapolis: Pegasus, 1974: 134-50; Martin Swales. *The German Bildungsroman from Wieland to Hesse.* Princeton: Princeton UP, 1978; Marianne Hirsch. "The Novel of Formation as Genre. Between *Great Expectations* and *Lost Illusions.*" *Genre* 12 (1979): 293-311.

[4]Alexander Pope. *An Essay on Man* in *Poetical Works.* Ed. Maynard Mack. London: Methuen, 1950, rpt. 1964.

[5]The notions of the individual's divine origin, social contact, and interrelations are as old as Plato and as new as E.F. Schumacher. "Toward an Appropriate Technology." *Atlantic Monthly* (April 1979): 92, or Lewis Thomas. *The Lives of a Cell.* New York: Viking, 1974.

[6]"Die Götter Griechenlands"(1800) ll. 87-88; see also ll. 166-68: "nature from whom the Gods have fled / serves the law of gravity slavishly / like the dead sound of the pendulum-clock!"

[7]These attributes of the clown are outlined by Suzanne Langer. *Feeling and Form: A Theory of Art.* New York: Scribner, 1953.

[8]See for example: Dennis Donaghue. *Jonathan Swift. A Critical Introduction.* Cambridge: UP, 1969: 163; Irvin Ehrenpreis. "The Meaning of Gulliver's Last Voyage." In Ernest Tuveson (Ed.). *Swift: A Collection of Critical Essays.* Englewood Cliffs, NJ: Prentice-Hall, 1964: 142; William Bragg Ewald, Jr. *The Masks of Jonathan Swift.* Cambridge: Harvard UP, 1954: 131; Joseph Horrell. "What Gulliver Knew." In: *Swift: A Collection of Critical Essays* 69; Maynard Mack. "Gulliver's Travels." In *Swift: A Collection of Critical Essays* 113; John Lawlor. "The Evolution of Gulliver's Character." In: *Essays and Studies 1955* (1956): 69; and Everett Zimmerman. *Swift's Narrative Satires. Author and Authority.* Ithaca: Cornell UP, 1983: 114 ff.

[9]Nigel Dennis (*Jonathan Swift: A Short Character.* New York: Macmillan, 1965) argues that Swift wrote *Gulliver's Travels* as a parody of *Robinson Crusoe.*

Chapter 3

[1]See Bénichou (I.1. n.57) 9; Octave Nadal (*Le Sentiment de l'amour dans l'oeuvre de Pierre Corneille.* Paris: Gallimard, 1948: 127) defines the crossroads as the "tragic and unavoidable moment when the exterior and interior events cross."

[2]On the reflection of the aristocratic values in Corneille's dramas, see: Bénichou 16, 33; Georges Couton. *Corneille.* Paris: Hatier, 1958: 47, 64, 71. While concurring, Bernard Dort (*Pierre Corneille.* Paris: L'Arche, 1957: 45, 49), Serge Doubrovsky (*Corneille et la dialectique du héros.* Paris: Gallimard, 1963: 29, 90, 98) and André Stegmann (*Héroisme cornélien: Genèse et signification.* Paris: Armand Colin, 1968: 2: 579-81); also see a breakdown of the older order founded on adherence to a rigid social code and a rise of a newer one,

based on individual initiative and accomplishment. On the debate of whether or not Racine's figures are free to make their own choices, see: H.T. Barnwell. *The Tragic Drama of Corneille and Racine: An Old Parallel Revisited.* Oxford: Clarendon P, 1982: 151; Barthes (I.1. n.82) 21, 37, 84, 112; Bettina L. Knapp. *Jean Racine: Mythos and Renewal in Modern Theater.* University, AL: U of Alabama P, 1971: 71; Jacques Scherer. *Racine et/ou la cérémonie.* Paris: PUF, 1982: 34; and Eléonore M. Zimmermann. *La Liberté et le destin dans le théâtre de Jean Racine.* Saratoga, CA: Anma Libri, 1982: 1-153.

[3]Nadal (130) points out that conversation forms a climate in which each understands the other in Corneille's plays.

[4]Nadal (280) distinguishes the two meanings of heart as affection and courage. Most critics have pointed out the immense role played by pride and the exaltation of the ego in Corneille's plays, especially as a characteristic of the hero. According to René Jasinski (*A travers le XVIIIe siècle.* Paris: Nizet, 1981: 38) this superiority is synonymous with a merited grace that absolves the hero from abiding common norms. But Doubrovsky (29, 206) points out that *Le Cid* actually portrays individual pride as illusive, in keeping with the destruction of the old values and rise of a new code. Nevertheless, the "enactment of power" (to reverse Cook's title) becomes an integral expression of the freedom of the will, which critics have viewed as the basis of Corneille's characters and without which no crossroads decision would be possible. See also William O. Goode. "Hand, Heart and Mind: The Complexity of the Heroic Quest in *Le Cid*." *PMLA* 91 [1976]: 44-53 on the fusion of hand, heart, and mind in the "quest" for power.

[5]On Corneille's use of surprise, cf. Barnwell 156; Bénichou 25; Dort 31, 113; Georges May. *Tragédie cornélienne, tragédie racinienne. Etude sur les sources de l'intérêt dramatique.* Urbana: U of Illinois P, 1948: 22, 78 ff.; and Robert J. Nelson. *Corneille: His Heroes and Their Worlds.* Philadelphia: U of Pennsylvania P, 1963: 276.

[6]For Andromaque's unique characterization within the canon of Racine's tragedies, see: Mary Lynne Flowers. *Sentence Structure and Characterization in the Tragedies of Jean Racine.* Rutherford: Associated UP, 1979: 56-57; Lucien Goldmann. *Le Dieu caché.* Paris: Gallimard, 1955: 356; Knapp 70. Barthes (84), in contrast, views Pyrrhus as Racine's most liberated figure.

[7]For the stifling role of passion and its immobilizing effects, see: Barthes 78-79; Albert Cook. *French Tragedy: The Power of Enactment.* Chicago: Swallow P, 1981: 47; Moore (I.1. n.59) 71-73; Eugène Vinaver. *Racine et la poésie tragique.* Paris: Nizet, 1963: 12. Charles Mauron (*L'Inconscient dans l'oeuvre et la vie de Racine.* Gap: Ophyrs, 1957: 332) stresses in contrast the positive energizing force of passion.

[8]On Racine's break with the old courtly (pastoral) portrayal of devoted, unrequited love, see Barthes 78-79; Bénichou 135-36.

[9]Critics are divided on the issue of the relative power of the word and the glance. See: Barthes 42-43; Goldmann 356; Knapp 81-82; Reinhard Kuhn. "The Palace of Broken Words: Reflections on Racine's *Andromaque.*" *Romance Review* 70 (1979): 336-45; Jean Starobinski. *L'Oeil vivant.* Paris: Gallimard, 1961: 76-89; Susan W. Tiefenbrun. *Signs of the Hidden: Semiotic Studies.* Amsterdam: Rodopi, 1980: 211-31; Louis van Delft. "Language and Power: Eyes and Words in *Britannicus.*" *Yale French Studies* 45 (1970): 102-12.

[10]L. Petit de Julleville in his introduction to *Horace* in *Théâtre choisi de Corneille* (Paris: Hachette, n.d.: 235) characterizes the crossroads as being shaped by the conflict between love and patriotism, in which the more "sublime" virtue of patriotism wins. See also Jasinski 38.

[11]Cf. Louis Herland (*Horace ou naissance de l'homme.* Paris: Editions de Minuit, 1952: 12), who characterizes the action as Roman, but not the characters; also Couton 63-64; Dort 50-51. Stegmann 583 characterizes Horace as the

only genuine hero, while Mary Jo Muratore ("Aphorism as Discursive Weaponry: Corneille's Language of Ammunition." *L'Esprit Créateur* 22. 3 [1982]: 20-26) identifies the heroic with recklessness, expressed in Corneille by the sharpness of the spoken word. Moore 68-69 names *Horace* Corneille's only "real tragedy."

[12]For Doubrovsky (142-54) Curace espouses the feminine values of sensibility expressed later by Camille, which Horace must combat in order to achieve the superior masculine values of mastery (*maîtrise*), which alone will lead to genuine heroism. By killing first Curiace, then Camille, Horace ascends as hero. On Camille's absolute insistence on her right to love and happiness, see Stegmann, 583-84. Doubrovsky 136-54 discusses the equilibrium that Camille and Curiace bring to Horace's courage and patriotism. Nadal 180-83 traces Camille's radical difference to her determination of placing love in the inner realm of the heart, not in the realm of public glory.

[13]Cf. Horst S. Daemmrich. "The Incest Motif in Lessing's *Nathan der Weise* and Schiller's *Die Braut von Messina.*" *Germanic Review* 42 (1967): 184-96.

[14]Dante. *The Divine Comedy.* Trans. Laurence Binyon. New York: Viking, 1947: 3.

[15]For research that locates Schiller's play in the tradition of fate tragedies and pursues indications that the basic dramatic configuration is determined by an inexplicable fate, see W.H. Carruth. "Fate and Guilt in Schiller's *Die Braut von Messina.*" *PMLA* 17 (1902): 105-24; Benno von Wiese. *Die deutsche Tragödie von Lessing bis Hebbel.* 5th ed. Hamburg: Hoffmann & Campe, 1961: 261; Friedrich Sengle. "Die Braut von Messina." *Deutschunterricht* 12 (1960): 72-89; G.A. Wells. "Fate, Tragedy and Schiller's *Die Braut von Messina.*" *Journal of English and Germanic Philology* 64 (1965): 191-212.

[16]Cf. Ilse Appelbaum-Graham. "Element into Ornament: The Alchemy of

Art." *Deutsche Beiträge zur geistigen Überlieferung* 4 (1961): 41-63; see also Herbert Seidler. "Schillers *Braut von Messina.*" *Literaturwiss. Jb. Görres-Gesellschaft* (1960): 27-52.

[17]The present analysis advances the findings in Horst S. Daemmrich. "The Sentient Heart: Motif Analysis of Goethe's *Tasso* III. iii." In John McCarthy, Albert A. Kipa (Eds.). *Aufnahme-Weitergabe. Literarische Impulse um Lessing und Goethe.* Hamburg: Buske, 1982: 153-64.

[18]Of special interest are: E.M. Wilkinson. "Goethe's *Tasso.* The Tragedy of a Creative Artist." *Publications English Goethe Society* 15 (1945): 96-127; —. "Tasso—ein gesteigerter Werther in the Light of Goethe's Principle of Steigerung." *Modern Language Review* 44 (1949): 305-28; Wolfdietrich Rasch. *Goethes 'Torquato Tasso.' Die Tragödie des Dichters.* Stuttgart: Metzler, 1954; Gerhard Neumann. *Konfiguration. Studien zu Goethes "Torquato Tasso."* München: Fink, 1965; Gerhard Kaiser. *Wandrer und Idylle.* Göttingen: Vandenhoeck & Ruprecht, 1977: 175-208; Herbert Kraft. "Goethes *Tasso.* Nachfrage zu einem Bündnis zwischen Kunst und Politik." *Goethe Jb.* 104 (1987): 84-95; T.J. Reed. "Tasso und die Besserwisser." In John L. Hibbert, H.B. Nisbet (Eds.). *Texte, Motive und Gestalten der Goethezeit.* Festschrift Hans Reiss. Tübingen: Niemeyer, 1989: 95-112.

[19]Wolfgang Kayser. "Entstehung und Krise des modernen Romans." *Deutsche Vierteljahrsschrift* 28 (1954): 13.

[20]See, for instance, P.J. Brenner. "Kritische Form: Zur Dialektik der Aufklärung in Wielands Roman *Don Sylvio von Rosalva.*" *Jb. Deutsche Schiller-Gesellschaft* 20 (1976): 162-183; K. Oettinger. *Phantasie und Erfahrung.* München: Fink, 1970; J.A. McCarthy. *Christoph Martin Wieland.* Boston: Twayne, 1979: 60.

[21]Christoph M. Wieland. *Sämtliche Werke.* Ed. J.G. Gruber. Leipzig: Göschen, 1824: 4: 35-37. All references to *Don Sylvio* are from this edition.

[22]Friedrich Klinger. "Vorrede zu den Romanen" (1798). *Klingers Werke.* Berlin: Aufbau, 1964: 2: 7.

[23]Klinger. *Fausts Leben, Taten und Höllenfahrt.* In*Werke* 2: 209.

[24]Christoph M. Wieland. *Werke.* Berlin: Aufbau, 1967: 2: 346.

[25]See Wieland. "Schwärmerei und Enthusiasmus" (1775). In *Sämtliche Werke.* 44: 53.

[26]Cf. Wulf Segebrecht. "Die tödliche Lösung 'Lang lebe der König.' Zu Schillers Ballade 'Der Taucher.'" In Gunter E. Grimm (Ed.). *Deutsche Balladen.* Stuttgart: Reclam, 1988: 108-32.

[27]Many scholars have criticized the ballad's abrupt conclusion that is, however, entirely consistent with the function of the motif. For a thorough and convincing interpretation, see Ferdinand Piedmont. "Ironie in Schillers Ballade 'Der Handschuh.'" *Wirkendes Wort* 16(1966): 105-12.

[28]For a systematic analysis and presentation, see: Horst Hartmann. *Egmont. Geschichte und Dichtung.* Berlin: Volk und Wissen, 1972; important aspects and differing views in E. M Wilkinson. "The Relation of Form and Meaning in Goethe's *Egmont.*" *Publications English Goethe Society* N.S. 18 (1949): 149-82; Jeffrey L. Sammons. "On the Structure of Goethe's *Egmont.*" *Journal of English and Germanic Philology* 62 (1963): 241-51; Roger A. Nicholls. "Egmont and the Vision of Freedom." *German Quarterly* 43 (1970): 188-98.

[29]Friedrich Schiller. "Über Egmont"(1788). *Sämtliche Werke.* München: Hanser, 1959: 5: 932-42.

Chapter 4

[1]For the often conflicting assessment of the tradition see: Erich A. Albrecht. *Primitivism and Related Ideas in 18th Century German Lyric Poetry.* Baltimore: Johns Hopkins University, 1950; A. Owen Aldridge. "The State of Nature, an Undiscovered Country in the History of Ideas." *Studies on Voltaire and the 18th Century* 98 (1972): 7-26; Richard Beitl. *Goethes Bild der Landschaft.* Berlin: de Gruyter, 1929; Alfred Biese. *Das Naturgefühl im Wandel der Zeiten.* Leipzig: Quelle, 1926; Ernst Robert Curtius. *Europäische Literatur und lateinisches Mittelalter* (I. 1. n. 29); Willi Flemming. *Der Wandel des deutschen Naturgefühls vom 15. zum 18. Jahrhundert.* Halle: Niemeyer, 1931; Gerald Gillespie. *Garden and Labyrinth of Time. Studies in Renaissance and Baroque Literature.* New York: Lang, 1988; Ernst Ulrich Grosse. *Sympathie der Natur.* München: Fink, 1968; Hans Ulrich Seeber, Paul Gerhard Klussmann (Eds.). *Idylle und Modernisierung in der europäischen Literatur des 19. Jahrhunderts.* Bonn: Bouvier, 1986; Leo Marx. *The Machine and the Garden.* New York: Oxford UP, 1964; Wolfgang Raible. "Literatur and Natur. Beobachtungen zur literarischen Landschaft." *Poetica* 11 (1979): 105-23; Helmut Rehder. *Philosophie der unendlichen Landschaft.* Halle: Niemeyer, 1932; Alexander Ritter (Ed.). *Landschaft und Raum in der Erzählkunst.* Darmstadt: Wiss. Buchges., 1975; Micheline Tison-Braun. *Poétique du paysage. Essai sur le genre descriptif.* Paris: Nizet, 1980.

[2]See Otto Gillen. "'Wo faß ich dich, unendliche Natur...' Goethes religiöses und mythisches Landschaftserlebnis." *Goethe-Jb.* 100 (1983): 260-65; Uwe-Karsten Ketelsen. *Die Naturpoesie in der norddeutschen Frühaufklärung. Poesie als Sprache der Versöhnung.* Stuttgart: Metzler, 1974; August Langen. "Verbale Dynamik in der literarischen Landschaftsschilderung des 18. Jahrhunderts." *Zeitschrift für deutsche Philologie* 70 (1947/49): 249-318; Francis Turner Palgrave. *Landscapes in Poetry from Homer to Tennyson.* London: Macmillan, 1987; Thomas Saine. *Von der Kopernikanischen bis zur französischen Revolution. Die Auseinandersetzung der deutschen Frühaufklärung mit der neuen Zeit.* Berlin: Schmidt, 1987; Barbara Stafford. "Toward Romantic Landscape Perception." *Studies in 18th Century Culture* 10 (1981): 17-75;

Carsten Zelle. *"Angenehmes Grauen."* *Literaturhistorische Beiträge zur Ästhetik des Schrecklichen im achtzehnten Jahrhundert.* Hamburg: Meiner, 1987.

[3]Cf. Bodo Assert. *Der Raum in der Erzählkunst.* Tübingen: Diss., 1973; Mikhail Bakhtin. "Zeit und Raum im Roman." *Kunst und Literatur* 22 (1974): 1161-91; Enzo Caramaschi. "Paysages impressionistes chez Balzac." *Arts visuels et littérature. De Stendhal à l'impressionisme.* Paris: Nizet, 1985: 47-80; Gail Finney. *The Counterfeit Idyll. The Garden Ideal and Social Reality in 19th-Century Fiction.* Tübingen: Niemeyer, 1984; Gail Finney. "Garden Paradigms in 19th Century Fiction." *Comparative Literature* 36 (1984): 20-33; Joseph Frank. "Spatial Form in Modern Literature." *Sewanee Review* 53 (1945): 221-40; Rainer Gruenter. "Landschaft." *Germanisch-Romanische Monatsschrift* 34 (1953): 110-20; Alice Kuzniar. "The Vanishing Canvas: Notes on German Romantic Landscape Aesthetics." *German Studies Review* 11 (1988): 359-376; Frank C. Maatje. "Versuch einer Poetik des Raumes." In Ritter. *Landschaft* 393-416.

[4]Margaret McGowan ("Racine's 'lieu théâtral.'" In *Form and Meaning. Aesthetic Coherence in 17th Century Drama.* Ed. William Howarth, Ian McFarlane, and Margaret McGowan. Amersham, Eng.: Avebury Publishing Co., 1982: 167) characterizes the settings of seventeenth-century theater as a natural extension of the audience's environment. Eléonore Zimmermann ("L'Innocence et la tragédie chez Racine: Le Problème de Bérénice." *Papers on French Seventeenth-Century Literature* 12 [1979/80]: 110) identifies the palace as providing both security for those who are "innocent" and entry for those who would persecute them.

[5]See Tiefenbrun (I. 3. n.9) 211-12 and Evert Van der Starre. *Racine et le théâtre de l'ambiguité. Etude sur Bajazet.* Leiden: UP, 1966: 220 on the oppressiveness of the imprisoning palace, in which according to Odette Mourges (*Autonomie de Racine.* Paris: Cortin, 1967: 44) space closes in on the character. Cynthia B. Kerr ("Temps, lieux et paradoxes dans *Sertorius* ." *Revue*

d'Histoire Littéraire 83 [1983]: 16) characterizes the palace in Corneille's
Sertorius as a temporary place of refuge. Catherine Huebert ("Locus. A Key to
the Tragic Art of Racine." Diss., U. Pittsburgh, 1970) differentiates between the
"closed locus" of Racine's "middle period" (*Andromaque* to *Mithridate*) and the
"open locus" of his later plays.

[6]Anne Ubersfeld ("The Space of Phèdre." *Poetics Today* 2:3 [1981]: 204)
calls the space outside the palace the void to which both Hippoyte and Phèdre aspire to flee but cannot.

[7]Richard L. Barnett ("Centripétence textuelle: La structuration convergente
du tragique racinien." Diss., Brandeis U., 1979) argues that Racine represents humans as universally and metaphorically entrapped by the forces colliding around
them and by the incommunicability of messages. Huebert maintains that the
centripetal movement of compression of space reaches a culmination in *Bajazet*
and *Phèdre*. Mourges (44) sees space as closing in on Racine's characters, yet
also providing individual figures with immense elasticity (51). Ubersfeld (206),
in contrast, cites Michel Hermon's creation of the snail-shaped stage setting for
Phèdre to point out the continuous spiraling movement from inner to outer
space in that play. Van der Starre (220) views Racine as a precursor of Beckett
and Sartre in claustration of characters.

[8]See Danielle and David Kaisergruber and Jacques Lempert (*Phèdre de
Racine: pour une sémiotique de la représentation classique*. Paris: Larousse,
1972: 44) on Phèdre filling the stage with her physical presence. Barthes
(I.1.n.82: 44) describes the space outside that of human interaction as "unpeopled
space."

[9]Knapp (I.3. n.2: 104) describes the palace as a mask for Néron.

[10]Thomas G. Pavel (*La Syntaxe narrative des tragédies de Corneille.
Recherches et propositions*. Paris: Klinksieck, 1976: 49) points out that all
major action takes place off stage. Nadal (I.3. n. 1: 130) places the climate of

tragedy in the dialogue of Corneille's tragedies.

[11]Nelson (I.3. n.5: 262) stresses the importance of the political environment in which Corneille has placed the action of his plays from *Le Cid* to *La
Mort de Pompée.*

[12]John C. Lapp ("Racine's Symbolism." In R.C. Knight [Ed.]. *Racine.*
London: Macmillan, 1969: 67) discusses the ambivalent function of the altar in
Iphigénie as a place of veneration, of struggle, of death, and of the union of
lovers. McGowan (172-77) points out that in those plays in which the palace
becomes the site for the protagonist's death, it is given physical substance:
closed doors, thick walls, etc.

[13]Jacques Garelli (*Le Recul et la dispersion.* Paris: Gallimard, 1978: 79)
defines Racine's procedure as the "derealization" of persons and things in order to
reconstitute them in the realm of the imaginary. Ubersfeld (206) discusses the
concepts of "displaced people," who, confined in a definable space, constantly
wish they were elsewhere and the "void of representation" giving a "concrete
non-picture" to *Phèdre.*

[14]See John Dryden. *Of Dramatic Poesie* (1688). In *The Dramatic Works.*
Ed. Montague Summers. New York: Gordian P., 1968: 14-15. See also John
M. Alden. "Dryden, Corneille and the Essay of Dramatic Poesy." *Review of
English Studies* n.s. 6 (1955): 147-56 and Pierre Leganis. "Corneille and Dryden
as Dramatic Critics." *Seventeenth Century Studies Presented to Sir Herbert
Grierson.* Oxford: Clarendon P, 1938.

[15]All quotations in the text are taken from the following texts: John
Dryden. *The Indian Queen* in *The Works of John Dryden.* Vol. 8. Berkeley, Los
Angeles: U California P, 1965; *The Indian Emperor* in *Works.* Vol. 9, 1966;
Aureng-Zebe in Dryden. *The Dramatic Works.* Vol. 4. New York: Gordian P,
1968. The latter text does not have numbered lines.

[16]Jean La Fontaine. *Oeuvres complètes* . Paris: Editions Du Seuil, 1965: 309-10.

[17]Alexander Pope. "Windsor-Forest" in *Poetical Works*. Oxford: Oxford UP, 1978.

[18]Christoph Martin Wieland. *Werke*. Berlin: Aufbau, 1967. 2: 496.

[19]Wieland. *Werke:* 2: 7.

[20]See especially the scenes in the house of Hippias and on the estate of Daenae. Goethe's youthful attack on the loss of vitality in Wieland's characters also points to the danger of a moderation that has become conventional in an idyllic rococo setting. See "Götter, Helden und Wieland." (JA 7: 125-39).

[21]Lieselotte Kurth-Voigt ("Der Sieg der Natur über die Schwärmerei." In Hansjörg Schelle [Ed.]. *Christoph Martin Wieland*. Darmstadt: Wiss. Buchges., 1981) and Marianne Thalmann ("Die horizontale und die vertikale Landschaft." *Neue Deutsche Hefte* 20 [1973]: 3-8 and "Der romantische Garten." *Journal of English and Germanic Philology* 48 [1949]: 329-42) have demonstrated that contemporaries of Goethe used similar techniques.

[22]The analysis is based on Horst S. Daemmrich. "Landschaftsdarstellungen im Werk Goethes. Erzählfunktion – Themen-bereiche – Raumstruktur." *Deutsche Vierteljahrsschrift* 66 (1993). See also Dieter Borchmeyer. *Die Weimarer Klassik*. 2 Bde. Königstein/Ts.: Athenäum, 1980; Eberhard Buchwald. *Naturschau mit Goethe*. Stuttgart: Kohlhammer, 1960; Horst Falk. *Der Leitgedanke von der Vollkommenheit der Natur in Goethes klassischen Werk*. Frankfurt/M.: Lang, 1980; Friedrich Hiebel. *Goethe. Die Erhöhung des Menschen. Perspektiven einer morphologischen Lebenschau*. Bern: Francke, 1961; Monika Hielscher. *Natur und Freiheit in Goethes Die Wahlverwandtschaften*. Frankfurt/M.: Lang, 1985; Franz Koch. *Goethes Gedankenform*.

Berlin: de Gruyter, 1967; Gerhard Neumann. *Konfiguration. Goethes "Torquato Tasso."* München: Fink, 1965, especially 67-69; Michael Niedermeyer. *Das Ende der Idylle. Symbolik, Zeitbezug, 'Gartenrevolution' in Goethes Roman "Die Wahlverwandtschaften."* Frankfurt/M.: Lang, 1992; Erich Trunz. "Goethes Entwurf 'Landschaftliche Malerei.'" *Weimarer Goethe-Studien.* Weimar: Böhlau, 1980: 156-202; Clemens Alexander Wimmer. *Geschichte der Gartentheorie.* Darmstadt: Wiss. Buchges., 1989.

[23]In such instances of *himmelhoch jauchzend, zum Tode betrübt,* Goethe assigns to Werther the conflicting sentiments expressed by Klärchen in *Egmont* and by multiple voices in his poems of the period.

[24]Cf. Gerhard Sauder. *Empfindsamkeit.* Stuttgart: Metzler, 1974. 1: 121, 137-43, 166 ft.

[25]Cf. Werner Danckert. *Offenes und geschlossenes Leben. Zwei Daseinsaspekte in Goethes Weltschau.* Bonn: Bouvier, 1963; Rüdiger Els. *Ralph Waldo Emerson und "Die Natur" in Goethes Werken.* Frankfurt/M.: Lang, 1977; Heinrich Henel. *Goethezeit. Ausgewählte Aufsätze.* Frankfurt/M.: Insel, 1980; Werner Keller. "Das Drama Goethes." In W. Hinck (Ed.). *Handbuch des deutschen Dramas.* Düsseldorf: Bagel, 1980: 133-56; and Arthur Koch. "Wirklichkeit in Poesie verwandeln. Betrachtungen über die Beziehung des Landschaftserlebens zum Dichtwerk bei Goethe." *Goethe Jb.* 91 (1974): 58-77, who emphasizes emotional aspects of the identification with nature.

[26]Cf. Johannes Flügge. "Goethes morphologische Naturanschauung und die Macht der exakten Naturwissenschaften." *Scheidewege* 12 (1982): 429-47; F.-J. von Rintelen. "Goethes Liebe zur Natur." *Philosophische Studien* 2 (1950/51): 53-66; Rolf Zimmermann. "Goethes Verhältnis zur Naturmystik am Beispiel seiner Farbenlehre." In R. Zimmermann (Ed.). *Epochen der Naturmystik.* Berlin: Schmidt, 1979: 333-63; Raimar Zons. "Ein Riß durch die Ewigkeit. Landschaft in Werther und Lenz." *Literatur für Leser* 4 (1981):

65-78.

[27]Cf. Goethe's observations on introspection and self-knowledge gained through active participation in life in "Winckelmann und sein Jahrhundert" (1805), "Betrachtungen im Sinne der Wanderer" (1829), and JA 4: 29, 100;18: 255; 38: 250. See also Andreas Wachsmuth. *Geeinte Zwienatur.* Berlin: Aufbau, 1966: 113-56.

[28]Note the similarities of the landscape to the designs of the English garden (park) advocated by landscape planners (W. Kent, C. Brown) and highly praised by Shaftesbury, *The Moralist* (1709), Pope (essay in the "Guardian," 1713), Defoe, *Tour Through Great Britain* (1724-26), G. Mason, *An Essay on Design in Gardening* (1768), and W. Mason, *The English Garden* (1779). For the critical function of nature in *Die Wahlverwandtschaften,* see: Richard Faber. "Parkleben. Zur sozialen Idyllik Goethes" in N. W. Bolz (Ed.). *Goethes Wahlverwandtschaften. Kritische Modelle und Diskursanalysen zum Mythos Literatur.* Hildesheim: Gerstenberg, 1981: 91-168; Finney. *Counterfeit Idyll* ; Hielscher. *Natur und Freiheit* ; Ulrike Weinhold. "Ebenbild und Einbildung. Zur Problematik des Garten-Motivs in Goethes *Wahlverwandtschaften." Neophilologus* 67 (1983): 419-31.

[29]The motifs of spatial restriction in Goethe's works differ from those developed in the writings of the Storm and Stress authors. Goethe points to reasons for individual limitations. Lenz, in contrast, accentuates an irreversible trend (See II. 3 "Realistic Space").

[30]Friedrich Schiller. "Was heißt und zu welchem Ende studiert man Universalgeschichte?" (1789). SA 13: 23 and *Über die ästhetische Erziehung des Menschen in einer Reihe von Briefen* (1795). Brief 6. SA 12: 22.

[31]SA 13: 9-11.

[32]For Schiller's reception of Shaftesbury see Benno von Wiese. *Friedrich Schiller.* Stuttgart: Metzler, 1963 and Käte Hamburger. "Schillers Fragment 'Der Menschenfeind' und die Idee der Kalokagathe." *Deutsche Vierteljahrsschrift* 30 (1956): 367-400.

Chapter 5

[1]For various critical assessments of this controversial tragedy, see, among others: Barthes (I.1. n.82) 60 ff.; Bénichou (I.1. n.57) 136; Cook (I.3. n. 7) 79; Goldmann (I.3. n.6) 394, 415-40; Kaisergruber et al. (I.4. n.8) 10 *passim* ; Moore (I.3. n.7) 78-79; Mourges (I.4. n.5) 152; Rousset (I.1. n.83) 162; and Vinaver (i.3. n.7) 77, who names Phèdre Racine's "purest heroine" because the gods have taken over her heart as their battlefield.

[2]On the alignment of the figures in *Mithridate* on a scale from possessiveness to renunciation, see Barthes 106-7; Bénichou 144; Knapp (I.3. n.2) 140-45; also Claude Bernet's word counts for *coeur* (57), *main* (32) and *intérêt* (9) (*Le Vocabulaire des tragédies de Jean Racine. Analyse statistique.* Genève, Paris: Slatkine, 1983). Lapp (I.4. n.12: 71) identifies Monime's bandeau as a mark of bondage.

[3]Cook (49) views Mithridate's final reassessment of both his political and personal power as the recognition of the aging process.

[4]See Anne T. Barbeau. *The Intellectual Design of John Dryden's Heroic Plays.* New Haven, London: Yale UP, 1970: 62-90, 149-61; and Derek Hughes. *Dryden's Heroic Plays.* Lincoln: U. of Nebraska P, 1981): 23-58 for the central role of passion in the rhythm, design, and characterization of *The Indian Queen* and *The Indian Emperour.* Since passion is always linked with possessiveness and frequently fatal, it must be eliminated or overcome.

[5]Barbeau (62) characterizes Dryden's plays as "plays of ideas." Thus, she ar-

gues (87), Guyomar and Cortez are two halves of a single hero in sharing a common political philosophy.

[6]Hughes (338) characterizes the figures in *The Indian Emperour* as helplessly caught in a past that they seek to transcend, while the figures in *The Indian Queen* grow in their altruistic capacity.

[7]Curiously, Bernet (231) found the highest word count for *oreille* (ear) to be in *Esther.*

[8]On the political implications of Addison's play, see J.M. Armistead. "Drama of Renewal: *Cato* and Moral Empiricism." *Papers on Language and Literature* 17 (1981): 281 and Michael M. Cohen. "The Imagery of Addison's *Cato* and The Whig Sublime." *CEA Critic* 38 (1976): 23-24. Donald O. Rogers ("Addison's *Cato:* Teaching through Imagery." *CEA Critic* 36 [1974]: 17-18) traces the antithetical characterizations of Caesar and Cato in the storm and mountain imagery.

[9]Wieland. *Werke.* 3: canto 6, stanzas 10-103.

[10]Cf. Günter Blöcker. *Heinrich von Kleist oder Das absolute Ich.* Berlin: Argon, 1960; Max Kommerell. "Die Sprache und das Unaussprechliche." *Geist und Buchstabe in der Dichtung.* 4th edition. Frankfurt/M.: Klostermann, 1956: 243-317; Gert Ueding. "Zweideutige Bilderwelt: Das Käthchen von Heilbronn." In Walter Hinderer (Ed.). *Kleists Dramen. Neue Interpretationen.* Stuttgart: Reclam, 1981: 172-87.

[11]Friedrich Heinrich Jacobi. *Eduard Allwills Papiere. Faksimiledruck.* Stuttgart: Metzler, 1962: 29. For a collection of Jacobi's observations on love and friendship, see Friedrich Heinrich Jacobi. *Fliegende Blätter und Sentenzen aus seinen Werken und Briefen.* Heidelberg: Sauer, 1965: 79-80.

[12]In *Deutschland* 3 (Stück 8): 185-213, the first section of *Woldemar* was published as "Freundschaft und Liebe" in 1777 (*Teutscher Merkur*); for a thorough discussion of the successive revisions and versions of 1781, 1794, and 1796, see Frida David. *Friedrich Heinrich Jacobis "Woldemar" in seinen verschiedenen Fassungen.* Leipzig: Voigtländer, 1913.

[13]JA 15: 140-78; for an analysis of the symbolism of the arts, see Emil Staiger. *Goethe.* Zürich: Atlantis, 1963. 2: 449-74.

[14]Cf. "Gott, Gemüt und Welt" (1815). JA 4: 1-7.

[15]Cf. renunciation in "Die Geheimnisse" (1785), "ein wunderbares Lied." JA 1: 293.

[16]Goethe. "Novelle" (1828). JA 16:357.

[17]*Dichtung und Wahrheit.* Buch 16 (1822). JA 25: 6.

Chapter 6

[1]For the proposition that Corneille intended Auguste's clemency to serve as a model to Louis XIII in his dealing with conspirators and rebels, see Couton (I.3. n.2) 67-71; Dort (I.3. n.2) 53-54; Nelson (I.3. n.5) 262-63. Doubrovsky (I.3. n.2: 214-16) calls Auguste's final apotheosis a moral and political victory that raises his clemency to the stature of the pardon of God, while Starobinski (I.3. n.9: 50-52) views Auguste's decision as an example of the mask donned by the protagonist who invents the self not according to what he is but what he wants to be. See also Jasinski's portrayal (I.3. n. 4: 56) of Corneille's figures as "heroes in mutation" who form a new will.

[2]See Tiefenbrun's study on surprise and illusion in *Cinna* (I.3. n.9: 181,

203) to show Corneille's conception of the human as not finished but in the act of becoming.

^{3}As Barthes points out (I.1. n.82: 58-59), modelling the past accentuates Racine's repetitive, circular treatment of time. See also Knapp (I.3. n.2)148 and Mourges (I.4. n.5)14. While Bénichou (I.1. n.57: 131-39) points out that Racine's tragedies are themselves innovative in breaking with literary conventions, Cook (I.1. n.7: 66-67) views Racine's continual references to the past as a sign of its importance in his drama, and Poulet (I.1. n.5: 154) identifies the subject of Racine's tragedy as the "ineluctable continuation of the past into the present." Buford Norman ("The Theme of Names and Its Relationship to Tragedy in Racine." *Papers on French Seventeenth-Century Literature* 12 [1979/80]: 84-86) discusses the notion of the model of excellence in Racine's plays as an "integral part of the theme of name" that is intimately connected with self-identity.

^{4}Barthes (78-79) sees *Andromaque* as focusing on the question of how to pass from the old to the new order, while Mourges sees the figures as obsessed with the past. Kuhn (I.3. n.9: 338) points out the irony that the future of Oreste, Hermione, and Pyrrhus depends upon a central past decision: that Astyanax has been doomed to die while Mourges sees the figures as obsessed with the past.

^{5}According to Zimmermann (I.3. n.2:18), Bajazet is willing to sacrifice external freedom to internal faith. Knapp (135) identifies the theme of *Bajazet* as Roxane snatching Bajazet from the void into the world of conflict and then sinking back with him into the quagmire. Mourges (40) argues that the future is destroyed in *Bajazet*. Tiefenbrun's analysis of the play as centering on the question of the unreliability of information (209) points out that without open communication, no future will be established. See also Van der Starre 206-07.

^{6} Many critics have interpreted this break positively, as coming-of-age and growth toward independence. See for example Barthes 89-90; Mauron (I.3. n.7) 75; Van Delft (I.3. n.9) 102. Knapp (104) shows that the "cognitive triad" of past, present, and future has been shattered, while Moore (I.3. n.7) 72) states that no one in *Britannicus* is master of the situation.

[7]Goldmann (I.3. n.6: 368) states that in her final walk, Junie enters the world of the gods.

[8]See Barthes 95; J.A. Dainard. "The Power of the Spoken Word in *Bérénice.*" *Romanic Review* 67 (1976): 163; Goldmann's identification of Rome as the "hidden god" that demands the sacrifice of Titus' private life (378); Knapp's interpretation of the sacrifice as the step initiating Titus' manhood by divesting himself of his individual personality in order to assume a collective consciousness (111-15); Zimmermann 22. Mourges (108-10) argues that the exemplariness of the characters in *Bérénice* destroys their humanity and paradoxically both approaches and distances them from the audience. Ingrid Heyndels (I.1. n.59: 29) interprets Titus' weeping at the end of the play as illustrative for Racine's subversion of the king's power in many of his plays.

[9]Barthes (56) places Xipharès, along with Iphigénie, among Racine's most "regressive" figures, imprisoned in the past, while he places Pharnace, alonge with Achille, among the "progressive" ones, liberated for the future. See also Bénichou's (146-47) identification of Xipharès with the old aristocratic patterns, while Pharnace represents the new, bourgeois mode of thought based on self-interest. The redemptive result of Mithridate's renunciation is emphasized by Flowers (I.3. n.6: 114), while Knapp (140-43) and Moore (77) stress that like an outdated god or social order, Mithridate is doomed to fade away.

[10]See Mauron 132.

[11]Barthes (115) points out the barbarity of preserving family and community at the expense of the individual life of Eriphile.

[12]See Johnson (I.1. n.40) 94-104; M.M. Kelsall. "The Meaning of

Addison's *Cato.*" *Review of English Studies* n.s. 17 (1966): 149 ff., Armistead (I. 5. n.8) 271-83.

[13]Cf. "Einfache Nachahmung der Natur, Manier, Stil" (1789). "Über die bildende Nachahmung des Schönen" (1788/89). "Über Wahrheit und Wahrscheinlichkeit der Kunstwerke" (1797). JA 33: 54-59; 60-64; 84-91. See also the influential study by Karl Philipp Moritz. *Über die bildende Nachahmung des Schönen* (1788). In "Deutsche Literaturdenkmale des 18. und 19. Jahrhunderts." Vol. 31. Heilbronn: Henninger, 1888, especially 31-32, 38 ff. Moritz discussed his theoretical considerations with Goethe in Rome, and Goethe accepted his basic premise of the autonomy of art. The definitive explanation of the classical view of freedom in appearance was advanced by Schiller in his letters to Christian Gottfried Körner of 2.18.1793 and 2.23.1793 in *Schillers Briefe* (I.1. n.72): 3: 254-80 and in *Über die ästhetische Erziehung des Menschen in einer Reihe von Briefen* (SA 12: 54-60, 76-120). Schiller agrees with Goethe that every individual has the potential for complete individuation. He also credits the antagonism of conflicting forces with stimulating cultural advance. In *Über die ästhetische Erziehung* he argues that the imbalance between sensuous impulses and rational aspirations contributes to individual failure and impedes the evolution of sociopolitical institutions.

[14]Cf. "Philosophische Studie" (1784/85). *Zur Natur und Wissenschaftslehre.* JA 39: 6-9; *Dichtung und Wahrheit.* Buch 9. JA 23: 166; also Buch 14. JA 24: 196 ff.; "Was wir bringen" (1814). JA 9: 235; "Wald und Höhle." *Faust* I. ll. 3217-3250; Goethe to Lavater, Sept. 20, 1780 in *Gedenkausgabe* 18: 532.

[15]"Aus Ottiliens Tagebuche." *Wahlverwandtschaften.* JA 21: 225.

[16]Among the many excellent interpretations of *Iphigenie*, the following prove especially helpful for thematic analysis: Liselotte Blumenthal. "Iphigenie von der Antike bis zur Moderne." In H. Holtzhauer (Ed.) *Natur und Idee. Festschrift für Andreas Wachsmuth.* Weimar: Böhlau, 1966: 9-40; Christa

Bürger. *Der Ursprung der bürgerlichen Kunst. Literatursoziologische Unter-
suchungen zum klassischen Goethe.* Frankfurt/M.: Suhrkamp, 1977: 177-207;
Dieter Borchmeyer. "*Iphigenie auf Tauris.*" In H. Müller-Michaelis (Ed.).
Deutsche Dramen. Königstein/Ts. : Athenäum, 1981: 52-86; James Boyd.
Goethe's Iphigenie auf Tauris. An Interpretation and Critical Analysis. Oxford:
Blackwell, 1942; R. M. Browning. "The Humanity of Goethe's *Iphigenie.*"
German Quarterly 30 (1957): 98-113; Sigurd Burckhardt. "Die Stimme der
Wahrheit und der Menschlichkeit: Goethes *Iphigenie.*" *Monatshefte* 48
(1956):49-71; Ulrich K. Goldsmith. "The Healing of Orestes in Goethe's
Iphigenie auf Tauris." *Studies in Comparison.* New York: Lang, 1989: 75-86;
Pierre Grappin. "Die Idee der Entwicklung im Spiegel des Goetheschen
Schauspiels *Iphigenie auf Tauris.*" *Goethe-Jb.* 99 (1982):32-40; Fritz Hackert.
"Iphigenie auf Tauris." In Walter Hinderer (Ed.) *Goethes Dramen.* Stuttgart:
Reclam, 1980: 144-68; Sylvia P. Jenkins. "The Image of the Godess in
Iphigenie auf Tauris." *Publications English Goethe Society* 21 (1952): 56-80;
Herbert Lindenau. "Die geistesgeschichtliche Voraussetzung von Goethes
Iphigenie. Zur Geschichte der Säkularisierung christlicher Denkformen in der
deutschen Dichtung des 18. Jahrhunderts." *Zeitschrift für deutsche Philologie*
75 (1956): 113-153; Peter Pfaff. "Die Stimme des Gewissens. Über Goethes
Versuch zu einer Geneologie der Moral, vor allem in der *Iphigenie.*" *Euphorion*
72 (1978): 20-42; Heinz Politzer. "No Man is an Island: A Note on Image and
Thought in Goethe's *Iphigenie.*" *Germanic Review* 37(1962):42-54;
Wolfdietrich Rasch. *Goethe's 'Iphigenie auf Tauris' als Drama der Autonomie.*
München: Beck, 1979; Susan Helen Reynolds. "Erstaunlich modern und un-
griechisch? Goethe's *Iphigenie auf Tauris* and Its Classical Background."
Publications English Goethe Society 57 (1986/87): 55-74; Ursula Segebrecht.
"Götter, Helden und Goethe. Zur Geschichtsdeutung in Goethes *Iphigenie auf
Tauris.*" In Karl Richter (Ed.). *Klassik und Moderne.* Stuttgart: Reclam,
1983: 175-93; Oskar Seidlin. "Goethe's *Iphigenie* and the Human Ideal."
Modern Language Quarterly 10 (1949): 307-20; Hans-Georg Werner. "Goethes
Iphigenie und die Antinomien eines idealen Humanitätskonzepts." *Text und
Dichtung. Analyse und Interpretation.* Berlin: Aufbau, 1984: 128-164;
Wolfgang Wittkowski. "Goethe's *Iphigenie.* Autonomous Humanity and the
Authority of the Gods in the Era of Benevolent Despotism." In Alexej

Ugrinsky (Ed.). *Goethe in the Twentieth Century.* New York: Greenwood,1987: 77-83.

[17]For critical evaluations of the thematic structure and relationship between individual and society, see: Ingrid G. Daemmrich. "Parallelism in Motifs and Theme. A Comparison of Schiller's 'Wilhelm Tell' and Zola's 'Paris.'" *Neuphilologische Mitteilungen* 82 (1981): 111-21; Louis Gouthier Fink. "Schillers *Wilhelm Tell.* Ein antijakobinisches republikanisches Trauerspiel. In Karl Eibl (Ed.). *Französische Revolution und deutsche Literatur.* Hamburg: Meiner, 1986: 57-81; Fritz Martini. "Wilhelm Tell, der ästhetische Staat und der ästhetische Mensch." *Deutschunterricht* 12 (1960): 90-118; Benno von Wiese. *Friedrich Schiller.* 3rd edition. Stuttgart: Metzler, 1963: 763-76.

Chapter 7

[1]On Dryden's deliberate introduction of the non-heroic in order to humanize his figures, see Hughes (I.5. n.4) 2, 12, 23, 47-48, 122-137.

[2]Gabriele Conesa. (*Le Dialogue molièresque: Etude stylistique et dramaturgique.* Paris: PUF, 1983: 289) cites this exchange as an example of a "pivotal term" that gives the dialogue cohesion. All line numbers in the text are from Molière. *Oeuvres complètes.* 2 vols. Ed. Georges Couton. Paris: Gallimard, 1971.

[3]W. G. Moore (*Molière: A New Criticism.* 6th ed. Oxford: Clarendon, 1968: 72) regards the struggle between the deceiver and the deceived, which is at times fused into a single character, as fundamental to Molière's dramatic structure, while Lionel Gossman (*Men and Masks: A Study of Molière.* Baltimore: The Johns Hopkins UP, 1963: 215) analyzes Molière's characters as bent on using others who retaliate with ruse and hypocrisy as "instruments of survival."

[4]Elaine D. Caucalon ("L'Inversion de l'amour courtois dans trois comédies de Molière." *Neophilologus* 56 [1972]: 134-45) demonstrates that Arnolphe's,

Alceste's, and Dom Juan's denigration of the women in their power is the inverse of the knightly code of honor. See also Konrad Schoell. "Abhängigkeit und Herrschaft in der Molièreschen Komödie." *Poetica* 12 (1980): 167-81, as well as two dissertations on plot in Molière: Biruta Cap. "Molière's Creative Process Studied through Recurring Patterns and Techniques." New Brunswick: Rutgers U, 1968 and Daniel Lawrence Eneman. "Unity in the Structure of Molière's Plays." Ann Arbor: U of Michigan, 1968. Roger Guichemerre ("Molière et la farce." *Oeuvres et critiques* 6 [1981]: 111-24) shows the derivation of Molière's conventionalized plots and figures from standard Italian farce. See also Marcel Gutwirth. *Molière ou l'invention comique. La Métamorphose des thèmes et la création des types.* Paris: Minard, 1966 and Hanns Heiss. *Molière.* Leipzig: Quelle und Meyer, 1929: 59-81.

[5]See Gossman (101-35) on the result of the complex collusion between the two domineering figures of *Tartuffe*. Ralph Albanese's identification of the prevailing economic concerns of *L'Avare* ("Argent et réification dans *L'Avare*." *Esprit Créateur* 21 [1981]: 35-50) can be applied to Tartuffe as well. See also Albanese's review article, "Molière devant la socio-critique." *Oeuvres et critiques* 6 (1981): 57-68; W.G. Moore (72); and Jack Yashinsky. "Métaphore, langage et mouvement dramatique dans *Le Misanthrope*." *Les Lettres Romanes* 34 (1980): 383.

[6]Many critics have analyzed this paradox in Alceste as blindness or self-deception, or even cold calculation. See, for example, Gossman 67-79; J. D. Hubert. *Molière and the Comedy of Intellect.* New York: Russell and Russell, 1962: 137; Robert McBride. *The Sceptical Vision of Molière.* London: MacMillan, 1977: 122.

[7]Critics have often pointed to the alienation from society incurred by the aggressiveness of the dominant figures as the mainspring of Molière's comedies. See, for example, Ramon Fernandez. "The Comedy of Will." In Jacques Guicharnaud (Ed.). *Molière: A Collection of Critical Essays.* Englewood Cliffs: Prentice-Hall, 1964: 50-53; Hubert 57; Robert J. Nelson. "The

Unreconstructed Heroes of Molière." In Guicharnaud 111-15; Richard L. Regosin. "Ambiguity and Truth in *Le Misanthrope*." *Romanic Review* 60 (1969): 265-72. Harold C. Knutson (*Molière: An Archetypal Approach.* Toronto: Toronto UP, 1976: 19, 43-110) develops the thesis that these old authoritarian "blocking" figures are "expelled" from the stage by the vital, young romantic figures who replace them.

[8]Critics have repeatedly traced the comic effect of Molière's figures to the strategically designed linguistic patterns of their speech. See, for instance, Anthony A. Ciccone. *The Comedy of Language: Four Farces by Molière.* Potomac: José Porrúa Turanzas, 1980: 12-34; Conesa 29-66; Fernandez 53; Robert Garapon. "Le Dialogue moliéresque: contribution à l'étude de la stylistique dramatique de Molière." *CAIEF* 16 (1964): 203-17; H. Gaston Hall. *Comedy in Context: Essays on Molière.* Jackson: UP of Mississippi, 1984: 27.

[9]Molière's use of the stick is a holdover from traditional farce. See Ciccone 62; Guichemerre 117; Hall 33. Schoell 170 discusses that servants, the objects of many beatings, are described only in relation with their masters.

[10]In "Molière comique ou tragique?" (*Revue d'Histoire Littéraire* 72 [1972]: 769-85), Raymond Picard points out that for seventeenth-century audiences accustomed to Italian *commedia del'arte*, the "pathetic language" of figures like Sganarelle or Arnolphe merely heightened the comic effect. For Fernandez (50-53), laughter signals the transition between freedom and automatic determinism, a view supported by Philip R. Berk in "The Therapy of Art in *Le Malade imaginaire*" (*French Review* 44, Spec. Issue 4 [1972]: 39). See also Gutwirth 99-109; Hall 25-29; also his tracing of the punning on names (90, 180), and the parodying of the courtly literature of tragedy (136-39, 153). McBride (141) traces comedy to the disparity between a narrow-minded idealism and the reality of human diversity.

[11]On Agnès's single-handed triumph, see Ralph Albanese. *Le Dynamisme*

de peur chez Molière: une analyse socio-culturelle de Dom Juan, Tartuffe et L'Ecole des femmes. University, Mississippi: Mississippi UP, 1976: 162-66; also Gutwirth 88. Knutson (13-14, 68-75) points out that the Agnès-Arnolphe conflict can be viewed in terms of the fertility – sterility motif sequence.

[12]For the significance of the secondary couple, especially the Philinte-Eliante relationship, see: Gossman 98; McBride 141; Moore 72; Merlin Thomas ("Philinte and Eliante." In W.D. Howarth, Merlin Thomas (Eds.) *Molière: Stage and Study.* Oxford: Clarendon, 1973: 73-92) defines the secondary couple as "a good deal more viable" than the dominant pair.

[13]On the secondary characters' adoption of the strategy and values of the dominant figures, see Albanese. "Argent et réification dans *L'Avare*" 37; Bénichou (I.1. n.57) 162, 167; Berk 40-44; Conesa 53, 95 ff., 289 ff., 334-35; Emmet J. Gossen, Jr. "'Les Femmes savantes': Métaphore et mouvement dramatique." *French Review* 45 (1971): 39-43; Hubert. *Molière and the Comedy of Intellect*: 149, 179, 250, 260; Knutson 73, 84, 96; Moore 72 ff.; Schoell 174, 180; Hiram Walker. "Action and Ending of 'L'Avare.'" *French Review* 34 (1961): 34.

[14]Jacques Arnavon (*Notes sur l'interprétation de Molière.* Paris: Librairie Plon, 1923: 114-22) hears a "cry of freedom" in the final statements of *Le Malade imaginaire,* while Berk (47-48) feels that though Argan "will never be cured of his malady . . . he will be ministered to by the loving and momentarily triumphant therapy of art." See also Conesa 162 on the accumulation and release of dramatic tension; William O. Goode. "The Comic Recognition Scene in 'L'Avare.'" *Romance Notes* 14 (1972): 123; Hall 25; and Knutson 64, 89 on the redemption of the dominant figures and their induction into a realm of fantasy at the end of a number of Molière's plays.

[15]On the role of language, dialogue, and repetition of key terms to determine action, character, and themes in Molière's plays, see especially Ciccone 3-34; Conesa 53-66; 254-294; 329 ff.; Garapon 213; Gossman 74; Hubert.

Molière and the Comedy of Intellect 118, 243-44; Regosin 265; and Bernd Spillner. "Pragmatische Analyse kommunikativ-komplexer Gesprächssituationen in den Komödien Molières." In Ernst W.B. Hess-Lüttich (Ed.). *Literatur und Konversation. Sprachsoziologie und Pragmatik in der Literaturwissenschaft.* Wiesbaden: Athenaion, 1980: 281. It is evident that contrary to Heiss's findings (50), Molière's language is highly stylized and carefully designed to convey precise messages to his spectators.

[16]A number of critics have pointed out that *Le Tartuffe* exhibits more levels of power than any other Molière play, among them, Albanese. *Le Dynamisme de la peur* 93 ff.; Arnavon 145-46; Gossman 141; Gutwirth 112; and especially Schoell 176-80.

[17]A number of critics, among them, Albanese ("Argent et réification dans 'L'Avare'") 43; Gutwirth 128; Hubert ("Theme and Structure in *L'Avare.*" *PMLA* 75 [1960]: 35); and Walker 35, point out that avarice has so thoroughly transformed Harpagon into a less-than-human creature that integration into the human community is impossible to conceive. But according to Hubert (36), Harpagon's assumption of all meanness, vanity, and indifference to the needs of others in the family makes it possible for the other members to establish a circle based on spontaneity, generosity, and affection.

[18]Knutson (84-89) traces the division of the family into two camps in *Tartuffe* and *Les Femmes savantes,* as well as the formation of the basis for a new society by the young couple and ensuing communal celebration.

[19]On the disturbing interference of the divine in the human sphere in *Amphitryon,* see Bénichou 162-64; Gossman 30; Hubert (*Molière and the Comedy of Intellect*) 179-82; Nelson 134.

[20]Critics have traced the downfall of the marital relationship to the couple's treatment of each other as objects (Gossman 154), as reflected in the written contract of the marriage (Hubert. *Molière and the Comedy of Intellect* 190-97).

Knutson (157) sees in *George Dandin* the "total inversion of the comic myth," because the dominating blocking character is included, not excluded as in other Molière plays.

[21]For a systematic study of the development of the novel in Germany after 1850, see Eva D. Becker. *Der deutsche Roman um 1780.* Stuttgart: Metzler, 1964.

[22]For a thorough assessment of the social relevance of the novels, see Peter Uwe Hohendahl. "Empfindsamkeit und gesellschaftliches Bewußtsein: Zur Soziologie des empfindsamen Romans am Beispiel von 'La vie de Marianne,' 'Clarissa,' 'Fräulein von Sternheim' und 'Werther.'" *Jb. Deutsche Schiller-Gesellschaft* 16 (1972): 176-207; Thilo Joerger. *Roman und Emanzipation.* Stuttgart: Heinz, 1981; Isabel Knautz. *Epische Schwärmerkuren. Johann Karl Wezels Romane gegen die Melancholie.* Würzburg: Königshausen & Neumann, 1990; A. von Rinsum. "Der Roman *Sophiens Reise* . . . als geistesgeschichtlicher und kulturhistorischer Ausdruck seiner Zeit." Diss. Marburg, 1949; Gerhard Steiner. "Nachwort." In Johann Karl Wezel. *Herrmann und Ulrike.* Leipzig: Insel, 1980: 823-82; Hans Peter Thurn. *Der Roman der unaufgeklärten Gesellschaft.* Stuttgart: Kohlhammer, 1973. The commentary in Helmut De Boor, Richard Newald. *Geschichte der deutschen Literatur.* 6: Sven Aage Jørgensen, Klaus Bohnen, Per Øhrgaard. *Aufklärung, Sturm und Drang.* München: Beck, 1990: 180-82, 187 ff. is cursory and partially inaccurate.

[23]See especially the principles that guide the education of children in the school founded by Sophie: Marie Sophie La Roche. *Geschichte des Fräuleins von Sternheim* (1771). In "Deutsche Literaturdenkmale des 18. und 19. Jahrhunderts." Vol. 138. Berlin: Behr, 1907: 202-228.

[24]La Roche 330-35. Cf. the sentiments expressed by Therese (Forster) Huber in *Adele von Senange* (1795), *Die Familie Seeldorf* (1795), and most succinctly in her letters to Humboldt in *Georg und Therese Forster und die*

Brüder Humboldt. Urkunden und Umriße von Albert Leitzmann. Bonn: Röhrscheid, 1936: 129, 131, 146. See also Michael Maurer (Ed.). *Ich bin mehr Herz als Kopf. Sophie von La Roche. Ein Lebensbild in Briefen.* München: Beck, 1983.

[25]Wezel 822.

[26]Adolph Knigge. *Geschichte des Amtsraths Gutmann, von ihm selbst geschrieben. (Sämtliche Werke 8).* Neudeln: KTO Press, 1978: 356-74.

[27]All citations in the text are to JA 17-20. The research on *Wilhelm Meister* and the tradition of the German *Bildungsroman* is very extensive. Arnold Bergstraesser's penetrating investigation (*Goethe's Image of Man and Society.* Freiburg: Herder, 1962) examines in detail the importance of the social realm for Wilhelm's growth. Jeffrey L. Sammons ("The Mystery of the Missing *Bildungsroman,* or: What Happened to Wilhelm Meister's Legacy." *Imagination and History.* New York: Lang, 1988: 7-31) questions the entire concept. Of topical interest are the excellent studies by: Ehrhard Bahr. "Wilhelm Meisters Wanderjahre oder Die Entsagenden." In Paul M. Lützeler (Ed.). *Goethes Erzählwerk. Interpretationen.* Stuttgart: Reclam, 1985: 363-95; Ernst Cassirer. *Goethe und die geschichtliche Welt.* Berlin: Cassirer, 1932; Wilhelm Emrich. "Das Problem der Symbolinterpretation im Hinblick auf Goethes 'Wanderjahre.'" *Deutsche Vierteljahrsschrift* 26 (1957): 331-52; Rudolf Grimminger. *Die Ordnung, das Chaos und die Kunst.* Frankfurt/M: Suhrkamp, 1986; Arthur Henkel. *Entsagung: Eine Studie zu Goethes Altersroman.* Tübingen: Niemeyer, 1954; Hans Dietrich Irmscher. "Beobachtungen zum Problem der Selbstbestimmung im deutschen Bildungsroman am Beispiel von Goethes Roman *Wilhelm Meisters Lehrjahre."* *Jb. Wiener Goethe Verein* 86/88 (1982/84): 135-72; Jürgen Jacobs. *Wilhelm Meister und seine Brüder. Untersuchungen zum deutschen Bildungsroman.* München: Fink, 1972; Ernst Jockers. *Soziale Polarität in Goethes Klassik.* Philadelphia: U Pennsylvania P, 1942; Anneliese Klingenberg. *Goethes Roman Wilhelm Meisters Wanderjahre oder Die Entsagenden. Quellen und Komposition.* Berlin: Aufbau, 1972;

Helmut Koopmann. "Wilhelm Meisters Lehrjahre (1795/96)." In Paul M. Lützeler (Ed.). *Goethes Erzählwerk. Interpretationen.* Stuttgart: Reclam, 1985: 168-91; Kurt May. "Wilhelm Meisters Lehrjahre, ein Bildungsroman?" *Deutsche Vierteljahrsschrift* 31 (1957): 1-37; Mathias Mayer. *Selbstbewußte Illusion. Selbstreflexion und Legitimation der Dichtung im 'Wilhelm Meister.'* Heidelberg: Winter, 1989; Mauro Ponzi. "Zur Entstehung des Goetheschen Motivs der Entsagung." *Zeitschrift für Germanistik* 7 (1986): 150-59; Gustav Radbruch. "Goethe. Wilhelm Meisters socialistische Sendung." *Gestalten und Gedanken.* Leipzig: Koehler & Amelang, 1944: 93-127; Bejamin C. Sax. "A Fairy Tale for the Industrial Age." *Goethe and the Problem of Self-Conception in the Nineteenth Century.* New York: Lang, 1987: 117-60; Ivar Sagmo. *Bildungsroman und Geschichtsphilosophie. Eine Studie zu Goethes Roman Wilhelm Meisters Lehrjahre.* Bonn: Bouvier, 1982; Hannelore Schlaffer. *Wilhelm Meister. Das Ende der Kunst und die Wiederkehr des Mythos.* Stuttgart: Metzler, 1980; Emil Staiger. *Goethe.* 3rd ed. Zürich: Atlantis, 1962: 1: 426-75; 2: 128-74; 3: 128-78; Hartmut Steinecke. "'Wilhelm Meister' und die Folgen. Goethes Roman und die Entwicklung der Gattung im 19. Jahrhundert." In Wolfgang Wittkowski (Ed.). *Goethe im Kontext.* Tübingen: Niemeyer, 1984: 89-111; Erich Trunz. "Die 'Wanderjahre' als 'Hauptgeschäft' im Winterhalbjahr 1828/29." In Helmut Holtzhauer (Ed.). *Natur und Idee. Andreas Wachsmuth zugeignet.* Weimar: Böhlaus Nachf., 1966: 242-62; Wilhelm Voßkamp. "Utopie und Utopiekritik in Goethes Romanen *Wilhelm Meisters Lehrjahre* und *Wilhelm Meisters Wanderjahre.*" *Utopieforschung.* Stuttgart: Metzler, 1982: 227-49; Max Wundt. *Goethes 'Wilhelm Meister' und die Entwicklung des modernen Lebens-Ideals.* Berlin: Göschen, 1913.

[28]Goethe's thinking anticipates the systematic sociological classification by Ferdinand Tönnies. *Gemeinschaft und Gesellschaft* (1887) and also the critical concern voiced by Max Weber in *Wirtschaft und Gesellschaft* (1922). For an excellent critical evaluation, see Carlo Antoni. *From History to Sociology.* Detroit: Wayne State UP, 1959.

[29]In "Selige Sehnsucht" (1814, JA 5: 16) Goethe expressed the identical

call for continuous transformation of the personality by evoking the image of a moth-butterfly consumed by the flame.

[30]Cf. "Maximen und Reflexionen." JA 4: 223: "Which government is the best? The one that teaches us to govern ourselves." The pragmatic approach to social reform in *Wilhelm Meister* corresponds to Knigge's views but differs from most proposals for reform during the period. Neither a proponent of the absolute, if enlightened state nor a champion of radical political change, Goethe outlines the features of a community that accommodates constant revisions.

[31]Cf. "Vorspiel zu Eröffnung des Weimarischen Theaters am 19. September 1807." JA 9: 194-203.

[32]For a thorough psychoanalytical examination of the sexual allusions, see K.R. Eissler. *Goethe. A Psychoanalytical Study.* Detroit: Wayne State UP, 1963: 2: 755-65, 828 ff. For other passionate embraces and kisses, see 17: 307. For allusions to the spirit of romanticism, cf. the affinity of Mignon's sentiments to those epxressed in Novalis. *Hymnen an die Nacht* (1797).

[33]"Aus Makariens Archiv" was originally appended to the edition of 1829. JA 4: 234-41; 35: 315-81; 38: 271-82; 39: 78-86.

[34]Cf. H. Rudolf Vaget. "Der Dilettant." *Jb. Deutsche Schiller-Gesellschaft* 14 (1970): 131-58.

[35]"Epochen geselliger Bildung" (1831). JA 38: 232-33; and "Wohlgemeinte Erwiderung" (1832). JA 38: 240-42.

Chapter 8

[1]See Mack's tracing of the image of the pebble thrown into the pond (I.2.

n.4) in his note on page 164 to Chaucer's *House of Fame* II: 280 ff.;
Shakespeare's *I Henry VI* I. ii. 133-35; Marvell's *Anniversary of the
Government under Oliver Cromwell;* Donne's *Love's Growth;*   and Pope's
Temple of Fame, as well as his parody in *The Dunciad* A. II. 373 ff.

[2]See Knutson's definition (I.7. n.7: 64) of the ending of the romantic comedy as the expulsion of the rigid authoritarian figure from the community.

[3]Northrop Frye. *The Anatomy of Criticism.*   Princeton: Princeton UP,
1957: 165. See also Ingrid G. Daemmrich. "The Cyclical Seasons of Humor in
Literature." *HUMOR: International Journal of Humor Research* 3 (1990): 421.

[4]17 January 1643 in *Recueil des lettres* (1647).

[5]Quoted by Johnson. *English Neoclassical Thought* (I.1. n.40) 99.

[6]See Addison. *Cato: A Tragedy.* London: Tonson, 1928: 7.

[7]See Armistead's interpretation (I.5. n.8: 281-83) of Cato's decision as an
appeal to political concord under Hanoverian rule.

[8]Critics have identified Polyeucte's exclusiveness as a feature of his superior
or aristocratic character, or the exaltation of his ego. See Bénichou (I.1. n.57)
16-33; Dort (I.3. n.2) 55; Doubrovsky (I.3. n.2) 243-49; Nadal (I.3. n.1)128. In
contrast, Stegmann (I.3. n.2: 588) views Polyeucte's decision for martyrdom as
a "detachment from the self."

[9]See Doubrovsky 179-83; Stegmann 583.

[10]Goldmann (I.3. n.6: 440) interprets Thésée's final announcement as a return of the mundane order.

[11]Barthes (I.1. n.82: 78) and Jules Brody ("Bajazet, or the Tragedy of Roxane." *Romanic Review* 60 [1969]: 278) point out the circularity of action in those Racinian tragedies which show no centripetal pattern (*Andromaque*, *Bajazet*). Goldmann (351-52) asserts that all tragic characters refuse both the future and the communal life. See also Mourges (I.4. n.5) 51. In contrast, Heyndels (I.1. n.59: 37) argues that Racine wrote his tragedies for an implied audience capable of joining his figures in moving toward the high level of sentiments.

[12]Goldmann (369) views Junie's act as tragic because she enters a silent, isolated realm from which no dialogue with the world would be possible.

[13]Barthes (58, 59) points to *Bérénice* as the best example of the exclusive, repetitive, immobile circular pattern of the binary relationship, which can only be broken by the inclusion of a third person. See also Knapp 114.

[14]See Knapp's interpretation (153) of the sacrifice as a release of the energy of the feminine *anima* which in turn strengthens the masculine power of the Greek army. Poulet (Ch. 6) suggests that in making contact with the human, the divine may lose its purity and existence.

[15]Goldmann (396) suggests that in the course of the play, Mithridate's vision and preoccupation are transformed from focusing on the past to viewing the future.

[16]Of topical interest are: Peter Boerner, Sidney Johnson (Eds.). *Faust Through Four Centuries. Retrospect and Analysis.* Tübingen: Niemeyer, 1989; Jens Kruse. *Der Tanz der Zeichen. Poetische Struktur und Geschichte im Faust II.* Königstein/Ts.: Hain, 1985; Victor Lange. "Faust. Der Tragödie zweiter Teil." In W. Hinderer (Ed.). *Goethes Dramen. Neue Interpretationen.* Stuttgart: Reclam, 1980: 281-312; Helmut Schanze. "Szenen, Schema, Schwammfamilie. Goethes Arbeitsweise und die Frage der Struktureinheit von Faust I und II." *Euphorion* 78 (1984): 383-400.

[17]For systematic, often conflicting interpretations of the figure, see: Albert Fuchs. "Méphistophèles." *Etudes Germaniques* 20 (1965): 233-42; Alfred Mann. "The Riddle of Mephistopheles." *Germanic Review* 24 (1949): 265-68; Eudo C. Mason. *Goethe's Faust. Its Genesis and Purport.* Berkeley: U California P, 1967: 195 ff.; Wolfgang Staroste. "Mephistos Verwandlung." *Germanisch-Romanische Monatsschrift* N.F. 11 (1961): 184-97; Walter Weiß. "Goethes Mephisto. Entwicklung und Wesen vom *Faust II* aus gesehen." Diss. Innsbruck, 1952.

[18]Horst Fritz. "Der Krieg des Menschen gegen die Natur. Zu einigen Vorahnungen Goethes." *Literatur für Leser* (1985): 116-31; Ilse Graham. "Kompromittierung und Wiedergutmachung. Ein Versuch zu Fausts Schlußmonolog." *Jb. Deutsche Schiller-Gesellschaft* 26 (1982): 163-203.

[19]See Liselotte Dieckmann. *Goethe's Faust. A Critical Reading.* Englewood Cliffs: Prentice Hall, 1972: 16 ff. ;and Ernst Loeb. *Die Symbolik des Wasserzyklus bei Goethe.* Paderborn: Schöningh, 1967: 133-94.

[20]See Horst S. Daemmrich. "Die Motivreihe Nebel-Licht im Werk Goethes." *Publications English Goethe Society* 42 (1972): 65-89.

[21]Cf. Heinz Moenkemeyer. "Zum Verhältnis von Sorge, Furcht und Hoffnung in Goethes *Faust.*" *German Quarterly* 32 (1959): 121-32; Harry Steinhauer. "Faust's Pact with the Devil." *PMLA* 71 (1956): 180-200; Paul Stöcklein. "Die Sorge im Faust." *Wege zum späten Goethe.* 2nd ed. Hamburg: Schröder, 1960: 93-162.

[22]Such sentiments also prevail in the ideal of "gesellige Bildung," the beneficial influence of social relations founded on respect for others. See for instance the observations of the baroness in *Unterhaltungen deutscher Ausgewanderten* (1795); JA 16: 179-81.

[23]"Bedeutende Fördernis durch ein einziges geistreiches Wort" (1823). JA 39: 49.

[24]"Betrachtungen im Sinne der 'Wanderer'" (1829). JA 4: 224; see also JA 4: 29, 100 and 38: 250-51.

[25]"Shakespeare und kein Ende" (1813-16). JA 37: 37.

[26]"Die Geheimnisse" (1785). JA 1: 287 ff.